SCUDDER'S

WHITE MOUNTAIN

VIEWING GUIDE

SCUDDER'S

WHITE MOUNTAIN

VIEWING GUIDE

Fifty-four Northern New England
Mountain Top
Viewing Diagrams

Brent E. Scudder

Second Edition
Revised

High Top Press

North Sutton, N.H.
2005

SCUDDER'S WHITE MOUNTAIN VIEWING GUIDE

First edition, first printing by High Top Press 1995
First edition, second printing by Bondcliff Books 2000
Second edition by High Top Press 2005

Manufactured in the United States of America
for High Top Press
by McNaughton & Gunn, Inc.

Cover: Photograph and diagram of view towards Mount Washington from the summit of Mount Jackson.

DISCLAIMERS: See Page 8

Publisher's Cataloging-in-Publication
(Provided by Quality Books, Inc)

Scudder, Brent E.
    [White Mountain viewing guide]
    Scudder's White Mountain viewing guide : fifty-four
northern New England mountain top viewing diagrams /
Brent E. Scudder. -- 2nd ed. rev.
    p. cm.
    Includes bibliographical references and index.
    LCCN 2005922167
    ISBN 0-9645856-3-4

    1. White Mountains (N.H. and Me.)--Guidebooks.
I. Title. II. Title: White Mountain viewing guide

F41.25.S28 2005   917.42'20444
                    QBI05-800251

FOR

REGGIE

TABLE OF CONTENTS

SCUDDER'S WHITE MOUNTAIN VIEWING GUIDE

DISCLAIMERS: Although some information pertaining to safety is included, the nature of this book is that of a viewing guide and not a hiking guide. Therefore neither the author of this book nor High Top Press is responsible for any omission of fact regarding convenience or safety. The information contained herein is current as of the publication date to the best of the author's knowledge. We assume no responsibility if a trip is wasted due to the closing, dismantling or destruction of a viewing platform.

While given hiking times are based upon a sophisticated set of guidelines, these are estimates. Some hiking times could be off by more than 15%. This is especially true for two sections of the Appalachian Trail: (1) from Mount Cube to South Kinsman Mountain and (2) along the Mahoosuc Range. Keep in mind that trail conditions, the darkness of night and the hiker's own ability can drastically affect the length of a hike.

GPS readings are in the WGS84 datum mode. Every effort has been made to ensure their accuracy. However, the author and High Top Press disclaim any responsibility for typographical errors in this regard. Even if there are no errors, the hiker should never rely on GPS as the sole method of navigation.

The author does not hold a medical degree. The medical statements in Appendix D are based upon his reading and experience. He disclaims any responsibility for omissions of fact or for omissions of necessary elaborations.

It is the responsibility of the user of the White Mountains not to exceed his or her physical capabilities. Knowledge of these capabilities involves extensive reading of current White Mountain literature and discussions with more experienced hikers. It is strongly recommended that anyone new to this activity engage in hikes with those who are more knowledgeable. Anyone who is not in reasonable physical condition should check with their doctor before attempting a mountain climb.

INTRODUCTION

Jerry Hill is 728 feet high, a molehill in relation to numerous loftier heights in New Hampshire. In 1953, a teacher took his charges on a hike to Jerry's summit and its observation tower. The view was spectacular for such a low elevation. There lay a long pond to the north and two smaller ones to the south. All around the horizon rose mountains of many profiles. One student in particular was fascinated the way the teacher could identify every peak he saw. Each name echoed forth the music of northern New England's early history of the settler and the Native American from Monadnock, Sunapee, Kearsarge, Moosilauke, Lafayette, Bean, Belknap and Rattlesnake to Pawtuckaway.

The teacher had mistaken Fort Mountain for one of the Pawtuckaways because the former stood in the way. The student was not aware but merely wished that he had the ability to identify what could be seen in this marvelous view. He assumed that a book existed identifying what could be seen from New Hampshire's higher peaks. Having never heard of the ancient works of Moses Sweetser, he thought no such book had ever been written. Would someone write one soon?

The observation tower has been removed from Jerry Hill, and trees obscure the summit. The two ponds to the south are one now having been joined by a rise in water level caused by the building of a dam. The sought-after book did not appear. It finally dawned upon the former pupil that he had to write it.

The making of *Scudder's White Mountain Viewing Guide* began as a hobby in 1967. By the mid-Eighties diagrams of the views from fifteen mountains had been assembled. If the book was ever to appear, the author had better give his creation a lot more of his time. The first edition appeared in 1995 featuring 43 mountains and sold out its print run within two years. A second printing appeared in 2000 thanks to Mike Dickerman of Bondcliff Books who assumed total responsibility for financing and marketing. Today, High Top Press has published the Second Edition with a vastly improved format and eleven additional mountains.

The diagrams contained herein are panoramas developed from overlapping photographs taken around the horizon from forty-seven mountain tops in New Hampshire and from seven other summits just beyond its borders. Prominent terrain features are labeled, and these allow the White Mountain hiker to become familiar with what can be seen from each peak.

Chapter by chapter, we describe a particular mountain followed by its corresponding summit view diagram. Hiking instructions are included only where it is felt such tips might supplement existing hiking guidebooks. THIS WORK SHOULD NEVER BE USED AS A SUBSTITUTE FOR A HIKING GUIDEBOOK.

While the summit view changes slightly with time, hiking instructions change rapidly. Trails fall into disuse or are relocated. Should the book be several years old, then use it only to show what can be seen from the top and seek all hiking instructions elsewhere.

The *WHITE MOUNTAIN GUIDE* published by the Appalachian Mountain Club (AMC) is available in New England bookstores and where outdoor goods are sold. The *GUIDE* is updated every three or four years. Much sage advice is sprinkled among the many trail descriptions and hiking maps.

We begin with Pack Monadnock Mountain located not far from the Massachusetts border. From chapter to chapter, we work our way northward weaving left and right to assure a continuum that allows each subsequent panorama to overlap the previous one.

From Pack Monadnock to Blue Job Mountain, we feature the southern New Hampshire area. The land is rather flat but with isolated mountains that are easy to recognize. Far to the north stand the White Mountains visible only on a day of remarkable clarity, their dark serrated outline arousing a sense of awe and mystery.

From Mount Major to Maine's Streaked Mountain, we cover the Lakes Region. Large island-studded bodies of water stand before us while the White Mountains, much nearer now, tower beyond. The southern White Mountain area follows. This is the Black Cap to Loon Mountain region. Here we skirt the "Sandwich Front," a range of mountains that separate the lowlands to the south from the high peaks to the north.

Central to the book is the Appalachian Trail. Starting with Mount Cube near the Connecticut River to Maine's Old Speck, we describe nineteen mountains located a day's hike apart on or near this famous path. While the day climber can choose his trips when the visibility is excellent, the Appalachian Trail hiker is stuck with whatever weather lies in store. By having charts of the views strung out at daily hiking intervals, the overnight backpacker can utilize at least some of the skyline diagrams.

Finally we come to the North Country featuring such peaks as The Horn, Sugarloaf and Magalloway. Towns are few. Forest is everywhere. The White Mountains, behind us now, shut us off from cities and civilization.

Not only are there difficult climbs included for the intrepid hiker, but simple ascents as well. Mount Adams takes four hours to reach while Pitcher's summit requires but fifteen minutes. Some heights can be reached by chair lift and by automobile. Yet such tops as Bond and Carrigain require the aspirant to be in good physical condition.

The overlapping photographs used to construct each chart are actually slides projected on paper with their profiles traced in ink. A "scale slide" was then prepared depicting one-degree intervals of compass azimuth and projected onto the same paper.

In order to identify distant summits, we pasted together topographical maps of adjacent areas in order to form a mosaic. On this composite map, we located the peak from which we were designing a skyline diagram for the book and called it the "featured mountain."

With a ruler and protractor we drew two sight lines from the featured mountain; the first line to a well-known peak seen on the slides, the so-called "reference mountain." The other sight line extended to the object that was to be identified, the "target mountain." Using simple drafting techniques, we took both sight lines and determined their compass direction in degrees relative to True North (the True Azimuth). The difference in azimuth between the reference mountain and target mountain represented the angle on the map that both peaks made with the featured mountain. To positively identify the target mountain, this "map" angle had to agree with the scale angle that had been traced on the paper.

Sight lines may cross as many as twelve topographical maps, each 16 ½ by 23 inches. Pasting together twelve such maps must give the reader a mental image of paper stretched across the entire floor of a barn or studio. Rather than doing the actual pasting of maps, consider that a sight line running off the edge of one map a certain distance up from the bottom will intersect the adjacent map the same distance up. This means that we can keep the charts separate and draw on them one at a time.

Drawing sight lines across individual charts got very tedious. It became necessary to speed up the process with a computer. Using software, we entered one-time basic data for the featured mountain and then typed in the predetermined azimuth angle to the target mountain. The computer calculated the point on each of the twelve maps that the sight line emerged. Only the final map interested us, because that one contained the target mountain. On that last chart, we took a ruler and protractor and drew the sight line. If it crossed the mountain in question, we had a positive identification.

It was not always apparent from the topographical maps whether one mountain completely hid another. For example, a line drawn 50 miles from New Hampshire's Mount Monadnock to Glastenbury Mountain, Vermont, passes over Mount Snow. Can one see Glastenbury from the top of Monadnock or is it hidden by Snow? A "Terrain eclipse" program was written to solve the problem. This program took into account the Earth's curvature and told us that Mount Snow totally hid Glastenbury from view. The Terrain Eclipse program did not allow for atmospheric refraction, a quantity that varies with the ever-changing density of the intervening air layers. But refraction gave us trouble only if the object was more than 100 miles away.

In order to observe all of the view shown in these diagrams, one needs a rare commodity, a day when the visibility is unlimited. If the featured mountain is free of fog, objects thirty or forty miles away are usually visible. An excellent day requires the visibility to be at or above 80 miles. Appendix A lists six weather forecasting rules that the layman can use to predict a super clear day. If these rules are followed properly, anyone can forecast excellent visibility with an accuracy of 95%.

If you limit your climbing experience to periods of crystal clear weather, you will not climb often. Certainly, you can use the charts on hazy days. But we are often stuck with rain, wind and fog where the charts lack any use at all. Even then there is temporary clearing revealing fantastic aspects as you look down upon clouds covering nearby slopes and hiding distant mountains – a marvelous landscape of vapor and forest, rising mists, brilliant rainbows and storm-tossed sunshine. You will miss much if you confine your hikes only to periods where the charts are at their best.

The panorama diagrams will amply reward your hiking experience. Before long, you will surprise yourself at how many mountains you can name without the use of the charts even from peaks that are not featured in this book. You will certainly surprise your hiking companions.

I would like to give thanks to Dan H. Allen who climbed two of the peaks and took slides for me. We have already mentioned Mike Dickerman's contribution. Thanks also go to Jeff Hare whose technical assistance on the preparation of diagrams saved a considerable amount of time. A special appreciation goes out to John B. Mulford for his comments on the first edition. Several persons (some unwittingly) were responsible for instilling in me a love of the White Mountains. Without them this book would not exist. These were my father W. Tracy Scudder II, Tudor Richards, Alan N. Hall, Harold (Smoky) Payson and Ransom B. True. But most of all, I would like to thank my wife Regina for proof-reading, editing, helping me on research and accompanying me on some of the climbs.

MOUNTAIN

LOCATION

MAPS

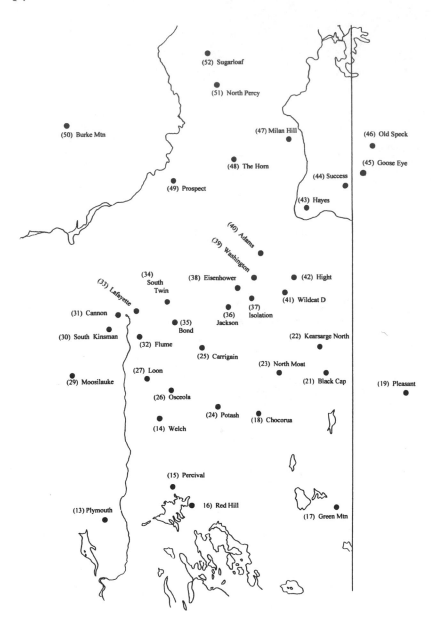

(52) Sugarloaf

(51) North Percy

(50) Burke Mtn

(47) Milan Hill

(46) Old Speck

(45) Goose Eye

(48) The Horn

(44) Success

(49) Prospect

(43) Hayes

(40) Adams

(39) Washington

(34) South Twin

(38) Eisenhower

(42) Hight

(33) Lafayette

(41) Wildcat D

(31) Cannon

(37) Jackson

(36) Isolation

(35) Bond

(30) South Kinsman

(22) Kearsarge North

(32) Flume

(25) Carrigain

(23) North Moat

(27) Loon

(21) Black Cap

(29) Moosilauke

(19) Pleasant

(26) Osceola

(24) Potash

(18) Chocorua

(14) Welch

(15) Percival

(13) Plymouth

16) Red Hill

(17) Green Mtn

Featured mountains in central New Hampshire

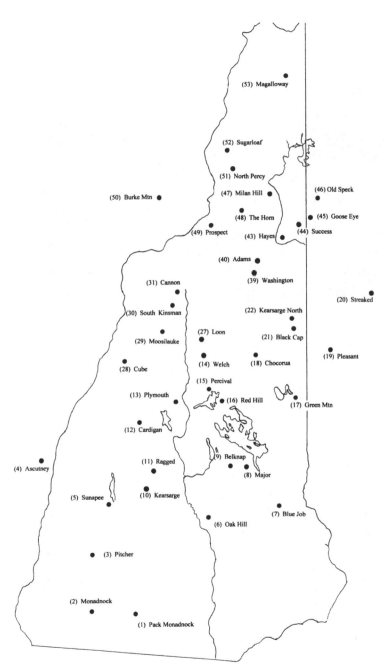

(54) Megantic

(53) Magalloway

(52) Sugarloaf

(51) North Percy

(47) Milan Hill

(50) Burke Mtn

(48) The Horn

(46) Old Speck

(45) Goose Eye

(49) Prospect

(43) Hayes

(44) Success

(40) Adams

(39) Washington

(31) Cannon

(20) Streaked

(22) Kearsarge North

(30) South Kinsman

(27) Loon

(21) Black Cap

(29) Moosilauke

(14) Welch

(18) Chocorua

(19) Pleasant

(28) Cube

(15) Percival

(13) Plymouth

(16) Red Hill

(17) Green Mtn

(12) Cardigan

(11) Ragged

(9) Belknap

(4) Ascutney

(8) Major

(5) Sunapee

(10) Kearsarge

(7) Blue Job

(6) Oak Hill

(3) Pitcher

(2) Monadnock

(1) Pack Monadnock

Featured Peaks in and about New Hampshire

Applachian Mountain Club hikers on
Mount Eisenhower.
Mount Washington is in the background.

Cathy and Dave Howell along with Andrew Curtis about to enter the clouds
from the saddle between Mount Lafayette and its north peak.

USING THE DIAGRAMS

The many panorama diagrams in the book cover overlapping territory allowing us to use them to extra advantage. For example, each chart has insufficient space to label every lump and bump on the horizon. Yet we can determine the names of some of the mountains that are left blank.

As you look from the summit of Kearsarge North (page 130), glance westward at the 28-mile distant Franconia Range. The diagram of that view labels only one mountain in this set, Lafayette. Between Kearsarge North and the Franconia Range stands Mount Bond. Take a look at Bond's chart depicting the Franconias now seen only six miles away (page 199). Many more labels appear namely Mounts Flume, Liberty, Little Haystack, Lincoln as well as Lafayette. In other words, the Franconia Range as seen from Bond represents a telescopic version of the view from Kearsarge North.

The large number of panoramas with overlapping territory allows us to recognize features seen from mountains that are not diagrammed in this book. We have developed no charts from the top of Boott Spur. Yet stand there during a clear day and glance southeastward towards Kearsarge North. Behind us rises Mount Washington for which we do have diagrams (page 226). Using the charts from that peak, is not the view to the southeast similar to what can be seen from Boott Spur? Now glance to the southwest. Mount Hight is behind us. Does not the prospect to the west-southwest seem to resemble what is observed from Mount Hight? (Page 241).

Although these charts were developed from photographs taken on crystal clear days, they may also be used on days when the visibility is less than perfect. A haze-hidden horizon results in a skyline of a different shape. On such a day, start out by identifying objects on the charts that are less than fifteen miles away. Slowly raise your gaze over ridge after ridge until you reach the farthest visible terrain. You will recognize today's restricted horizon as one of the nearer ridges.

The diagrams are fairly self-explanatory. Yet the style of labeling each mountain should be discussed.

Consider the entry: Mt Madison (5366) 41

We are looking at Mount Madison, the elevation of which is 5366 feet and located 41 miles away.

Consider: (5) Mt Sunapee(2730) 13

The underline means that a diagram was prepared for the view from Mount Sunapee and is located elsewhere in the book, namely in Chapter (5).

Jeffers Mtn (The Hogsback) (2994) 45

Sometimes a mountain has more than one label. What is perceived to be the more common name is listed first.

Puzzle Mtn ME (3133) 40

A state abbreviation appears whenever the sighted mountain is located in a different state than the featured mountain. Exceptions appear for the sake of chart brevity, and these are explained on the diagrams themselves.

Sentinel Mtn, Tuftonboro quad (1690) 14

In our area of study, there are three Sentinel Mountains. This one happens to be located on the topographic map entitled "Tuftonboro." The "quad" is short for the word quadrangle and tells us that Tuftonboro is the title of a United States Coast and Geodetic Survey (USCGS) map and not the name of a terrain feature.

An enormous number of peaks are nameless. Most of these are terrain projections of little note. But what has been observed as an insignificant lump from a valley clearing often becomes a sharp profile when seen from another mountaintop. Such nameless summits can be mistaken for well-known peaks. We could have tagged these "unnamed mountain" but chose instead to give them temporary designations. An asterisk allows the reader to spot each.

McCutcheon Hill* (2215) 4.6

The best example of the need to label an unnamed mountain involves the view from our 29th peak. Anyone who religiously climbs our tops chapter-by-chapter never sees Canada until he or she arrives at the crest of Moosilauke. A small piece of Canada is visible, a nameless summit. Suppose that later one climbs our northernmost peak, Mt. Megantic. That person may wish to locate that same nameless height visible from Moosilauke. Because we had called it Mt. Fullerton* on both charts, we have no problem locating it from Megantic.

The name sources for the temporary labels are the names of nearby lakes, river, towns or districts. Many peaks are officially named in just this way. Mounts Success, Pemigewasset, Plymouth and Sandwich Mountains are all named after nearby places. In continuing this practice, we saw that Hobbs Brook ran down the side of one nameless hill. Whimsically, we assigned the label "Hobbs Knob." We later discovered that it appears on the Chocorua Mountain Club's panorama as Hobbs Mountain.

It is hoped that the purist does not take offense at this treatment of mountain names.   It is merely a device to organize a pattern of inconsistencies into coherence. The nameless peaks, that we honored, make up a small percentage of the total labels on the many charts and even fail to appear on some. The casual climber will hardly notice them.

The list of temporary designations along with their locations appears in Appendix E. A further discussion of our style of mountain labeling continues in Appendix F.

The eight principal compass directions of N, NE, E, SE, S, SW, W, and NW appear in big letters near the base of the panorama charts. These directions are relative to True North. But compasses point to Magnetic North or about sixteen degrees to the left of True. Some hikers would have preferred that we had placed these direction letters relative to Magnetic North in order to agree with the compass.

We chose True North because most maps are squared up with True North, East, South and West. People also tend to think in these terms. In order to use the compass, merely orient it so that the needle points towards 344 degrees (a little over half the angular distance towards north-northwest). The letters on the rim of that instrument will now point in the True directions.

Should you ever lose your way in the forest, your increased knowledge of mountain identification will serve as an aid. It is not necessary to be atop a featured summit in order to recognize a particular land shape. Once I was not sure of my bearings. I stepped out on an open ledge and spotted the conical Kearsarge North. That landmark seemed like a friend telling me that I was not lost. The ability to recognize mountains in the offing inspires confidence and raises the enjoyment as well as the safety of hiking.

GLOBAL POSITIONING – GPS

Lord Nelson of the Royal Navy would have killed in order to obtain a GPS unit. In the early days, one determined the latitude through measurement of the angles that the stars sun or moon made with the horizon. Longitude was a bigger problem for you needed an extremely accurate clock. And you still had to work out your position by hand using tedious logarithmic tables. GPS units receive signals from orbiting satellites and integrate them into your exact position on the Earth's surface give or take a few feet. Recently, such units have become small enough to be hand-held and light enough to put in your backpack. Many outdoor stores offer these units in the $100 to $550 range. A wrist model sells for $150.

Latitude and longitude are distances across the world measured in units of degrees, parts of degrees called minutes and parts of minutes called seconds. Sixty seconds makes a minute and sixty minutes makes a degree.

Latitude is a distance north or south from the Equator. A degree is slightly over 69 statute miles. One minute equals about 6060 feet with a second only 101 feet. New Hampshire begins at nearly 43 degrees from the Equator and ends a little beyond 45. These degree units are derived from an angle drawn from one's location to the center of the Earth and back to the Equator along a north-south line that passes through the starting location.

Longitude (a distance east or west) varies depending upon how far one is from the Equator. In central New Hampshire a longitude degree is about 50 miles. One minute measures 4208 feet with a second only 70 feet. These distances diminish by 2.4% from Massachusetts to Canada. Longitude units are reckoned from an angle determined by a line drawn from the Earth's surface perpendicularly to the spin axis and then back to a point east or west of the first point. By international agreement the zero-degree line (the Prime Meridian) passes through the Greenwich Observatory near London, England. As a result, New Hampshire lies mainly between 71 and 72 degrees west of Greenwich.

During the nationally chauvinistic years of the Nineteenth Century, Italian maps placed the Prime Meridian through Rome while France placed theirs through Paris. Even early United States maps ran theirs through Washington. Eventually, the Greenwich Observatory became the accepted location for the zero-degree longitude line.

A trip consists of waypoints (points along the way), positions that define the path one takes. Waypoints are plotted as dots on a map. Connecting the waypoints gives a person an approximate route of travel.

GPS waypoints are often given in units of latitude and longitude. You have to install these positions using the manual that came with your unit. Only then can GPS tell you that you are located at a certain compass bearing and distance from each waypoint.

This book lists the waypoints of all the featured mountain summits (save one). We use degrees, minutes and decimal parts of minutes. Your GPS unit may be set up differently. If such is the case, Appendix G on page 334 demonstrates not only how to convert your waypoints to and from the ones used in this book, but also how to use a topographical map to determine the latitude and longitude of a waypoint. Most GPS units will convert waypoint readings automatically with the push of a button.

We also list the positions for at least one trailhead per mountain. This helps you locate where to start your hike. If this book is several years old, then use these positions for reference, but do not rely upon them! Trails get rerouted over time and so do their beginnings. However you may continue to rely on the waypoints of the mountain tops. Most summit waypoints were hand calculated and should be accurate to within 200 feet. Waypoints along the trail and at the trailheads were measured with an older unit (No WAAS) and should be correct to within 50 feet.

The complete latitude/longitude coordinates of each mountain top are listed at the beginning of each chapter. For purposes of brevity, waypoints within the chapter lack the degree designation. Thus a trailhead latitude reading of 44 degrees, 32.221 minutes North would merely be listed as 32.221 minutes North with the 44 degrees understood. If the degree value differs from that listed at the head of the chapter, it will be so noted.

Use GPS to establish the location of where you parked your car for the hike. This helps you return to it. No calculation is needed to set a waypoint when you are at its actual location. One merely presses a couple of buttons on the unit.

We need to be concerned with something called "datum." A datum is a standard reference point. Maps are constructed so that every spot on that map is located at a certain distance and elevation from that datum point. Unfortunately, Different sets of maps use different datums. If you ignore the datum concept while using our waypoints, you could be 125 feet off the mark, particularly in and east or west direction.

Recently manufactured GPS units have been given a default setting at the factory to list waypoints in the so-called WGS84 datum mode. All waypoints in this book use WGS84. If your unit was programmed at the factory to use a different datum mode as the default setting, consult the instruction book so that you can alter it to WGS84 with the push of a few buttons. This mode should not change (even with the unit turned off) until you convert it back. However check what mode you are in after each battery change.

Should your GPS lack this conversion feature, consult pages 338 and 340 in order to convert manually among the three most commonly used datums.

There are two additional sources of discrepancy when comparing your GPS reading with our waypoints: (1) The hiker may have keyed in the wrong numbers (Heaven forbid!). (2) The hiker may not be standing in exactly the same spot that the author did when he took the reading for this book. Such a discrepancy is especially true at trailheads and on broad summits such as Moosilauke or Black Cap.

Remember that the direction and distance to a waypoint is a straight line. Between you and the waypoint could lie deep ravines or tall ridges, cliffs you cannot climb or descend, rushing streams impossible to cross not to mention impenetrable brush.

Yet you could lose the trail and determine from the map that such obstacles (except for the brush) do not exist. Then it might be possible to bushwhack in a straight line to your destination. But often you can determine to which side you strayed from the trail. Try to find the trail first. Locating it will get you home more quickly.

Each time I turn on my GPS, the following disclaimer appears: "Do not rely on this product as your primary source of navigation." One could be using the wrong datum. Batteries could be old and you forgot to bring spares. Mishaps along the trail may cause the unit to be damaged or even lost. **Never lose your ability to navigate using map and compass alone.**

(1) PACK MONADNOCK MOUNTAIN

(SOUTH PACK MONADNOCK)

N 42° 51.708'
W 71° 52.704'

(Elevation 2300 feet)

Between Manchester and Keene, New Hampshire, the land is hilly and forested abounding in small lakes and streams. This is the transition between the Atlantic Coastal Plain and the Appalachians. Small mountains poke up here and there. One range in particular, the Wapacks, begins with Mount Watatic in Massachusetts and reaches northward into south central New Hampshire past Barrett Mountain, Temple Mountain and the Pack Monadnocks. The larger Pack Monadnock has views in all directions.

The three charts that follow show the panorama from Pack's summit tower. We see the Wapack Range itself approaching from the south. Off to the west stands the famous Grand Monadnock. To its right but farther off appear the ski trails of Mount Snow and Stratton Mountain, Vermont. On the northern horizon stretch the White Mountains capped by Mount Washington 101 miles away. We feature many of these peaks later on, and several are visible from here.   First, look for the nearly tree-hidden lean-to shelter 100 yards north of the tower. Mount Kearsarge rears up on the horizon just beyond its roof. To its left and farther off stands Mount Cardigan. The peak called Moosilauke cannot be seen for it is blocked by Kearsarge. But line up the right wall of the shelter with a distant apex, and we discover Mount Lafayette 90 miles away.

Pack Monadnock is part of Miller State Park. One reaches it by taking Route 101 westward out of Milford, New Hampshire. After nine miles the road begins a steady ascent of the Wapack Range up into a pass separating Pack Monadnock from Temple Mountain. At 13.8 miles from Milford, just beyond the top of the pass, the base parking area shows up to the right (N 51.010 min, W 53.216 min). At this point visitors can either drive the paved automobile road to the summit or else get their daily exercise by hiking up from the base. During winter, the road is not maintained.   Fees are charged from May 1st through October 31st as well as during weekends from April through mid-December. Ascent on foot takes about 35 minutes.

Climb Pack Monadnock in April and note at least three snow-capped mountains along with five others with visible ski trails. All the rest are blanketed by forest. If you desire to become adept at mountain identification, learn a few names at a time. During the April climb, concentrate on learning only the snow mountains. This quickly gives you the ability to identify eight important summits.

Already we have mentioned Mounts Washington, Lafayette and Cardigan. These are the snow-capped peaks. Previously we had pointed out the ski trails on Stratton Mountain and Mount Snow. Look to the south and see more ski trails on Wachusett Mountain as well as the nearer Watatic. The Temple Mountain ski area (no longer in business) stands right at our feet. These are the eight summits to learn.

What can be seen of the hills in western Massachusetts? In the Connecticut River Valley, we observe neither Mount Tom nor the Holyoke Range. Too many tall hills located west of the Quabbin Reservoir block the way. But the Bay State's highest, Mount Greylock, does appear, standing to the left of Grand Monadnock about two thirds of the way over towards Little Monadnock. Greylock's attendant peaks of Mounts Fitch and Saddleball are also visible.

As we advance from chapter to chapter, let us gradually develop a list of mountains that are easy to recognize from most summits in the region. I call these "reference landmark mountains." By knowing each landmark, one can use his or her slowly acquired geographical knowledge to identify summits adjacent to the landmark as well as nearby lakes, rivers and towns. At the head of the list is that tall Grand Monadnock to the west, the highest point in southernmost New Hampshire. From almost any hill within seventy miles, a person merely glances in the direction of Grand Monadnock and is able to name it immediately.

The view from Pack Monadnock is one of peace. As a person drinks in the scene of distant field and forest, lake and mountain, the mind may be allowed to drift freely. It becomes a time of pleasant reflection either with one's self or with a companion. This is why so many people climb.

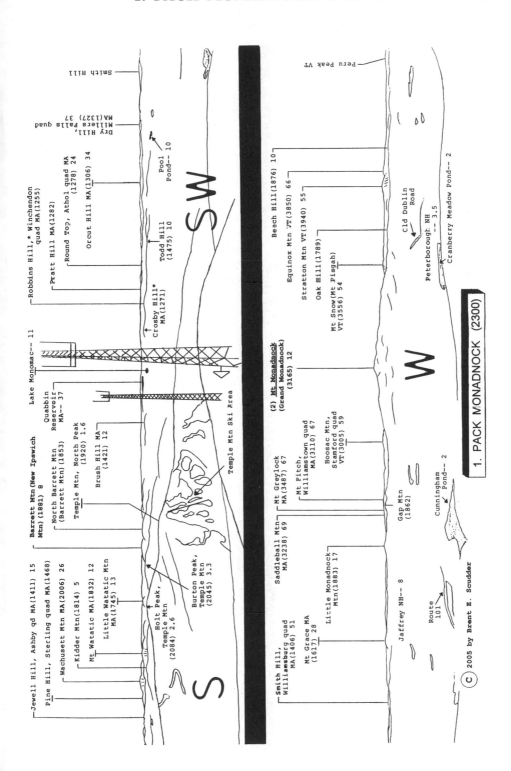

1. PACK MONADNOCK (2300)

© 2005 by Brent E. Scudder

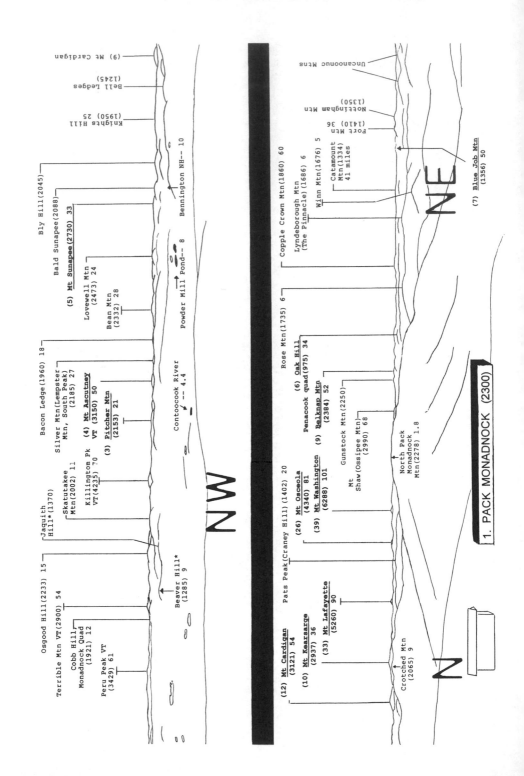

NW

NE

N

1. PACK MONADNOCK (2300)

(9) Mt Cardigan
Bell Ledges (1245)
Knights Hill (1950) 25
Bly Hill (2045)
Bald Sunapee (2088)
(5) Mt Sunapee (2730) 33
Bennington NH-- 10
Lovewell Mtn (2473) 24
Bean Mtn (2332) 28
Powder Mill Pond-- 8
Bacon Ledge (1960) 18
Silver Mtn (Lempster Mtn, South Peak) (2185) 27
(4) Mt Ascutney VT (3150) 50
Pitcher Mtn (2153) 21
(3) Contoocook River -- 4.4
Jaquith Hill* (1370)
Skatutakee Mtn (2002) 11
Killington Pk VT (4235) 70
Osgood Hill (2233) 15
Terrible Mtn VT (2900) 54
Cobb Hill Monadnock Quad (1921) 12
Peru Peak VT (3429) 61
Beaver Hill* (1285) 9

Uncanoonuc Mtns
Nottingham Mtn (1350)
Fort Mtn (1410) 36
Catamount Mtn (1334) 41 miles
(7) Blue Job Mtn (1356) 50
Copple Crown Mtn (1860) 60
Lyndeborough Mtn (The Pinnacle) (1686) 6
Winn Mtn (1676) 5
Rose Mtn (1735) 6
(6) Oak Hill
Penacook quad (975) 34
(9) Belknap Mtn (2384) 52
Gunstock Mtn (2250)
Mt Shaw (Ossipee Mtn) (2990) 68
North Pack Monadnock Mtn (2278) 1.8
Pats Peak (Craney Hill) (1402) 20
(26) Mt Osceola (4340) 81
(39) Mt Washington (6288) 101
(12) Mt Cardigan (3121) 54
(10) Mt Kearsarge (2937) 36
(33) Mt Lafayette (5260) 90
Crotched Mtn (2065) 9

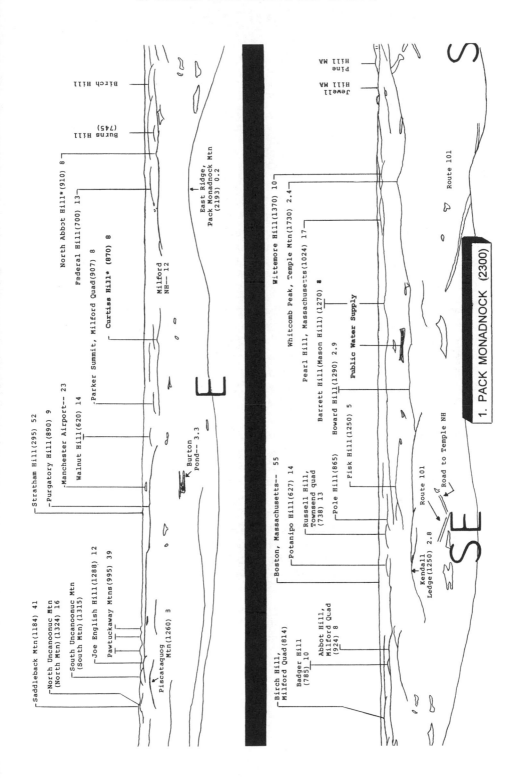

(2) MOUNT MONADNOCK

(GRAND MONADNOCK MOUNTAIN)

N 42° 51.692'
W 72° 06.488'

(Elevation 3165 feet)

"Quick! Push someone off! I want to get on!" This was the feeling we had during one sunny Columbus Day weekend as we emerged from the woods and faced the summit of Mount Monadnock. Hundreds of people were gathered on top as if to hear an outdoor concert. It has been suggested that Monadnock is the second most frequently climbed mountain in the world. Japan's Mount Fuji places first.

Monadnock is popular because it lies within a day's drive of several cities ranging from Boston and Manchester down to Hartford and New Haven. Certain New York suburbanites can set their alarms for 4 a.m., be up to southern New Hampshire and back by evening. The summit view is excellent. One can see all the way over to Mount Tom near Springfield, Massachusetts; Mount Greylock in the Berkshires; Killington Peak in the Green Mountains and Mount Washington in the Whites. Boston is visible through binoculars.

Geologically speaking, a monadnock is an isolated mass of rock or hill rising above the peneplain. Other monadnocks include Kearsarge, Vermont's Ascutney and a northern Mount Monadnock. A slang word for a policeman's nightstick is monadnock. With such an object, one can receive a mad knock on the head!

One approach to this popular peak is to head west out of Jaffrey on Route 124. Turn right onto Dublin Road and drive about a mile or so until you pass the Monadnock Bible Conference Center. Take the first left. Drive a half mile to the trailhead parking located in Monadnock State Park where one pays a small fee (N 50.755 min, W 05.360 min). The climb takes two hours.

On busy weekends, there may be no parking space at the State Park. In that case drive west from Jaffrey 5.2 miles or southeast out of Marlborough 7.3 miles to a height of land and parking to the north of the road at the Old Halfway House trailhead (N 50.127 min, W 06.833 min). Also expect a two-hour climb. Other approaches are listed in the Appalachian Mountain Club's *Southern New Hampshire Trail Guide.*

To avoid the summit crowds, pick a weekday for climbing or else hike between late October and Memorial Day. During winter, snowshoes with crampons may be required.

While at the top, let us increase our list of peaks that do not require the panorama charts – the "reference landmark mountains." Look northward towards Dublin Lake. Across its left stands a prominent height in the middle distance, Mount Kearsarge. Kearsarge's signature is a smaller mountain joined on the left when observed from the south and east, but connected on the right when seen from the north and west. From nearly every mountain featured in this book we can spot either Kearsarge or Mount Washington – often both.

Ascutney is to be added to the list of reference landmarks. After viewing Kearsarge, turn your head to the left and look past several ponds. The obvious protrusion on the horizon is Mount Ascutney – very easy to spot.

The eight "snow" mountains seen from Pack Monadnock are still visible. Gaze eastward across the town of Peterborough and pick up North Pack Monadnock at the left end of the Wapack Range. Run your eye to the right past South Pack, the triple peaks of Temple Mountain, Kidder Mountain, the three Barretts, and finally ending up with Mount Watatic in Massachusetts. Beyond and farther right is Wachusett Mountain standing abruptly on the horizon. Some snow mountains are not as easy to locate because their angle has changed, their ski slopes less visible. But we found some of them merely by taking out the diagram and counting peaks along the Wapack Range.

To the west, we observe Vermont's Mounts Snow and Stratton seen just as before. Climb Monadnock during the early spring and easily spot the three snow mountains of Washington, Lafayette and Cardigan. But wait! There is a fourth "whitecap." The nearer mountain on the left is Cardigan. The other, beyond and farther left, is Moosilauke, nearly five thousand feet high and eighty-one miles away.

We stand on the roof of southern New Hampshire commanding a view of at least three states. By reaching Monadnock, we have struck a toehold in the Granite State. Perhaps when we return, we shall have time to drive much farther north into regions so lonely that one may fail to encounter another hiker all day long.

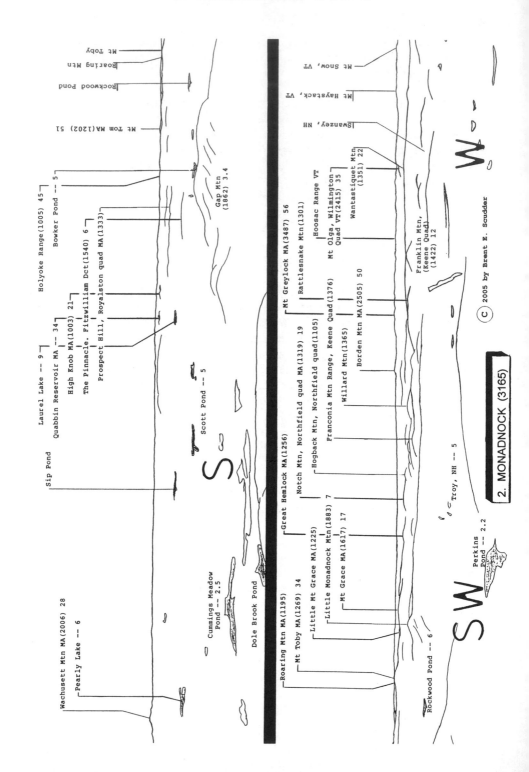

Wachusett Mtn MA(2006) 28
Pearly Lake -- 6
Sip Pond
Laurel Lake -- 9
Quabbin Reservoir MA -- 34
High Knob MA(1003) 21
The Pinnacle. Fitzwilliam Dct(1540) 6
Prospect Hill, Royalston quad MA(1333)
Holyoke Range(1005) 45
Bowker Pond -- 5
Mt Tom MA(1202) 51
Rockwood Pond
Roaring Mtn
Mt Toby
Gap Mtn (1862) 3.4
Scott Pond -- 5
Cummings Meadow Pond -- 2.5
Dole Brook Pond

Roaring Mtn MA(1195)
Mt Toby MA(1269) 34
Little Mt Grace (1225)
Little Monadnock Mtn(1883) 7
Mt Grace MA(1617) 17
Great Hemlock MA(1256)
Notch Mtn, Northfield quad MA(1319) 19
Hogback Mtn, Northfield quad(1105)
Franconia Mtn Range, Keene Quad(1376)
Willard Mtn(1365)
Mt Greylock MA(3487) 56
Rattlesnake Mtn(1301)
Hoosac Range VT
Mt Olga, Wilmington Quad VT(2415) 35
Borden Mtn MA(2505) 50
Wantastiquet Mtn (1351) 22
Franklin Mtn, (Keene Quad). (1422) 12
Swanzey, NH
Mt Haystack, VT
Mt Snow, VT

Rockwood Pond -- 6
Perkins Pond -- 2.2
Troy, NH -- 5

S
SW
W

2. MONADNOCK (3165)

© 2005 by Brent E. Scudder

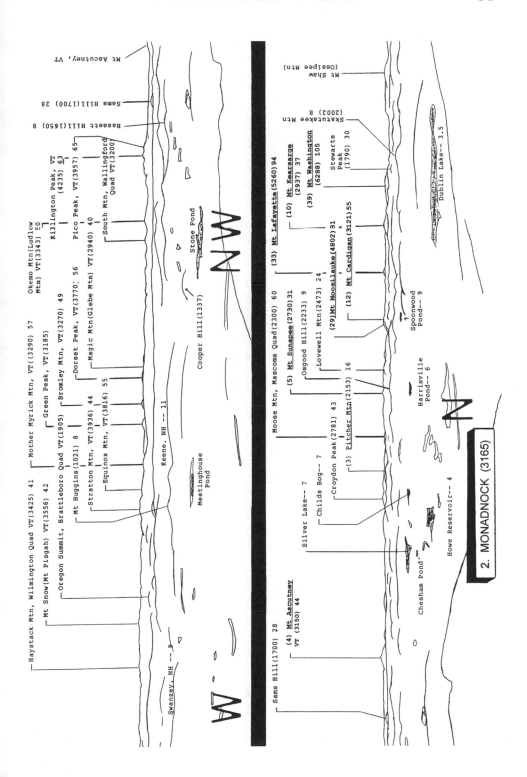

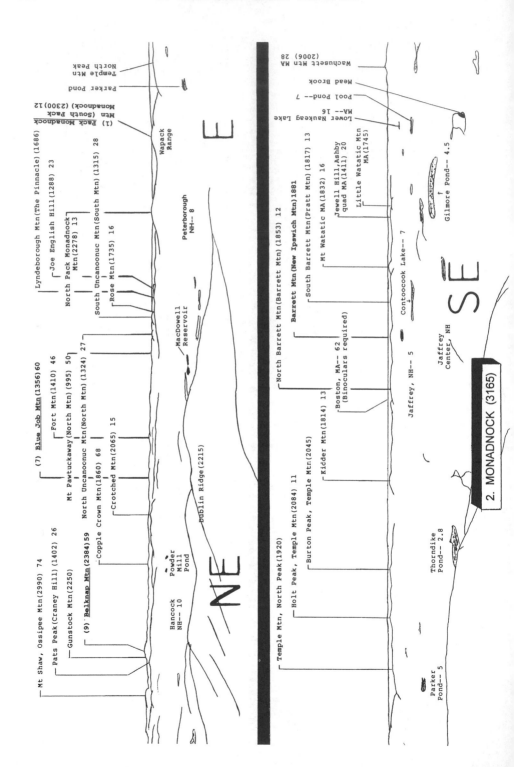

NE panorama (upper, inverted labels reading E):

Temple Mtn North Peak
Parker Pond
Pack Monadnock Mtn (South Mtn) (2300) 12
(1) Pack Monadnock Mtn (South Pack Monadnock) (2300) 12
Lyndeborough Mtn (The Pinnacle) (1686)
Joe English Hill (1288) 23
North Pack Monadnock Mtn (2278) 13
South Uncanoonuc Mtn (South Mtn) (1315) 28
Rose Mtn (1735) 16
Wapack Range
Peterborough NH-- 8
MacDowell Reservoir

NE panorama (lower):

Mt Shaw, Ossipee Mtn (2990) 74
Pats Peak (Craney Hill) (1402) 26
Gunstock Mtn (2250)
(9) Belknap Mtn (2384) 59
(7) Blue Job Mtn (1356) 60
Fort Mtn (1410) 46
Mt Pawtuckaway (North Mtn) (995) 50
North Uncanoonuc Mtn (North Mtn) (1324) 27
Copple Crown Mtn (1860) 68
Crotched Mtn (2065) 15
Powder Mill Pond
Hancock NH-- 10
Dublin Ridge (2215)

NE

SE panorama (upper):

Wachusett Mtn MA (2006) 28
Mead Brook
Pool Pond -- 7
MA -- 16
Lower Naukeag Lake
Jewell Hill, Ashby quad MA (1411) 20
Little Watatic Mtn MA (1745)
Gilmore Pond -- 4.5

SE panorama (lower):

Temple Mtn, North Peak (1920)
North Barrett Mtn (Barrett Mtn) (1853) 12
Barrett Mtn (New Ipswich Mtn) 1881
South Barrett Mtn (Pratt Mtn) (1817) 13
Mt Watatic MA (1832) 16
Contoocook Lake -- 7
Holt Peak, Temple Mtn (2084) 11
Burton Peak, Temple Mtn (2045)
Kidder Mtn (1814) 13
Boston, MA -- 62 (Binoculars required)
Jaffrey, NH -- 5
Jaffrey Center, NH
Parker Pond -- 5
Thorndike Pond -- 2.8

SE

2. MONADNOCK (3165)

(3) PITCHER MOUNTAIN

N 43° 05.652'
W 72° 08.113'

(Elevation 2153 feet)

More people are beginning to hear of Pitcher Mountain. Hiking guides now mention it. Local people know it well. The peak lies along a continuous trail system that starts at Rising Corner, Connecticut and extends all the way to Ragged Mountain located six miles north of Mount Kearsarge. The Metacomet-Monadnock trail connects with the Monadnock-Sunapee Greenway which in turn runs into the Sunapee-Ragged-Kearsarge Greenway. It has been proposed to extend this trail system northward to connect with the Appalachian Trail near Smarts Mountain located not far from White River Junction, Vermont.

Pitcher Mountain has a fantastic view and is easy to reach. This elevation is one of many hills of similar height representing the uplands of Cheshire County, New Hampshire. Ponds are everywhere while Highland Lake dominates the view to the east.

One may reach this elevation from Route 9 northeast of Keene by turning northwest towards Stoddard on Route 123 and driving 4.7 miles to a parking lot on the right (N 05.575 min, W 08.377 min). The lot may also be reached from Route 10 by turning east on 123 near Marlow and driving 3.1 miles. A white-blazed path leads off to the right. The climb takes but 15 minutes.

A fire tower stands on top. When open, the public may climb to the cab, enjoy the view and talk with the fire ranger. If the tower is closed, one can still reach the floor below the cab and look about.

Should the view look unfamiliar, locate the reference landmark mountains, an idea developed in the first chapter. First locate Grand Monadnock, familiar to most as Mount Monadnock. It stands to the south as a huge massif. In order to find Kearsarge, gaze towards the northeast at a nearby rounded peak. We now ask you to become a human protractor. Stretch out the left hand at full length in front of your face with the palm down and the fingers spread. Line up the middle finger with the nearer rounded peak, and your thumb will point to the more distant Kearsarge. The third reference landmark mountain, Ascutney, appears prominently a little north of northwest in the middle distance standing alone.

Add two more landmarks to the list. The first is the nearby rounded hill that we used to locate Mount Kearsarge – Lovewell Mountain. The other landmark is Killington Peak, Vermont. Return your gaze to Mount Ascutney. Become a left-handed human protractor once more. Place the forefinger on Ascutney. The little finger gives you Killington.

How accurate is the human protractor? Outstretched fingers on small hands would seem to subtend a smaller angle than those on large hands. But a large hand is assumed to be at the end of the long arm of a taller person and thus farther from the eye. The angle subtended should be nearly identical.

Climb Pitcher in the early spring and still see several peaks with snow-whitened ski trails. Vermont's Stratton Mountain looms large to the west. On the left, Mount Snow is less visible due to it being partially blocked by a nearer ridge. Our lower elevation lessens the ability to pick out the ski mountains along the Wapack Range. But look directly southeast. To the right stands Pack Monadnock and then Temple Mountain, its trails barely visible. Watatic in Massachusetts is but a bump on the horizon and easily confused with other heights. Osgood Hill hides Wachusett.

Another ski mountain looms into view. Left of Pack Monadnock lies a nearby pond containing islands (Island Pond, of course!) Farther left on the horizon stands Crotched Mountain with an upper trail in view.

We now see only one of the northern snow-capped peaks, Lafayette, located "two fingers" to the left of Lovewell Mountain. This crest is hard to recognize unless there is an unusual combination of weather conditions. A storm must be centered to the southeast of Cape Cod causing cloudiness to spread well into southern New Hampshire. Any precipitation must remain to the south. These conditions produce a north wind that results in excellent visibility. What we seek is a foreground deep in cloud shadow and a snow-covered Lafayette bathed in sunlight. It will be distant and tiny but gleaming white on the horizon 77 miles away.

Take a picnic lunch and enjoy the day. Do some side hikes from the top. Pitcher is a mountain for all of the family from the oldest to the youngest. You will all return home with pleasant memories.

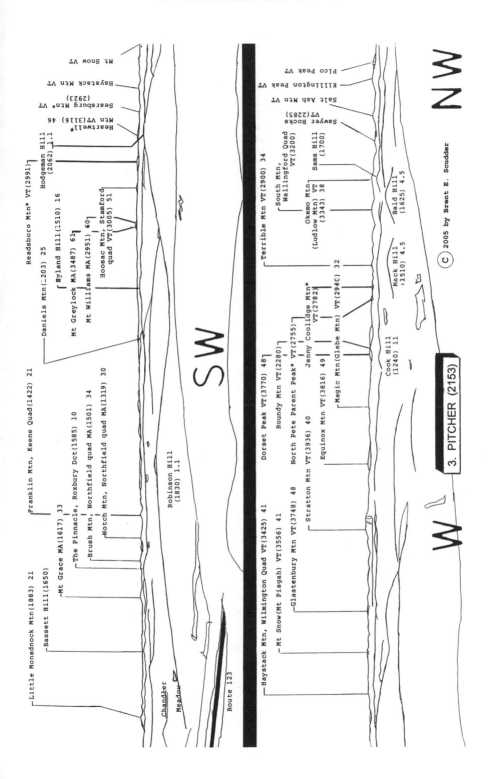

3. PITCHER (2153)

NW

SW

W

© 2005 by Brent E. Scudder

Mt Snow VT
Haystack Mtn VT
Searsburg Mtn* VT (2923)
Heartwell* Mtn VT(3116) 46
Hodgeman Hill (2062) 1.1
Readsboro Mtn* VT(2991)
Daniels Mtn(~203) 25
Hyland Hill(1510) 16
Mt Greylock MA(3487) 61
Mt Williams MA(2951) 60
Hoosac Mtn, Stamford, quad VT(3005) 51

Little Monadnock Mtn(1883) 21
Bassett Hill(1650)
Mt Grace MA(1617) 33
The Pinnacle, Roxbury Dct(1585) 10
Brush Mtn, Northfield quad MA(1501) 34
Notch Mtn, Northfield quad MA(1319) 30
Franklin Mtn, Keene Quad(1422) 21
Robinson Hill (1830) 1.1

Chandler Meadow
Route 123

Pico Peak VT
Killington Peak VT
Salt Ash Mtn VT
Sawyer Rocks VT(2285)
South Mtn, Wallingford Quad VT(3200)
Sams Hill (1700)
Bald Hill (1625) 4.5
Okemo Mtn (Ludlow Mtn) VT (3343) 38
Terrible Mtn VT(2900) 34
Mack Hill (1510) 4.5
Jenny Coolidge Mtn* VT(2782)
Magic Mtn(Glebe Mtn) VT(294C) 32
Cook Hill (1240) 11
Equinox Mtn VT(3936) 40
North Pete Parent Peak* VT(2755)
Roundy Mtn VT(2280)
Dorset Peak VT(3770) 48
Stratton Mtn VT(3748) 48
Glastenbury Mtn VT(3556) 41
Mt Snow(Mt Pisgah) VT(3425) 41
Haystack Mtn, Wilmington Quad VT(3425) 41

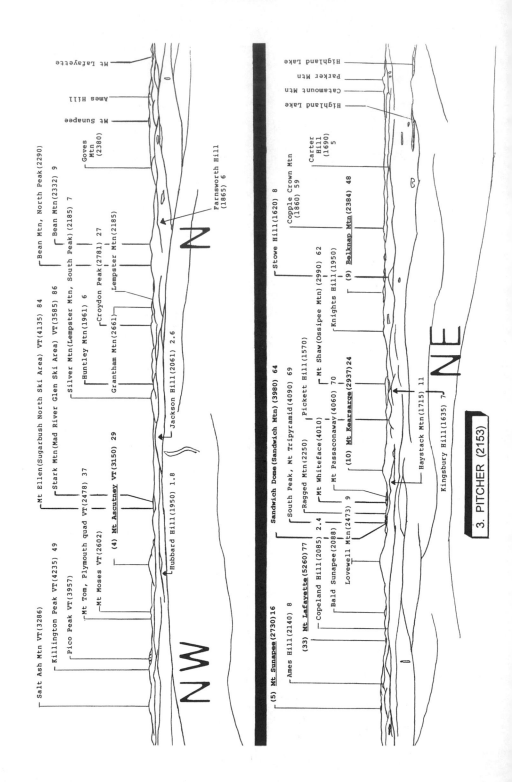

Salt Ash Mtn VT(3286)
Killington Peak VT(4235) 49
Pico Peak VT(3957)
Mt Tom, Plymouth quad VT(2478) 37
Mt Moses VT(2602)
Mt Ellen(Sugarbush North Ski Area) VT(4135) 84
Stark Mtn(Mad River Glen Ski Area) VT(3585) 86
Silver Mtn(Lempster Mtn, South Peak) (2185) 7
Huntley Mtn(1961) 6
Croydon Peak(2781) 27
Lempster Mtn(2185)
Grantham Mtn(2661)
Bean Mtn, North Peak(2290)
Bean Mtn(2332) 9
Goves Mtn (2380)
Mt Sunapee
Ames Hill
Mt Lafayette
(4) Mt Ascutney VT(3150) 29
Hubbard Hill(1950) 1.8
Jackson Hill(2061) 2.6
Farnsworth Hill (1865) 6

N

NW

(5) Mt Sunapee (2730)16
Ames Hill(2140) 8
(33) Mt Lafayette (5260)77
Copeland Hill(2085) 2.4
Bald Sunapee(2088)
Lovewell Mtn(2473) 9
Sandwich Dome (Sandwich Mtn) (3980) 64
South Peak, Mt Tripyramid(4090) 69
Ragged Mtn(2250)
Mt Whiteface(4010)
Mt Passaconaway(4060) 70
(10) Mt Kearsarge (2937)24
Pickett Hill(1570)
Mt Shaw(Ossipee Mtn) (2990) 62
Knights Hill(1950)
Haystack Mtn(1715) 11
Kingsbury Hill(1635) 7
Stowe Hill(1620) 8
Copple Crown Mtn (1860) 59
(9) Belknap Mtn (2384) 48
Carter Hill (1690) 5
Highland Lake
Catamount Mtn
Parker Mtn
Highland Lake

NE

3. PITCHER (2153)

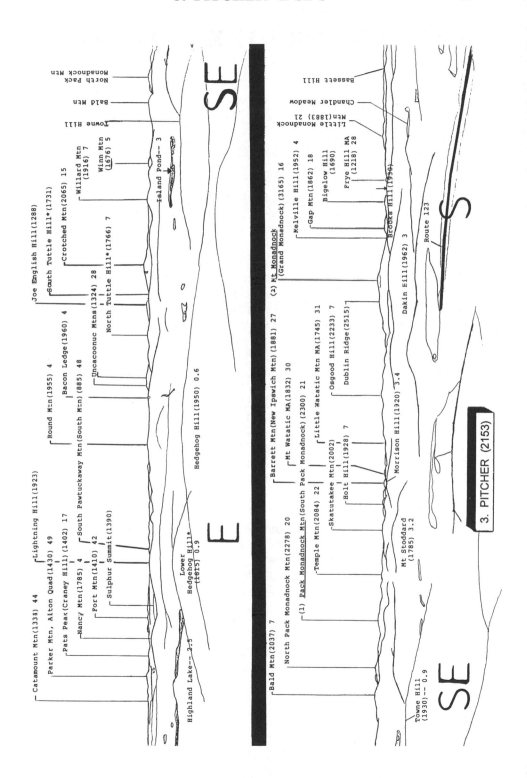

3. PITCHER (2153)

(4) MOUNT ASCUTNEY, VERMONT

N 43° 26.628'
W 72° 27.257'

(Elevation 3150 feet)

Chutney, Putney and Ascutney: these names would suggest a British origin. Yet the Algonquin word "Ascutegnik" meaning "a meeting of the waters" appears to be the source for the title of this peak.

Ascutney startles the viewer by its abrupt solitary presence that towers above the Connecticut River. Much of its mass is quartz syenite, rocks that resist erosion and glaciers well. Over the millennia the surrounding countryside washed away to lower elevations. Ascutney remained. Great ice sheets flowed over and around the peak plucking away boulders and dropping them as far away as Massachusetts.

This monadnock has a long history. It was one of the first higher peaks to have been encountered by encroaching Colonial civilization. Rock quarries were an early industry with Ascutney building stones having been shipped as far as Montreal, New York and Ohio. A hiking trail was established in 1825. Around the turn of the Twentieth Century, James P. Taylor climbed Ascutney frequently. He later founded the Green Mountain Club which built the path that runs the length of Vermont, the Long Trail. This in turn inspired the establishment of the Appalachian Trail.

When gazing from the summit tower, see Mount Moosilauke beyond the top of Ascutney's north summit. Mount Lafayette appears just beyond and to the right of Moosilauke. Only 100 feet of Mount Washington looms over the top of the nearer Carr Mountain. Mounts Osceola, Tecumseh, Tripyramid and Sandwich Dome appear in succession followed by the closer Cardigan. Our eyes then rest upon nearby Grantham Mountain and Croydon Peak.

There are four trails to the top. The Futures Trail and a toll road commence at the entrance to Ascutney State Park. This road is open daily from the middle of May to the middle of October. Parking is found within a mile of the summit which means that the individual must complete the final ascent on foot, a gentle climb lasting about 35 minutes.

To reach the State Park, get off of I-91 at Exit 8 and drive east a short distance to the intersection of Routes 12 and 5. Go left on 5 and proceed 1.2 miles to Back Mountain Road (Route 44A) which angles left. Take that road for 1.1 miles to the Park entrance. The Futures Trail starts at the base of the mountain near the Park campground's site #22 (N 26.089 min, W 24.454 min). Expect to climb a rather steep slope for 4.6 miles taking about 2 hours and 40 minutes to arrive at the top.

From the observation tower, let us review the easy-to-spot reference landmark mountains covered thus far. Mount Monadnock stands alone on the horizon between southeast and south. Kearsarge, with its characteristic attendant peak to the right, looms up in the middle distance slightly south of due east. Find Lovewell Mountain between the two appearing as a slight bump beyond the long Sunapee Mountain ridge to the southeast. Almost directly in back of us is Killington Peak with a few ski trails visible. Let us add Okemo Mountain to the reference landmark list. Turn left from Killington past the nearby Salt Ash Mountain until your eyes reach a ski-trailed profile only fifteen miles away. That is Okemo.

The panoramic view is of patchwork fields with higher mountains rearing upwards farther away. Looking south, we can see Mount Grace and Crag Mountain, both in Massachusetts. To the west, Buck and Erebus Mountains near Lake George in New York State poke the horizon. Most of the principal peaks in Vermont may be seen from here. To the southwest, there is Mount Snow, then Magic, Stratton, Equinox and Dorset Mountains. To the north find Mounts Wilson, Abraham, Ellen, Camels Hump and Mansfield.

Hike to Ascutney's West Peak on a windy day and watch hang gliding. Ski on the northwest slopes that start down from about two-thirds the way up. The mountain has a variety of recreational activity.

A person wonders why Ascutney is not used more by the public. I-91 makes it perhaps the most accessible higher peak when traveling from the cities of the lower Connecticut River Valley. The view is magnificent. Ascutney's toll road for easy access is a feature that Grand Monadnock lacks. Yet Monadnock is far more popular.

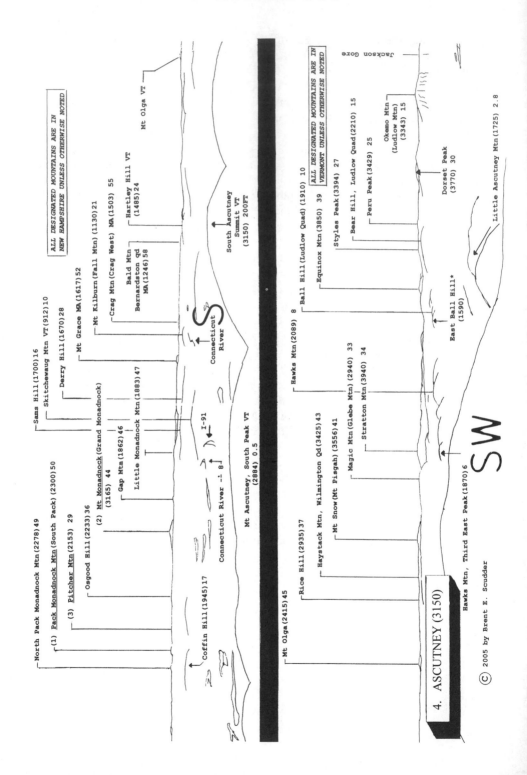

ALL DESIGNATED MOUNTAINS ARE IN
NEW HAMPSHIRE UNLESS OTHERWISE NOTED

Mt Olga VT

Hartley Hill VT (1485) 24

Bald Mtn
Bernardston qd
MA (1246) 58

Crag Mtn (Crag West) MA (1503) 55

Mt Kilburn (Fall Mtn) (1130) 21

Mt Grace MA (1617) 52

Derry Hill (1670) 28

Skitchewaug Mtn VT (912) 10

Sams Hill (1700) 16

North Pack Monadnock Mtn (2278) 49

(1) Pack Monadnock Mtn (South Pack) (2300) 50

(3) Pitcher Mtn (2153) 29

Osgood Hill (2233) 36

(2) Mt Monadnock (Grand Monadnock) (3165) 44

Gap Mtn (1862) 46

Little Monadnock Mtn (1883) 47

Coffin Hill (1945) 17

Connecticut River

South Ascutney
Summit VT
(3150) 200FT

I-91

Connecticut River –⁏ 8

Mt Ascutney, South Peak VT
(2884) 0.5

S

ALL DESIGNATED MOUNTAINS ARE IN
VERMONT UNLESS OTHERWISE NOTED

Jackson Gore

Okemo Mtn
(Ludlow Mtn)
(3343) 15

Dorset Peak
(3770) 30

Little Ascutney Mtn (1725) 2.8

Peru Peak (3429) 25

Bear Hill, Ludlow Quad (2210) 15

Styles Peak (3394) 27

Equinox Mtn (3850) 39

Ball Hill (Ludlow Quad) (1910) 10

Hawks Mtn (2089) 8

East Ball Hill*
(1590)

Rice Hill (2935) 37

Haystack Mtn, Wilmington Qd (3425) 43

Mt Snow (Mt Pisgah) (3556) 41

Magic Mtn (Glebe Mtn) (2940) 33

Stratton Mtn (3940) 34

Mt Olga (2415) 45

Hawks Mtn, Third East Peak (1870) 6

SW

4. ASCUTNEY (3150)

© 2005 by Brent E. Scudder

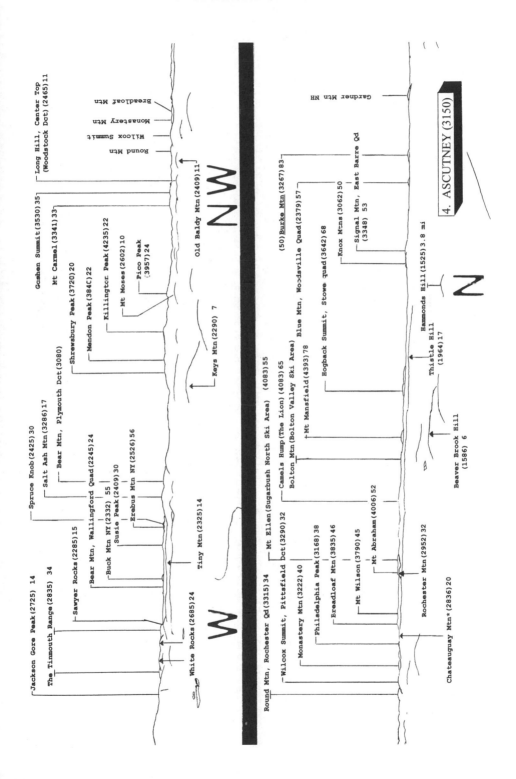

4. ASCUTNEY (3150)

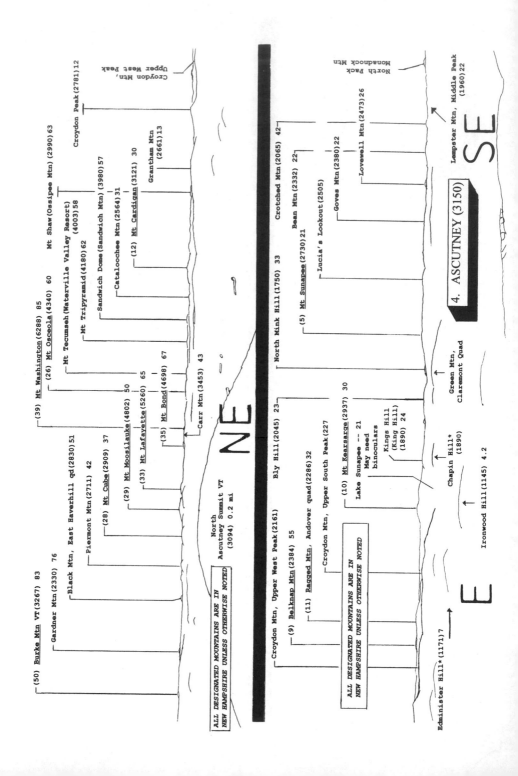

NE

(50) <u>Burke Mtn</u> VT (3267) 83

Gardner Mtn (2330) 76

Black Mtn, East Haverhill qd (2830) 51

Piermont Mtn (2711) 42

(28) <u>Mt Cube</u> (2909) 37

(29) <u>Mt Moosilauke</u> (4802) 50

(33) <u>Mt Lafayette</u> (5260) 65

(35) <u>Mt Bond</u> (4698) 67

Carr Mtn (3453) 43

(39) <u>Mt Washington</u> (6288) 85

(26) <u>Mt Osceola</u> (4340) 60

Mt Tecumseh (Waterville Valley Resort)
                    (4003) 58

Mt Tripyramid (4180) 62

Sandwich Dome (Sandwich Mtn) (3980) 57

Cataloochee Mtn (2564) 31

(12) <u>Mt Cardigan</u> (3121) 30

Grantham Mtn
        (2661) 13

Croydon Peak (2781) 12

Croydon Mtn,
Upper West Peak

North
Ascutney Summit VT
(3094) 0.2 mi

ALL DESIGNATED MOUNTAINS ARE IN
NEW HAMPSHIRE UNLESS OTHERWISE NOTED

E

Edminister Hill* (1171) 7

Croydon Mtn, Upper West Peak (2161)

(9) <u>Belknap Mtn</u> (2384) 55

(11) <u>Ragged Mtn</u>, Andover quad (2286) 32

Croydon Mtn, Upper South Peak (227

Bly Hill (2045) 23

(10) <u>Mt Kearsarge</u> (2937) 30

Lake Sunapee -- 21
May need
binoculars

Kings Hill
(King Hill)
(1890) 24

Chapin Hill*
(1890)

Ironwood Hill (1145) 4.2

North Mink Hill (1750) 33

Crotched Mtn (2065) 42

Bean Mtn (2332) 22

(5) <u>Mt Sunapee</u> (2730) 21

Lucia's Lookout (2505)

Goves Mtn (2380) 22

Lovewell Mtn (2473) 26

Green Mtn,
Claremont Quad

ALL DESIGNATED MOUNTAINS ARE IN
NEW HAMPSHIRE UNLESS OTHERWISE NOTED

SE

4. ASCUTNEY (3150)

Lempster Mtn, Middle Peak
                (1960) 22

North Pack
Monadnock Mtn

(5) MOUNT SUNAPEE

N 43° 18.830'
W 72° 04.451'

(Elevation 2730 feet)

"I've been up on Sunapee. I did not see all that." This will be the reaction of most visitors if they examine the diagrams that follow. They never saw the entire view. Nor will they ever. That is unless a summit observation tower is built.

In the 1970s, it was possible to take in the entire horizon by merely moving about the mountain top. But over the years the growth of trees has been swallowing up one of the best views in New England bit by bit. A person can still see much. Climb to the balcony of the Summit Lodge and get a complete scan of Vermont with Mount Snow to the southwest; Okemo, Ascutney and Killington to the west and Mount Ellen to the northwest. Hike a little ways down the ski trails and behold most of the magnificent scenery across Lake Sunapee to the north and east.

Most of Sunapee's view was diagrammed with photographs taken from the top in 1971 when the trees were smaller. Even then a ridge blocked what could be seen to the southeast. To learn what was visible in that direction, we physically got around the blocking ridge and filmed the remaining expanse from White Ledges (N 18.550 min, W 03.833 min.)

It is a common practice in this book to create 360-degree panoramas by assembling partial views seen from different viewing positions on or near each summit. Such a procedure causes problems with any nearby hill visible from two separate lookouts. In the diagram, said hill will appear to be in the proper position when viewed from one site but several degrees to the left or right when viewed from the other. The short distance to such a hill produces little difficulty in identification.

Prepare to see a fantastic view—the best one so far! We can gaze over Lake Sunapee all the way to the 4802-foot Mount Moosilauke. Append Moosilauke to your list of reference landmark mountains. Also add Mount Cardigan which lies closer in but to Moosilauke's right. Farther east, one sees the entire White Mountain panorama extending from Lafayette to South Twin, Bond, Washington, and Chocorua.

Sunapee Mountain is actually a multi-crested range seven miles long that is from south to north.   Joining Sunapee near its upper end from the southwest is a similar but longer range, Lempster Mountain. The peak called Mount Sunapee lies near the convergence of these two long ridges and is the highest elevation in the complex. It is there that we have Mount Sunapee State Park complete with ski trails, open slopes and ski lifts. During summer, the tourist may ride the chair lift. For days and hours of operation check www.mountsunapee.com

The climber can shun the casual tourist for most of his hike by choosing the Andrew Brook Trail, a climb that includes White Ledges. If driving north on I-89, get off at Exit 9 and head west on Route 103 away from Warner. After 12.1 miles, turn left on Mountain Road. Proceed another 1.2 miles. Park on the side shoulder (N 17.880 min, W 02.286 min). There is a tiny sign, but the trail is clearly seen heading westward into the woods to the right of Andrew Brook. It crisscrosses this stream several times on the way up to lovely Lake Solitude, the 2520-foot elevation of which makes it the highest body of water in southern New Hampshire. Continue climbing until the trail swings out and back to bring you to the top of White Ledges. During this latter segment, you pass Jack and June Junction, the meeting place of the the Monadnock-Sunapee Greenway and the Sunapee-Ragged-Kearsarge Greenway trails.

Behold the view! On the left stands Mount Kearsarge with its smaller attendant summit just to its south. Directly before us are seen the Mink Hills capped by Stewarts Peak. Several lakes spread out before us with such names as Blaisdell, Todd and Massasecum. Sprinkle among them the towns of South Newbury and Bradford, and the background is complete. Placid Lake Solitude lies beneath us with Crotched Mountain easy to find beyond. Pack Monadnock requires careful scrutiny but can be identified off to the right. Farther west, the rounded Lovewell pops up 8 miles away followed by Monadnock and Pitcher Mountains.

Onward to the top! You will need two hours to get from car to summit. Again the view is unfamiliar. But seek the reference landmark mountains. We have mentioned every one. Soon all of this wonderful view falls into place.

Be a casual tourist, skier or hiker. With the large lake in the foreground and the White Mountains beyond, the view from Mount Sunapee is a must.

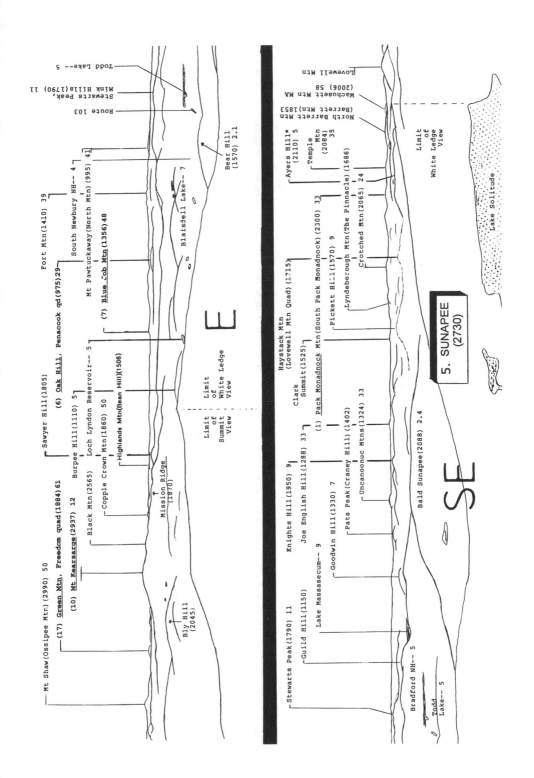

5. SUNAPEE
(2730)

Mt Shaw(Ossipee Mtn) (2990) 50

(17) Green Mtn, Freedom quad(1884) 61

(10) Mt Kearsarge(2937) 12

Black Mtn (2565)

Copple Crown Mtn(1860) 50

Highlands Mtn(Bean Hill)(1506)

Mission Ridge (1870)

Bly Hill (2045)

Sawyer Hill(1805)

(6) Oak Hill, Penacook qd(975)29

Burpee Hill(1110) 5

Loch Lyndon Reservoir-- 5

Limit of Summit View

Limit of White Ledge View

Mt Shaw(Ossipee Mtn) (2990) 50

Fort Mtn(1410) 39

South Newbury NH-- 4

Mt Pawtuckaway(North Mtn) (995) 41

(7) Blue Job Mtn (1356)48

Blaisdell Lake- 7

Bear Hill (1570) 2.1

Todd Lake-- 5

Mink Hills(1790) 11

Stewarts Peak,

Route 103

E

Haystack Mtn (Lovewell Mtn Quad) (1715)

Clark Summit (1525)

(1) Pack Monadnock Mtn(South Pack Monadnock) (2300) 33

Pickett Hill(1570) 9

Lyndeborough Mtn(The Pinnacle) (1686)

Crotched Mtn(2065) 24

Ayers Hill* (2110) 5

Temple Mtn (2084) 35

North Barrett Mtn (Barrett Mtn)1853

Wachusett Mtn MA (2006) 58

Lovewell Mtn

Limit of White Ledge View

Lake Solitude

SE

Stewarts Peak(1790) 11

Guild Hill(1150)

Lake Massasecum-- 9

Knights Hill(1950) 9

Joe English Hill(1288) 33

Goodwin Hill(1330) 7

Pats Peak(Craney Hill) (1402)

Uncanoonuc Mtns(1324) 33

Bald Sunapee(2088) 2.4

Bradford NH-- 5

Todd Lake-- 5

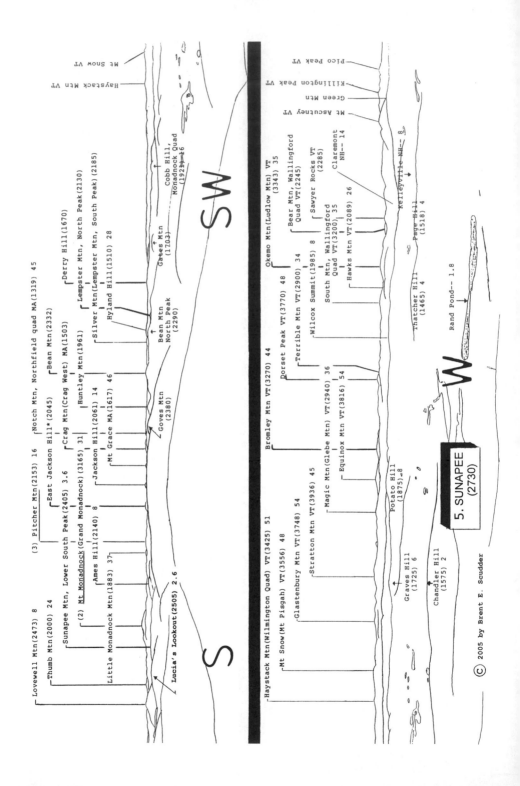

Lovewell Mtn(2473) 8
Thumb Mtn(2000) 24
Sunapee Mtn, Lower South Peak(2405) 3.6
(2) Mt Monadnock(Grand Monadnock)(3165) 8
Ames Hill(2140) 8
Little Monadnock Mtn(1883) 37

(3) Pitcher Mtn(2153) 16   Notch Mtn, Northfield quad MA(1319) 45
East Jackson Hill*(2045)   Bean Mtn(2332)
Crag Mtn(Crag West) MA(1503)
Jackson Hill(2061) 14   Huntley Mtn(1961)
Mt Grace MA(1617) 46   Silver Mtn(Lempster Mtn, South Peak)(2185)
                          Lempster Mtn, North Peak(2130)
                          Derry Hill(1670)
Goves Mtn
(2380)   Hyland Hill(1510) 28
             Bean Mtn   Gates Mtn
             North Peak   (1703)
             (2290)   Cobb Hill,
                                  Monadnock Quad
                                  (1924) 16

Lucia's Lookout (2505) 2.6

Mt Snow VT
Haystack Mtn VT

S

SW

Haystack Mtn(Wilmington Quad) VT(3425) 51
Mt Snow(Mt Pisgah) VT(3556) 48
Glastenbury Mtn VT(3748) 54
Stratton Mtn VT(3936) 45
Magic Mtn(Glebe Mtn) VT(2940) 36
Equinox Mtn VT(3816) 54

Bromley Mtn VT(3270) 44
Dorset Peak VT(3770) 48
Terrible Mtn VT(2900) 34
Wilcox Summit(1985) 8
Potato Hill
(1875) 8

Okemo Mtn(Ludlow Mtn) VT
(3343) 35
Bear Mtn, Wallingford
Quad VT(2245)
Sawyer Rocks VT
(2285)
South Mtn, Wallingford   Claremont
Quad VT(3200) 35   NH-- 14
Hawks Mtn VT(2089) 26

Kelleyville NH-- 8

Page Hill
(1518) 4
Thatcher Hill
(1465) 4

Rand Pond-- 1.8

Pico Peak VT
Killington Peak VT
Green Mtn
Mt Ascutney VT

Graves Hill
(1725) 6
Chandler Hill
(1575) 2

W

5. SUNAPEE
(2730)

© 2005 by Brent E. Scudder

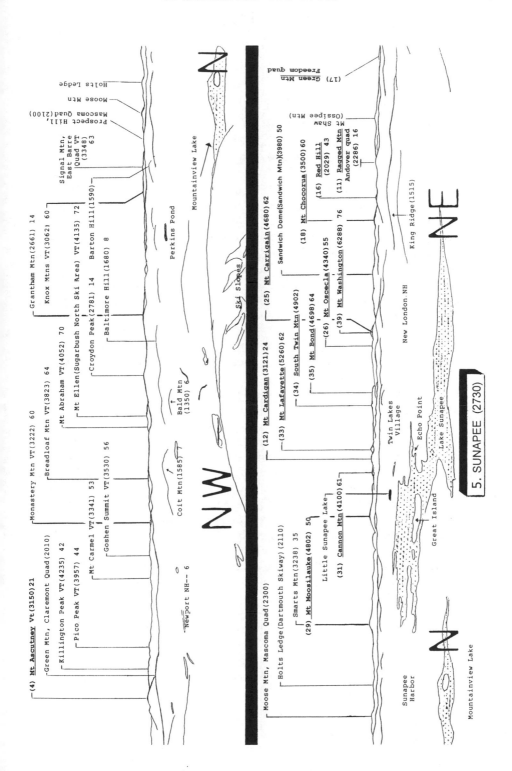

5. SUNAPEE (2730)

(6) OAK HILL

Penacook Quadrangle

N 43° 16.752'
W 71° 30.330'

(Elevation 975 feet)

It is time to interrupt our progress northward through New Hampshire and cross over to the east. We alight upon a summit of low elevation, yet one from which one sees all of the upper Merrimack Valley. Oak Hill, located five miles northeast of Concord, is representative of numerous low summits in southern New Hampshire found at the doorstep of most of its inhabitants. Many towns have an "Oak Hill" serving as a Sunday afternoon climb for the family. In East Derry, it is Warner Hill. In Stratham, it is Stratham Hill and outside of Milford, Federal Hill. Sometimes "Oak Hill" is just a place where the road passes over a ridge surrounded by open fields allowing for a fantastic view of the lakes and the mountains.

New Hampshire has eight real Oak Hills. The one near Concord is not surrounded by hills of similar height, and so a view of the White Mountains unfolds. Easily visible are Mounts Osceola, Carrigain and Chocorua, summit panoramas that we feature later on. Towering above these is Mount Washington shimmering white in winter.

Our low elevation precludes spotting many of the reference landmark mountains previously designated. Moosilauke, Killington, Okemo and Ascutney are absent. But we spot them later in the book many times. Visible is Monadnock, that massive summit distant to the southwest. Kearsarge looms far to the right, its characteristic attendant peak now seen to the left. Lovewell Mountain is harder to find. To the left of Kearsarge at an angle of about 1 ¾ hand spans lies a ridge that is at the same distance as Kearsarge. These are the Mink Hills capped by Stewarts Peak. Seek the tallest rounded summit farther off but immediately to the left. That is Lovewell. Return to Kearsarge now and measure the same distance to the right that the Mink Hills are to the left. There stands Mount Cardigan with characteristic attendant peaks on both sides.

Oak Hill is a gentle thirty minute climb from Oak Hill Road. To reach it take Route I-93 to Exit 16, the off-ramp for East Concord. Go East. If you leave a Mobile gas station to your right you will be on Shawmut Street. After 0.7 miles Shawmut veers left to become Oak Hill Road. Go an additional 3.3 miles and look to the right for a white house with an octagonal observation loft built on to it. The trail commences across the road from there beyond a locked gate (N 16.379 min, W 29.240 min). You will need to park along the road and hike up. Private property surrounds the area, so please park unobtrusively, that is, near a property boundary rather than directly in front of someone's house. A couple we know leaves their car in nearby Loudon and hikes up from there.

At the top, let us add to the list of reference landmarks. Glance northward but to the east of the White Mountains. Notice two nearer rounded bumps. The right hand bump is Belknap Mountain. Not only do we see Belknap again and again later on, but we have seen it four times already. Now look southward just to the left of Concord and behold a pair of twin hills sharply defined against the sky. These are the Uncanoonuc Mountains located just west of Manchester. To the right is another rounded summit in sharp relief – Joe English Hill. As with Belknap Mountain, we have seen and shall see this trio repeatedly.

To the right of the trio, we notice that the Wapack Range is farther away. If we gaze to the right, Pitcher Mountain is hard to spot for it is easy to confuse among the many hills of Cheshire County. What about the Jerry Hill featured in the Introduction? Jerry is lined up in front of Crotched Mountain, but its treetops virtually merge with those of the nearer Rattlesnake Hill. Jerry's observation platform once gave it away.

Not to live in the Appalachian foothills means not having an "Oak Hill" at your doorstep, not having a unique way of enjoying close at hand the "greening" of spring, the haze of summer, the rampant reds and oranges of autumn and the whiteness and stillness of winter. Not having an "Oak Hill" nearby means being unable to take an hour or two from daily activity to behold the ever-changing shadows and hues of the eternal lakes and mountains. If you ever move to the Appalachian foothills, look for that "Oak Hill" nearby. A walk from your domicile may represent too distant a hike, but it is seldom beyond a fifteen-minute drive.

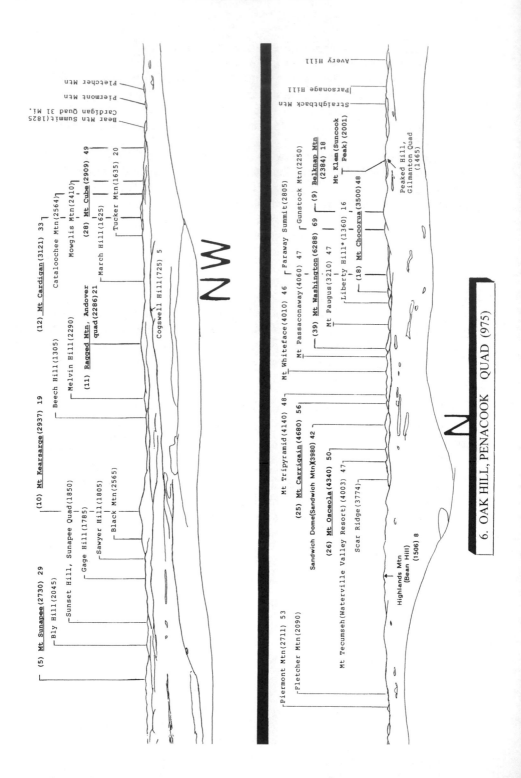

6. OAK HILL, PENACOOK QUAD (975)

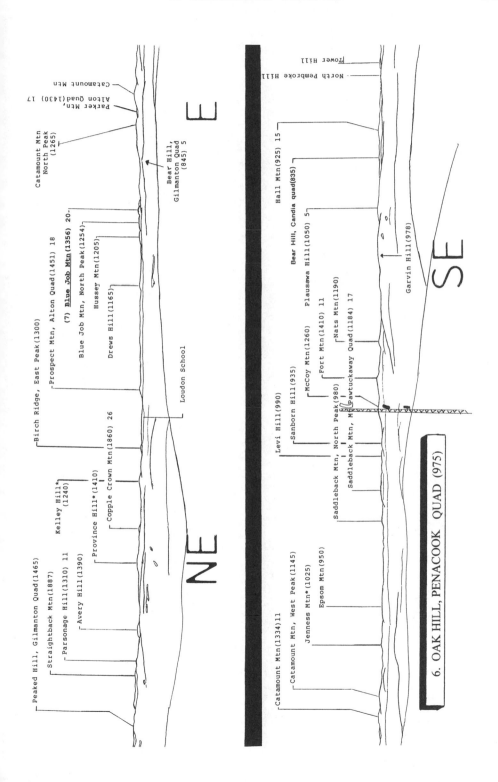

6. OAK HILL, PENACOOK QUAD (975)

NE

E

SE

Peaked Hill, Gilmanton Quad(1465)
Straightback Mtn(1887)
Parsonage Hill(1310) 11
Avery Hill(1390)
Birch Ridge, East Peak(1300)
Prospect Mtn, Alton Quad(1451) 18
(7) Blue Job Mtn(1356) 20
Blue Job Mtn, North Peak(1254)
Hussey Mtn(1205)
Drews Hill(1165)
Catamount Mtn
North Peak
(1265)
Parker Mtn, (1430) 17
Alton Quad
Catamount Mtn
Bear Hill,
Gilmanton Quad
(845) 5
Loudon School
Kelley Hill*
(1240)
Province Hill*(1410)
Copple Crown Mtn(1860) 26

Catamount Mtn(1334)11
Catamount Mtn, West Peak(1145)
Jenness Mtn*(1025)
Epsom Mtn(950)
Levi Hill(990)
Sanborn Hill(935)
McCoy Mtn(1260)
Fort Mtn(1410) 11
Nats Mtn(1190)
Pawtuckaway Quad(1184) 17
Saddleback Mtn, North Peak(980)
Saddleback Mtn, M
Plausawa Hill(1050) 5
Bear Hill, Candia quad(835)
Hall Mtn(925) 15
North Pembroke Hill
Tower Hill
Garvin Hill(978)

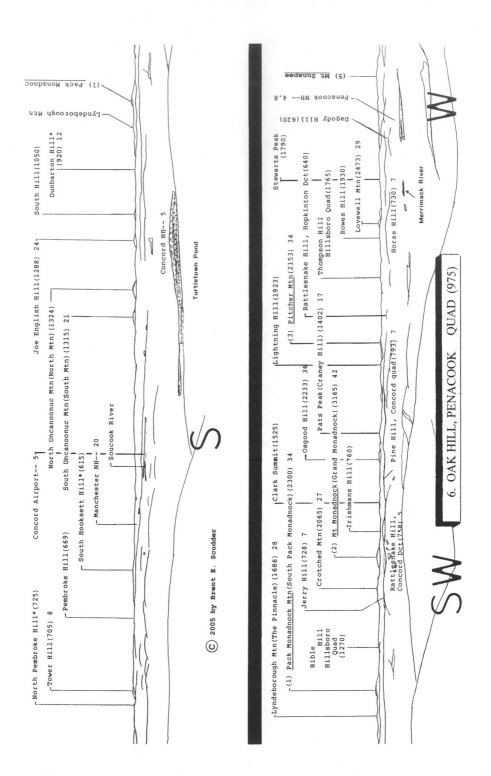

North Pembroke Hill* (725)
Tower Hill (705) 8
Pembroke Hill (669)
South Hooksett Hill* (615)
Manchester NH-- 20
Soucook River
Concord Airport-- 5
North Uncanoonuc Mtn (North Mtn) (1324)
South Uncanoonuc Mtn (South Mtn) (1315) 21
Joe English Hill (1288) 24
South Hill (1050)
Dunbarton Hill* (920) 12
Lyndeborough Mtn
(1) Pack Monadnoc

Turtletown Pond

Concord NH-- 5

(c) 2005 by Brent E. Scudder

S

Bible Hill Hillsboro Quad (1270)
Jerry Hill (728) 7
Crotched Mtn (2065) 27
(2) Mt Monadnock (Grand Monadnock) (3165) 42
Irishmans Hill (760)
Rattlesnake Hill, Concord Qct (758) 5
(1) Pack Monadnock Mtn (South Pack Monadnock) (2300) 34
Clark Summit (1525)
Osgood Hill (2233) 36
Pats Peak (Craney Hill) (1402) 17
(3) Pitcher Mtn (2153) 34
Lightning Hill (1923)
Rattlesnake Hill, Hopkinton Dct (640)
Thompson Hill Hillsboro Quad (1765)
Rowes Hill (1930)
Lovewell Mtn (2473) 29
Stewarts Peak (1790)
Dagody Hill (620)
Penacook NH-- 4.8
(5) Mt Sunapee

Pine Hill, Concord quad (793) 7
Horse Hill (730) 7
Merrimack River
Lyndeborough Mtn (The Pinnacle) (1686) 28

SW

6. OAK HILL, PENACOOK   QUAD (975)

W

(7) BLUE JOB MOUNTAIN

N 43° 19.901'
W 71° 06.984'

(Elevation 1356 feet)

Continuing eastward, we arrive at Rochester's "Oak Hill," a fifteen-minute drive from the center of town.   The   climb is easy, unrepresentative of the tribulations of the biblical Job. Given a crystal clear day, we can even see Mount Washington, and in the opposite direction, Boston.

Blue Job Mountain lies along the northern half of a range of hills that stretches eleven miles from Strafford to Farmington.   It is not the highest elevation along the range. But it is the only one with a fire tower and thus a fine view.

From the top, glance west-southwest and see Mount Monadnock well into the distance. The slightly nearer Crotched Mountain appears immediately to its right with Pack Monadnock some distance to the left. Other familiar features in this direction are blocked by high ground.

Looking westward, we recognize Mount Kearsarge.   Using the left hand as a protractor, the way we did in Chapter Three, place the palm down and spread the fingers. Put the thumb up against Kearsarge, and the little finger will point not only to the nearer Lovewell Mountain on the horizon but also to the nearer Oak Hill. Split the angle between Kearsarge and Lovewell and see Mount Sunapee 48 miles away.

Driving to the base of Blue Job involves coming north on the Spaulding Turnpike and passing around the west side of Rochester. Get off at Ten Rod Road (Exit 14) and turn right just at the bottom of the ramp followed by a quick right on to Main Street. Just shy of a Burger King, turn right onto Twombley Street. At the end of the road, make a fourth right onto Walnut Street, Route 202A. Proceed 2.3 miles to where the highway forks left, but you continue straight for another 5.6 miles. If the leaves are off the trees one can see Blue Job on the right capped by a cell phone tower. A red house lies to the left. Park on the right but do not block the adjacent locked gate (N 19.679 min, W 07.323 min).

There may be a sign on a utility pole indicating Blue Job. The two trails up the mountain both take 20 minutes. Both start about fifty feet in from the parking lot. The left hand trail is prettier for it climbs through young birch.

Look out at the view and see two domes rise up to the northwest. The higher one is Belknap Mountain. Look two thirds of the angle from Kearsarge over to Belknap and recognize Mount Cardigan low on the horizon. Moosilauke is still hidden by higher terrain.

One sees Mount Washington to the north dominating the skyline sixty-five miles away. Immediately to Washington's left is Mount Chocorua and to its right the steep defile of Carter Notch. By knowing the geography of the area, one is aware that Wildcat Mountain forms the west wall of the notch while Carter Dome forms the east.

Two more reference landmark mountains are to be added. Copple Crown, fourteen miles away, is the first mountain to the right of Carter Dome. Now measure the same angle to the left of Mount Washington as Copple Crown is to the right. Half way to the horizon stands Mount Shaw, the highest point in the Ossipee Range.

For the first time we see into Maine and have our best view of Mount Agamenticus. Over the centuries, Agamenticus has served as an excellent landmark for fishermen and coastal sailing vessels. It rises abruptly above the York countryside and can be mistaken for no other.

Be on Blue Job by 11 a.m. and the sun will light up the Atlantic, Great Bay and the Isles of Shoals. At 12:30, it will be the turn of Massachusetts Bay to be illuminated. Later in the day the water, as seen through the haze, becomes the same color as the land and is therefore hard to spot. Boston lies due south with the Prudential Building easily seen through binoculars. To the right and closer by stand the Pawtuckaway Mountains which are three hills in Nottingham, New Hampshire. The State Park associated with the Pawtuckaways with its summits and lake afford a variety of recreation.

The elevation where we stand may seem insignificant. But if we can identify objects 65 miles away to the north and 80 miles away to the south, then Blue Job is well worth the effort.

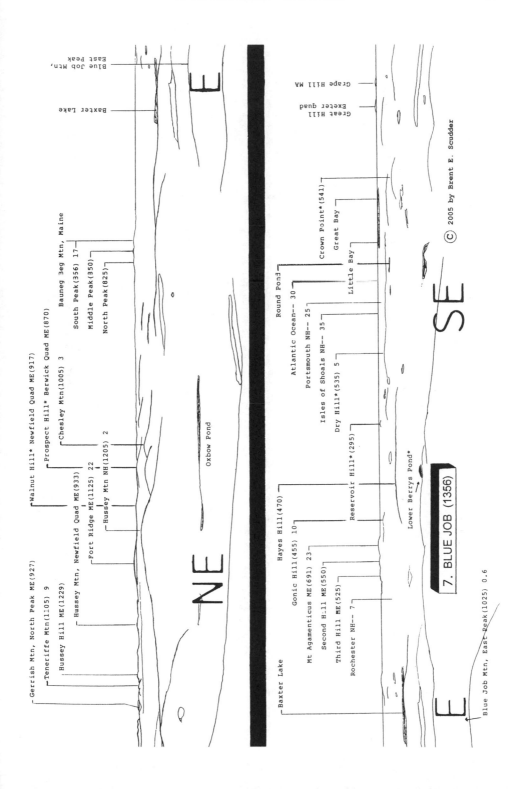

Gerrish Mtn, North Peak ME(927)
Teneriffe Mtn(1105) 9
Hussey Hill ME(1229)
Hussey Mtn, Newfield Quad ME(933)
Fort Ridge ME(1125) 22
Hussey Mtn NE(1205) 2
Walnut Hill* Newfield Quad ME(917)
Prospect Hill* Berwick Quad ME(870)
Chesley Mtn(1005) 3
Bauneg Beg Mtn, Maine
South Peak(356) 17
Middle Peak(350)
North Peak(825)

Oxbow Pond

Blue Job Mtn, East Peak
Baxter Lake

NE

Baxter Lake
Hayes Hill(470)
Gonic Hill(455) 10
Mt Agamenticus ME(691) 23
Second H.ll ME(550)
Third Hill ME(525)
Rochester NH-- 7
Reservoir Hill*(295)
Dry Hill*(535) 5
Isles of Shoals NH-- 35
Portsmouth NH-- 25
Atlantic Ocean-- 30
Round Pond
Crown Point*(541)
Great Bay
Little Bay
Grape Hill MA
Great Hill
Exeter quad

Lower Berrys Pond*

7. BLUE JOB (1356)

E

SE

Blue Job Mtn, East Peak(1025) 0.6

© 2005 by Brent E. Scudder

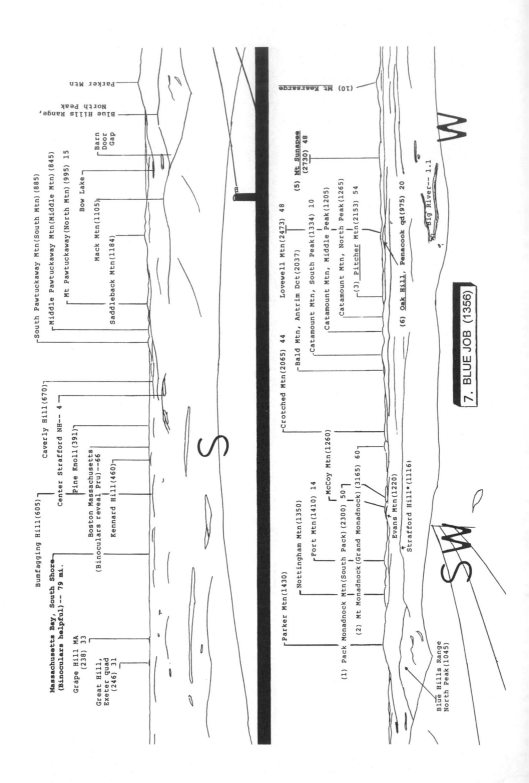

7. BLUE JOB (1356)

Labels (as appearing in the panorama):

Parker Mtn

Blue Hills Range, North Peak

Barn Door Gap

Bow Lake

Mack Mtn(1105)

Saddleback Mtn(1184)

Mt Pawtuckaway(North Mtn)(995) 15

Middle Pawtuckaway Mtn(Middle Mtn)(845)

South Pawtuckaway Mtn(South Mtn)(885)

Caverly Hill(670)

Bumfagging Hill(605)

Center Strafford NH-- 4

Pine Knoll(391)

Boston Massachusetts
(Binoculars reveal Pru)--66

Kennard Hill(460)

Massachusetts Bay, South Shore
(Binoculars helpful)-- 79 mi.

Grape Hill MA
(238) 33

Great Hill,
Exeter quad
(246) 31

(10) Mt Kearsarge

(5) Mt Sunapee
(2730) 48

Lovewell Mtn(2473) 48

Bald Mtn, Antrim Dct(2037)

Catamount Mtn, South Peak(1334) 10

Catamount Mtn, Middle Peak(1205)

Catamount Mtn, North Peak(1265)

(3) Pitcher Mtn(2153) 54

Crotched Mtn(2065) 44

McCoy Mtn(1260)

Fort Mtn(1410) 14

Nottingham Mtn(1350)

Parker Mtn(1430)

(1) Pack Monadnock Mtn(South Pack)(2300) 50

(2) Mt Monadnock(Grand Monadnock)(3165) 60

Evans Mtn(1220)

Strafford Hill*(1116)

(6) Oak Hill, Penacook qd(975) 20

Big River-- 1.1

Blue Hills Range
North Peak(1045)

S

SW

W

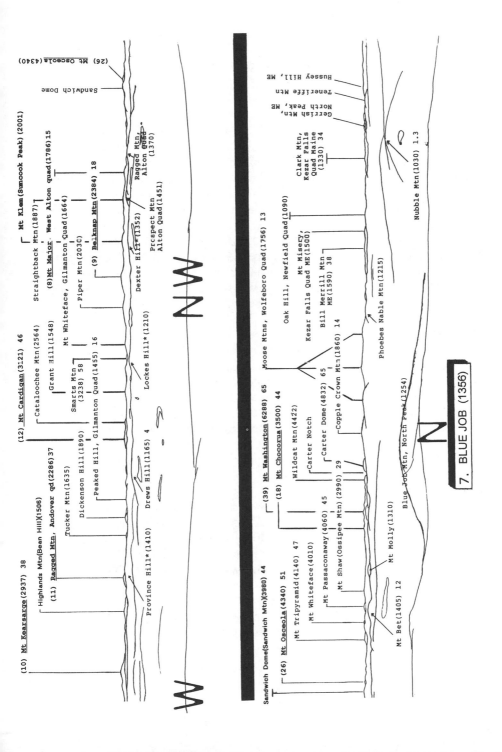

(10) Mt Kearsarge(2937) 38

Highlands Mtn(Bean Hill)(1506)

(11) Ragged Mtn, Andover qd(2286) 37

(12) Mt Cardigan(3121) 46

Cataloochee Mtn(2564)

Grant Hill(1548)

Tucker Mtn(1635)

Smarts Mtn (3238) 58

Dickenson Hill(1890)

Mt Whiteface, Gilmanton Quad(1664)

Peaked Hill, Gilmanton Quad(1455) 16

Piper Mtn(2030)

Straightback Mtn(1887)

(8)Mt Major, West Alton Quad(1786)15

Mt Klem(Suncook Peak) (2001)

Sandwich Dome

(26) Mt Osceola (4340)

Ragged Mtn,
Alton Quad (1370)

Dexter Hill*(1352)

(9) Belknap Mtn(2384) 18

Prospect Mtn
Alton Quad(1451)

Province Hill*(1410)

Drews Hill(1165) 4

Lockes Hill*(1210)

NW

W

N

Sandwich Dome(Sandwich Mtn)(3980) 44

(26) Mt Osceola (4340) 51

Mt Tripyramid(4140) 47

Mt Whiteface(4010)

Mt Passaconaway(4060) 45

Mt Shaw(Ossipee Mtn) (2990) 29

(39) Mt Washington(6288) 65

(18) Mt Chocorua (3500) 44

Wildcat Mtn(4422)

Carter Notch

Carter Dome(4832) 65

Copple Crown Mtn(1860) 14

Moose Mtns, Wolfeboro Quad(1756) 13

Oak Hill, Newfield Quad(1090)

Mt Misery,
Kezar Falls Quad ME(1500)

Bill Merrill Mtn
ME(1590) 38

Phoebes Nable Mtn(1215)

Gerrish Mtn,
North Peak, ME

Clark Mtn,
Kezar Falls
Quad Maine
(1330) 34

Teneriffe Mtn

Hussey Hill, ME

Nubble Mtn(1030) 1.3

Mt Molly(1310)

Mt Bet(1405) 12

Blue Job Mtn, North Peak(1254)

7. BLUE JOB (1356)

(8) MOUNT MAJOR

N 43° 30.812'
W 71° 17.231'

(Elevation 1786 feet)

"Awesome!"

This is the expression that some children still use to refer to everything out of the ordinary, regardless of whether the event is of great magnitude or merely the focusing of attention on something slightly unusual. Those who hike the trail from the parking lot see only surrounding forest most of the way up. But climb out onto the summit ledges and a fantastic view unfolds. A full half of the foreground is covered by giant Lake Winnipesaukee with its bays, coves, peninsulas and (what is rumored to be) 365 islands. Beyond loom the White Mountains in all their glory from Moosilauke eastward to Kearsarge North. Mount Washington is there, but one sees only a small bit of it peeping over the top of the Ossipee Mountains. Even the person who seldom uses the youngster's all-purpose expression can describe the scene with only one word – awesome!

A curious summit feature is the remains of an old stone cabin. George Phippen built it. He bought land that included the summit back in 1914 for $125. It took him eleven years before he could afford to build the cabin which he opened to hikers. During the following winter the top blew off. Six months later he replaced it with a sturdier roof . The second effort lasted two winters before northwest gales sent it flying off the ledges also. George could not afford a third roof. In 1929, the Great Depression hit. Mr. Phippen defaulted on his taxes, and he lost the property to the stewardship of the town of Alton. In 1956, Alton donated the land to the State of New Hampshire and so it remains today a state park.

To reach the beginning of the trail, drive west out of the village of Alton Bay on Route 11 for a distance of 4.2 miles. A big sign for Mount Major indicates parking on the left (N 31.149 min, W 16.440 min). Do not attempt to navigate in a direct line between the two GPS points given in this chapter. A very steep slope intervenes which gets very slippery when wet or icy. Stick to the trails.

The trail goes straight in, bears right and splits – the two splits running parallel to each other before joining up farther on. After having hiked 0.7 miles to an altitude of 940 feet, the trail divides again. The blue-blazed Mount Major

Trail turns left and ascends rather steeply. The gentler choice is the yellow-blazed Brook Trail which continues straight, loops around and climbs the mountain from behind. The latter course is recommended during slippery conditions. The main trail should take about 80 minutes from parking lot to summit. Should you elect the easier Brook Trail, add another 25 minutes to your climb.

If bad weather threatens, get off the summit! Get down to where the trees are. Sudden rain and snow squalls can chill you rapidly. During an electrical storm, one should not be using the remains of the cabin as a windbreak. Lightning has a special propensity for Mount Major.

But today is crystal clear. Try to determine the number of islands in the lake. Look northwest and see Mount Moosilauke 45 miles away. Turn your head to the right and encounter South Kinsman Mountain, South Twin, Tripyramid, Whiteface, Passaconaway and Mount Washington, the last being 52 miles away. In the middle distance stand Red Hill, Sandwich Dome and Mount Shaw. You see neither Mount Lafayette nor Mount Chocorua.

One sees many elevations in Maine. To the northeast there arise Albany and Pleasant Mountains, Douglas Hill and Clark Mountain. To the east-southeast stands a curious phenomenon. Look at Bauneg Beg Mountain 27 miles away, seen a little to the left of nearby Echo Point. You see a series of three hills. The northern hill is smallest, the middle one taller and the southern height the highest. Now look to the right and pick out Mount Agamenticus. Again there are three hills rising in succession from north to south. Let the geologist explain that coincidence.

Southwest lie the two Uncanoonuc Mountains near Manchester. Looking west we have the Belknap mountains among which Straightback and Klem are the nearer heights with Mounts Belknap and Rowe being farther away. East Quarry Mountain hides Gunstock.

Mount Major is a wonderful starter mountain, the favorite of many schools and camps. If this magnificent view fails to inspire the young to seek further climbing adventure, nothing will.

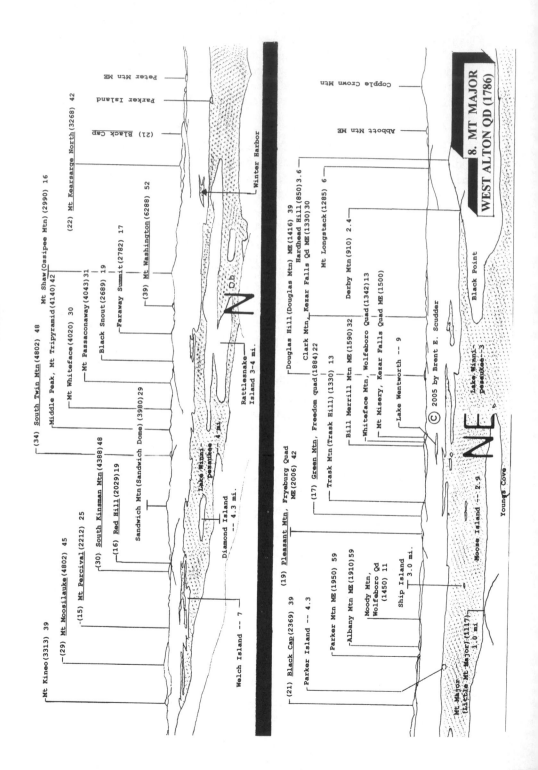

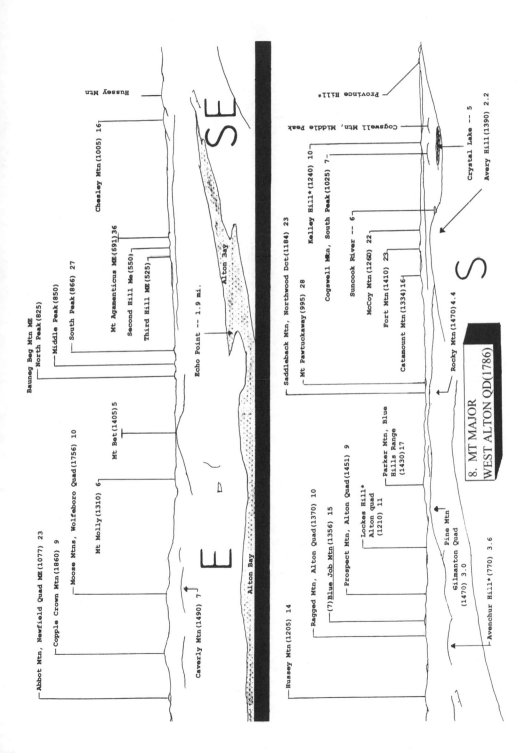

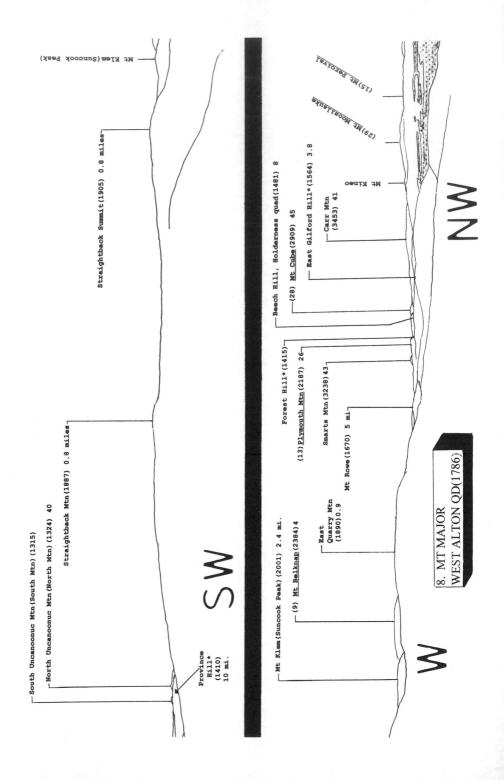

South Uncanoonuc Mtn (South Mtn) (1315)

North Uncanoonuc Mtn (North Mtn) (1324) 40

Straightback Mtn (1887) 0.8 miles

Straightback Summit (1905) 0.8 miles

Mt Klem (Suncook Peak)

Province Hill* (1410) 10 mi.

SW

Mt Klem (Suncook Peak) (2001) 2.4 mi.

(9) Mt Belknap (2384) 4

East Quarry Mtn (1890) 0.9

Forest Hill* (1415)

(13) Plymouth Mtn (2187) 26

Smarts Mtn (3238) 43

Mt Rowe (1670) 5 mi.

Beech Hill, Holderness quad (1481) 8

(28) Mt Cube (2909) 45

East Gilford Hill* (1564) 3.8

(15) Mt Percival

(29) Mt Moosilauke

Mt Kineo

Carr Mtn (3453) 41

W

NW

8. MT MAJOR
WEST ALTON QD(1786)

(9) BELKNAP MOUNTAIN

N 43° 31.059'
W 71° 22.156'

(Elevation 2384 feet)

If a hiking group places one car at Mount Major's parking lot and another at Gunstock's, Belknap Mountain can become part of an exhausting 8-hour 12-mile hike over nine peaks. However this highest elevation along the way may also be reached in half an hour from a third parking lot outside of Gilford. From the top of Belknap a hiker sees Lake Winnipesaukee once again covering half of the horizon with the White Mountains serving as a backdrop. The view exceeds that of the previous chapter because you stand 600 feet higher.

Geologically, the Belknap Mountains form what is known as a ring dike complex. Over a hundred million years ago, a somewhat circular section of the Earth's crust settled over a liquid magma chamber lying below. This settling is similar to pushing an undersized cork into a test tube of water. As the plug settles, water is pushed up around the sides to cover the top of the cork. The magma rose up around the settled crust forming volcanism in the form of a ring. It then hardened to form the so-called ring dike. This wall prevented erosion from inside the dike while the land on the outside wore away. The dike eroded also but only down to the level of the land contained within. By that time the surrounding terrain had been washed away to a much lower elevation. The result is a circular set of mountains several miles across. There are so many summits that most remain nameless. The result of all this geological activity can be seen nearby to the north, east and south of Belknap Mountain.

Approach this summit by taking route 11A to Gilford Village. Turn south on Belknap Mountain Road. Drive 0.9 miles and bend left. After traveling an additional half a mile, the road turns right. When the trip odometer out of Gilford Village reads 2.5, fork left onto the Belknap Carriage Road and go an additional 500 yards to a gate that is open except in winter. Beyond the gate, the last 0.7 miles is a steep dirt road that will give two-wheel drive vehicles difficulty in mud. Once you have parked the car, hike over to the Fire Warden's garage, the start of the green-blazed Green Trail (N 31.038 min, W 22.725 min). When reaching the top, make sure you notice where the trail ended. A number of paths converge upon the fire tower. It is easy to start back down the wrong trail.

The summit view scans four states. Naturally we see into New Hampshire with the twin Uncanoonucs and Joe English Hill to the south-southwest. Extend the left arm as we did in Chapter Three with the palm turned down and the fingers spread. Point the ring finger at the right hand Uncanoonuc. The forefinger should be aiming at Mount Watatic in Massachusetts some sixty-three miles away.

Vermont is visible. Using that same human measuring stick, place the thumb on New Hampshire's Mount Cardigan now seen across the upper half of Winnisquam Lake. Along the right edge of the ring finger stands Pico Peak with Killington farther left. If the thumb points to Pico, the right side of the ring finger reveals Mount Ascutney.

The fourth state is Maine, the border of which passes just twenty miles to the east. We recognize Douglas Hill beyond the southern half of Winnipesaukee's huge Rattlesnake Island followed by Stone and Pleasant Mountains appearing past the northern half.

We do not have the room in the diagrams to label all the islands in the lake nor all the peaks on the horizon. We name enough of them so that the experienced can fill in the gaps. Mount Moosilauke rears up beyond the town of Meredith. To the right, South Kinsman dominates the horizon followed by Sandwich Dome, Tecumseh, Tripyramid, Whiteface, Passaconaway and Washington. Mount Chocorua is nearly blocked by the Ossipee Mountains. But we still see its tiny apex beyond them above Moultonborough Neck.

The reference landmark list to this point stands at fourteen. The fifteenth peak rears up across Winnipesaukee just to the right of Red Hill – Sandwich Dome. The Dome's nearly four thousand-foot elevation makes it stand apart from other mountains. Thus it is easily spotted from miles away in all directions.

The expanse from here is the best found in southern New Hampshire. Other views come close. Should your vacation time be short, choose Belknap.

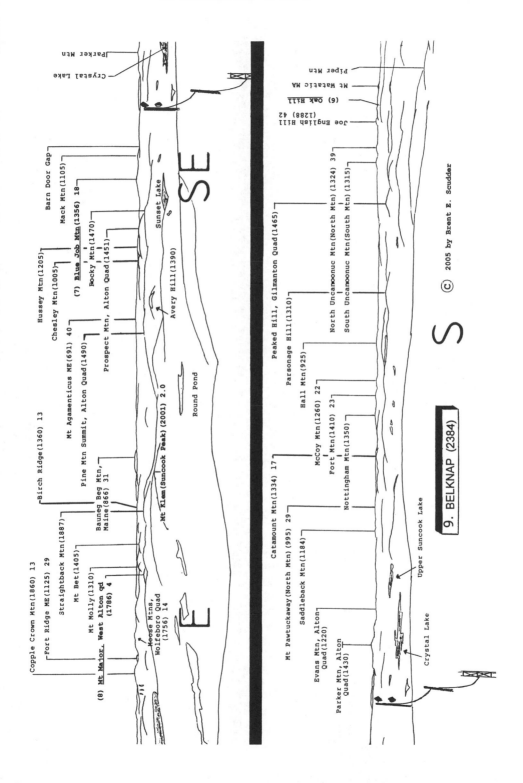

Parker Mtn

Crystal Lake

Barn Door Gap

Mack Mtn(1105)

Hussey Mtn(1205)

Chesley Mtn(1005)

(7) Blue Job Mtn(1356) 18

Rocky Mtn(1470)

Prospect Mtn, Alton Quad(1451)

Mt Agamenticus ME(691) 40

Pine Mtn Summit, Alton Quad(1490)

Birch Ridge(1360) 13

Bauneg Beg Mtn, Maine(866) 31

Mt Klem (Suncook Peak) (2001) 2.0

Copple Crown Mtn(1860) 13

Fort Ridge ME(1125) 29

Straightback Mtn(1887)

Mt Bet(1405)

Mt Molly(1310)

Mt Major, West Alton qd (1786) 4

(8) Mt Major, West Alton qd

Moose Mtns, Wolfeboro Quad (1756) 14

Sunset Lake

Avery Hill(1390)

Round Pond

SE

E

Piper Mtn

Mt Watatic MA

Oak Hill (6)

Joe English Hill 42 (1288)

Peaked Hill, Gilmanton Quad(1465)

North Uncanoonuc Mtn(North Mtn)(1324) 39

South Uncanoonuc Mtn(South Mtn)(1315)

Parsonage Hill(1310)

Hall Mtn(925)

McCoy Mtn(1260) 22

Fort Mtn(1410) 23

Nottingham Mtn(1350)

Catamount Mtn(1334) 17

Mt Pawtuckaway(North Mtn) (995) 29

Saddleback Mtn(1184)

Evans Mtn, Alton Quad(1220)

Parker Mtn, Alton Quad(1430)

Crystal Lake

Upper Suncook Lake

S

9. BELKNAP (2384)

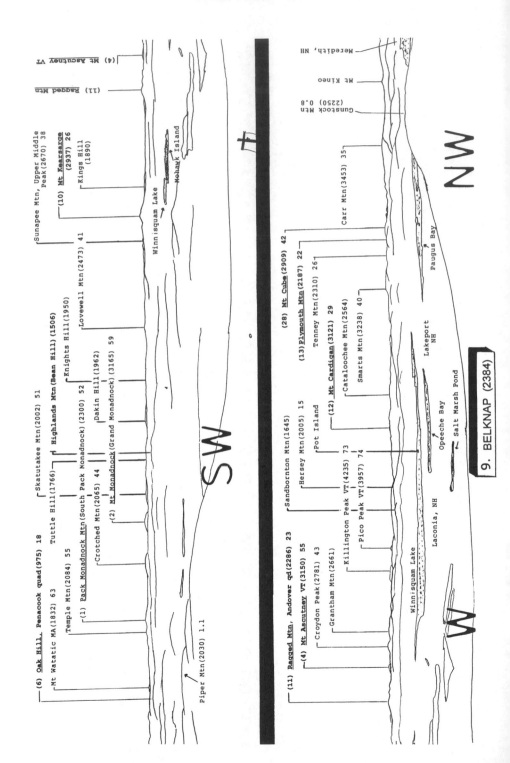

9. BELKNAP (2384)

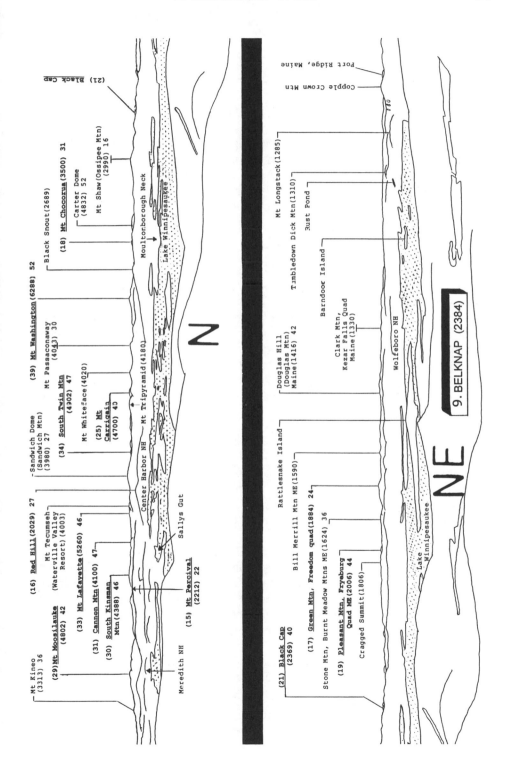

Mt Kineo (3313) 36

(16) Red Hill (2029) 27

(29) Mt Moosilauke (4802) 42

Mt Tecumseh (Waterville Valley Resort) (4003)

(33) Mt Lafayette (5260) 46

(31) Cannon Mtn (4100) 47

(30) South Kinsman Mtn (4388) 46

Meredith NH

(15) Mt Percival (2212) 22

Black Snout (2689)

(18) Mt Chocorua (3500) 31

Carter Dome (4832) 52

Mt Shaw (Ossipee Mtn) (2990) 16

(21) Black Cap

(39) Mt Washington (6288) 52

Mt Passaconaway (4043) 30

Sandwich Dome (Sandwich Mtn) (3980) 27

(34) South Twin Mtn (4902) 47

Mt Whiteface (4020)

(25) Mt Carrigain (4700) 40

Mt Tripyramid (4180)

Center Harbor NH

Sallys Gut

Moultorborough Neck

Lake Winnipesaukee

N

(21) Black Cap (2369) 40

(17) Green Mtn, Freedom quad (1884) 24

Stone Mtn, Burnt Meadow Mtns ME (1624) 36

(19) Pleasant Mtn, Fryeburg Quad ME (2006) 44

Cragged Summit (1806)

Bill Merrill Mtn ME (1590)

Rattlesnake Island

Douglas Hill (Douglas Mtn) Maine (1416) 42

Clark Mtn, Kezar Falls Quad Maine (1330)

Barndoor Island

Wolfeboro NH

Timbledown Dick Mtn (1310)

Rust Pond

Mt Longstack (1285)

Copple Crown Mtn

Port Ridge, Maine

Lake Winnipesaukee

NE

9. BELKNAP (2384)

(10) MOUNT KEARSARGE

N 43° 22.991'
W 71° 51.444'

(Elevation 2937 feet)

We are driving northward on New Hampshire's I-93 during a Saturday in January. The Hooksett Tolls have been left not far behind. Around us, car roofs are bedecked with skis. A nearby SUV sags in the rear. Within it sprouts a full compliment of children, adults and equipment. Passing it easily on the left is a small import carrying a driver and one pair of skis. Spread out before them is a valley with highlands beyond. Nearby to the left is Jerry Hill. Commanding the scene is one huge mountain – Kearsarge.

If we continue north on I-93, we seldom see the mountain again. But branch left on I-89 and Mount Kearsarge keeps getting bigger and bigger and bigger.

The origin of the name Kearsarge is obscure. John Mudge's book THE WHITE MOUNTAINS, *Names, Places and Legends,* mentions several possibilities. Kesough in Algonquin means "Born of the hill that first shakes hands with the morning light." Some feel that the mountain name came from a local eighteenth century hunter Hezekiah Sargent, hence Kiah Sarge's mountain. Other sources dispute this suggesting that the name Kearsarge preceeded the hunter by at least a generation.

During the warmer months, Mount Kearsarge is ideal for the mixed climbing groups that most families represent. We can drop the more hardy and adventurous off at Winslow State Park on the north slope to make the hour and a quarter climb up the Barlow Trail (a portion of the Sunapee-Ragged-Kearsarge Greenway). Winslow State Park (N 23.388 min, W 52.034 min) is easily reached from I-89's Exit 10 by following the signs.

The less hardy can then drive around the mountain to Rollins State Park where a toll road brings the party to a parking lot that is within 1/4 mile of the summit (N 22.726 min, W 51.531 min). Drive into the center of Warner by leaving I-89 at either Exit 8 or 9. Turn north on Kearsarge Mountain Road. The toll portion is closed during most of the off season. Either call 603-456-3808 or visit www.nhstateparks.org to determine when the road is open.

From the barren summit of Kearsarge, we can see all of the reference landmark mountains.   Looking south, one can easily pick out the Uncanoonucs and Joe English Hill.   Farther right stands Mount Monadnock.   Lovewell Mountain looms large to the southwest, and Ascutney is seen across Lake Sunapee. To Ascutney's right, Okemo and Killington appear in the distance. Glance north. On the left is Mount Cardigan beyond West Andover. Farther right is Moosilauke. Discover Sandwich Dome to the right of the more distant Mount Washington with Mounts Shaw, Belknap and Copple Crown appearing in succession towards the east.

We can make out 20 ski mountains especially if their trails are snow-whitened. Look south again and locate Pat's Peak on the left and Crotched Mountain on the right. To the west, Mount Sunapee is spotted. Vermont's Stratton Mountain stands just to the right of Sunapee and farther right Okemo and Killington. The ski trails on Haystack and Mount Snow face us, but these are practically hidden by Sunapee Mountain.

The 12 remaining ski mountains are not easily identified because their trails face away from us. To the left of nearby Kings Hill are Vermont's Magic and Bromley Mountains. To the right lies Mount Ascutney and Pico Peak along with Sugarbush's Mount Ellen and Lincoln Peak. As we continue to turn our head in the same direction, New Hampshire's Holts Ledge (Dartmouth Skiway) appears. And then come Tenney, Cannon, and Ragged Mountains. Waterville Valley's Tecumseh follows and then Gunstock Mountain.

Are all the previously climbed summits visible? We cannot see Mount Major. Pack Monadnock is visible over the top of Crotched Mountain. Pitcher is but a tiny bump on the horizon to the left of Lovewell. Oak Hill is hard to make out in the middle distance, but we discover it framed by the nearer Greenough and Walker Ponds. Blue Job is another horizon bump above the town of Salisbury. We can see eight summits featured in the earlier chapters along with twenty-one others that follow later in this book.

On crystal clear days binoculars reveal Boston on the horizon just to the left of the nearer Uncanoonuc Mountains. Portions of Maine are visible but not any notable hills.

While the view from Kearsarge lacks the magnificence of what can be observed from Belknap and Major, it is far more comprehensive. From no other summit does a person see so much of southern New Hampshire.

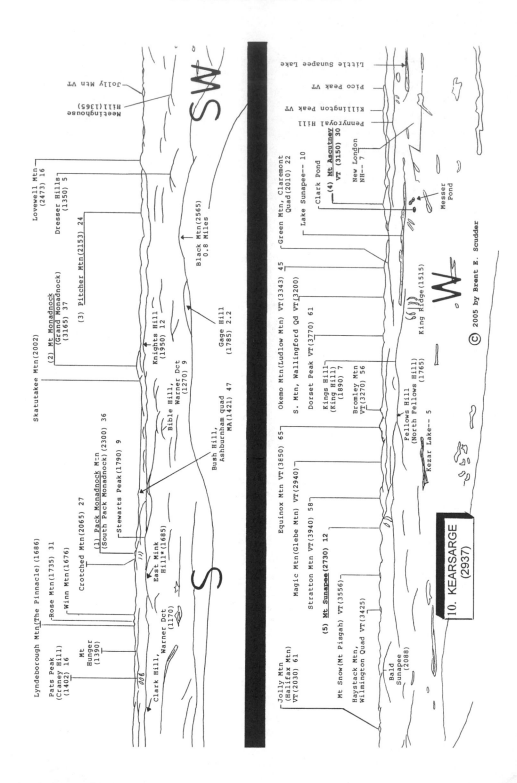

Lyndeborough Mtn(The Pinnacle) (1686)

Pats Peak (Craney Hill) (1402) 16

Rose Mtn(1735) 31

Winn Mtn(1676)

Mt Hunger (1390)

Crotched Mtn(2065) 27

Clark Hill, Warner Dct (1170)

(1) Pack Monadnock Mtn (South Pack Monadnock) (2300) 36

Stewarts Peak(1790) 9

East Mink Hill* (1685)

Lovewell Mtn (2473) 16

Dresser Hills (1350) 5

(2) Mt Monadnock (Grand Monadnock) (3165) 37

(3) Pitcher Mtn(2153) 24

Skatutakee Mtn(2002)

Jolly Mtn VT

Meetinghouse Hill (1365)

Knights Hill (1950) 12

Bible Hill, Warner Dct (1270) 9

Bush Hill, Ashburnham quad MA(1421) 47

Black Mtn(2565) 0.8 Miles

Gage Hill (1785) 2.2

SW

S

Jolly Mtn (Halifax Mtn) VT(2030) 61

Magic Mtn(Glebe Mtn) VT(2940)

Stratton Mtn VT(3940) 58

(5) Mt Sunapee (2730) 12

Mt Snow(Mt Pisgah) VT(3556)

Haystack Mtn, Wilmington Quad VT(3425)

Bald Sunapee (2088)

Equinox Mtn VT(3850) 65

Okemo Mtn(Ludlow Mtn) VT(3343) 45

S. Mtn, Wallingford Qd VT(3200)

Dorset Peak VT(3770) 61

Kings Hill (King Hill) (1890) 7

Bromley Mtn VT(3270) 56

Fellows Hill (North Fellows Hill) (1765)

Kezar Lake-- 5

Green Mtn, Claremont Quad(2010) 22

Lake Sunapee-- 10

Clark Pond

(4) Mt Ascutney VT (3150) 30

New London NH-- 7

Pennyroyal Hill

Killington Peak VT

Pico Peak VT

Little Sunapee Lake

Messer Pond

King Ridge (1515)

W

10. KEARSARGE (2937)

© 2005 by Brent E. Scudder

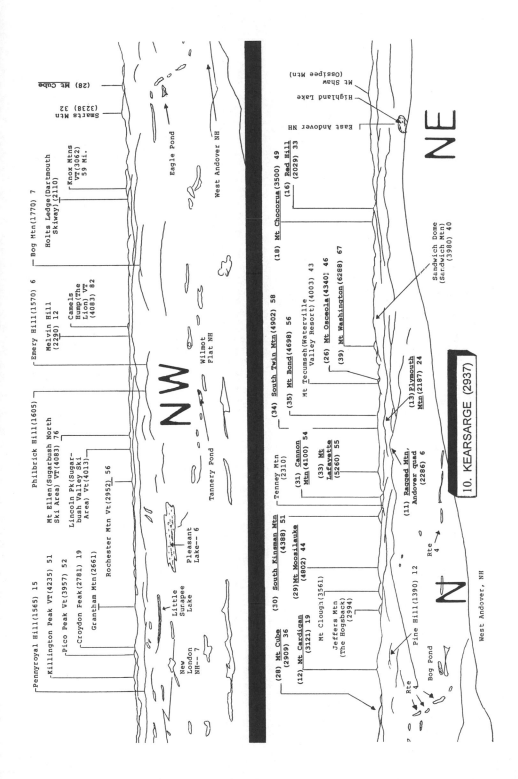

Pennyroyal Hill(1565) 15

Philbrick Hill(1605)

Mt Ellen(Sugarbush North Ski Area) VT(4083) 76

Mt Cube (28)

Smarts Mtn (3238) 32

Knox Mtns VT(3062) 59 Mi.

Bog Mtn(1770) 7

Holts Ledge(Dartmouth Skiway)(2110)

Emery Hill(1570) 6

Melvin Hill (2290) 12

Camels Hump(The Lion) VT (4083) 82

Eagle Pond

West Andover NH

Killington Peak VT(4235) 51

Pico Peak Vt(3957) 52

Croydon Peak(2781) 19

Grantham Mtn(2661)

Lincoln Pk(Sugar-bush Valley Ski Area) Vt(4013)

Rochester Mtn Vt(2952) 56

Wilmot Flat NH

NW

New London NH-- 7

Little Sunapee Lake

Pleasant Lake-- 6

Tannery Pond

Mt Chocorua (3500) 49

Red Hill (2029) 33

Mt Shaw (Ossipee Mtn)

Highland Lake

East Andover NH

NE

Sandwich Dome (Sandwich Mtn) (3980) 40

South Twin Mtn (4902) 58

Mt Bond(4698) 56

Mt Tecumseh(Waterville Valley Resort) (4003) 43

Mt Osceola(4340) 46

Mt Washington(6288) 67

Plymouth Mtn(2187) 24

(34) South Twin Mtn (4902) 58

(35) Mt Bond(4698) 56

(26) Mt Osceola(4340) 46

(39) Mt Washington(6288) 67

(13) Plymouth Mtn(2187) 24

(18) Mt Chocorua (3500) 49

(16) Red Hill (2029) 33

Tenney Mtn (2310)

Cannon Mtn(4100) 54

Mt Lafayette (5260) 55

(31) Cannon Mtn(4100) 54

(33) Mt Lafayette (5260) 55

Ragged Mtn, Andover quad (2286) 6

(11) Ragged Mtn, Andover quad (2286) 6

South Kinsman Mtn (4388) 51

Mt Moosilauke (4802) 44

(30) South Kinsman Mtn (4388) 51

(29) Mt Moosilauke (4802) 44

Mt Cube (2909) 36

Mt Cardigan (3121) 19

Mt Clough(3561)

Jeffers Mtn (The Hogsback) (2994)

(28) Mt Cube (2909) 36

(12) Mt Cardigan (3121) 19

Pine Hill(1390) 12

N

Rte 4

Bog Pond

Rte 4

West Andover, NH

10. KEARSARGE (2937)

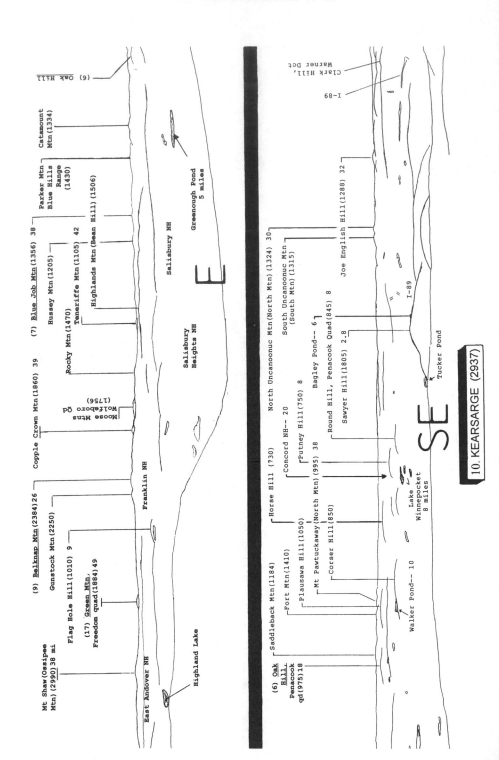

10. KEARSARGE (2937)

Mt Shaw(Ossipee Mtn) (2990) 38 mi
(9) Belknap Mtn(2384) 26
Gunstock Mtn(2250)
Copple Crown Mtn(1860) 39
(7) Blue Job Mtn(1356) 38
Parker Mtn
Blue Hills Range (1430)
Catamount Mtn(1334)
(6) OAK HILL

Flag Hole Hill(1010) 9
(17) Green Mtn, Freedom quad(1884) 49
Rocky Mtn(1470)
Hussey Mtn(1205)
Teneriffe Mtn(1105) 42
Highlands Mtn(Bean Hill) (1506)

Moose Mtns Wolfeboro Qd (1756)

Franklin NH
Salisbury Heights NH
Salisbury NH

East Andover NH
Highland Lake
Greenough Pond 5 miles

(6) Oak Hill Penacook qd(975)18
Saddleback Mtn(1184)
Fort Mtn(1410)
Plausawa Hill(1050)
Mt Pawtuckaway(North Mtn) (995) 38
Corser Hill(850)
Horse Hill (730)
Concord NH-- 20
Putney Hill(750) 8
Bagley Pond-- 6
Round Hill, Penacook Quad(845) 8
Sawyer Hill(1805) 2.8
North Uncanoonuc Mtn(North Mtn) (1324) 30
South Uncanoonuc Mtn (South Mtn) (1315)
Joe English Hill(1288) 32
Clark Hill, Warner Dct
I-89

Walker Pond-- 10
Lake Winnepocket 8 miles
Tucker Pond
SE
I-89

(11) RAGGED MOUNTAIN

Andover Quadrangle

(Elevation 2286 feet)

Welcome to the Sunapee-Ragged-Kearsarge Greenway! The SRKG is a 75 mile loop trail which takes in all three mountains along with lesser hills such as Bog Mountain. It travels through state parks and town forests but also through extensive private property. The landowners have been extremely generous in allowing the path to travel through their domains. The ninth trail section of the SRKG begins in Wilmot, passes over several summits of Ragged and then goes downhill to Proctor Academy in Andover.

The SRKG passes into extensive forest, past ponds, wetlands and over many ledges. There are often fine views in one direction or another but rarely can one see in all directions. Similarly, there is no all-encompassing panorama from the top of Ragged Mountain. But take the view from the top of the ski area's main chair lift, combine it with the prospect from the west peak, another vista from an outlook near that peak and a fourth scene from Balanced Rock, and it becomes possible to construct a 360 degree diagram.

Hikers can park one car at either end of the trail section, drive a second car to the other end and make it a through hike of nearly six miles. Expect to take five hours due to the trek being unexpectedly rough. There are numerous ascents and descents along the ridge line which slow the hiker considerably.

Up-and-back hikers should start in Andover, leaving their cars in the Farrell Field House parking lot of Proctor Academy located across Route 4 & 11 from some white-fenced playing fields. The trail begins to the right of the tennis courts (**N 43 degrees** 26.311 minutes, **W 71 degrees** 49.633 minutes) and ascends initially as a cross-country ski trail maintained by the School. Look for either white-painted tree blazes or small sheets of aluminum tacked to trees both in the shape of a trapezoid. After the trail goes 0.2 miles, the ski trail bends to the right. The SRKG goes straight.

When you are near the top, seek the Balanced Rock sign which points you to the right. One soon arrives at a huge 19-foot boulder situated in a precarious equilibrium (N 27.860 min, W 49.872 min). From here you can look to the southeast and make out Highland Lake, Elbow, Adder and Horseshoe Ponds in the foreground; along with the Blue Hills Range and the Oak Hill of a previous chapter in the background.

Return to the trail and continue climbing until a sign beckons you to divert left to an outlook that faces south (N 28.011 min, W 49.991 min). We call this the view from "near the west peak." From this spot you can see the twin Uncanoonucs on the horizon along with Joe English Hill to the right. You also look down into Andover with the Proctor Academy ski slopes beyond and Bradley Lake over the top. Mount Kearsarge arrests the eye six miles away.

The next stop is the west peak itself (N 28.028 min, W 50.060 min). This view includes Kearsarge but pans to the right past Mounts Monadnock, Sunapee, Ascutney, Killington and Pico finally reaching the main ski peak of Ragged Mountain itself – your final destination.

Drop steeply over 200 feet into the col between the west peak and the main ski peak. Reclimb roughly the same elevation, and you will arrive at the point where the ski trails and ski lift converge (N 28.352 min, W 50.702 min).

Here is the best view of all. To the left are the Moose Mountains of western New Hampshire along with Mount Cardigan. Moosilauke rises due north followed by many mountains on or near the Appalachian Trail. Mount Washington is 61 miles away. If we scan farther right, our eyes pick out the Sandwich Range from Sandwich Dome to Chocorua. The Ossipee Mountains come next followed by the Belknaps.

The main and west peaks of Ragged Mountain obscure what can be seen farther over. At this point we introduce a graphic technique that we call "looking through the mountain." The dashed line on page 77 represents the profile of Ragged's main and west peaks as seen from the top of the main ski lift. The solid lines represent the view as though the main and west peaks were absent. But we already saw that view – not from the top of the ski lift, but from Balanced Rock. This graphic technique of super-imposition is used several times in this book.

As of this writing, Ragged Mountain is mentioned in few guidebooks. A complete trail description of this section may be found in the SRKG TRAIL GUIDE. One can also download the description from srkgc.com.

The climb up from Andover and back is a pretty hike, certainly worth a day when the visibility is excellent. Allow about two hours to ascend. In wet or icy conditions, beware of the steep drop beyond the west peak. Other than that this eastern portion of Section Nine of the Sunapee-Ragged-Kearsarge Greenway is fairly easy.

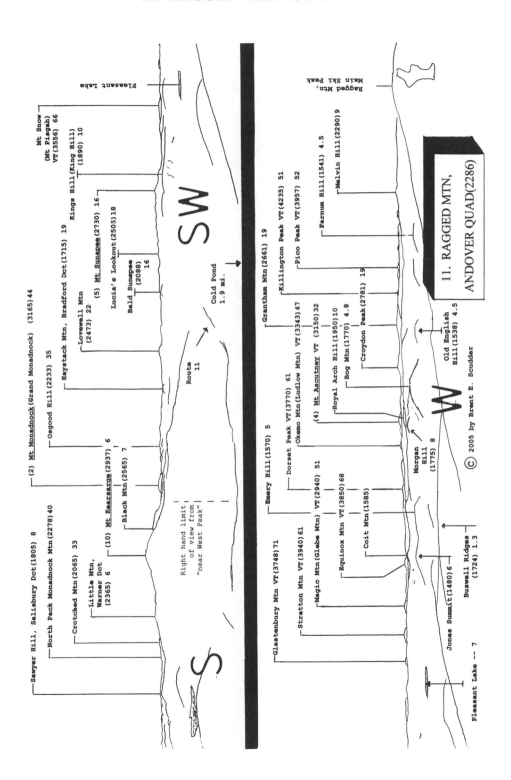

11. RAGGED MTN,
ANDOVER QUAD(2286)

© 2005 by Brent E. Scudder

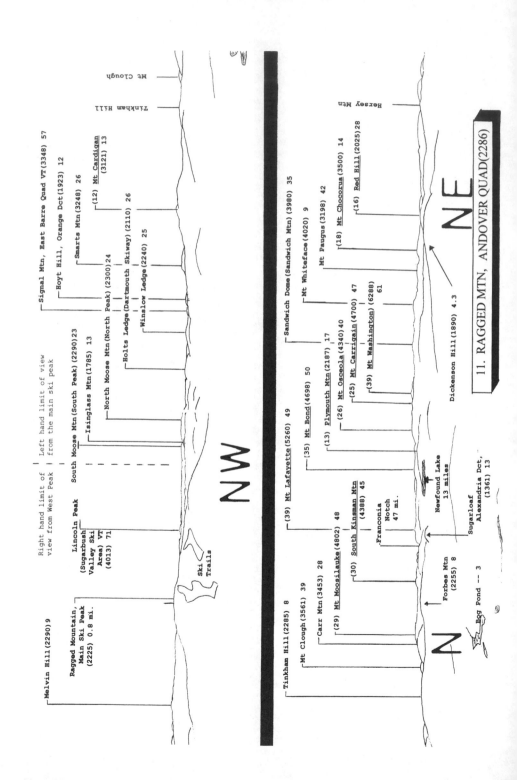

11. RAGGED MTN, ANDOVER QUAD(2286)

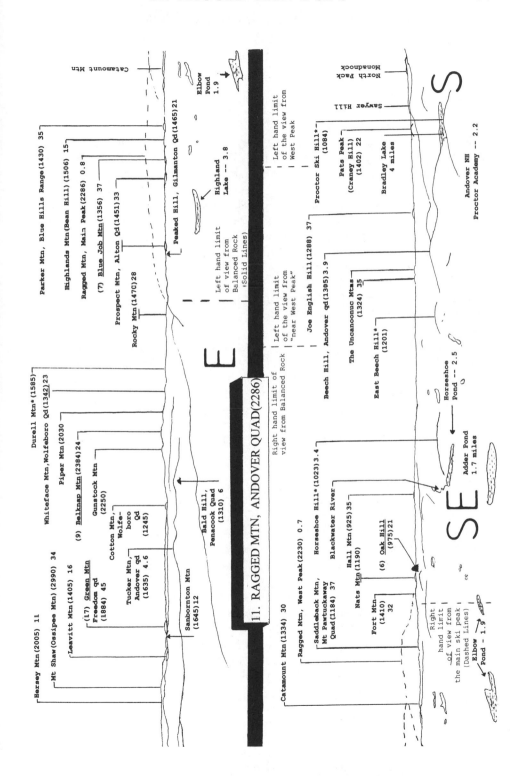

11. RAGGED MTN, ANDOVER QUAD(2286)

(12) MOUNT CARDIGAN

N 43° 38.964'
W 71° 54.850'

(Elevation 3121 feet)

Mount Kearsarge is not the first peak beyond Hooksett seen when traveling northward on I-93. After the tolls, look for Milepost 31.6. If there is 42 miles of visibility, that small protuberance on the horizon is Mount Cardigan.

This summit stands at the center of a crescent-shaped range of hills with the concave side facing eastward towards Newfound Lake. Towards the bottom of the crescent lies Brown Mountain followed by tops with such names as Church, Crane and Gilman. Descend from Cardigan along the top of the crescent past Firescrew and Mowglis and soon you will reach Oregon Mountain.

Firescrew was named for a spectacular tornado of flame caused by a forest fire in 1855. Orientals call this type of flaming whirl a "dragon twist."

Massive Mount Moosilauke prevails to the north. We spot it easily because Jeffers Mountain and Mount Clough serve as stepping stones approaching from the left. Where is the well-renowned Appalachian Trail? In our mind's eye, we see it passing from left to right over the twin peaks of Moose Mountain, on to Holts Ledge, behind Winslow Ledge, up and over Smarts Mountain and extending on to Mount Cube. From there it drops down in front of Piermont, up over Moosilauke, South Kinsman, Lafayette and South Twin and then eventually to Mount Washington.

It is easiest to climb Mount Cardigan from the west. Take Route 118 northeast out of Canaan, New Hampshire. Within half a mile turn right onto Cardigan Mountain Road. In another 3.1 miles you will pass a gate which is closed in winter. During warmer months one can drive an additional half mile to the parking lot which marks the start of the West Ridge Trail (N 36.648 min, W 56.108 min). A 75-minute climb should bring the hiker out of the forest onto the bare summit.

Be more adventurous and climb the eastern slope. Proceed westward out of the village of Alexandria and turn right onto another Cardigan Mountain Road. At a point 3.7 miles from the turn, the paved road makes a sharp turn to the right and goes downhill while a dirt road continues straight. Continue straight on the dirt road for 1.5 miles to arrive at the Appalachian Mountain Club's Cardigan

Mountain Lodge (N 38.962 min, W 52.680 min). The lodge is open to the public but reservations are strongly recommended. To make a reservation, visit www.outdoors.org. A number of trails begin near the Lodge. The Elizabeth Holt Trail is only a two-hour climb, but it is steep. Avoid it during wet weather. The gentler Clark Trail takes a half hour longer.

To the east, we see the open end of the crescent created by the Cardigan Mountain system. Beyond lies Newfound Lake. Mount Chocorua and the Ossipees stand far away on the left. Between them and beyond, 60 miles away arises Pleasant Mountain in Maine. Pleasant's tabletop profile allows for easy recognition from here as well as from several peaks featured later on. To the left of the Ossipees, one locates the nearer Squam Lake and, to the right, Lake Winnipesaukee.

Behold Vermont's Green Mountains to the west. We see Stratton and Ascutney to the left; Okemo, Killington and Pico in front with Mount Ellen and Camels Hump to the right. Close in are the gentle lakes and villages of western New Hampshire.

If we look south, the Uncannoonucs and Joe English are almost eclipsed by the nearer Ragged Mountain. Kearsarge is just to the right. Pack Monadnock stands almost behind Crotched Mountain. One cannot mistake Grand Monadnock followed by the nearer Lovewell and Sunapee Mountains.

Cardigan is a good mountain. It can be a day trip from either side and one can stay overnight at the Cardigan Mountain Lodge. The view from the top is quite similar to the views from Kearsarge and Ragged. But Cardigan's panorama reveals a wilder part of New Hampshire.

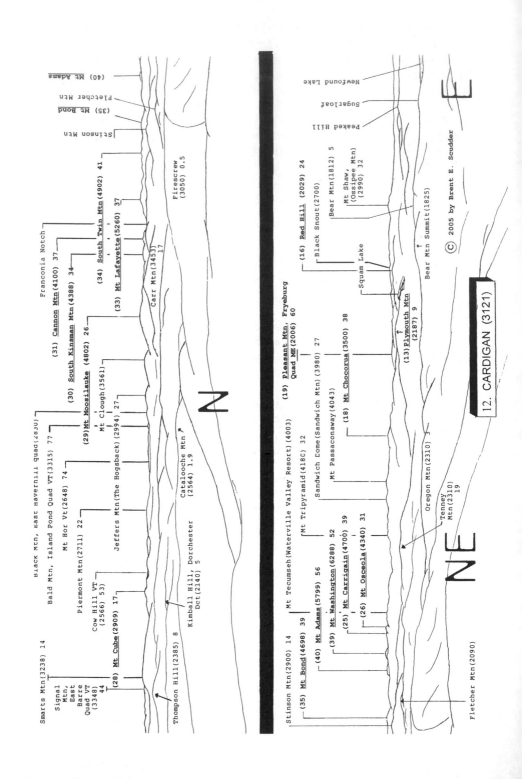

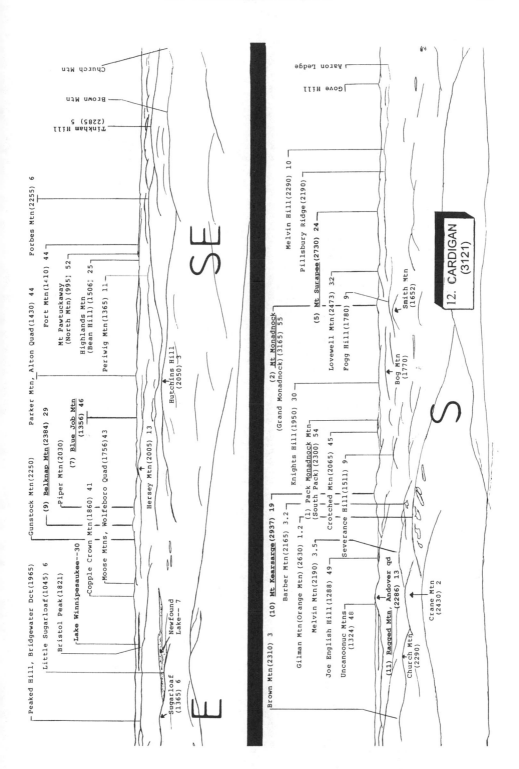

E

Peaked Hill, Bridgewater Oct(1965)
Little Sugarloaf(1045) 6
Bristol Peak(1821)
Lake Winnipesaukee--30
Copple Crown Mtn(1860) 41
Moose Mtns, Wolfeboro Quad(1756)43
Gunstock Mtn(2250)
(9) Belknap Mtn(2384) 29
Piper Mtn(2030)
(7) Blue Job Mtn
    (1356) 46
Hersey Mtn(2005) 13
Parker Mtn, Alton Quad(1430) 44
Forbes Mtn(2255) 6
Fort Mtn(1410) 44
Mt Pawtuckaway
(North Mtn) (995) 52
Highlands Mtn
(Bean Hill) (1506) 25
Periwig Mtn(1365) 11
Hutchins Hill
(2050) 3
Tinkham Hill
(2285) 5
Brown Mtn
Church Mtn
Sugarloaf
(1365) 6
Newfound
Lake--7

SE

Brown Mtn(2310) 3
(10) Mt Kearsarge (2937) 19
Barber Mtn(2165) 3.2
Gilman Mtn(Orange Mtn) (2630) 1.2
Melvin Mtn(2190) 3.5
Joe English Hill(1288) 49
Uncanoonuc Mtns
(1324) 48
(11) Ragged Mtn, Andover qd
        (2286) 13
Church Mtn
(2290)
Severance Hill(1511) 9
(1) Pack Monadnock Mtn
    (South Pack) (2300) 54
Crotched Mtn(2065) 45
Knights Hill(1950) 30
(2) Mt Monadnock(3165) 55
(Grand Monadnock) (3165) 55
Lovewell Mtn(2473) 32
Fogg Hill(1780) 9
(5) Mt Sunapee (2730) 24
Bog Mtn
(1770)
Smith Mtn
(1652)
Melvin Hill(2290) 10
Pillsbury Ridge(2190)
Gove Hill
Aaron Ledge
Crane Mtn
(2430) 2

S

12. CARDIGAN
    (3121)

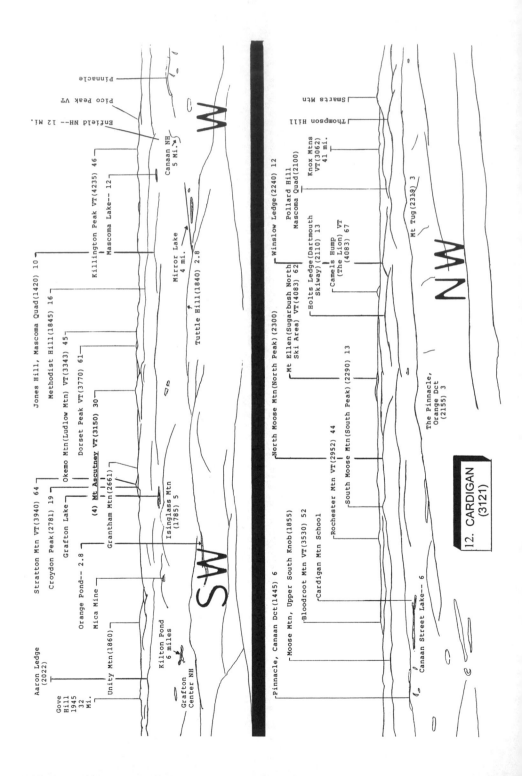

(13) PLYMOUTH MOUNTAIN

N 43° 42.543'
W 71° 43.406'

(Elevation 2187 feet)

Plymouth Mountain stands at the corner of two intersecting ranges. Extending away to the northwest are such mountains as Tenney and Fletcher. To the south one sees Bridgewater Mountain and Peaked Hill. These two ranges form the south edge of the Baker River Valley and the west side of the Pemigewasset River Valley respectively.

As with the Sunapee diagram, Plymouth's skyline chart was constructed with partial panoramas obtained by moving about this forested peak and taking pictures from various outlooks. However the photography was done some twenty years ago. Since then considerable forest growth has obscured a large part of the horizon. The view taken from a location three quarters of the way up the trail has vanished. Another prospect located 100 yards southwest of the top (N 42.506 min, W 43.459 min) is perhaps 50% obscured by pine in the winter and by additional foliage during the summer. However, hike 130 feet eastward from the summit and stand on an open ledge with fine views throughout the year (N 42.552 min, W 43.378 min). Close at hand are the steep rises and falls of the White Mountains and, on the right, large island studded lakes.

Locate the trailhead by leaving I-93 at Exit 23 and driving west on Route 104. In Bristol, the highway eventually turns left while Route 3A goes straight. Drive north on 3A a distance of 8.7 miles to an intersection. Signs to Hebron and Groton invite you to turn left. Turn right instead. This is Pike Hill Road, a dirt road along which parking is questionable due to increasing private development in the area. Some wide spots still exist where you may park without blocking other traffic. Should you lack 4-wheel drive, avoid this road during wet or icy conditions. Alternatively one may park near the intersection with 3A and add one hour to the 70-minute ascent. Pike Hill road bears left after the first 0.2 miles slowly climbing as it heads north. After traveling an additional 1.1 miles, you will come to a fork where the road makes a sharp left while a logging road goes straight (N 42.580 min, W 44.835 min). Walk up the logging road 100 yards and look for an open field to the right. To find the trailhead, cross this field to the far right hand corner. Trail blazes consist of signs that are nailed to trees featuring the logo of nearby Camp Mowglis, a black wolf.

At a point half way up the mountain, look for cliffs on the left. When the trail has climbed a short distance around them (N 42.576 min, W 44.097 min), you can bushwhack uphill about fifty yards, look from the top and get some glimpses of Newfound Lake especially during the colder months when foliage is lacking.

As of this writing, the trail maintenance near the summit has been less than perfect. Path finding taxes the utmost in ones hiking abilities but more so during the winter. (Be sure to bring map and compass). At one point (N 42.616 min, W 43.698 min), the trail appears to go straight when actually it turns right. Eventually one reaches a false summit (N 42.616 min, W 43.587 min). The true summit, containing a benchmark plate embedded in rock, lies 0.2 miles to the southeast.

At the top, bushwhack eastward to the ledge and take in the vast view. All the way around to the right stand the profiles of the Uncanoonucs and Joe English Hill more than fifty miles away. If we pan to the left, we discover the multi-summited Hersey Mountain close at hand along with the nearby ski trails on Burleigh. Lake Winnipesaukee comes next with the Ossipees guarding the north end. We can see into Maine with Fort Ridge standing a little south of due east.

To the northeast we scan the Sandwich Range from Mount Chocorua on the right to Sandwich Dome on the left. West of that and farther away is the Franconia Range. The spectacular steep-sided Franconia Notch follows and then Cannon Mountain, South Kinsman and Moosilauke.

The view from this ledge alone is well worth the climb.

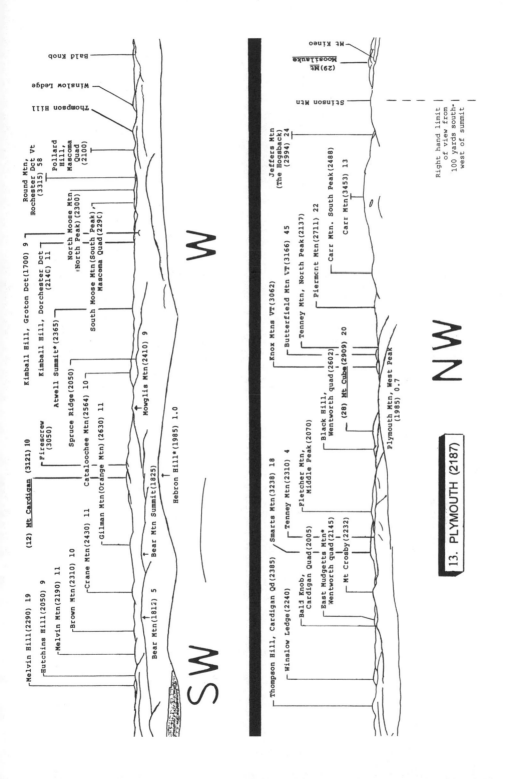

13. PLYMOUTH (2187)

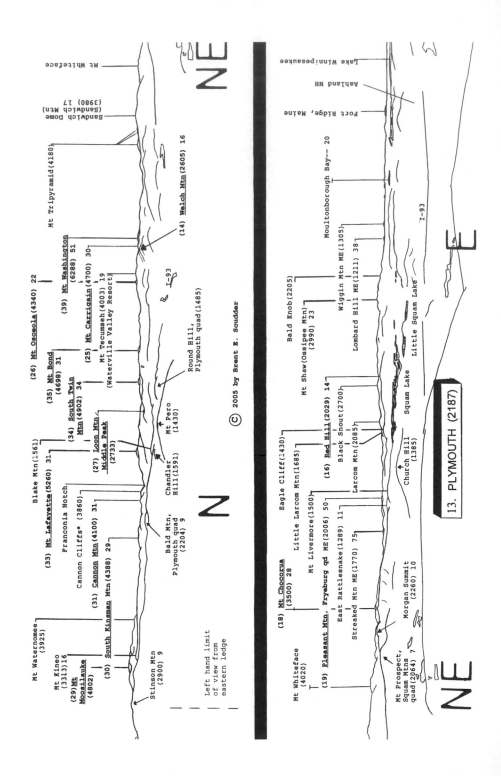

13. PLYMOUTH (2187)

© 2005 by Brent E. Scudder

Mt Whiteface

Sandwich Dome
(Sandwich Mtn)
(3980) 17

Mt Tripyramid(4180)

(26) Mt Osceola(4340) 22

(35) Mt Bond
(4698) 31

(34) South Twin
Mtn (4902) 34

(39) Mt Washington
(6288) 51

(25) Mt Carrigain(4700) 19

Mt Tecumseh(4003) 19
(Waterville Valley Resort)

(14) Welch Mtn (2605) 16

Blake Mtn(1561)

(33) Mt Lafayette(5260) 31

Franconia Notch

Cannon Cliffs* (3860)

(31) Cannon Mtn(4100) 31

(27) Middle Peak
(2733)

Loon Mtn
Mtn

I-93

Round Hill,
Plymouth quad (1485)

Mt Pero
(1430)

Chandler
Hill(1591)

N

Mt Waternomee
(3925)

Mt Kineo
(3313)16

(29) Mt
Moosilauke
(4802)

(30) South Kinsman Mtn(4388) 29

Stinson Mtn
(2900) 9

Bald Mtn,
Plymouth quad
(2204) 9

Left hand limit
of view from
eastern ledge

Lake Winnipesaukee

Ashland NH

Fort Ridge, Maine

Moultonborough Bay-- 20

Bald Knob(2205)

Wiggin Mtn ME(1305)

Lombard Hill ME(1211) 38

Mt Shaw(Ossipee Mtn)
(2990) 23

I-93

E

Eagle Cliff(1430)

Little Larcom Mtn(1685)

Mt Livermore(1500)

(16) Red Hill (2029) 14

Black Snout(2700)

Larcom Mtn(2085)

Squam Lake

Little Squam Lake

Church Hill
(1385)

(18) Mt Chocorua
(3500) 28

(19) Pleasant Mtn, Fryeburg qd ME(2006) 50

East Rattlesnake(1289) 11

Streaked Mtn ME(1770) 75

Mt Whiteface
(4020)

Mt Prospect,
Squam Mtns
quad(2064) 7

Morgan Summit
(2260) 10

NE

NE

NE

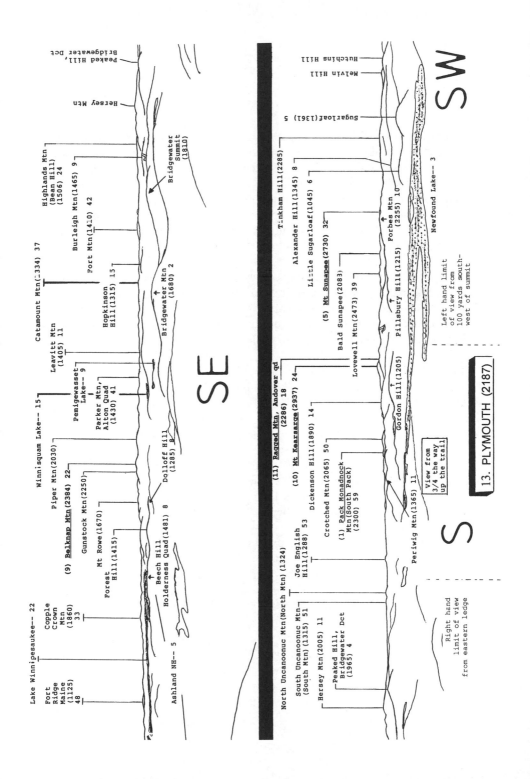

(14) WELCH MOUNTAIN

N 43° 55.154'
W 71° 34.538'

(Elevation 2605 feet)

Welcome to the White Mountain National Forest! Welch Mountain lies just within the southwest perimeter of this vast tract of land set aside by the United States Congress in 1911 for the enjoyment of all for all time. However, from the top of Welch, we are unable to see as many of the White Mountains as we can from lower elevations farther south. This is because our featured summit, though modest in height, stands up against a range of much higher elevation. This tall skyline blocks much of the view to the north and east, a range the author prefers to call the "Sandwich Front."

The "Sandwich Front" begins with Loon Mountain, near the town of Lincoln, and extends eastward over Scar Ridge, Osceola, Kancamagus and Scaur Peak; past the Tripyramids, the Sleepers, Mounts Whiteface, Passaconaway and Paugus finally terminating with Chocorua. This range separates the lowlands to the south from the highlands to the north.

From Welch's summit, gaze a little to the west of due south and see the area from which we have come. To the left appear Kearsarge, Ragged and Plymouth Mountains ranging from forty to sixteen miles away. In the center, I-93 curves towards us up the Pemigewasset Valley. On the right follows Tenney and Cardigan, the latter being twenty-five miles into the distance.

Looking west, we see nothing of Vermont. Mountains such as Carr, Kineo and Cushman block the way. Northwestward towers the massive Moosilauke nearly five thousand feet high. Its bare summit is white during the colder months allowing for easy identification.

Between northwest and north, our view is blocked by nearby Dickey Mountain. Repeating what was done in preparing the Ragged Mountain chapter, we utilize once again the graphic feature that we call "looking through the mountain." The profile of Dickey Mountain, as seen from Welch, is represented on the chart by a dashed line. If Dickey were absent, we could observe what is represented on the same chart by the solid lines below it. We can make Dickey Mountain disappear from the view by merely taking twenty minutes to cross over to it (N 55.387 min, W 34.722 min) and looking beyond.

From the top of Dickey, we see Mount Wolf, the Kinsmans, Cannon Mountain and the Franconia Range capped by Mount Lafayette.

To reach Welch Mountain, drive north on I-93 to exit 28, the Campton Exit. Drive eastward through Campton on Route 49. Four and a half miles after the Campton traffic light, turn left onto Mad River Road. Go 0.6 miles and turn right on to Orris Road. Another 0.7 miles takes you to trailhead parking on the right (N 54.273 min, W 35.309 min) while Orris Road bends left.

There is a cost for parking at all trailheads of the White Mountain National Forest. Fees are collectable at each parking lot (bring singles) and your ticket allows you to park at any of their other parking lots for the remainder of that day. One may purchase one-week tags or annual stickers at various outlets such as a gas station convenience store, general store, or place that sells outdoor goods such as EMS or L.L. Bean. Seniors can obtain a life long pass for a nominal processing fee from Forest Service information centers.

The trail goes into the woods a short distance and then divides with the right fork climbing Welch Mountain and the left ascending Dickey. You can reach the Welch's summit in an hour and 45 minutes. The trail to the top of Dickey takes ten minutes longer but is less steep. To climb one trail and descend the other is a popular option.

We see much of the western part of the "Sandwich Front." From Dickey's summit we see Loon Mountain and Scar Ridge. Back on Welch, Mount Tecumseh hides Osceola. As we swing our gaze to the right, we see in succession Kancamagus, Scaur Ridge, the Tripyramids, the Sleepers and Mount Whiteface. Note the rockslides on Tripyramid's South Peak.

Looking east and southeast, behold the massive Sandwich Dome followed by the lower mountains towards the lakes. The several summits of nearby Mount Weetamoo almost hide our next objective, the Squam Range. On the horizon stand the Belknap Mountains thirty miles away.

One often looks for easy climbs amid the towering masses of the White Mountains. Welch and Dickey Mountains in combination serve as one such hike. We have others in later chapters. The summit view is unusual in that we look up at taller forested masses in several directions.

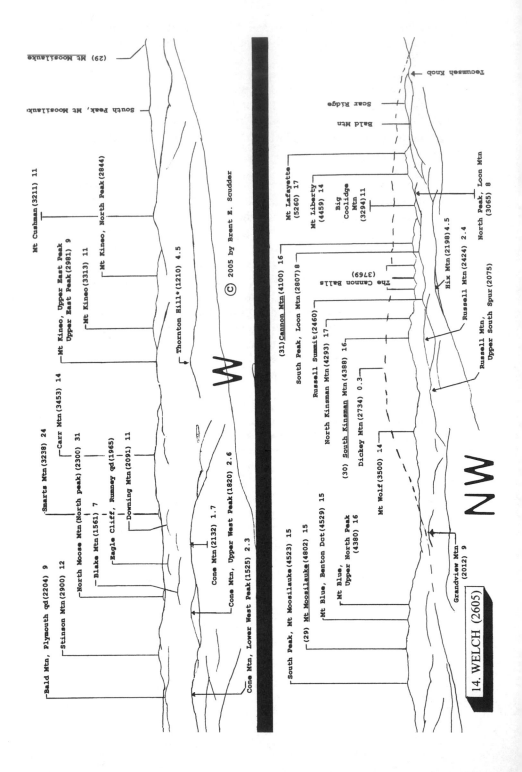

© 2005 by Brent E. Scudder

14. WELCH (2605)

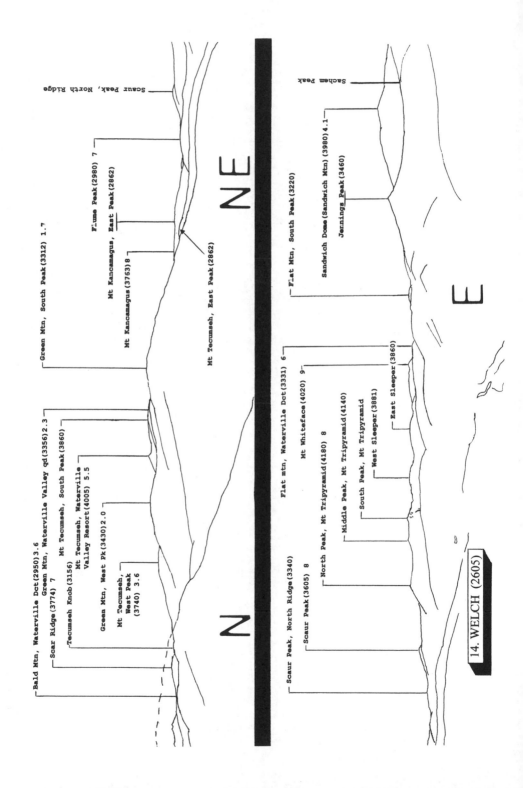

14. WELCH (2605)

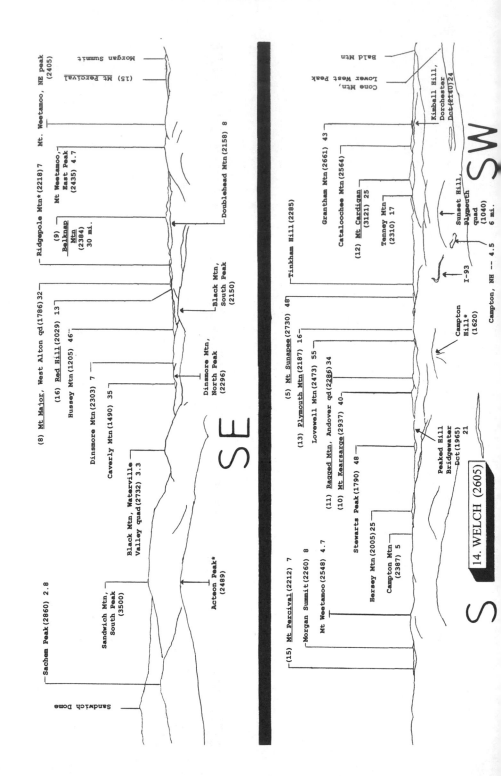

(15) MOUNT PERCIVAL

N 43° 48.562'
W 71° 33.416'

(Elevation 2212 feet)

"Amazing! Does that not look like Squam Lake?"

We were watching the opening scenes of the movie ON GOLDEN POND starring Katharine Hepburn and Henry Fonda. I had not been near Squam in 30 years. But I would swear that the filmmakers had been shooting from Eagle Cliff westward across Sandwich Bay. Three decades before, I had photographed what appeared to have been the same view. As I watched the screenplay unfold, I felt I needed one more definitive scene to positively identify the lake. But I had been away from Squam too long. Even so, the vegetation provided important clues. We saw white pine, pitch pine, white birch and maple. The lake may not have been Squam, but filming had to have taken place between Maine and New York's Adirondacks.

Mount Percival lies across Squam Lake from Eagle cliff and represents a small bump astride a nine-mile range known as the Squam Mountains. The Squams start with Mount Livermore to the west and extend in an arc around the north end of Squam Lake to Mount Israel. If we gaze at the lake, the numerous islands, bays and coves suggest many boating excursions in which one never sees the same view twice. To the north and northeast, the White Mountains stand tall.

From the top of Mount Percival, look to the southwest and note the tallest part of the Squam Range, Morgan Summit.* The true Mount Morgan (N 48.218 min, W 33.966 min) lies beyond. The view in this direction is obscured by the presence of Morgan Summit. Again we used the technique called "looking through the mountain" the same way we did on Ragged and Welch. We crossed over to Mount Morgan and took pictures of its view to the southwest – the very scenery that Morgan Summit hides from Percival. It became a simple matter to fold the hidden scenery into the Percival diagram with Morgan Summit represented there as a dashed line.

---

* Morgan summit is not an official name. See Appendix F starting on page 331.

To view the entire horizon, the hiker must climb both Percival and Morgan. From the top of either mountain, take twenty minutes to cross over to the other top and descend on the other trail. Both paths emerge on the road about a quarter of a mile apart

Directions to this mountain require you to take I-93 to Exit 24 – the Ashland/Holderness exit. Drive towards Holderness 4.6 miles and turn left onto Route 113. In another 5.1 miles, you will pass the turnoff to Rockywold and Deephaven Camps. Continue straight on 113 another half mile and park at the Mount Morgan trailhead. Hike farther down the road an additional quarter mile and see a sign for the Mount Percival trailhead (N 47.499 min, W 32.699 min) Allow a little over an hour for the climb.

At the top, look south for the Uncanoonuc Mountains and Joe English Hill seen on the horizon slightly to the right of White Oak Pond. Nearer ridges gobble up most of their altitude preventing this trio from cutting their familiar stark horizon profiles. You may need binoculars. Farther right is Kearsarge in sharp relief accompanied by a distant Monadnock on its left 71 miles away.

Many of the northern mountains are blocked by the "Sandwich Front" defined in the last chapter. Yet we can still identify Moosilauke, South Kinsman, Lafayette, Hancock and Carrigain. Sandwich Dome is close by and then the mountains appear farther and farther away in the forms of Whiteface, Paugus and Chocorua.

The Squam Range lies in the foreground from the nearest, Mount Squam to the farthest, Mount Israel. The Rattlesnakes, two humpbacked ridges, suggest a serpent the body of which arches upward as it slithers along the nearby lake shore.

The lakes, of course, arrest the eye. One can study the boating activity and follow the curved lines of many islands and peninsulas for a long time. If you are staying either at Squam Lake or Lake Winnipesaukee, it may not be too difficult to spot your location.

By the way, ON GOLDEN POND was indeed filmed at Squam Lake.

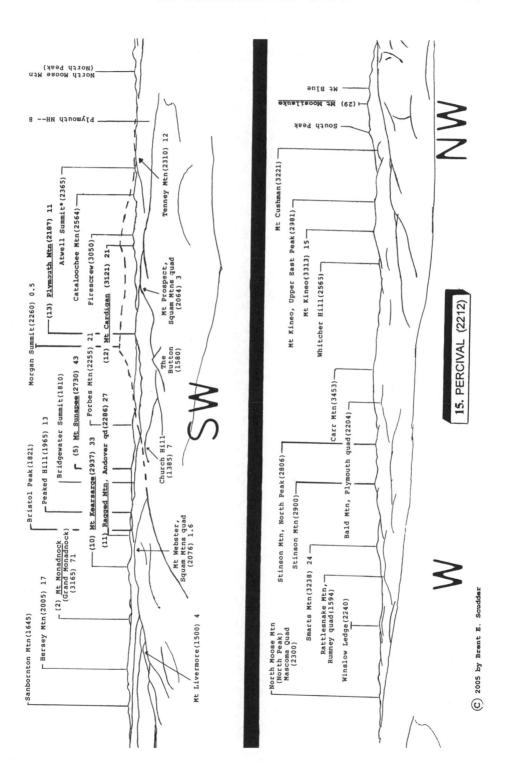

15. PERCIVAL (2212)

SW

W

NW

Sanbornton Mtn(1645)
Hersey Mtn(2005) 17
(2) Mt Monadnock (Grand Monadnock) (3165) 71
Bristol Peak(1821)
Peaked Hill(1965) 13
Bridgewater Summit(1810)
(5) Mt Sunapee(2730) 43
(10) Mt Kearsarge(2937) 33
(11) Ragged Mtn, Andover qd(2286) 27
Forbes Mtn(2255) 21
(12) Mt Cardigan (3121) 21
Morgan Summit(2260) 0.5
(13) Plymouth Mtn(2187) 11
Atwell Summit*(2365)
Cataloochee Mtn(2564)
Firescrew(3050)
Mt Webster, Squam Mtns quad (2076) 1.6
Mt Livermore(1500) 4
Church Hill (1385) 7
The Button (1580)
Mt Prospect, Squam Mtns quad (2064) 3
Tenney Mtn(2310) 12
Plymouth NH--8
North Moose Mtn (North Peak)

North Moose Mtn (North Peak) Mascoma Quad (2300)
Stinson Mtn, North Peak(2806)
Stinson Mtn(2900)
Smarts Mtn(3238) 24
Rattlesnake Mtn, Rumney quad(1594)
Winslow Ledge(2240)
Bald Mtn, Plymouth quad(2204)
Carr Mtn(3453)
Mt Kineo, Upper East Peak(2981)
Mt Kineo(3313) 15
Whitcher Hill(2565)
Mt Cushman(3221)
South Peak
(29) Mt Moosilauke
Mt Blue

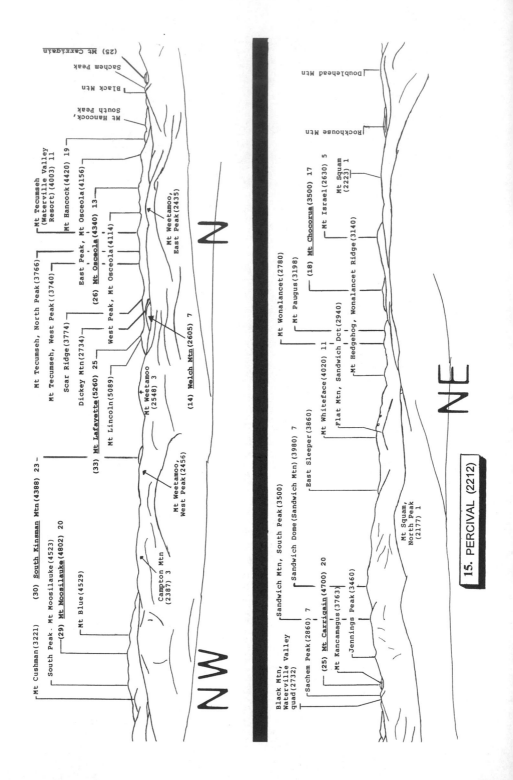

15. PERCIVAL (2212)

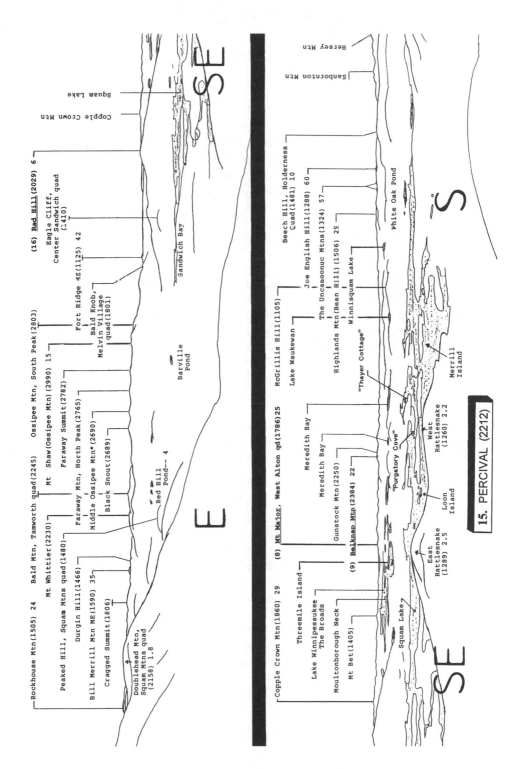

15. PERCIVAL (2212)

(16) Red Hill (2029) 6
Copple Crown Mtn
Squam Lake
Eagle Cliff, Center Sandwich quad (1410)
Fort Ridge 4E(1125) 42
Bald Knob, Melvin Village quad(1801)
Sandwich Bay
SE

Rockhouse Mtn(1505) 24
Bald Mtn, Tamworth quad(2245)
Ossipee Mtn, South Peak(2803)
Mt Whittier(2230)
Mt Shaw(Ossipee Mtn) (2990) 15
Peaked Hill, Squam Mtns quad(1480)
Faraway Summit(2782)
Durgin Hill(1466)
Faraway Mtn, North Peak(2765)
Bill Merrill Mtn ME(1590) 35
Middle Ossipee Mtn*(2690)
Cragged Summit(1806)
Black Snout(2689)
Doublehead Mtn, Squam Mtns quad (2158) 1.8
Red Hill Pond-- 4
Barville Pond
E

Copple Crown Mtn(1860) 29
(8) Mt Major, West Alton qd(1786)25
McGrillis Hill(1105)
Beech Hill, Holderness Quad(1481) 10
Threemile Island
Lake Waukewan
Joe English Hill(1288) 60
Lake Winnipesaukee The Broads
Meredith Bay
The Uncanoonuc Mtns(1324) 57
Moultonborough Neck
Meredith Bay
Highlands Mtn(Bean Hill) (1506) 29
Gunstock Mtn(2250)
Winnisquam Lake
White Oak Pond
Mt Bet(1405)
(9) Belknap Mtn(2384) 22
"Thayer Cottage"
"Purgatory Cove"
Merrill Island
Squam Lake
West Rattlesnake (1260) 2.2
East Rattlesnake (1289) 2.5
Loon Island
Sanbornton Mtn
Hersey Mtn
SE
S

15. PERCIVAL (2212)

(16) RED HILL

N 43° 45.344'
W 71° 27.458'

(Elevation 2029 feet)

Long a favorite of children's camps during the weekdays of July and August, Red Hill has the combination of providing an easy climb with an overwhelming view. To the south lies Lake Winnipesaukee with its supposed 365 islands. (Tongue-in-cheek legend has it that during Leap Year, the lake level drops to reveal a 366th!) Westward, Squam Lake stands forth with numerous islets of its own. To the north stands the "Sandwich Front" separating the lesser hills of the Lakes Region from the high country to the north.

Stand on the top of Red Hill, look east and behold New Hampshire's most perfectly formed geological ring dike complex, the Ossipee Mountains. The disk shape of this range is not immediately apparent because parts of these hills are represented on four separate charts. But join these maps together so as to form a mosaic and a nearly perfect circle emerges. Even Red Hill is a ring dike complex, albeit smaller and less circular. Yet it has the same characteristic of numerous nameless tops that stand slightly below the main summit.

Red Hill is well named. Take a canoe out upon Squam Lake late on a sunny autumn afternoon when the foliage is at its peak. Look to the east and discover the subtle reds that oak trees produce.

To get to the trailhead, enter the town of Center Harbor from the south and proceed one block past the intersection with Route 25B. Turn left on to Bean Hill Road. At a point 1.4 miles out of town, make a right turn at Silbey Road. At 2.7 miles from Center Harbor, veer left onto Red Hill Road. After an additional 0.2 miles, park opposite a gate that shuts off a jeep road leading to the east. This jeep road is the start of the trail (N 44.341 min, W 27.784 min).

From the summit, look at the horizon to the right of Lake Kanasatka and note that the Pack Monadnocks and Mount Kearsarge are still visible. Sunapee is but a pip seen over the top of the right portion of Ragged Mountain. Cardigan appears to the west-southwest with Plymouth Mountain nearer and on its right. Across the lake to the west and extending around to the north stands the entire Squam Range. One can easily see why an all-encompassing view does not exist on either Mount Morgan or Mount Percival. Tree-covered Morgan Summit rises forcibly between.

Northwestward stands Mount Moosilauke, its several component peaks easily noted. Nearby to the north is Sandwich Dome so covered with forest that it hides one of New Hampshire's best summit views.

The "Sandwich Front" hides most of what lies beyond including Mount Washington. The western part of the Front is blocked by Sandwich Dome. But it emerges to the right of the Dome in the forms of Tripyramid, the Sleepers, Whiteface, Passaconaway, Paugus and Chocorua. Beyond it we see only Mounts Hancock and Carrigain.

South of Chocorua, glance down the Bearcamp River Valley and find Pleasant Mountain in Maine along with two Mounts Tom, one of them 63 miles away. To the right of the Ossipee Mountains, more can be seen of the Pine Tree State in the shape of Ossipee Hill, Abbot Mountain and Fort Ridge.

We return to the pride of the view Lake Winnipesaukee, framed in the background by the Moose Mountains on the left and by the Belknaps on the right. Among the islands in the lake are Twin and Little Huck on the left and then Long and Steamboat in the center. To the right is Threemile Island upon which is located a family style camp open to all and operated by the Appalachian Mountain Club. Why should an island have a name like that? Consider that from left to right we have Sixmile Island, Fivemile Island, Threemile Island and Mile Island easily seen as stepping stones into Center Harbor. A fisherman returning late at night in the fog need only identify one of these outcroppings to know exactly his distance from home.

As chapter follows chapter, we slowly progress northward from mountain to mountain. The climbs become tougher, the panoramas more dearly bought. But even half way up the Granite State, we still have magnificent scenes such as from Red Hill that can be viewed with so little effort.

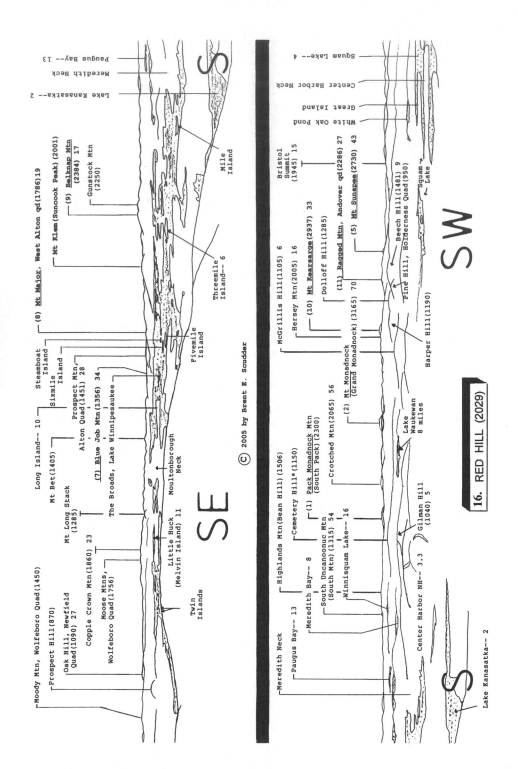

© 2005 by Brent E. Scudder

16. RED HILL (2029)

SE panel labels:

Paugus Bay-- 13
Meredith Neck
Lake Kanasatka-- 2
(9) Belknap Mtn (2384) 17
Gunstock Mtn (2250)
Mt Klem (Suncook Peak) (2001)
(8) Mt Major, West Alton qd(1786)19
Mile Island
Threemile Island-- 6
Fivemile Island
Long Island-- 10
Steamboat Island
Sixmile Island
Prospect Mtn, Alton Quad(1451) 28
(7) Blue Job Mtn(1356) 34
The Broads, Lake Winnipesaukee
Moultonborough Neck
Mt Bet(1405)
Mt Long Stack (1285)
Copple Crown Mtn(1860) 23
Moose Mtns, Wolfeboro Quad(1756)
Oak Hill, Newfield Quad(1090) 27
Prospect Hill(870)
Moody Mtn, Wolfeboro Quad(1450)
Little Buck (Melvin Island) 11
Twin Islands

SW panel labels:

Squam Lake-- 4
Center Harbor Neck
Great Island
White Oak Pond
Bristol Summit (1945) 15
(9) Ragged Mtn, Andover qd(2286) 27
(5) Mt Sunapee (2730) 43
Squam Lake
Beech Hill(1481) 9
Pine Hill, Holderness Quad (950)
McGrillis Hill(1105) 6
Hersey Mtn(2005) 16
(10) Mt Kearsarge (2937) 33
Dolloff Hill(1285)
(11) Ragged Mtn, Andover qd(2286) 27
Harper Hill(1190)
(2) Mt Monadnock (Grand Monadnock) (3165) 70
Highlands Mtn(Bean Hill) (1506)
Cemetery Hill*(1150)
(1) Pack Monadnock Mtn (South Pack) (2300)
Crotched Mtn(2065) 56
Lake Waukewan 8 miles
South Uncanoonuc Mtn (South Mtn) (1315) 54
Winnisquam Lake-- 16
Gilman Hill (1040) 5
Meredith Neck
Paugus Bay-- 13
Meredith Bay-- 8
Center Harbor NH-- 3.3
Lake Kanasatka-- 2

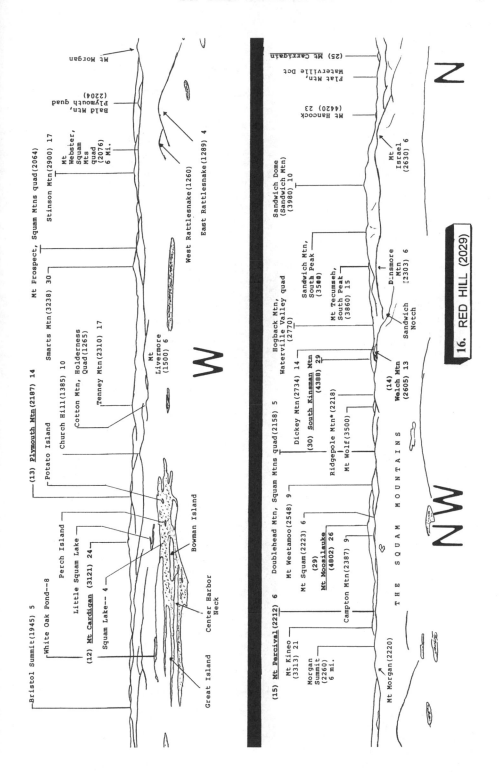

16. RED HILL (2029)

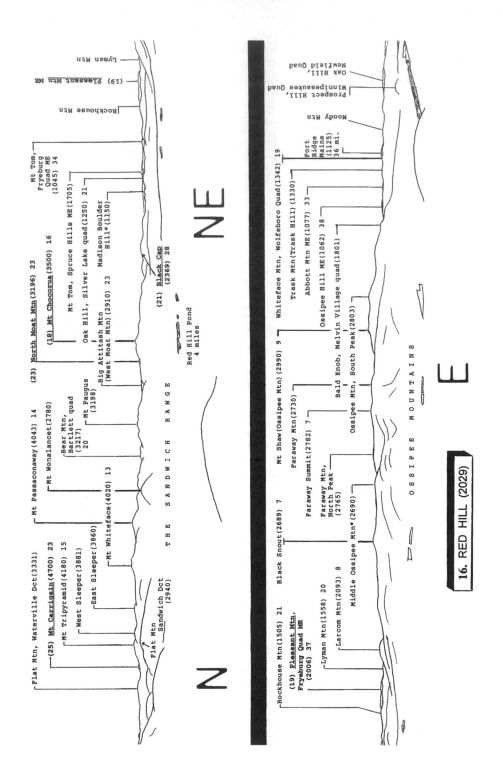

(17) GREEN MOUNTAIN

Freedom Quadrangle

N 43° 46.055'
W 71° 02.210'

(Elevation 1884 feet)

We continue eastward over and beyond the Ossipee Range and see ahead of us the smallest of six New Hampshire hills designated as Green Mountain. As with Red Hill, this summit is also a favorite of children's camps during the weekdays of July and August. Indeed, the author himself once led a group of pre-teens up the trail when he had been working as a counselor at Camp Copithorne formerly located on Danforth Bay.

Green Mountain is little known for it is tucked away in the southeastern corner of Carroll County. Mountain climbers and tourists alike pass it on their way north to more exotic heights. But the view from its fire tower is startling. Lakes stretch out in all directions. That big pond to the west is Ossipee Lake. Its associated bays and channels extend around to the northwest and north. To the southeast lies Province Lake and, farther on, Great East Lake.

To the north, we are no longer blocked by the "Sandwich Front." Mounts Liberty and Lafayette have reappeared. Bondcliff along with Mounts Nancy and Field are seen for the first time. Over the top of nearby Rockhouse Mountain, we look directly up the Saco River valley flanked on the west by the huge Moat Range and on the east by the pointed Kearsarge North. At the horizon stands the complete Presidential Range never glimpsed in its entirety until now. From Mount Webster on the left to Mount Madison on the right, the Presidentials tower majestically. We also have our initial view of the higher mountains in Maine such as Puzzle and Old Speck. Indeed the nearer terrain no longer shuts us in.

Green's summit lies only two miles from the Maine border. To the northeast stands Pleasant Mountain, its Shawnee Peak a notable ski area. Farther east may be found the Saddleback Hills, the same hills that flank the southwest shores of Sebago Lake. We see Sebago itself, 22 miles away just to the right of the Saddlebacks. During a crystal clear summer day, try to reach Green Mountain's fire tower before ten o'clock. One will see the Atlantic catching the glint of the morning sun just to the left of Maine's Ossipee Hill.

Across the left portion of Province Lake stands Mount Agamenticus. "Aggie" is now but a tiny bump on the horizon immediately to the right of Bauneg Beg Mountain. If we scan to the right, we come to the Moose and Belknap Mountains. The largest Moose easily hides Blue Job. Pieces of Lake Winnipesaukee appear to the southwest but its spectacular appearance is diminished by distance. To the right of the Belknaps, one sees far away the familiar mountains of Lovewell, Kearsarge and Sunapee.

The Ossipee Mountains eclipse Red Hill. From Mounts Major and Belknap we could spot Red Hill and Green Mountain simultaneously. We also saw the Ossipees rising forcibly between.

In seeking Green Mountain, take Route 16 northward to Center Ossipee. Follow Route 25 eastward approximately five miles and see a sign pointing out Route 153 leading to the left. Instead, turn right onto Green Mountain Road. After 1.2 miles angle left on a side road and after 0.2 more miles turn more sharply left. Drive east a mile until you pass the Lakeview Neuro-rehabilitation Center. When the paved road turns to dirt, proceed another tenth of a mile to a wide spot where there is parking. Look to the right and see a sign saying High Watch Preserve. The trailhead is here (N 47.034 min, W 02.765 min). This path is well marked as it skirts part way around the rehab center soon to bend left uphill into the forest. One can reach the top in less than an hour.

Green Mountain is the tallest and easternmost crest of a short range of hills oriented in the unusual direction of east to west. This orientation aids in identifying it from other summits. But for the Ossipees 12 miles to the west, Chocorua 17 miles to the northwest and Pleasant Mountain 21 miles to the northeast, no elevation competes with Green Mountain. Therein lies the secret of its marvelous view.

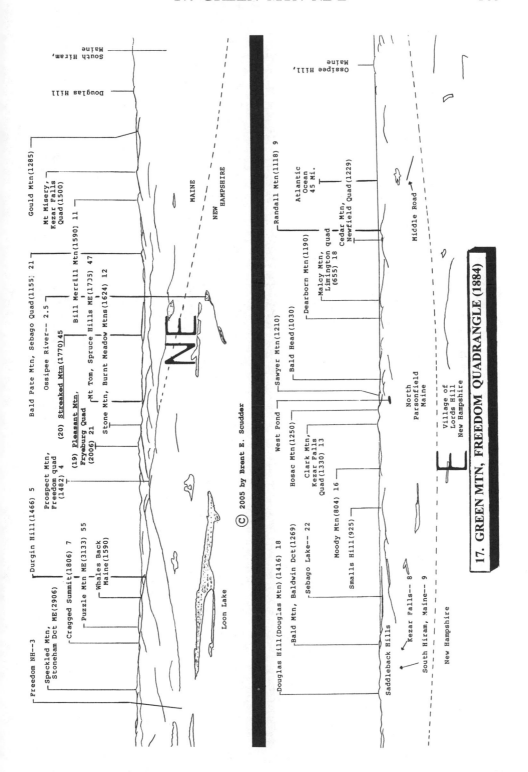

© 2005 by Brent E. Scudder

17. GREEN MTN, FREEDOM QUADRANGLE (1884)

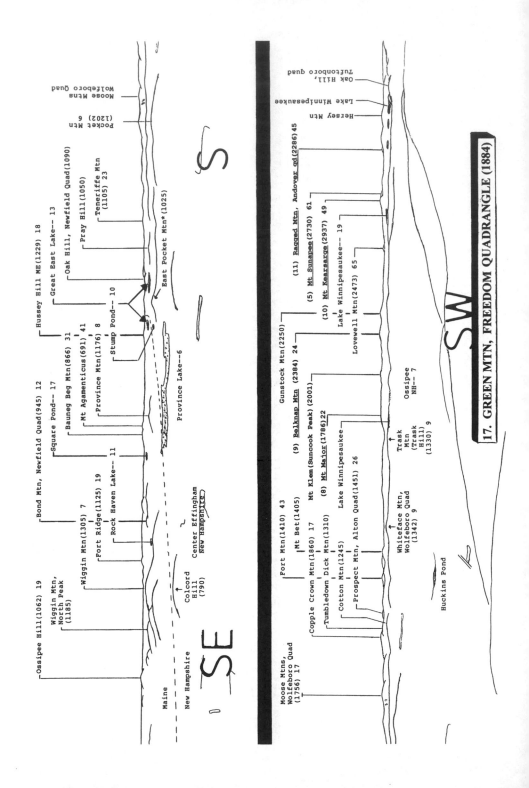

17. GREEN MTN, FREEDOM QUADRANGLE (1884)

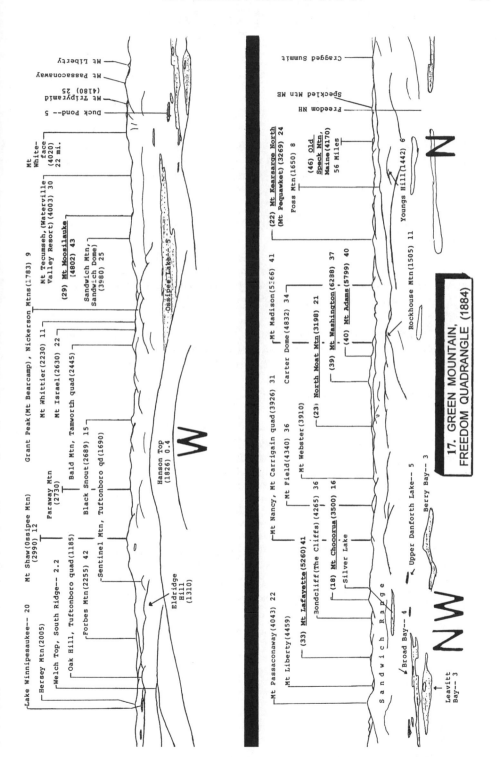

17. GREEN MOUNTAIN,
FREEDOM QUADRANGLE (1884)

(18) MOUNT CHOCORUA

N 43° 57.260'
W 71° 16.386'

(Elevation 3500 feet)

"Take a look at that!" We are standing somewhere along the Bearcamp River. The day is overcast. We look to the north. Before us, suspended in mid-air hanging from the sky appears a peak of bare granite. Nothing supports it – only cloud.

LeGrand Cannon, Jr.'s LOOK TO THE MOUNTAIN, a novel of early New Hampshire settlement, describes the fictitious Coruway Mountain. The hero has lost his way in a trackless forest near "Great Ossipy Pond." Murky skies hide all highland landmarks. He climbs a tree in order to find the peak that serves as his pilot beacon. The clouds open slightly and he beholds this ethereal sight. Only one mountain fits this description – Chocorua.

Your first glimpse of Chocorua may not resemble a sacred work of Michelangelo. But the august profile of a rocky crag leaps up against the sky. Drive north from down state on Route 16. You first see Chocorua as a pointed peak shortly after you have crossed the town line into Ossipee. As you continue, Chocorua sneaks up on you looming taller and taller.

Mount Chocorua was named for a tribal chief who, in fleeing the European settlers, swore that he would never be taken alive. Legends about him vary, but supposedly he was chased to the top of the pinnacle where he jumped off and landed in the lake that later bore his name. While geographical reality suggests that this was highly improbable, who knows? Strange things happen in legends.

From the top, we scan the entire White Mountains to discover a startling landscape of steep rises and falls. Mount Washington, the tallest, lies twenty-two miles away. To the left stretches the rugged Pemigewasset Wilderness. In earlier chapters, we saw Mount Carrigain as a slight horizon protrusion above nearer hills. Now behold its huge gambrel profile. Left of Carrigain appears the gigantic cone of Passaconaway. Osceola rises between. For once we see that Tripyramid is actually triple-peaked.

Due south lie the Ossipee Mountains, appearing lower now for we stand much higher. Observe Green Mountain on the left and Red Hill on the right. Beyond the Ossipees, we see pieces of the Belknap Mountains including one that we climbed. Gaze at the horizon beyond Black Snout. A tiny North Uncanoonuc Mountain announces itself along with Joe English Hill 72 miles away.

You can see farther but may need binoculars. On Joe's right stands the Bay State's Mount Wachusett 106 miles off into the distance. Vermont is visible. Okemo Mountain is but a slight apex on the horizon between the nearer Mount Cardigan and Sandwich Dome.

Of the many routes up Chocorua, hikers often choose the Piper Trail which leads away to the west from Route 16 exactly five miles north of Chocorua Village. This trail starts behind Davie's General Store and Campground (N 56.429 min, W 13.750 min). White Mountain National Forest fees are charged for parking here. (See page 89). Select this approach and you face 2700 feet of vertical ascent, which is higher than on any previously featured hike. The climb takes more than three hours.

A gentler route starts from a higher elevation resulting in only 2270 feet of ascent. Drive farther north on Route 16 and turn left onto the Kancamagus Highway. Drive 11.5 miles to the Champney Falls trailhead (N 59.404 min, W 17.943 min). Parking fees are charged here also. The climb can be done in under three hours. If you visit the Falls, be extremely careful. Numerous slipping accidents have occurred.

From the top we see more of Maine, a confused tumble of mountains extending away to the northeast. Farther right lay the lowlands with table-topped Pleasant Mountain at the forefront. Arrive at Chocorua's crest before 10 a.m. when the sun is out and catch its glimmer off the Atlantic Ocean. Numerous lakes are seen. More startling is the gentle countryside in one direction and the steep pitches in the other.

Few New Hampshire climbers have missed this summit. The sight of Chocorua becomes an obsession relieved only after its height has been achieved. Is it the lonely pinnacle behind a lake that inspires us or is it something primordial? Look to the Mountain. Chocorua beckons.

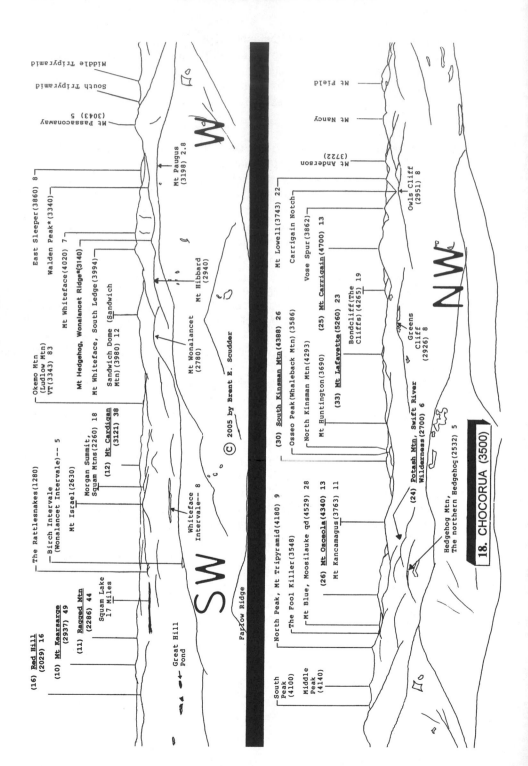

Middle Tripyramid

South Tripyramid

Mt Passaconaway (3043) 5

Mt Paugus (3198) 2.8

East Sleeper (3860) 8

Walden Peak* (3340)

Okemo Mtn (Ludlow Mtn) VT(3343) 83

Mt Hedgehog, Wonalancet Ridge* (3140) 7

Mt Whiteface(4020)

Mt Whiteface, South Ledge (3994)

Sandwich Dome (Sandwich Mtn) (3980) 12

Mt Hibbard (2940)

Mt Wonalancet (2780)

The Rattlesnakes(1280)

Birch Intervale (Wonalancet Intervale)-- 5

Mt Israel(2630)

Morgan Summit, Squam Mtns(2260) 18

(12) **Mt Cardigan** (3121) 38

(16) **Red Hill** (2029) 16

(10) **Mt Kearsarge** (2937) 49

(11) **Ragged Mtn** (2286) 44

Squam Lake 17 Miles

Whiteface Intervale-- 8

Great Hill Pond

Farlow Ridge

SW

W

© 2005 by Brent E. Scudder

(30) **South Kinsman Mtn**(4388) 26

Osseo Peak(Whaleback Mtn) (3586)

North Kinsman Mtn(4293)

Mt Huntington(3690)

(33) **Mt Lafayette**(5260) 23

(24) **Potash Mtn, Swift River Wilderness**(2700) 6

Hedgehog Mtn, The northern Hedgehog(2532) 5

North Peak, Mt Tripyramid(4180) 9

The Fool Killer(3548)

Mt Blue, Moosilauke qd(4529) 28

(26) **Mt Osceola**(4340) 13

Mt Kancamagus(3763) 11

South Peak (4100)

Middle Peak (4140)

Mt Lowell(3743) 22

Carrigain Notch

Vose Spur(3862)

(25) **Mt Carrigain**(4700) 13

Bondcliff(The Cliffs) (4265) 19

Greens Cliff (2926) 8

Mt Field

Mt Nancy

Mt Anderson (3722)

Owls Cliff (2951) 8

NW

18. CHOCORUA (3500)

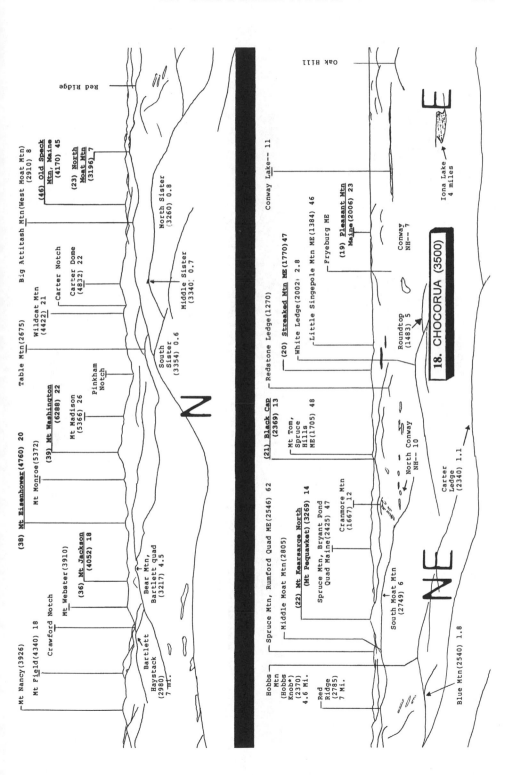

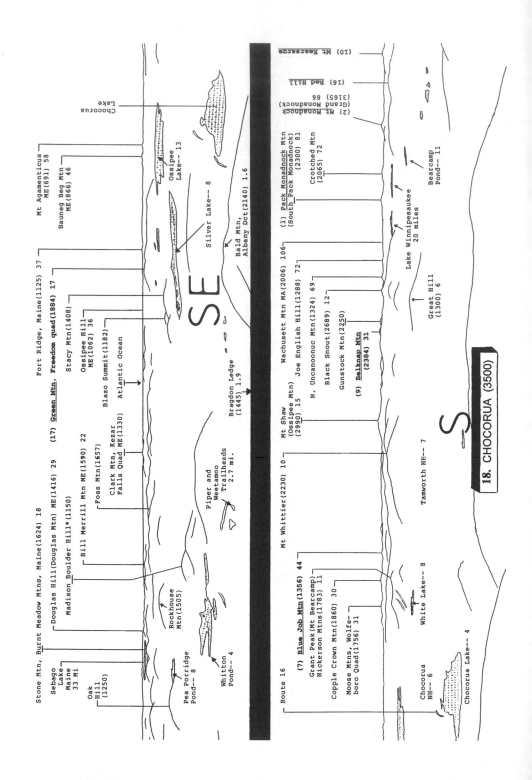

18. CHOCORUA (3500)

SE

S

Stone Mtn, Burnt Meadow Mtns, Maine(1624) 18
Sebago Lake Maine 33 Mi
Oak Hill (1250)
Douglas Hill(Douglas Mtn) ME(1416) 29
Madison Boulder Hill*(1150)
(17) Green Mtn, Freedom Quad(1884) 17
Bill Merrill Mtn ME(1590) 22
Foss Mtn(1657)
Clark Mtn, Kezar Falls Quad ME(1330)
Port Ridge, Maine(1125) 37
Stacy Mtn(1408)
Ossipee Hill ME(1062) 36
Blazo Summit(1182)
Atlantic Ocean
Mt Agamenticus ME(691) 58
Bauneg Beg Mtn ME(866) 46
Chocorua Lake
Ossipee Lake-- 13
Silver Lake-- 8
Bald Mtn, Albany Dct(2140) 1.6
Bragdon Ledge (1445) 1.9

Mt Kearsarge (10)
Red Hill (16)
Mt Monadnock (Grand Monadnock) (3165) 86 (2)
Pack Monadnock Mtn (South Pack Monadnock) (2300) 81 (1)
Crotched Mtn (2065) 72
Bearcamp Pond-- 11
Lake Winnipesaukee 20 miles

Pea Porridge Pond-- 8
Whitton Pond-- 4
Rockhouse Mtn (1505)
Piper and Weetamoo Trailheads 2.7 mi.

Route 16
(7) Blue Job Mtn(1356) 44
Grant Peak(Mt Bearcamp) Nickerson Mtns(1783) 11
Copple Crown Mtn(1860) 30
Moose Mtns, Wolfe-boro Quad(1756) 31
White Lake-- 8
Chocorua NH-- 6
Chocorua Lake-- 4
Mt Whittier(2230) 10
Mt Shaw (Ossipee Mtn) (2990) 15
Tamworth NE-- 7
Wachusett Mtn MA(2006) 106
Joe English Hill(1288) 72
N. Uncanoonuc Mtn(1324) 69
Black Snout(2689) 12
Gunstock Mtn(2250)
Belknap Mtn (2384) 31 (9)
Great Hill (1300) 6

(19) PLEASANT MOUNTAIN

Fryeburg 15' Quadrangle
Pleasant Mountain 7 ½' Quadrangle
Maine

N 44° 01.616'
W 70° 49.360'

(Elevation 2006 feet)

So far, the White Mountains have been introduced by approaching them chapter-by-chapter from the south utilizing views that become progressively closer to them. This design is in keeping with the fact that the majority of the readership lives to the south. But suppose as a child you attended summer camp in Maine or else grew up there. Your first taste of climbing may have come from a Fourth Grade outing where you took a picnic lunch to ascend Bradbury Mountain near Portland, or else Rattlesnake Mountain or Douglas Hill near Sebago Lake. In the distance, the White Mountains would appear entirely different than to those who approach them from the south.

Pleasant Mountain will give you a good taste of how the Whites appear from Maine. From the summit fire tower, one observes most of New Hampshire's higher peaks. We can see clear across the Granite State to the Franconia Range. On the left there is Chocorua, Passaconaway, Osceola and Carrigain. To the right stands the Presidential Range from Mount Jackson to Adams with Mount Washington towering between.

But we make out many of the higher mountains in Maine itself. Look to the north and behold Goose Eye, Old Speck, the Baldpates, Saddleback and Abraham. Maine's highest, Katahdin, is still too far away.

We can also see into Vermont. Mount Ascutney pricks the horizon 91 miles away to the left of Mount Cardigan.

To reach Pleasant Mountain from the west, pick up route 302 in Conway, New Hampshire, and drive into Maine. In Fryeburg, Route 5 forks left. Stay on 302 for another 8.8 miles and turn right on Mountain Road, a road that passes the Shawnee ski area. Mountain Road may also be reached from the east by driving to Bridgeton, Maine, on Route 302 and continuing to follow

302 for another five miles or so until you reach the lake-sized Moose Pond. Mountain Road is the second left past the pond. Turn there. Drive 3.2 miles to the Ledges trailhead which disappears into the woods on the right. Ample parking may be found on the left across from the trail (N 01.458 min, W 47.846 min). Expect nearly a two-hour climb.

At the top, we stand at the highest point of a four-mile long mountain range oriented north to south. Shawnee Peak is found at the north end with its ski area. Then comes Big Bald Peak. The ridge passes under us as it extends away to the southwest.

One truly realizes that he or she is in lake country. Scanning from left to right in a southerly direction, one sees Sebago Lake, Hancock, Sand, Moose, Granger and Rattlesnake Ponds. To the west lies Pleasant and Lovewell Ponds, the Saco River, Lower Kimball Pond, Kezar Pond and Kezar Lake. Looking east we see Highland Lake, Long Lake and Wood Pond. The westerly ponds with the towering White Mountains beyond create a marvelous view.

The hiker should spend some time with these lesser mountains. One tests not only his or her equipment and stamina before tackling the high peaks, but also the ability to navigate through dense forest.

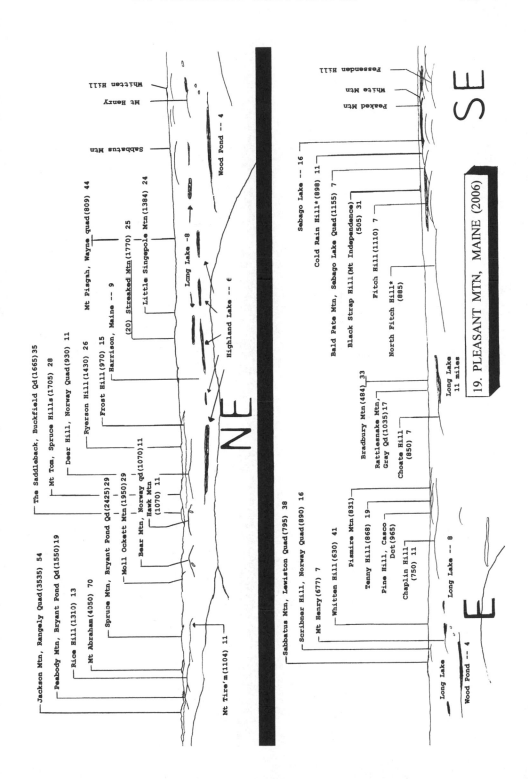

19. PLEASANT MTN, MAINE (2006)

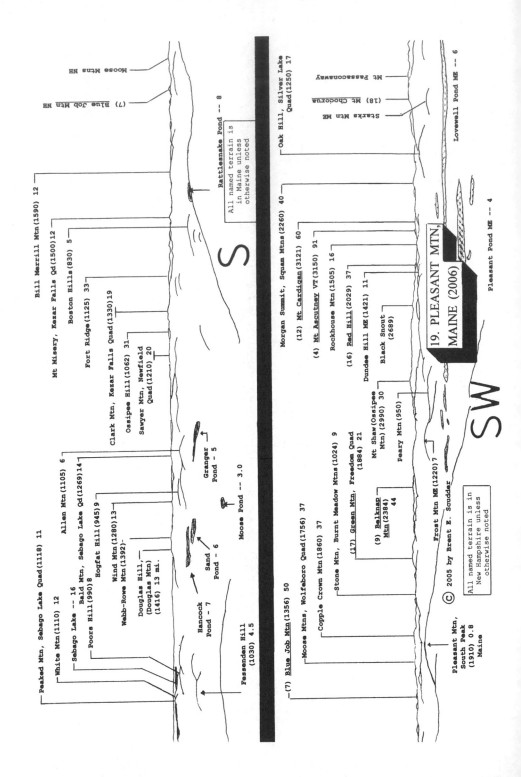

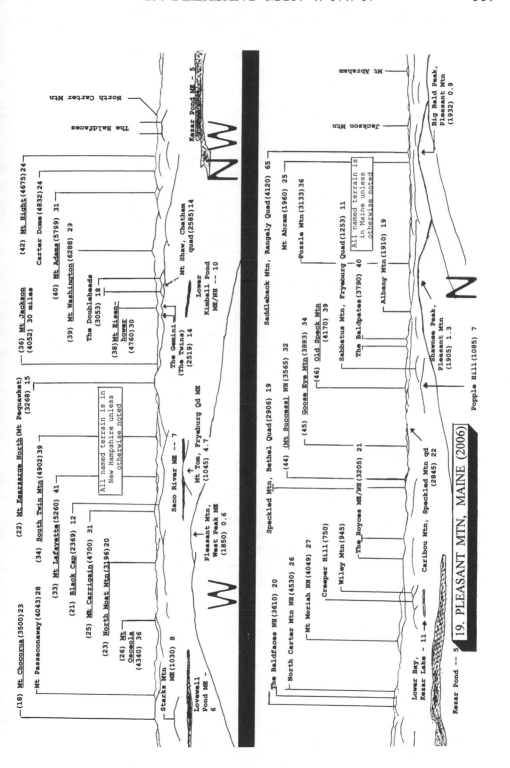

19. PLEASANT MTN, MAINE (2006)

(20) STREAKED MOUNTAIN

N 44° 15.006'
W 70° 25.413'

(Elevation 1770 feet)

Streaked Mountain's summit view includes a part of Maine that is little known except by area vacationers and, of course, residents. Lakes and ponds are profuse in number with large hills located mostly away from the coast. Strange town names such as China, Paris, Peru, Poland and Norway abound in all directions. Streaked Mountain is a short thirty minute climb but with a fine view. Detracting from the scenery are at least nine large antennas giving the top the look of a porcupine. Most of these towers were there before the advent of the cell phone. But we can hike around the summit placing the eyesores behind us as we look out upon the countryside.

One arrives at the trailhead by driving north on Route 26 to Norway, Maine and turning right onto Route 117. Proceed 6.1 miles to Streaked Mountain Road where you turn right again. Another half mile brings you to a dip in the road. The trailhead (N 14.779 min, W 25.901 min) is not immediately apparent. On the left is a fence perpendicular to the road that is fairly close to a house. A path seems to go to the left of the fence. If you look more closely you will see the Streaked Mountain sign leading up that trail.

The red-blazed trail maintained by Hebron Academy climbs through woods until it comes out onto ledges (N 14.816 min, W 25.639 min). Then you achieve an ever-expanding prospect of the White Mountains as you climb. The top has scattered trees that force you to hike about to get the view.

If we look southwest, we find the elongated Pleasant Mountain of the last chapter. To the right follows New Hampshire's Mount Cardigan 85 miles away. The White Mountains appear farther over. Kearsarge North with its cone shape appears over the top of nearby Pennesseewassee Lake with the Presidential Range even farther right.

An auspicious double peak appears to the west-northwest. The top on the left is Maine's Goose Eye Mountain. Everything to the right is in Maine with Old Speck being the highest elevation visible.

Towards the north, look for Tumbledown Dick Mountain, a fairly low elevation to the right of Peru township's Black Mountain. The name source for Tumbledown Dick is obscure, but perhaps we can shed some light. One possible explanation given in Robert and Mary Julyan's *Place Names of the White Mountains,* is that a horse named Dick tumbled down the mountain. Apparently he tumbled down not only this mountain, but a Tumbledown Dick near Gilead Maine, another in Brookfield, New Hampshire not to mention a Tumble Dick Mountain in the Dixville Notch area. The true source of the name may somewhat indelicate.

"Tumbledown Dick" was a slang expression used during the Seventeenth Century. As an example, in his *A History of the English Speaking Peoples,* Winston Churchill discusses Oliver Cromwell's takeover of English government authority. Oliver had to have been a strong personality without scruples to be able to achieve his goal. When Oliver approached death's door, he named his son Richard to succeed him. Churchill described the son: "*Tumbledown Dick*, as his enemies nicknamed him, was a respectable person with good intentions, but without the force and capacity required by the severity of the times."

Assuming that the slang meaning of the second word has not changed over the centuries, "Tumbledown Dick" would refer to a male in a perpetual state of detumescence, the implication being that Richard Cromwell was rather effeminate. Were the Colonial settlers naming these mountains after Richard? Perhaps not. All four mountains have one thing in common. Their horizon profiles are rather flaccid.

Beyond and to the right of Peru's Tumbledown Dick, we see more of Maine's higher peaks, namely Saddleback and Abraham. The hills then become smaller as we approach the coast. To the east lies a piece of Androscoggin Lake along with Mount Pisgah near Winthrop. Farther right lie the Camden Hills tiny on the horizon 67 miles away.

The remainder of the view was diagrammed from the south peak of Streaked Mountain (N 14.778 min, W 25.208 min), which is a bushwhack of 3/10 of a mile to the south-southeast. From the south peak we continue our gaze to the right and spy Lake Auburn eleven miles away followed by Ben Barrows Hill, Bradbury Mountain and Blackstrap Hill. The Sebago Lake area is next in line with Rattlesnake Mountain and Douglas Hill adjacent.

Having traveled this far eastward to climb a mountain, we turn back west to our next objective, North Conway's Black Cap in New Hampshire.

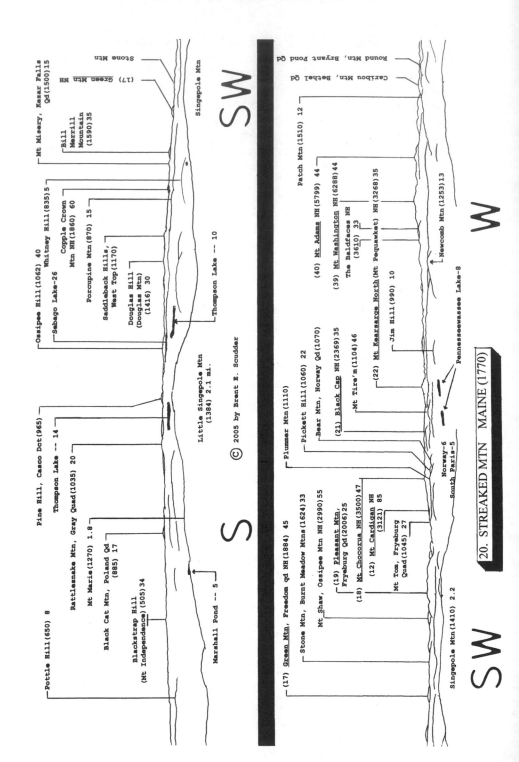

© 2005 by Brent E. Scudder

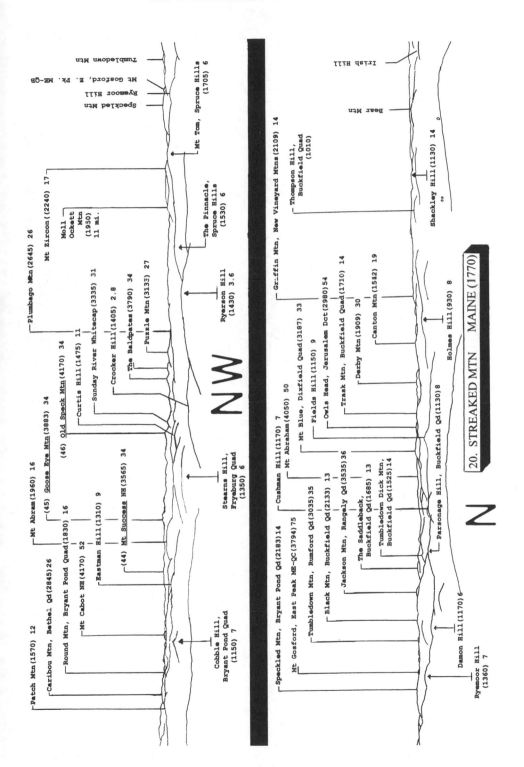

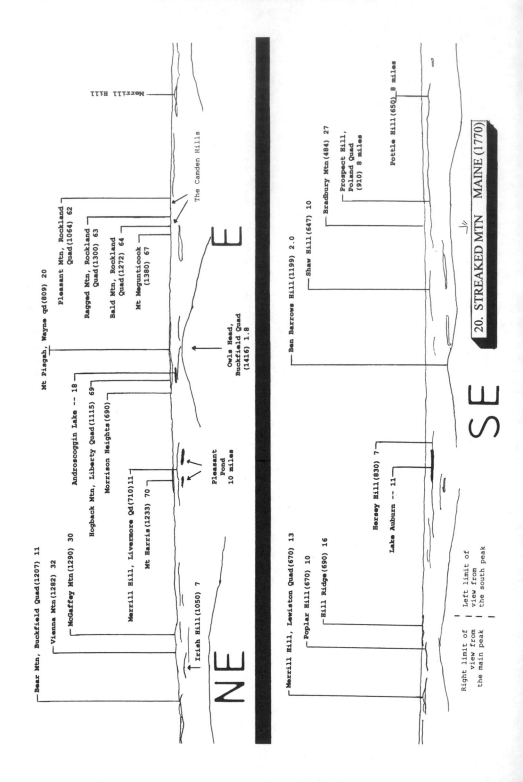

Bear Mtn, Buckfield Quad(1207) 11
Vienna Mtn(1282) 32
McGaffey Mtn(1290) 30
Hogback Mtn, Liberty Quad(1115) 69
Morrison Heights(690)
Merrill Hill, Livermore Qd(710)11
Mt Harris(1233) 70
Irish Hill(1050) 7

Mt Pisgah, Wayne qd(809) 20
Pleasant Mtn, Rockland Quad(1064) 62
Ragged Mtn, Rockland Quad(1300) 63
Bald Mtn, Rockland Quad(1272) 64
Mt Megunticook (1380) 67
Androscoggin Lake -- 18

Merrill Hill

The Camden Hills

Owls Head, Buckfield Quad (1416) 1.8

Pleasant Pond 10 miles

NE

E

Merrill Hill, Lewiston Quad(670) 13
Poplar Hill(670) 10
Hill Ridge(690) 16
Hersey Hill(830) 7
Lake Auburn -- 11

Ben Barrows Hill(1199) 2.0
Shaw Hill(647) 10
Bradbury Mtn(484) 27
Prospect Hill, Poland Quad (910) 8 miles
Pottle Hill(650) 8 miles

20. STREAKED MTN MAINE (1770)

SE

Right limit of view from the main peak

Left limit of view from the south peak

(21) BLACK CAP

N 44° 03.343'
W 71° 04.005'

(Elevation 2369 feet)

Take a thirty-five mile jump to the west to an elevation located near the eastern edge of the White Mountains. To the east we observe what has been seen in the last two chapters – gentle hills and lakes that make up southwestern Maine, for this is Maine. But we have returned to New Hampshire. Look west and behold a startlingly different aspect of huge rises and falls in the land with steep sides and precipitous cliffs. The western view is but a telescopic magnification of what was seen from Streaked Mountain.

As a person advances in age, he or she cannot fail to notice the detrimental effects that result from the expanding population. The increase in noise, water and air pollution, of course, is well documented. More subtle is the reaction of a person of means to shut out the encroaching horde and create his own paradise. His nirvana may consist of a house and yard on a 1/3-acre plot surrounded by a tall hedge or a high wood fence. Or else it may be a hundred acres of beautiful forest posted against trespassers. If the enclaves are few, then there is little effect upon the wanderer. But as the population increases, so do these private holdings. The free spirit is further restricted.

Many states are heavily endowed with thousands of square miles of mountains, forests, lakes and streams. Much of the freedom to explore such wilderness is closed to you and me through private ownership. Less affected is the Granite State. New Hampshire has over two million acres of national, state and town forest. In addition, many landowners allow hiking, fishing and other forest recreation. It is not the roadside attraction for the children such as Six Gun City or Santa's Village that brings us to New Hampshire. It is not even the majestic mountain visible across an azure lake that we see from the road. It is the freedom to roam.

Many people resident and non-resident alike have worked to continue this freedom. A typical case involved the generosity of Anna Stearns and the efforts of Eve Endicott, Katherine Billings and others who took almost thirty years to acquire the Green Hills Preserve. This land, now under the stewardship of the Nature Conservancy, is open to everyone.

The highest elevation in the Green Hills is Black Cap, a top with many open ledges. By moving about one can see in all directions. We see lakes to the northeast and south and make out the White Mountains from Chocorua to Washington. The other Green Hills stretch out below us starting in the southwest with Redstone Ledge and extending northward past Rattlesnake, Peaked, Cranmore and Hurricane Mountains.

Nearby Cranmore Mountain has a colorful ski history starting from the time when skiers were still a small fraternity. In 1938, Harvey Gibson was able to negotiate with the Nazis and liberate from the Reich Austrian skimeister Hannes Schneider and bring him to the United States. Together they developed Cranmore's ski slopes. Hannes made American sports history by introducing the Arlberg Technique, the first modern ski method to change skiing from a mishmash of gangly downhill missiles and sitzmarks to a ballet of gentle curving and swaying over the slopes.

The way to Black Cap requires driving north on Route 16 through North Conway. At 1.8 miles north of the Eastern Slope Inn, turn right onto Hurricane Mountain Road. Drive 3.7 miles to a parking lot found at the top of a hill (N 04.087 min, W 04.321 min). The latter part of Hurricane Mountain road is steep (15% grade) and, if wet, may give trouble to a two-wheel drive vehicle. This steep section is closed during winter. Our trail leads away from the parking lot into the woods. Allow 35 minutes for the climb.

At the top we look across the Saco River Valley beyond Cranmore and North Conway and see the Moat Range. In front of it stand White Horse and Cathedral Ledges, meccas, for the rock climber. Beyond the Moats lies the heart of the White Mountains capped by Mounts Carrigain, Bond, South Twin and Field. The Presidential Range arises farther north starting with Mount Webster on the left and extending all the way northeast to Mount Madison. Nearby Kearsarge North blocks much of the Carter Range. To the right the taller mountains disappear into Maine.

In order to look off to the east, one must take a paint-blazed spur trail a short distance to another ledge (N 03.381 min, W 03.961 min). From here we see the previously featured Pleasant Mountain nearby along with the more distant Streaked Mountain both in Maine. We also see a myriad of waters from Kezar Lake to Lovewell Pond.

When seekers of the White Mountains skip Black Cap, they miss much – they lose what is seen from a lesser height – the towering majesty of the wild country they will soon encounter.

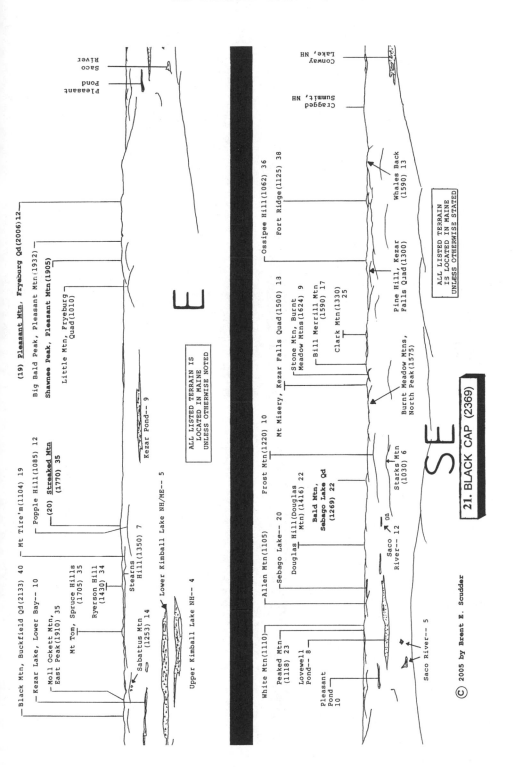

© 2005 by Brent E. Scudder

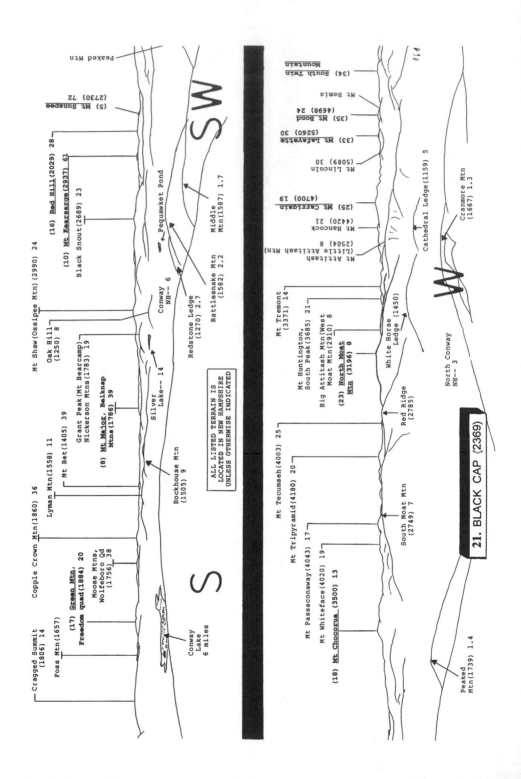

21. BLACK CAP (2369)

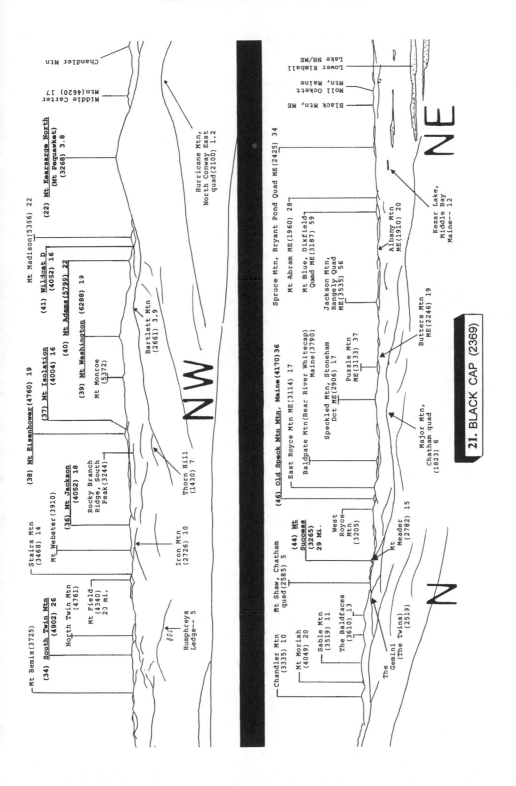

21. BLACK CAP (2369)

(22) MOUNT KEARSARGE NORTH

(Mount Pequawket)

N 44° 06.340'
W 71° 05.649'

(Elevation 3268 feet)

Kearsarge North stands as a lone sentinel on the northeast corner of the Saco River Valley. In viewing this mountain from various angles, one would not consider that it is actually part of a ridge that extends northeastward to include such tops as Rickers Knoll, The Gemini, Chatham's Mount Shaw and Walter Mountain. Kearsarge North stands so much higher than these that it seems to be a single entity, its cone shape a dead giveaway from any direction.

Considerable historic debate is connected with the name of this summit. A number of early maps called it Pequawket after a tribe of Native Americans inhabiting the area. Yet early settlers referred to the mountain as Kearsarge. Editorial debate of the Nineteenth Century contained sharply divided opinion as to whether the mountain should have one name or the other. There were those who regarded this mountain as the "true" Kearsarge and not that "upstart" peak to the southwest. But the opposition was gaining momentum and, by 1915, the United States Board of Geographic Names declared Pequawket as the official label.

The name did not stick. In 1957, the Board reversed itself somewhat. In order to avoid confusion with the southern Kearsarge, they renamed it Kearsarge North.

To reach this controversial elevation, once again drive northward out of North Conway on Route 16 and turn right onto Hurricane Mountain Road. This time one goes only 1.3 miles. The 15% uphill grade of the last chapter will not be encountered. Park by the Kearsarge North trailhead found on your left (N 04.529 min, W 06.541 min).

This mountain is a good conditioning climb in the early spring. The lower half of the trail faces south where the snow melts quickest. A good view greets the climber at ledges half way up. The trail then winds around to the north side where melting is slower. Until May 1st, snowshoes with crampons may still be required.

The view from the top is fantastic! During the summer months, be on the crest by 10:30 a.m. and see the sun's sparkle off the ocean. Portland, Maine is visible through binoculars. To the southwest we discover that "upstart" Kearsarge just to the left of Chocorua. We see little of the 100-mile distant Monadnock but can spot it lined up with Roundtop and Hopkinson Hill.

Westward, we gaze across the Moat Mountains and up the Saco River Valley to see Moosilauke and the Franconia Range. Northwest is the awe-inspiring view of Mount Washington, snow-covered during the colder months. To the right lies Wildcat Mountain and the deep indentation of Carter Notch.

Glance north-northeast and spot Maine's Speckled Mountain. This region has many tops with outstanding views. Start in New Hampshire with North and South Baldface and turn right letting your eyes pass into Maine past East Royce, Caribou, Speckled, Blueberry and Albany Mountains. All seven peaks have open summits making a climb on each well worth the trip.

Beyond and to the right of the Baldfaces we spot Maine's fourth highest peak Old Speck, thirty-two miles away. We see Mount Blue, its concical profile easily recognized particularly from mountain tops farther north.

At our present elevation there are mountains that we may suspect are visible but due to intervening ranges are not. Belknap is stashed behind the Ossipee Range. Sandwich Dome is hidden by Passaconaway. Among the Presidential Peaks, Mount Clay is blocked by Mount Washington, and Jefferson crouches behind Nelson Crag.

Yet the view is among the best. Kearsarge North, by standing apart from other mountains of similar size, allows for a sweeping summit panorama. With lakes to the east and south and mountains elsewhere, Kearsarge North has a view that lingers in the mind for days.

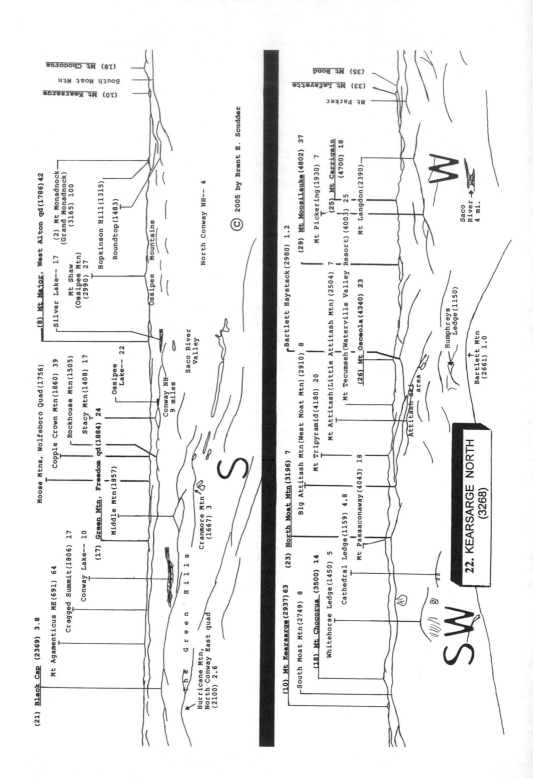

© 2005 by Brent E. Scudder

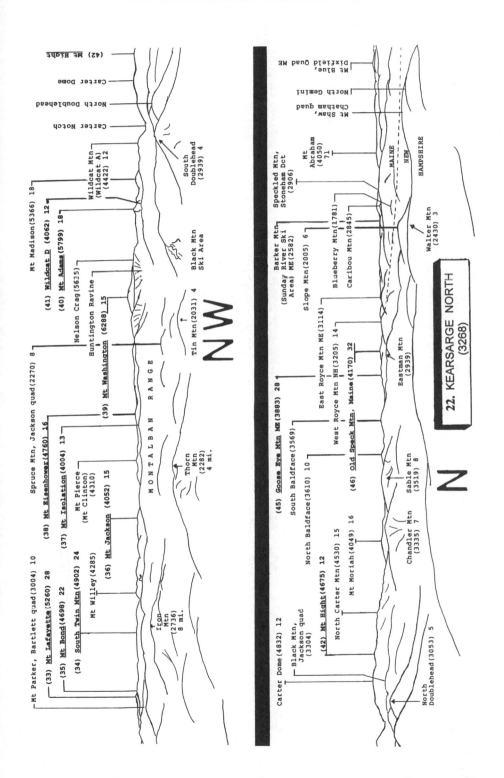

NW

N

22. KEARSARGE NORTH (3268)

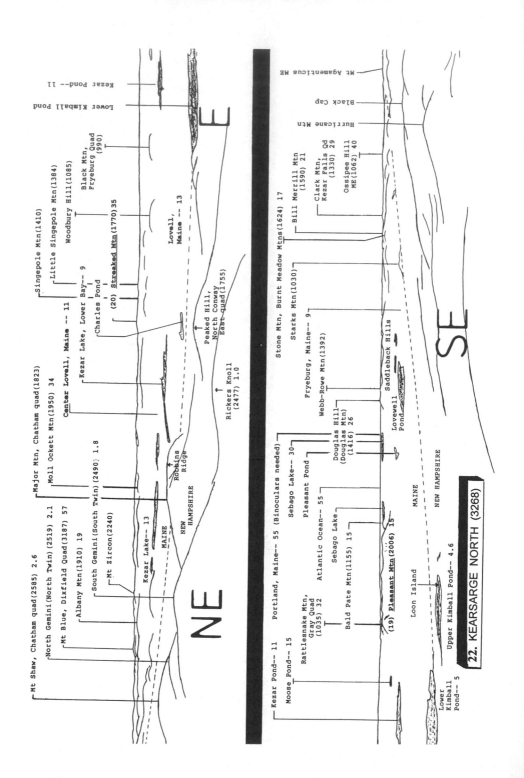

(23) NORTH MOAT MOUNTAIN

N 44° 02.584'
W 71° 12.882'

(Elevation 3196 feet)

We complete our visit to North Conway by climbing what forms the western wall of the Saco River Valley – the Moat Range. One thinks of moats as channels of water barring passage. According to Robert and Mary Julyan's *Place Names of the White Mountains,* the "Moats" originally referred to a series of ponds caused by beaver dams on streams that coursed down these mountains. "Going over the Moats" indicated a trip to this area. Eventually the expression referred to going over the range itself.

One thinks of the Moat Mountains in terms of what is visible from North Conway, namely South Moat, Middle Moat, Red Ridge and North Moat. But the range also runs westward behind these four peaks to include the Attitashes, Table Mountain and Bartlett's Bear Mountain. Extensive views are found along the eastern Moat Range due to a forest fire that burned out the summit trees during the Nineteenth Century.

At the top of North Moat, we can look down state and identify the southern Moats along with the flat profile of Green Mountain which cuts the horizon beyond. Ossipee Lake is visible just 18 miles away. Turn the head clockwise and you will be able to spot the Ossipee Range along with a tiny point of Belknap Mountain appearing beyond and between Mount Shaw and Faraway Summit. Closer in, the magnificent sharp-crested Chocorua rises up just seven miles away. Much of the back side of the Sandwich Range appears including Mounts Paugus, Passaconaway, The Sleepers and Tripyramid.

To the west and north lies the center of the White Mountains – steep ups and downs, rugged profiles, land that prefers to be vertical rather than horizontal. This chewed up tumult of rock and forest diminishes the majesty of the farther and taller Moosilauke, Lafayette, Bond and the Twins. The nearer Carrigain, Vose Spur, Mounts Lowell, Anderson and Nancy form a roller coaster of terrain profile rearing majestically.

Students who lack "wheels" can hike the 2.3 mile course out to the trailhead from North Conway. In driving out there, enter North Conway from the south on Route 16 and turn left at the Eastern Slope Inn. After 1.5 miles, you will see the road leading left to Cathedral Ledge. Do not turn but continue straight an additional 0.8 miles to arrive at a rather large parking lot to the left of the road (N 04.471 min, W 09.852 min).   A wide trail leads into the woods and intersects with a gravel road near the mill site of Diana's Baths, so called because of a set of circular stone depressions along Lucy Brook. The principal trail leaves from here and advances along the stream towards the west-southwest. After an additional 1.8 miles, the trail divides. The left fork takes you straight up the mountain. Allow three and a half hours to hike from car to summit.

From the top, look towards the northwest. The Presidential Range begins to the east of Crawford Notch. Sweep your eyes to the right past Mounts Webster, Jackson, Pierce, Eisenhower, Franklin, Monroe, Washington, Adams and Madison.   A little of Huntington Ravine is visible, but the glacial cirques on Mount Washington are mostly hidden.

Due north stands Wildcat Mountain followed by Carter Notch and the range of that name to the right. We see little of Maine's higher mountains, but there stands Old Speck and Baldpate in the distance. To the east, Maine's coastal hills appear between Kearsarge North and Black Cap. Immediately before us, Cranmore Mountain displays the many ski trails that converge upon its summit. If you arrive at the top by 10 a.m. during July and August, you may once again see the Atlantic Ocean lit up by the sun. As the season progresses, the sun's bearing shifts, and it becomes necessary to reach the summit sooner. In early September, be there by 9 a.m. Two months later the ocean cannot be seen after 7 a.m.

It is difficult to say which mountain in this region has the best view. Frequent climbers develop their favorites. Several routes assail the Moat Range upon which there are many open ledges. The numerous combinations of trails attract climbers back here again and again.

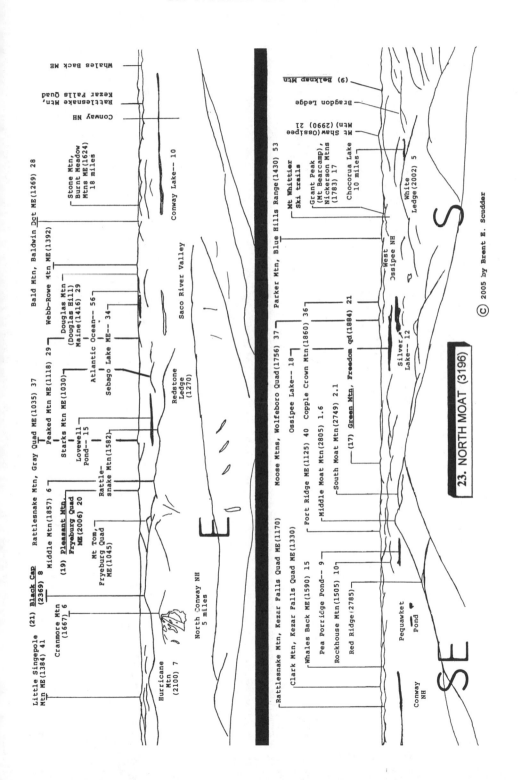

Little Singepole (21) **Black Cap**
Mtn ME(1384) 41   (2369) 8

Cranmore Mtn
(1667) 6

Middle Mtn(1857) 6

(19) **Pleasant Mtn**,
Fryeburg Quad
ME(2006) 20

Mt Tom,
Fryeburg Quad
ME(1045)

Rattlesnake Mtn, Gray Quad ME(1035) 37

Peaked Mtn ME(1118) 29

Starks Mtn ME(1030)

Lovewell
Pond-- 15

Rattle-
snake Mtn(1582)

Bald Mtn, Baldwin Oct ME(1269) 28

Webb-Rowe Mtn ME(1392)

Douglas Mtn
(Douglas Hill)
Maine(1416) 29

Atlantic Ocean-- 56

Sebago Lake ME--' 34

Stone Mtn,
Burnt Meadow
Mtns ME(1624)
18 miles

Conway Lake-- 10

Whales Back ME

Rattlesnake Mtn,
Kezar Falls Quad

Conway NH

Hurricane
Mtn
(2100) 7

North Conway NH
5 miles

Redstone
Ledge
(1270)

Saco River Valley

Rattlesnake Mtn, Kezar Falls Quad ME(1170)

Clark Mtn, Kezar Falls Quad ME(1330)

Whales Back ME(1590) 15

Pea Porridge Pond-- 9

Rockhouse Mtn(1505) 10

Red Ridge(2785)

Conway
NH

Pequawket
Pond

Moose Mtns, Wolfeboro Quad(1756) 37

Port Ridge ME(1125) 40

Middle Moat Mtn(2805) 1.6

Copple Crown Mtn(1860) 36

Ossipee Lake-- 18

South Moat Mtn(2749) 2.1

(17) **Green Mtn**, Freedom qd(1884) 21

Parker Mtn, Blue Hills Range(1430) 53

Mt Whittier
Ski trails

Grant Peak
(Mt Bearcamp)
Nickerson Mtns
(1783) 17

West
Ossipee NH

Silver
Lake-- 12

Mt Shaw(Ossipee
Mtn)(2990) 21

Chocorua Lake
10 miles

White
Ledge(2002) 5

Bragdon Ledge

(9) Belknap Mtn

23. NORTH MOAT (3196)

SE

S

© 2005 by Brent E. Scudder

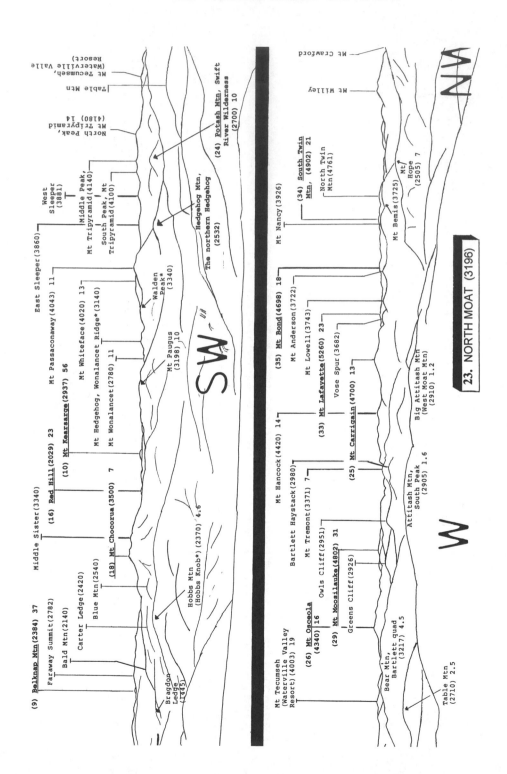

23. NORTH MOAT (3196)

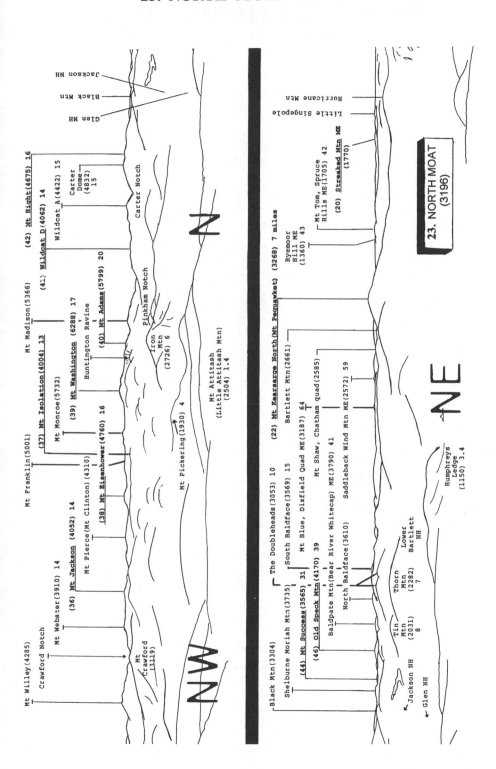

23. NORTH MOAT (3196)

(24) POTASH MOUNTAIN

Swift River Wilderness

N 43° 58.919'
W 71° 23.435'

(Elevation 2700 feet)

Early in one's experience of the White Mountains, a person might consider tackling a low elevation. From such a summit, the true size of the higher mountains becomes apparent. Reaching the top of Potash requires a hike of about two hours. But even from here, one is still dwarfed by the likes of Passaconaway, Whiteface, the Sleepers and the three peaks of Tripyramid. To the north, Mount Carrigain reveals itself as a hefty day's climb.

The Potash trailhead (N 59.648 min, W 22.163 min) begins on the south side of a parking lot located off the Kancamagus Highway 21.2 miles from the I-93 Exit ramp in Lincoln and 14.2 miles from the intersection with Route 16 in Conway. The trail goes into the woods for fifty feet and then makes a sharp right turn that is not well marked. After 0.3 miles it crosses Downes Brook and thereafter is easy to follow. It climbs around Potash Mountain finally to approach the summit from the opposite side.

At the top there is no one spot where you can see in all directions. You have to move about. Even so, a fifteen degree patch of the horizon to the northeast is obscured by trees. We can see all of what is missing from the summit view at an outlook along the trail located at about the 2120-foot level (approximately N 59.10 min, W 23.05 min). We made the missing patch part of the summit diagram but omitted stating where one view ends and the other view begins. This is simply because so little of the horizon is obscured.

Look along the skyline and discover that the farthest object visible stands no more than thirty miles away. This is the consequence of being on a low summit surrounded by giants. Therefore, reserve Potash Mountain for a relatively hazy day. It would be wise for the vacationer to save the crystal clear day for the higher mountain.

The Potash view is spectacular in its own way. One finds difficulty in spotting any sign of human intrusion in all that he or she sees. Forest, cliff and rock slide greet the viewer as he or she takes in Carrigain Notch, the

Presidential Range, the Wildcats and Carter Dome. Hemming us in on the east are Bear Mountain, the Moat Range and the several peaks of Chocorua and Paugus. Through a break lies Maine's Pleasant Mountain twenty-eight miles away. Earlier we mentioned the tall wall to the south beginning with Passaconaway. We also noted the three peaks of Tripyramid.

Climbing parties of the Nineteenth Century lacked the proper maps for scaling Tripyramid. More than once they reached another summit only to gaze across a deep abyss that separated them from their destination. This false summit soon came to be called The Fool Killer. Today, hiking groups climb The Fool Killer on purpose every few years to celebrate none other than April Fool's Day.

Farther right one sees Mounts Osceola, Kancamagus and Liberty. Liberty is the most distant of three peaks that stand one behind the other. The nearest summit in line is the west peak of Mount Huntington. Behind it rises Mount Flume. So little of Flume is visible that our chart resolution does not allow us to show it. You might discern Flume with binoculars but only on days when suitable light contrasts are present such as those caused by patches of cloud shadow.

Mount Hancock and its component peaks complete this wilderness view of little human activity. There is the occasional smudge of black smoke to the left side of Mount Washington and a small visible section of the Kancamagus Highway. Other than that, there is no sign of man.

Not all White Mountain ascents have to be herculean. Climbing Potash is an excellent example.

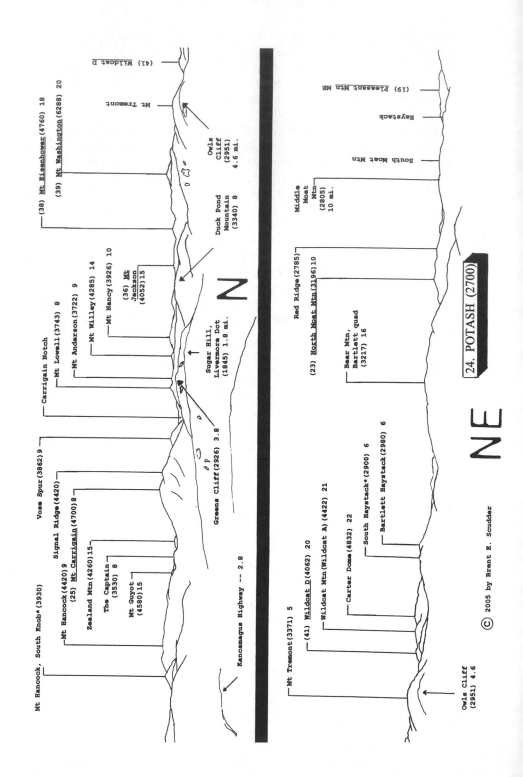

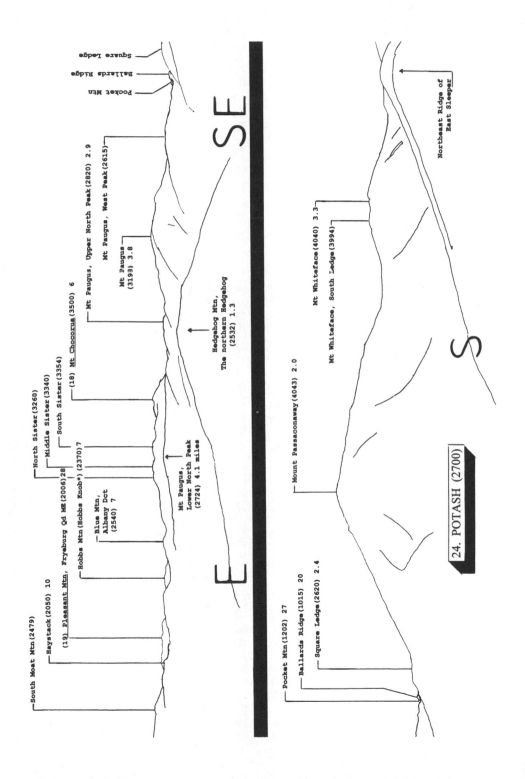

24. POTASH (2700)

SE

E

S

South Moat Mtn (2479)
Haystack (2050) 10
(19) Pleasant Mtn, Fryeburg Qd ME (2006) 28
North Sister (3260)
Middle Sister (3340)
South Sister (3354)
Hobbs Mtn (Hobbs Knob*) (2370) 7
Blue Mtn, Albany Dct (2540) 7
(18) Mt Chocorua (3500) 6
Mt Paugus, Upper North Peak (2820) 2.9
Mt Paugus, West Peak (2615)
Mt Paugus (3193) 3.8
Mt Paugus, Lower North Peak (2724) 4.1 miles
Hedgehog Mtn, The northern Hedgehog (2532) 1.3

Pocket Mtn
Ballards Ridge
Square Ledge

Pocket Mtn (1202) 27
Ballards Ridge (1015) 20
Square Ledge (2620) 2.4
Mount Passaconaway (4043) 2.0
Mt Whiteface (4040) 3.3
Mt Whiteface, South Ledge (3994)
Northeast Ridge of East Sleeper

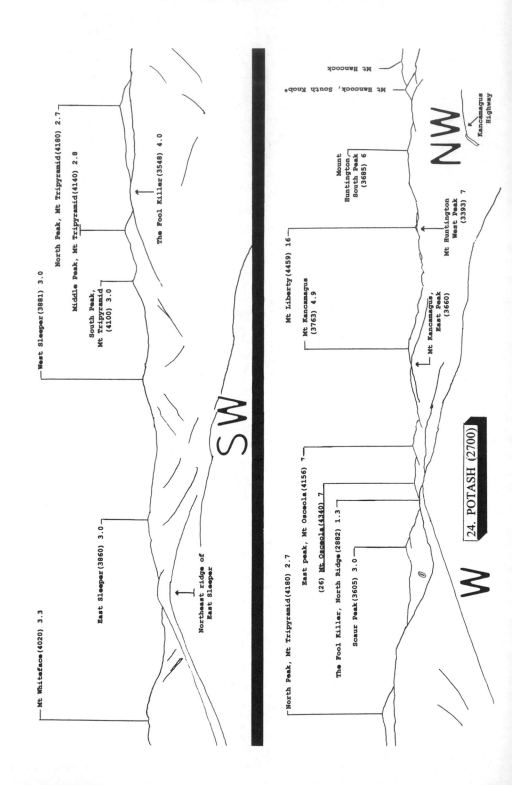

Mt Whiteface (4020) 3.3

West Sleeper (3881) 3.0

North Peak, Mt Tripyramid (4180) 2.7

Middle Peak, Mt Tripyramid (4140) 2.8

South Peak, Mt Tripyramid (4100) 3.0

The Fool Killer (3548) 4.0

East Sleeper (3860) 3.0

Northeast ridge of East Sleeper

SW

Mt Liberty (4459) 16

Mt Kancamagus (3763) 4.9

Mt Kancamagus, East Peak (3660)

Mt Hancock, South Knob*

Mt Hancock

NW

Kancamagus Highway

Mount Huntington South Peak (3685) 6

Mt Huntington West Peak (3393) 7

North Peak, Mt Tripyramid (4180) 2.7

East peak, Mt Osceola (4156) 7

(26) Mt Osceola (4340) 7

The Fool Killer, North Ridge (2882) 1.3

Scaur Peak (3605) 3.0

24. POTASH (2700)

W

(25) MOUNT CARRIGAIN

N 44° 05.609'
W 71° 26.800'

(Elevation 4700 feet)

What a difference an extra two thousand feet of elevation makes! We cannot compare the previous view from Potash Mountain with the prospect from Carrigain. The transformation is total. From the top of Carrigain, Potash is seen standing before Passaconaway as a bump on a low ridge.

Yet look south from Carrigain's observation platform and note that the Sandwich Range still forms a barrier. Starting with Chocorua on the left, our eyes sweep all the way over to Mount Osceola. The scene of distant mountains to the west is partially obscured by the Franconia Range. Northward the view is blocked not only by the Bonds and the Twins but also the Presidentials. To the east the Moat Range forms a wall.

Yet it is the high elevation of Mount Carrigain that causes its summit view to be among the best found in New England. Generally, we can see over and around the barriers mentioned above. Between Sandwich Dome and Osceola, we can make out Mount Monadnock 91 miles away. Westward, Vermont's Pico and Killington Peaks are visible. We see for the first time several of the Green Mountains located not far from Canada. The Bald Mountain found near Island Pond is but 17 miles south of the border while the northern Monadnock stands eight miles from Quebec. Eastward we look well into Maine. The Spruce Hills appear clearly along with Pleasant Mountain and Sebago Lake. Around the horizon over 300 terrain features are visible.

Despite Carrigain's isolation from human activity, there is not a great deal of distance required to "hike in." From the center of Bartlett, drive west 4.0 miles on Route 302. Turn left on Sawyer River Road. Proceed 2.0 miles up this dirt road to find a parking lot to the left just beyond a concrete bridge. The Signal Ridge Trail (N 04.217 min, W 23.014 min) starts just before the bridge and leads away from the north side of the road.

Once you are upon Signal Ridge, a fine view of the summit leaps forth. If the season is around Labor Day, there are blueberries aplenty. The top of the mountain is wooded, but the observation platform looks easily over the trees.

Being the highest mountain climbed thus far, it is also the most strenuous. The vertical rise is 3300 feet surpassing Chocorua's Piper Trail by 560 feet. Estimate a climb of four hours.

The most breathtaking part of the view is the tortured nature of the land. We gaze from the tower southeastward beyond Signal Ridge and note the steep profiles of nearby Bartlett Haystack, Tremont and Bear Mountains. Now look southwest at Osceola and Tecumseh and turn right towards Mount Hancock. We see a similar twist of terrain.

The value of the panorama diagram becomes especially apparent. Look between Osceola and its west peak. Note the tiny protrusion of a distant mountain above and beyond the ridge. Without the diagram the novice does not know what that peak is. But neither does the frequent climber. The latter cannot see enough of that mysterious mountain to determine a characteristic profile. Neither can he or she relate the distant summit to something near it. Without the diagram, even the expert can only guess.

Map, protractor and ruler reveal the mystery peak to be Mount Cardigan. The diagram of the view from Cardigan's top reveals Carrigain in just the same manner.

At the left of Mount Washington look down. One beholds a majestic hump that many hikers mistake for Vose Spur. Actually the protrusion is Carrigain's north peak. Vose Spur could not be seen from the earlier observation platform from which this skyline diagram was developed. When standing on the present platform, seek the spur just beyond the adjacent ridge line in the direction of North Carter Mountain. It is still possible that Vose Spur is not visible.

The view from Mount Carrigain gives you the true nature of the White Mountain Wilderness. From the steep defiles extending away in all directions to the never ending forest, this peak will give you a good sense of the view during Colonial times.

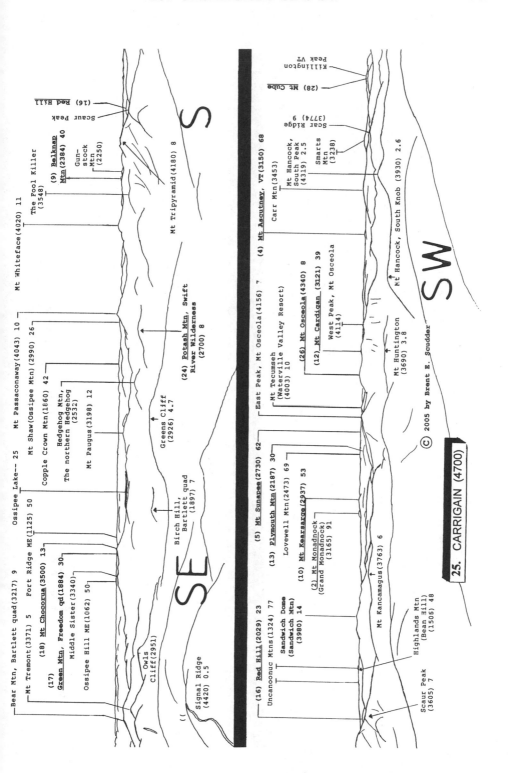

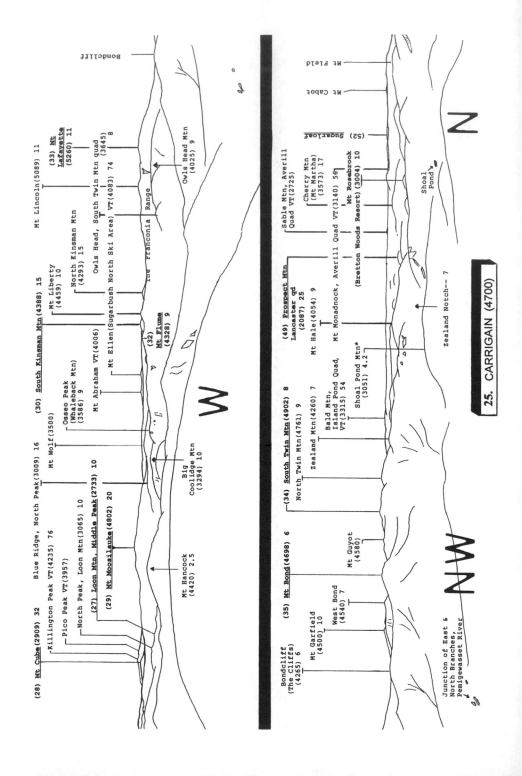

25. CARRIGAIN (4700)

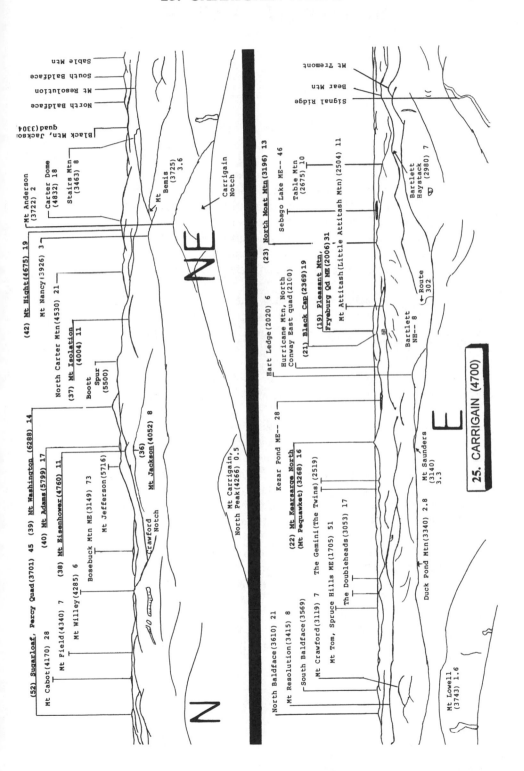

25. CARRIGAIN (4700)

(26) MOUNT OSCEOLA

N 44° 00.084'
W 71° 32.128'

(Elevation 4340 feet)

Why call a New Hampshire mountain Osceola? The name belongs to a Florida Seminole Native American leader who had fought off the settlers for years until his capture in 1837. Similarly, nearby Mount Tecumseh honored a Shawnee of distant Ohio. Indian tales were rife in the early Nineteenth Century. Why should the early settlers not name two peaks looming above the forest after two wilderness notables who towered above the people in the recesses of their imaginations? These men were their celebrities.

This mountain stands near the eastern end of a long ridge that begins near Lincoln. Osceola has steep slopes to the north, east and south giving the observer a sense of being "pulled off" into space. Although the feeling is unsettling, it seldom lasts long.

Osceola's panorama diagram was created from photographs taken from the top of the former fire tower located at the GPS coordinates stated above. Without the platform, trees block part of the view. Still, one can gaze to the north past Galehead and South Twin Mountains all the way around to the east and south past Chocorua, Tripyramid, Sandwich and Tecumseh. Now walk to Osceola's true summit fifty yards to the west and bushwhack a few feet to the north. The view from this latter perch begins with Mount Moosilauke and then takes in the Kinsman Range, Cannon Mountain and the Franconias. It also overlaps the other view. We have recovered 5/6 of what could be seen from the dismantled fire tower.

The southern approach to Osceola requires driving towards Waterville Valley and turning left on the road leading to the main ski area. After 1.2 miles, look for a narrow paved road that angles right. Take this new road 3.3 miles to a height-of-land. Just beyond the crest, locate the trailhead on your right (N 43 deg 59.012 min, W 71 deg 33.522 min). A gate stands at the height-of-land that is closed at times during the Spring and Autumn. In this case, park at a wide spot in the road and hike from there. Climbing takes slightly more than two hours.

Alternatively, one may drive to the trailhead from the west by getting off I-93 at Exit 31 to drive east on Tripoli Road (mostly dirt) for 6.7 miles. This approach is closed in winter.

Once you are at the top, look south. The village and ski slopes of Waterville Valley arrest the eye. One easily notes the golf course and the long sinuous ski trails flanking the east slope of Tecumseh. Beyond the village, Sandwich Dome rises up and hides most of the Belknap Range. On the very horizon stands Blue Job Mountain and farther right our old friends the Uncanoonucs and Joe English Hill. Almost in line with Tecumseh, the southern Kearsarge and Mount Monadnock march away into the skyline.

Look west-northwest and see a bit of Vermont. Camel's Hump dents the horizon 71 miles away. The state's highest point, Mount Mansfield, lies just to the left of Scar Ridge and exhibits a flat unimpressive profile.

Snaking along below the Franconia Mountains slithers the well-known Kancamagus Highway. Raise the eye. Beyond Mount Garfield, take note of Gore Mountain 65 miles away. Gore is but six miles from Canada. The nearer South Twin Mountain and the Bonds dominate the view to the north, while to the northeast, the Presidential Range tops all.

Eastward we see far into Maine with the Spruce Hills' Mount Tom appearing on the horizon at a range of 58 miles. Close by we note the cone-shaped Kearsarge North and, farther right, the Moat Range. Beyond the Moats stands Maine's Pleasant Mountain, a landmark easy to recognize. Chocorua and Passaconaway come next, the latter almost hidden by Tripyramid's North Peak.

Despite trees blocking the view to the southwest, climbing Mount Osceola is well worth the effort. A person sees the raggedness of the Pemigewassett Wilderness from another direction and again becomes aware of how most of New Hampshire once looked. Behind you comes the intrusion of mankind, a gentle intrusion in the form of a golf course and ski slopes set amid mountain and forest. Osceola is the favorite mountain of many.

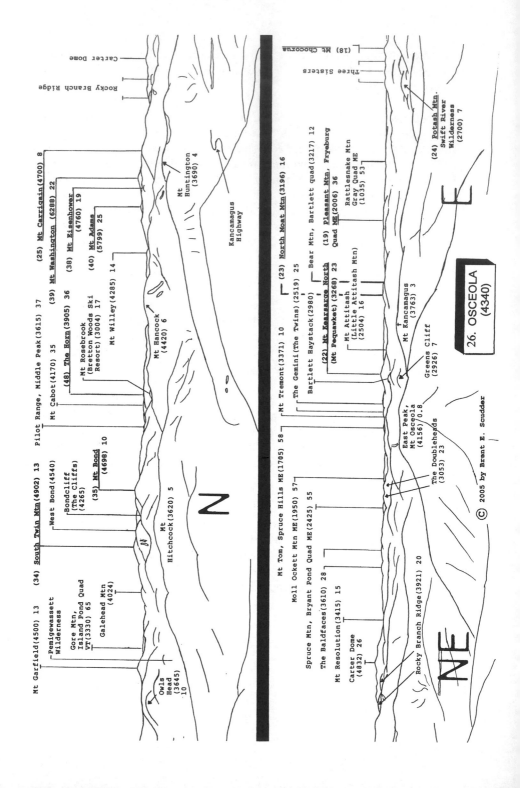

© 2005 by Brent E. Scudder

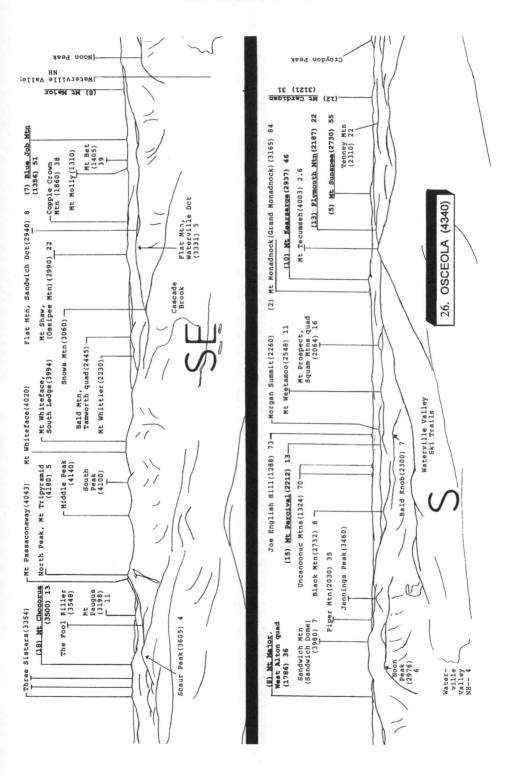

SE

Three Sisters(3354)
Mt Passaconaway(4043)   Mt Whiteface(4020)
(18) Mt Chocorua   North Peak, Mt Tripyramid   Mt Whiteface,   Flat Mtn, Sandwich Dct(2940) 8   **(7) Blue Job Mtn**
(3500) 13   (4180) 5   South Ledge(3994)   (1356) 51
The Fool Killer   Middle Peak   Mt Shaw,   Copple Crown
(3548)   (4140)   (Ossipee Mtn)(2990) 22   Mtn (1860) 38
Mt   South   Snows Mtn(3060)   Mt Molly(1310)   Mt Bet
Faugus   Peak   (1405)
(3198)   (4100)   Bald Mtn,   39
11   Tamworth quad(2445)   Flat Mtn,
Mt Whittier(2230)   Waterville Dct
(3331) 5
Cascade
Brook
Scaur Peak (3605) 4

S

Joe English Hill(1288) 73   Morgan Summit(2260)   (2) Mt Monadnock(Grand Monadnock) (3165) 84   Croydon Peak
Mt Weetamoo(2548) 11
(15) Mt Percival (2212) 13   (10) **Mt Kearsarge**(2937) 46   Mt Cardigan 31
Uncanoonuc Mtns(1324) 70   Mt Prospect,   (3121)
(8) Mt Major,   Squam Mtns quad   Mt Tecumseh(4003) 2.6   **(12)**
West Alton quad   Black Mtn(2732) 8   (2064) 16   **(13) Plymouth Mtn**(2187) 22
(1786) 36   Piper Mtn(2030) 35   **(5) Mt Sunapee**(2730) 55
Sandwich Mtn   Jennings Peak(3460)   Tenney Mtn
(Sandwich Dome) 7   (2310) 22
(3980)   Bald Knob(2300) 7   Waterville Valley
Ski Trails
Noon
Peak   Waterville Valley, NH
(2976)   Noon Peak
Water-
ville
Valley
NH--4

26. OSCEOLA (4340)

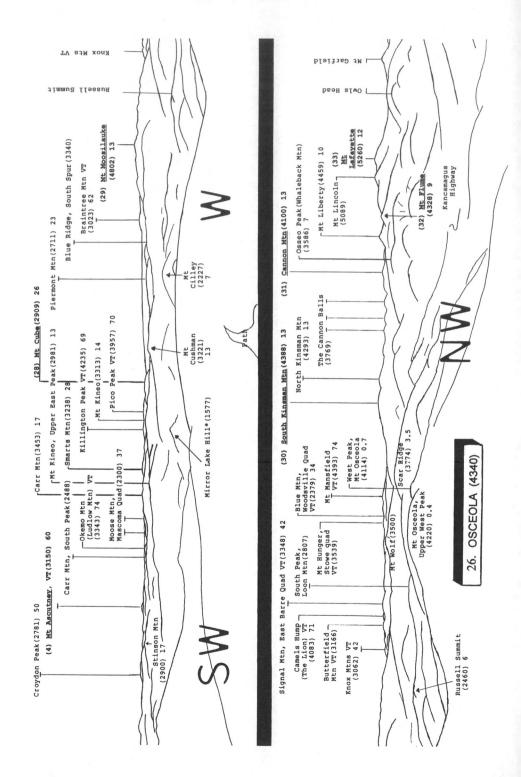

Croydon Peak (2781) 50

(4) **Mt Ascutney, VT** (3150) 60

Carr Mtn, South Peak (2488)

Carr Mtn (3453) 17

Mt Kineo, Upper East Peak (2981) 13

(28) **Mt Cube** (2909) 26

Smarts Mtn (3238) 28

Piermont Mtn (2711) 23

Blue Ridge, South Spur (3340)

Braintree Mtn VT (3023) 62

(29) **Mt Moosilauke** (4802) 13

Okemo Mtn (Ludlow Mtn) VT (3343) 74

Killington Peak VT (4235) 69

Mt Kineo (3313) 14

Pico Peak VT (3957) 70

Moose Mtn, Mascoma Quad (2300) 37

Mt Cilley (2227) 7

Mt Cushman (3221) 13

Mirror Lake Hill* (1577)

Stinson Mtn (2900) 17

SW

W

Russell Summit

Knox Mts VT

Path

Signal Mtn, East Barre Quad VT (3348) 42

South Peak, Loon Mtn (2807)

Camels Hump (The Lion) VT (4083) 71

Butterfield Mtn VT (3166)

Knox Mtns VT (3062) 42

Blue Mtn, Woodsville Quad VT (2379) 34

Mt Mansfield VT (4393) 74

West Peak, Mt Osceola (4114) 0.7

(30) **South Kinsman Mtn** (4388) 13

North Kinsman Mtn (4293) 13

The Cannon Balls (3769)

(31) **Cannon Mtn** (4100) 13

Osseo Peak (Whaleback Mtn) (3586) 7

Mt Liberty (4459) 10

(33) **Mt Lafayette** (5260) 12

Mt Lincoln (5089)

(32) **Mt Flume** (4328) 9

Owls Head

Mt Garfield

Kancamagus Highway

Mt Wolf (3500)

Mt Osceola, Upper West Peak (4220) 0.4

Scar Ridge (3774) 3.5

Russell Summit (2460) 6

NW

26. OSCEOLA (4340)

(27) LOON MOUNTAIN MIDDLE PEAK

N 44° 02.284'
W 71° 37.673'

(Elevation 2733 feet)

The Osceola climber may feel unhappy that trees hide the magnificent view towards the southwest. Bushwhack then along the tops of Scar Ridge and, after nearly six miles, arrive at Loon Mountain's North Peak. Descend on the Sunset Ski Trail until you see a large knoll appearing on the right. This nameless hump which we are calling Loon Mountain's Middle Peak, features an observation tower. When viewing from its top, we see some of Osceola's missing scenery.

The prospect from this knoll is similar to that seen from Potash Mountain. Loon's low elevation amid giants causes the hiker to gaze up at the surrounding world. Nearby mountains take on a great majesty, something not recognized from the much higher Osceola. Skip ahead to the charts showing the view from the 4698-foot Mount Bond (Page 199). Note how small West Bond seems. From Loon Mountain, West Bond looms massively in its own right. The same may be said for Moosilauke, the Kinsmans and the Franconia Range. From our lesser height these peaks seem the tall alps that they really are.

Save yourself the six-mile bushwhack and arrive at Loon by driving up I-93 to Exit 32 at Lincoln. Proceed east through town and the first miles of the Kancamagus Highway. Look for Loon Mountain Ski area signs and drive into their parking lot (N 03.376 min, W 37.808 min). Except during their winter season, ascent may be made on any of the ski trails or, if open, the gondola lift. Check for operating times of the lift at www.loonmtn.com

Skiers are able to choose a number of lifts including the one to the higher North Peak. But North Peak's commanding view faces north alone. From the middle peak, not only are we able to look northward into the distance but in most other directions as well. As of this writing, the observation tower is closed during the winter. The skier will have to be content with the prospect from the various trails. Yet it was what could be seen from these trails that led this skier to include Loon Mountain's panorama in this book.

At the top of the observation tower, something familiar has been mounted beneath the windows – a panorama chart facing west, north and east. So why repeat the process with a chapter in this book? The following diagrams are filled with more detail and can be studied in advance of a trip to Loon. With the tower closed in winter, the skier obviously has no access to their charts.

The skyline charts found in Loon's Tower omit a view to the south. Our charts include the southern outlook featuring the Sandwich and Squam Ranges on the left with Plymouth Mountain and the southern Kearsarge on the right. Look not for the familiar Uncanoonucs, Joe English Hill nor Monadnock. Loon's low elevation combined with the vertical angle depression caused by the Earth's curvature allows intervening terrain to hide all four.

Look westward and see the huge Moosilauke ten miles away attended by the adjacent Mounts Blue, Jim, Waternomee and South Peak. Across Big Loon Pond, we barely see our next objective, Mount Cube, peeping over the saddle between Mount Cushman and Blue Ridge.

To the northwest, we make out the extension of I-93, the Franconia Notch parkway, disappearing into the mountain pass of that name. Beyond arises Mount Wolf and, to the right, the Kinsmans, the Cannon Balls and then Cannon Mountain itself. We stand south of the Franconia Range and perceive the tall steep Mounts Liberty, Lincoln and Lafayette almost in line.

Looking northeastward now, we have an extensive outlook of the White Mountains from South Twin to and beyond Mount Washington. The southern Presidential Range is barely visible due to its summits being backed up against higher terrain beyond. Yet all are taller than many of our well-defined nearer heights.

Mount Carrigain appears to the right of Hancock. To the right of Hancock, the land drops down into Hancock Notch and rises up the other side to reveal Mount Huntington. Well hidden is Mount Kancamagus, it being nearly in line with North Peak.

Loon Mountain demonstrates that one need not be on the highest top for a spectacular view. Its skiers seldom mention the magnificent outlooks for these have been blended into a total magical experience.

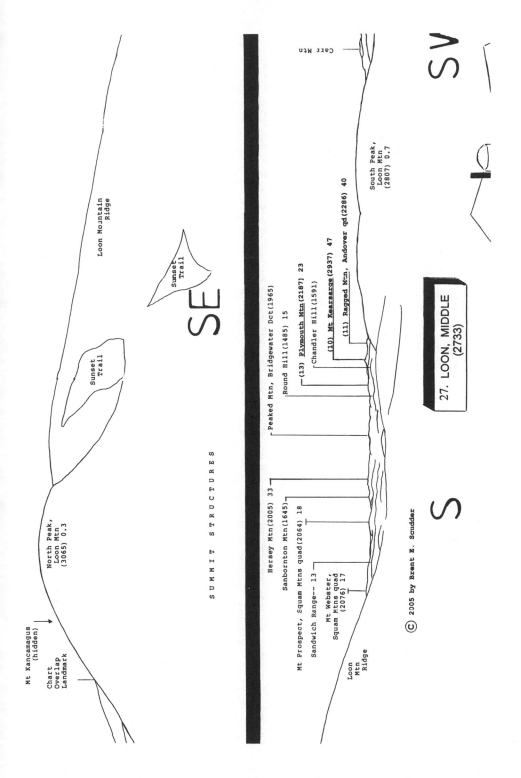

S U M M I T   S T R U C T U R E S

SE

S

SW

Mt Kancamagus
(hidden)

Chart
Overlap
Landmark

North Peak,
Loon Mtn
(3065) 0.3

Loon Mountain
Ridge

Sunset
Trail

Sunset
Trail

Peaked Mtn, Bridgewater Dct(1965)

Round Hill(1485) 15

(13) Plymouth Mtn(2187) 23

Chandler Hill(1591)

(10) Mt Kearsarge(2937) 47

(11) Ragged Mtn, Andover qd(2286) 40

Carr Mtn

South Peak,
Loon Mtn
(2807) 0.7

Hersey Mtn(2005) 33

Sanbornton Mtn(1645)

Mt Prospect, Squam Mtns quad(2064) 18

Sandwich Range-- 13

Mt Webster,
Squam Mtns quad
(2076) 17

Loon
Mtn
Ridge

27. LOON, MIDDLE
(2733)

© 2005 by Brent E. Scudder

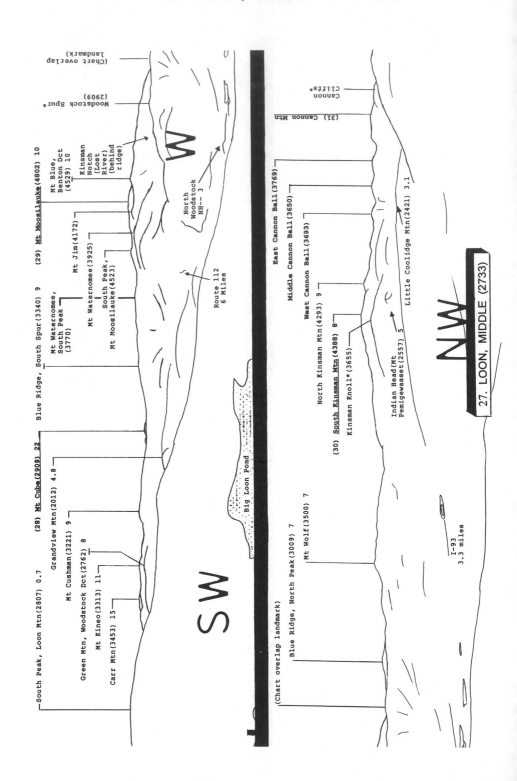

South Peak, Loon Mtn(2807) 0.7

(28) Mt Cube(2909) 22

Grandview Mtn(2012) 4.8

Mt Cushman(3221) 9

Green Mtn, Woodstock Dct(2762) 8

Mt Kineo(3313) 11

Carr Mtn(3453) 15

Blue Ridge, South Spur(3340) 9

Mt Waternomee,
South Peak
(3770)

Mt Waternomee(3925)

South Peak,
Mt Moosilauke(4523)

(29) Mt Moosilauke(4802) 10

Mt Jim(4172)

Mt Blue,
Benton Dct
(4529) 10

Kinsman
Notch
(Lost
River)
(behind
ridge)

North
Woodstock
NH-- 3

Route 112
6 Miles

(Chart overlap
landmark)

Woodstock Spur*
(2909)

SW

Big Loon Pond

(Chart overlap landmark)

Blue Ridge, North Peak(3009) 7

Mt Wolf(3500) 7

Kinsman Knoll*(3655)

(30) South Kinsman Mtn(4388) 8

North Kinsman Mtn(4293) 9

West Cannon Ball(3693)

Middle Cannon Ball(3650)

East Cannon Ball(3769)

Cannon
Cliffs*

(31) Cannon Mtn

Indian Head(Mt
Pemigewasset(2557) 5

Little Coolidge Mtn(2421) 3.1

I-93
3.3 miles

NW

27. LOON, MIDDLE (2733)

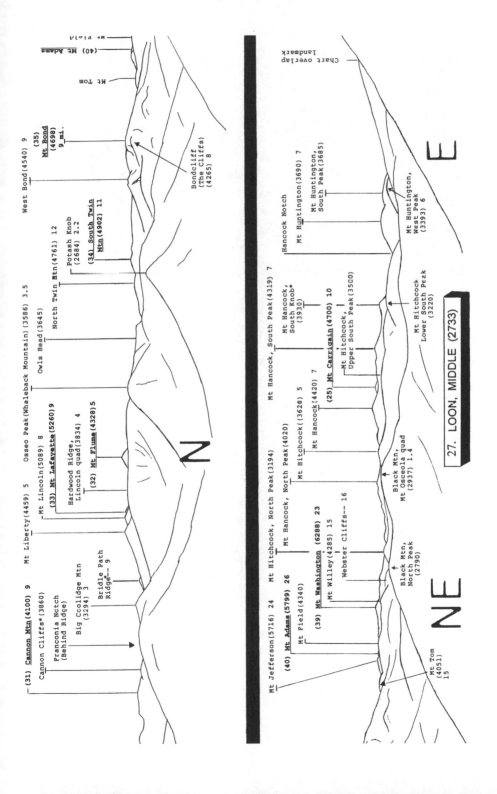

27. LOON, MIDDLE (2733)

Seven year-old Rob Gillis looks eastward towards
the Saco River Valley from the top of North Moat Mountain.
Thorn Mountain, the Doubleheads and the Baldfaces decorate the background

Youngster approaches the summit of Mount Major
on a cold, raw, windy day in early April.
Lake Winnipesaukee visible beyond.

THE APPALACHIAN TRAIL

Welcome to the A. T. This path emanates from Georgia's Springer Mountain and winds up 2173 miles later at Maine's Mount Katahdin. During the next nineteen chapters, we shall progress northeastward across New Hampshire into Maine featuring mountains that are on or close to this famous path. These peaks lie sufficiently near one another to allow the backpack-encumbered A.T. Trail hiker to have at least one diagrammed view available daily.

Each mountain was also selected with an eye to the summer day hiker who wishes to pack a lunch, a sweater and possible rain gear.

Caution is advised especially on the higher peaks. Be in good health and physical shape. A person new to mountain hiking may not be aware of his or her physical limits. Heart attacks claim climbers annually. It is wise first to try some of the lesser summits that are featured in this book. Too frequently, people take on the Presidential Range with a severe case of "got-to-get-there-itus." A worse disease is called "got-to-get-there-before-two-o'clock-itus." Being out of shape, being in a hurry and being in the mountains is a very nasty combination.

Check the weather beforehand. Snow means slippery. Ice means slippery. Rain means slippery. Even wet ground following rain or mist means slippery. If the forecast calls for thunderstorms, you need to be aware. Lightning renders pointed summits and knife-edged ridges particularly vulnerable. Get off the ridge. Get back into the woods. The proverbial advice during electrical activity is not to get under a tree. In a forest lightning has thousands upon thousands of trees from which to choose. The few trunks you stand near would be in little danger.

Begin the climb early enough in the day so that darkness does not find you still in the woods. Solo hiking has its merits but also its hazards. Hike in company until you are well seasoned.

While suggesting that the New Hampshire Appalachian Trail section is for the hardy, three mountains on or near the trail, namely Cannon, Wildcat D and Washington are available to the casual tourist via tramway, chairlift, automobile or cog railway.

In terms of overnight accommodation, the New Hampshire hiker has three options.   There is, of course, the tent. He or she might camp in the woods or else at one of several tent platform sites set up for the purpose.   Second, the hiker might consider a string of lean-to shelters.   Third, the Appalachian Mountain Club (AMC) operates eight huts and two visitor's centers with overnight sleeping arrangements that are open to the public. The term "hut" is misleading. AMC huts are actually lodges offering sumptuous boarding house style meals and bunk room sleeping. The Visitors' Centers are open not only to the climber but also casual tourists and their families. At these centers you need not don a single hiking boot yet still get a feeling for the ambiance of staying in an AMC hut. These ten facilities are located a day's hike apart on or near the A.T. One could walk much of this section and never carry a tent or a sleeping bag.

As we proceed from chapter to chapter along the Appalachian Trail, this book creates the unavoidable misconception that one is free to stop overnight unannounced at any of the above AMC facilities.   This would be in keeping with the free spirit of the wanderer. Unfortunately the enormous popularity of mountain hiking limits this freedom, particularly during the summer season and during the weekends of spring and autumn. The lean-to shelters and tentsites are available on a first-come-first-served basis while AMC huts are booked up with reservations often months in advance.   Last minute cancellations sometimes allow the walk-in accommodation, but there are no guarantees. The freest backbacker carries his tent, cookery, food and sleeping bag and needs not push beyond the limits of severe weather or fatigue.

Yet the tenter is somewhat limited. A few areas are not open for random camping due to their popularity and resulting damage to ground cover. Other areas have come under restricted use. There is no intention to diminish the enjoyment of the campers but rather to spatially spread out their use of the forest in order to give ground cover damage time to repair itself.

The tenter has certain responsibilities. That person should leave no trace that he or she has ever camped at one spot. Cooperation with this advice has been admirable over the years, and it shows. Yes, litter is sometimes found along the first hundred yards of popular trails. Late night revelers who had parked their cars nearby may have left behind such trash. Farther up the trail there is no litter. If you step aside from the trail for purposes of necessity, there will be no sign that anyone had ever been there.

During the summer, a caretaker attends some of the tentsites and lean-to shelters. If such is the case, expect to pay a small fee for purposes of upkeep.

All of the AMC huts are open during the summer months with full accommodation meaning that meals are served (except lunch), and that pillows and blankets are provided for the bunkrooms. (Hikers can usually purchase trail mix and candy bars to see them through the midday hours). Fees are far below that of a motel and restaurant existence.

Half way into and out of the off-season, the huts remain open more cheaply on a self-service basis; that is, bring your own sleeping bag and food. Three huts remain open all year. Under self-service status, the Club will provide the bunks, the water, and the cooking fuel, along with serving utensils and pots and pans. Minimal housekeeping chores are requested by the club taking no more than five minutes of your time during times of "full-service," and fifteen minutes (in addition to food preparation) during the off-season. For information and reservations, either call 1-800-262-4455 or else visit the AMC website, the latter containing a wealth of material including a listing of the huts and when they have vacancies. Punch in www.outdoors.org

We must not overlook the efforts of the Appalachian Trail Conference (ATC), an organization based in West Virginia. They oversee the upkeep and improvement of the A.T including giving support to the local hiking clubs that help maintain it. This support includes the maintenance of shelters, bridges and trail signs. They run the ATC Land Trust that acquires and conserves land near the Trail. They publish excellent guidebooks, each of which handles a section of the A.T. Each trail is described as though you were hiking it in either direction. Profile maps give the hiker a graphic sense of the gentleness or severity of the planned hike. For information, contact (304)-565-6331 located at P.O. Box 807, Harpers Ferry WV 25425-0807 or else visit www.appalachiantrail.org

Let us begin with a peak of modest elevation and then travel along the Appalachian Trail over New England's highest mountains.

(28) MOUNT CUBE

N 43° 53.148'
W 72° 01.395'

(Elevation 2909 feet)

Mount Cube forms a short range with Smarts Mountain to the south. This range, located twelve miles northeast of Hanover, New Hampshire, is a favorite of the Dartmouth Outing Club. Cube's charm is not immediately apparent. From the road, the summit seems low and forested. But from Cube's higher southern peak, a person has a clear prospect towards the east, south and west. From the nearby northern peak (N 53.363 min, W 01.365 min), one can look north and northeast. A hundred yards farther along the trail is seen the northwest prospect. We used all three positions to develop the full panorama.

Monopolizing the view to the northeast is the extensive mass of Mount Moosilauke. The White Mountains extend farther east. To the south arises Smarts Mountain and, to the west, the splendid expanse of Vermont's Green Mountains from Stratton to Jay Peak. Look due north and see, for the first time, the steep-sided Mounts Hor and Pisgah which flank Vermont's spectacular Lake Willoughby gap.*

In order to locate one of the Mount Cube trailheads, go east on Route 25A out of Orford, New Hampshire for a distance of 6.2 miles. At a sign for Schoolhouse Gardens, turn right onto the unpaved Baker Road and travel an additional 0.9 miles (N 53.150 min, W 02.856 min). The Cross-Rivendell Trail leads away to the left. Parking may be found a little before and at the trailhead. There is space to turn around 0.3 miles beyond. The ascent is along a blue-blazed trail and takes 90 minutes or more. Near the top you join the Appalachian Trail and will know it by the white blazes.

Those who began their trek at Springer Mountain Georgia, may have spend the previous night at the Hexacuba Shelter. They will need 90 minutes to reach Cube's summit and an additional 6 1/2 hours to arrive at the next night's destination, the Jeffers Brook Shelter located beyond Oliverian Notch. Due to

---

* The notch which brackets Lake Willoughby has no name. Therefore the word "gap" is in the lower case. In a similar vein, sometimes a mountain, let us say Bald Mountain, has a single nameless trail flanking its slopes. I refer to the path as the Bald Mountain trail ("trail" in the lower case) meaning the trail up Bald Mountain.

the length of the hike, one might consider camping out near Mount Mist and then, the next day, push on to the more distant Beaver Brook Shelter. The Ore Hill Shelter, a three hour hike from the summit of Mount Cube, is closer than Mount Mist, but staying there would make it too long a trek tomorrow to reach a mountain with a diagrammed view. If tomorrow's forecast calls for low clouds and rain, then there is no need to push beyond Ore Hill tonight.

Mount Cube's view will be somewhat unfamiliar to the person accustomed to climbing in central New Hampshire. Yet several old friends remain. One can still see Sandwich Dome, Whiteface, Tripyramid and Carrigain.

You might climb Mount Cube on a seemingly clear day and discover one cloud and one cloud only standing beyond and to the right of Mount Waternomee. The cloud never grows, shrinks or moves. This is the Mount Washington cloud cap and it may be the only cloud in the entire State. If the cloud is absent, Mount Washington should be visible, but only as a tiny pip over the high ridge of Waternomee.

To the east, Stinson and Carr Mountains hide such landmarks as Red Hill and the Ossipee Range. Southeastward, we still have our Belknaps, Plymouth Mountain and the southern Kearsarge. Smarts Mountain eclipses other landmarks. We see no Sunapee or Monadnock.

In the opposite direction are Vermont's Green Mountains. To the southwest are Ascutney, Stratton, Okemo, Killington and Pico. Okemo hides Mount Equinox. To the northwest lie Mounts Abraham, Ellen and the magnificent Camels Hump. Farther on we see Mount Mansfield, the Knoxes and the Jays. The apex of Mansfield may be hidden. Yet the presence of a considerable amount of atmospheric refraction which bends light rays may allow it to appear. If such is the case, then look for Mansfield from Cube's southern peak.

Nearby are the beautiful ponds and towns in small valleys that extend to the horizon. One sees mostly forest, but fields and other open spaces are lightly sprinkled amid the view.

If you manage to get over to the western part of New Hampshire, consider Mount Cube. Even if you are not into backpacking along the Appalachian Trail, think of this summit along with the next eighteen peaks in this series as successive day trips to be hiked over the course of several months. Some climbs are as easy as Mount Cube. Others are rough. But all nineteen will give you the entire spectrum of the White Mountains.

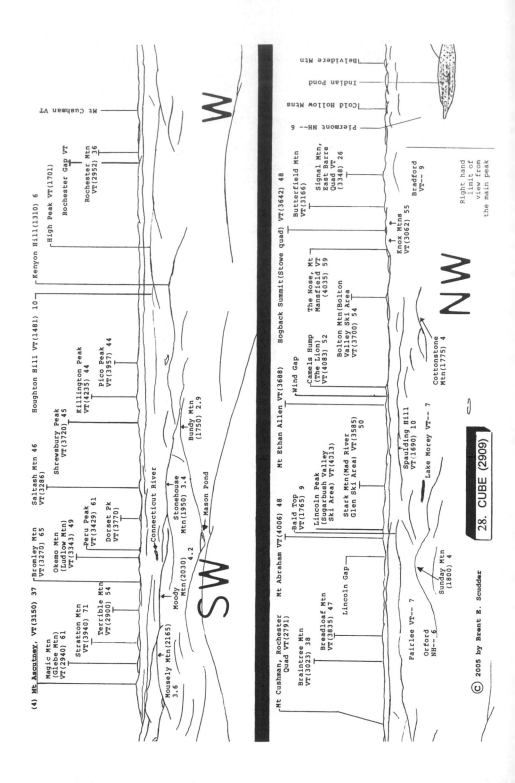

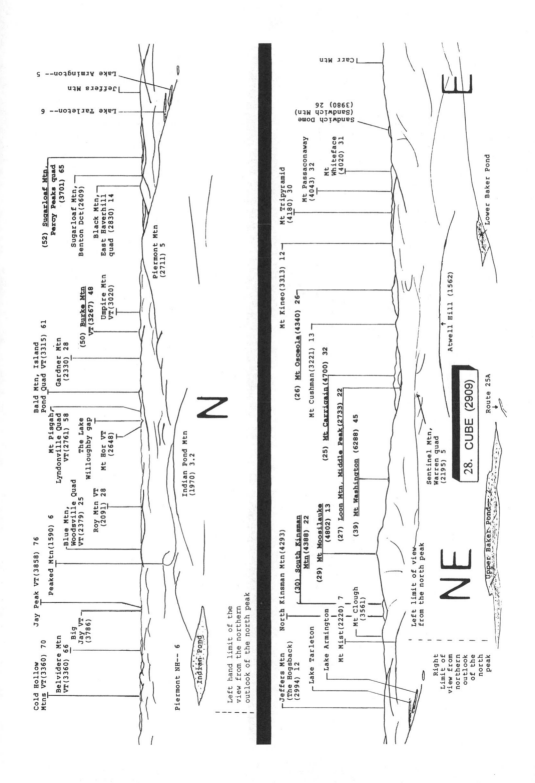

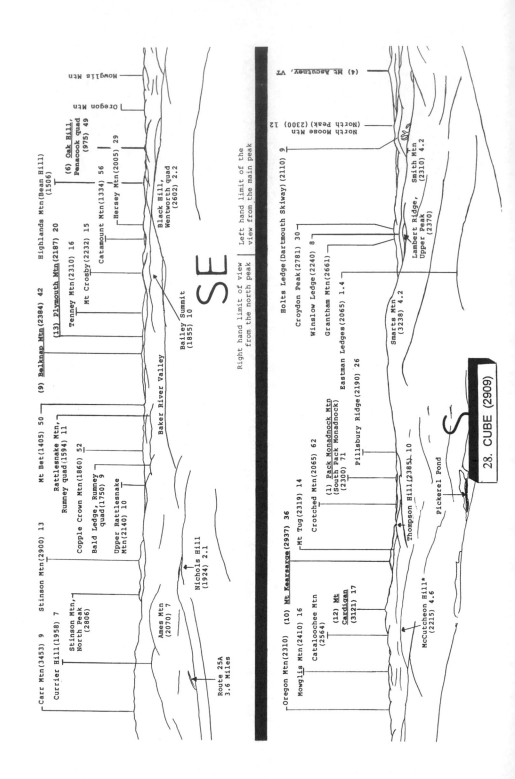

(29) MOUNT MOOSILAUKE

N 44° 01.444'
W 71° 49.858'

(Elevation 4802 feet)

HELP US TO MAKE MOOSILAUKE
NEW ENGLAND'S HIGHEST PEAK.
CARRY A ROCK TO THE TOP.
ONLY 1486 FEET TO GO.

The above sign once stood at the beginning of Moosilauke's Gorge Brook Trail. Guessing that each climber could carry a 45 pound rock and estimating the volume needed for a 28% pitch as well as projecting the forecasts for the annual number of climbers, beating Mount Washington would take over a million years. Perhaps that is why I have not seen the sign of late.

Moosilauke impresses you with its shear bulk. The attendant Mounts Blue, Jim, Waternomee and South Peak are actually part of the great massif. At least five square miles stand above 3000 feet with about two square miles exceeding 4000. This summit is not only the highest peak achieved thus far in this book but also the highest elevation encountered by the northbound Appalachian Trail (A.T) user since southern Virginia.

At the top we get our first glimpse of a mountain located entirely in Canada. For that it is necessary to become a human protractor once again as we did in Chapter Three. Using the skyline diagram, locate the village of Lisbon a little to the west of due north. Extend your left arm. With the palm down, spread the hand. Line up the end of your forefinger with Lisbon and the tip of your ring finger will point to an extremely faint mountain on the horizon 82 miles away. You are looking at the northern-most peak of the Sutton Range near St-Malo, Quebec, a summit temporarily designated as Mt. Fullerton.

To the northeast we recognize the White Mountains. Nearby stands the Cannon-Kinsman Range with the Franconias off to the right. Over the top of the Franconias are seen the Presidential and Carter Ranges respectively.

A.T. aspirants headed for Maine have just experienced a strenuous climb. Yet they must endure the visible ascents and descents that stretch away to the horizon along with the numerous ups and downs that cannot be seen from here. If they camped out last night near Mount Mist, they will need five and a half hours to reach Moosilauke's Crest. Tonight's shelter, Beaver Brook, lies but 90 minutes beyond.

The day hiker should drive west on Route 112 out of North Woodstock and fork left onto Route 118. Continue 7.2 miles and turn right on the road that leads to Ravine Lodge. Drive 1.9 miles to the end and park where you will not block other cars. Do not park in the turnaround circle. The trails begin beyond the circle (N 43 deg 59.634 min, W 71 deg 48.883 min). Climbers generally go up one trail and down another. Assume an ascent time of nearly three hours.

The Ravine Lodge, run by the Dartmouth Outing Club (DOC), is open to the public during the warmer months except for three weeks in September due to DOC trips. It takes three hours to reach the lodge from the A.T. by using the Hurricane Trail.   For reservations, telephone 603-764-5858. Their web site is www.Moosilauke.Ravine.Lodge@Dartmouth.edu

At the summit one discovers the wind chill to be worse than expected. The oft gale-swept top is barren, devoid of trees for some distance down. Bring plenty of warm clothing. Retire early should thunderstorms threaten.

The long flat ridge of Moosilauke blocks the view in two directions. Consequently, the skyline diagram was designed from partial panoramas observed from two locations 150 yards to the northeast of the summit and from two more locations the same distance to the southwest. Hopefully the hiker is now accustomed to the angle shift that this method causes nearer peaks.

Note the towns of North Woodstock and Lincoln to the east.   Loon Mountain's North Peak is just to the right. Loon's middle peak of an earlier chapter snuggles in beneath North Peak. Other featured mountains stand nearly in line. Note Kearsarge North on the left and North Moat on the right. To the south, the southern Kearsarge is visible along with three bumps on the horizon more than seventy miles away – the Uncanoonucs and Joe English Hill.

From the top of Moosilauke, Vermont's Green Mountains now are seen from a much higher elevation than in earlier chapters.   Note Dorset Peak 78 miles away and Stratton Mountain 85 miles into the distance.

We have taller peaks to climb where the view becomes even more expansive. Save the higher mountains for those days of incredible visibility. The reward of waiting is several-fold.

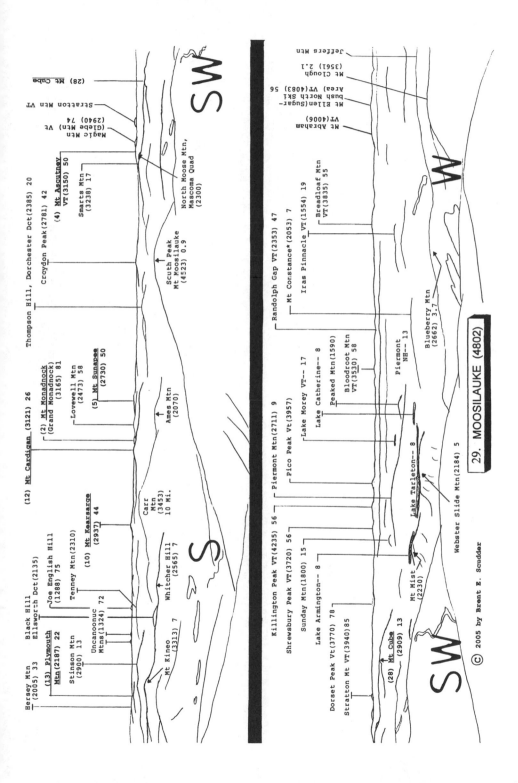

29. MOOSILAUKE (4802)

© 2005 by Brent E. Scudder

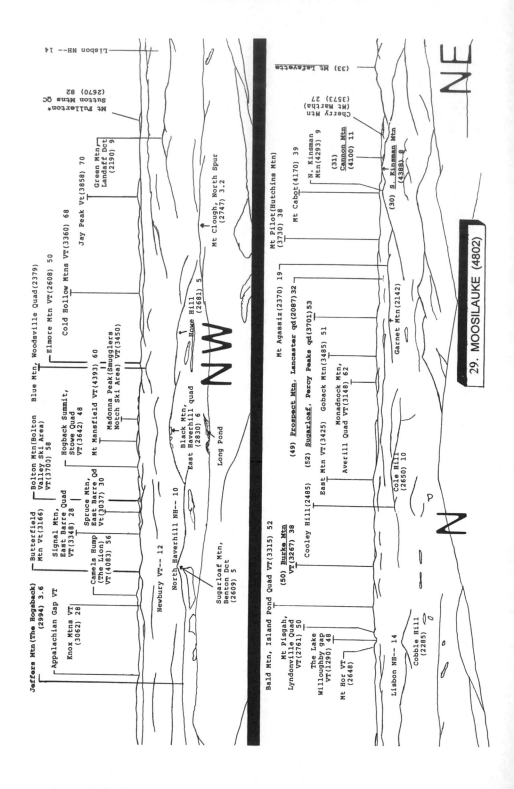

NE

NW

N

29. MOOSILAUKE (4802)

Lisbon NH-- 14

(33) Mt Lafayette

Mt Fullerton*
Sutton Mtns QC
(2670) 82

Green Mtn,
Landaff Dct
(2190) 9

Cherry Mtn
(Mt Martha)
(3573) 27

N. Kinsman
Mtn(4293) 9

Jay Peak Vt(3858) 70

(31)
Cannon Mtn
(4100) 11

Mt Clough, North Spur
(2747) 3.2

(30) S. Kinsman Mtn
(4381) 8

Elmore Mtn VT(2608) 50

Mt Cabot(4170) 39

Blue Mtn, Woodsville Quad(2379)

Cold Hollow Mtns VT(3360) 68

Mt Pilot(Hutchins Mtn)
(3730) 38

Howe Hill
(2681) 5

Mt Agassiz(2370) 19

Garnet Mtn(2142)

Bolton Mtn(Bolton
Valley Ski Area)
VT(3700) 58

Hogback Summit,
Stowe Quad
VT(3642) 48

(49) Prospect Mtn, Lancaster qd(2087)32

Madonna Peak(Smugglers
Notch Ski Area) VT(3450)

Mt Mansfield VT(4393) 60

(52) Sugarloaf, Percy Peaks qd(3701)53

Goback Mtn(3485) 51

Butterfield
Mtn Vt(3166)

Black Mtn,
East Haverhill quad
(2830) 6

Monadnock Mtn,
Averill Quad VT(3148) 62

Signal Mtn,
East Barre Quad
VT(3348) 28

Spruce Mtn,
East Barre Qd
Vt(3037) 30

Long Pond

East Mtn VT(3425)

Cole Hill
(2650) 10

Jeffers Mtn(The Hogsback)
(2994) 3.6

Camels Bump
(The Lion)
VT(4083) 56

Newbury VT-- 12

Cooley Hill(2485)

Appalachian Gap VT

North Haverhill NH-- 10

(50) Burke Mtn
VT(3267) 38

Knox Mtns VT
(3062) 28

Sugarloaf Mtn,
Benton Dct
(2609) 5

Bald Mtn, Island Pond Quad VT(3315) 52

Cobble Hill
(2285)

Mt Pisgah,
Lyndonville Quad
VT(2761) 50

Lisbon NH-- 14

The Lake
Willoughby gap
VT(1290) 48

Mt Hor VT
(2648)

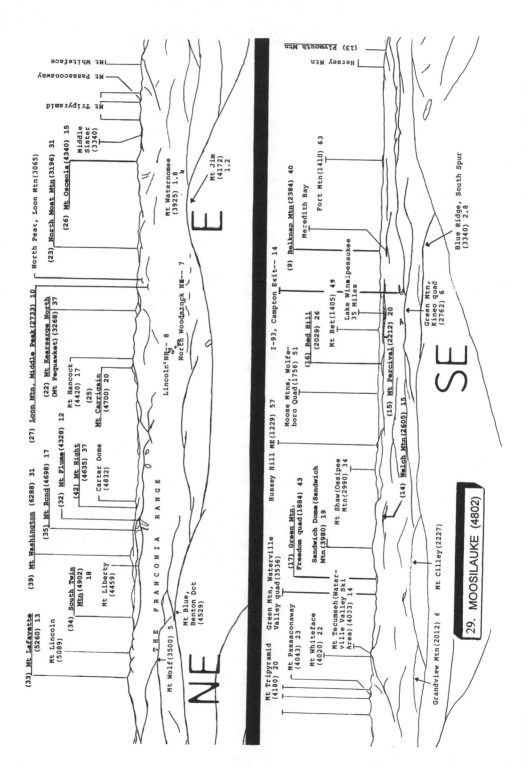

(30) SOUTH KINSMAN MOUNTAIN

N 44° 07.360'
W 71° 44.248'

(Elevation 4388 feet)

South Kinsman Mountain has two tops located 80 yards apart. Should you stand on the eastern summit, the western top appears to be the taller of the pair. Now go the western apex and perceive the eastern to rise higher.

What causes such an optical illusion? If the landscape is more vertical than horizontal, the organs of the inner ear are easily fooled. Steep terrain profiles nearby cause us to think that the direction called "down" is pointing in a slightly different direction than the true nadir. This shift affects our perception of the relative altitudes of surrounding peaks. Over on Mount Lafayette, one gazes at Carrigain. The latter is nearly 600 feet lower and yet it seems taller. Near Salt Lake City, Utah, there is a road located half way up the side of a canyon that travels more-or-less horizontally. A car parked in neutral will begin to roll backwards uphill...or so it seems.

South Kinsman's summit cairn is found on the western top suggesting that it is higher than the eastern crest. Hiking altimeters confirm that west beats east by about thirty feet. But the United States Coast and Geodetic Survey people placed their summit benchmark* on the eastern top. The latest topographical chart shows that the 4358-foot benchmark lies within the highest contour line, a line that embraces both tops. Without further scrutiny, I would say that South Kinsman's elevation is 4358 feet. Now if I draw a line from the benchmark to the top of nearby North Kinsman, I get a bearing of 359 degrees relative to True North. But on the panorama diagram developed from South Kinsman's higher western summit, North Kinsman bears 6 ½ degrees farther right. Conclusion? The benchmark is on the lower eastern apex and South Kinsman has to be about thirty feet higher.

If we look east, we are awed by the grandeur of the Franconia Range. Lafayette dominates followed on the right by Mounts Lincoln, Little Haystack, Liberty and Flume in descending crescendo. The shear steepness is apparent here. Little vegetation grows, and past rock slides appear everywhere.

---

* A benchmark is a small metal disc embedded in rock to facilitate mapping surveys.

While this grand mountain wall forms the eastern side of Franconia Notch, the Cannon-Kinsman Range forms the western. Gaze to the right of North Kinsman and note the three rounded Cannon Balls, two of them barely appearing over the ridge. Cannon Mountain rises beyond. The land then flattens out for nearly twenty-five miles until the King-Waumbek or Pliny Range rises up against the skyline.

Loon Mountain stands to the southeast, its ski trails marking the middle and North Peaks. I-93 waves its way south into the haze. Mount Kearsarge is farther right followed by the nearer Cardigan. On Cardigan's left stands Mount Monadnock low on the horizon 89 miles away.

The northbound backpacker may have spent the previous night at either the Beaver Brook Shelter located beyond Kinsman Notch or else the Eliza Brook Shelter on this side of Mount Wolf. The hiking time from the former is 7 1/2 hours and from the latter, two hours. If the following night is to be spent at the Kinsman Pond Shelter, it will take you an hour to reach it. The Pond itself is visible to the right of North Kinsman Mountain. The more distant Lonesome Lake AMC Hut requires two hours of hiking from here.

Day climbers can approach South Kinsman from the Lafayette Campground's south parking lot on the west side of the Franconia Notch Parkway (N 08.527 min, W 41.188 min). Climb the Lonesome Lake Trail and continue around the lake of that name to the AMC hut. Now gaze east across the lake and discover one of the loveliest views in the White Mountains. Beyond the blue lake are forest and the majestic Franconia Range beyond. Now proceed up the Fishin' Jimmy Trail to the base of North Kinsman's summit cone. A mad scramble over that mountain brings you to South Kinsman. Estimate 3 1/2 hours from car to crest.

To the west, northwest and north, we see into Vermont. Camels Hump's sharp profile is diminished by being partially hidden behind the nearer mountains east of Barre. We have no problem finding Mount Mansfield, the Jays and the Lake Willoughby gap. Behold Vermont's Monadnock 55 miles away appearing to the right of North Kinsman. Deer Mountain Summit stands 78 miles distant in far northern New Hampshire and, to the right, Maine's Saddleback at a distance of 83 miles.

While recognizing such distant landmarks may be satisfying, the nearby terrain – the Franconias, the Moosilauke heights and the companion North Kinsman give our mountain its tremendous view. The hike is longer than many but well worth it.

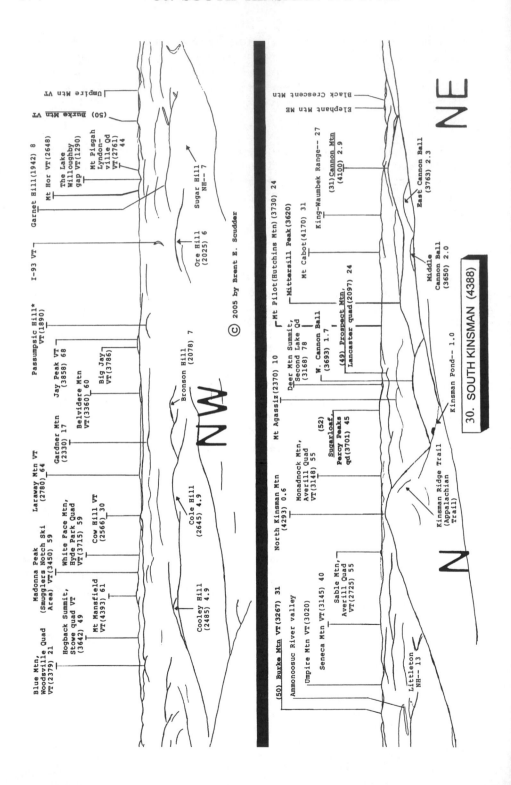

© 2005 by Brent E. Scudder

30. SOUTH KINSMAN (4388)

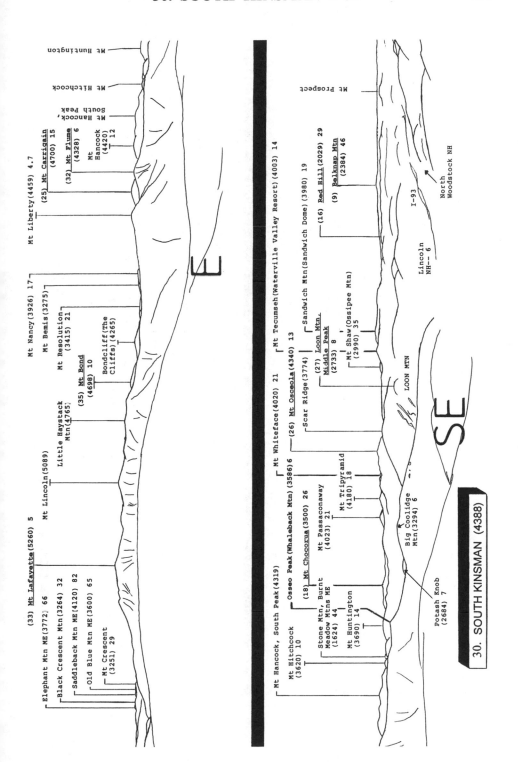

30. SOUTH KINSMAN (4388)

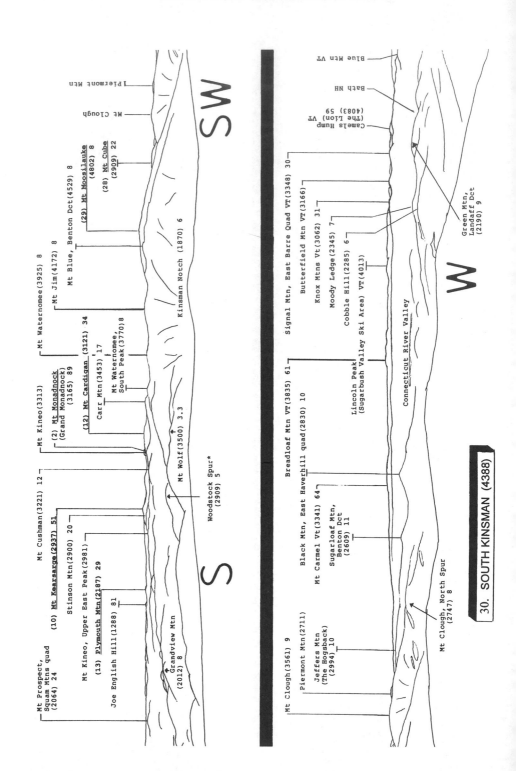

SW

Piermont Mtn

Mt Clough

(29) Mt Moosilauke (4802) 8

Mt Blue, Benton Dct(4529) 8

(28) Mt Cube (2909) 22

Mt Waternomee(3925) 8

Mt Jim(4172) 8

Kinsman Notch (1870) 6

Mt Kineo(3313)

(2) Mt Monadnock (Grand Monadnock) (3165) 89

(12) Mt Cardigan (3121) 34

Carr Mtn(3453) 17

Mt Waternomee, South Peak(3770) 8

Mt Cushman(3221) 12

(10) Mt Kearsarge(2937) 51

Stinson Mtn(2900) 20

Mt Kineo, Upper East Peak(2981)

(13) Plymouth Mtn(2187) 29

Joe English Hill(1288) 81

Mt Prospect, Squam Mtns quad (2064) 24

Grandview Mtn (2012) 8

Mt Wolf(3500) 3.3

Woodstock Spur* (2909) 5

S

Blue Mtn VT

Bath NH

Camels Hump (The Lion) VT (4083) 59

(4802) 8

W

Green Mtn, Landaff Dct (2190) 9

Signal Mtn, East Barre Quad VT(3348) 30

Butterfield Mtn VT(3166)

Knox Mtns Vt(3062) 31

Moody Ledge (2345) 7

Cobble Hill(2285) 6

Lincoln Peak (Sugarbush Valley Ski Area) VT(4013)

Connecticut River Valley

Breadloaf Mtn VT(3835) 61

Black Mtn, East Haverhill quad(2830) 10

Mt Carmel Vt(3341) 64

Sugarloaf Mtn, Benton Dct (2609) 11

Mt Clough(3561) 9

Piermont Mtn(2711)

Jeffers Mtn (The Hogsback) (2994) 10

Mt Clough, North Spur (2747) 8

30. SOUTH KINSMAN (4388)

(31) CANNON MOUNTAIN

N 44° 09.402'
W 71° 41.923'

(Elevation 4100 feet)

The Friday evening of May 2, 2003 was foggy and misty. Hikers camping in Franconia Notch awoke to a loud crash of falling rock. Saturday dawned crisp and clear. Two State Park workers engaged in early morning chores happened to glance up at the Cannon cliffs. One of the workers, Amy Cyrs, later told *Concord Monitor* reporter Jennifer Skalka, "We both side-stepped, thinking we're just not seeing something right." Indeed they were not. New Hampshire's state symbol, the Old Man of the Mountain, had vanished.

The Old Man had been a rock profile of a man's face looking eastward across Franconia Notch perhaps since 8000 BC, but at least since Francis Whitcomb and Luke Brooks discovered it in 1805. Nathaniel Hawthorne immortalized the Old Man in his short story *The Great Stone Face*. The profile was ephemeral, visible from only one location. If you moved about, you no longer saw it.

New Hampshire is not the first state to continue using as their symbol something that has ceased to exist. An 1869 hurricane blew down Connecticut's Charter Oak, an emblem that appears on their 1999 quarter.

There is at least one other "Old Man" in the world. In Ontario, Canada, just north of Wiarton's Colpoys Bay, a high-cliffed peninsula faces Georgian Bay. A similar profile, easily seen from a boat, juts out from the cliff.

We selected Cannon Mountain for the casual visitor, the skier and the hiker. The visitor and the skier has New Hampshire's only aerial tramway which whisks him or her up the slope in a matter of minutes. Many tourists do not bother to walk the additional 150 yards to the summit platform. As a result, the hiker sees little of the commercialism and has most of the trails all to himself.

We selected Cannon for the view. From the summit, one sees Vermont's Camels Hump, Mount Mansfield, Jay Peak, the steep-sided Lake Willoughby gap, as well as the northern Monadnock. Close beneath us lie the New Hampshire towns of Franconia and Littleton. To the northeast, lies the village of Twin Mountain and, well beyond it, several mountains in Maine. New

Hampshire's Presidential Range begins to the right with Mounts Adams and Jefferson. Then the Franconia Range takes over the horizon hiding not only the southern Presidentials but Mount Washington as well.

The Franconias boldly rise far above our level as they extend away to the east and southeast. Its tallest, Mount Lafayette, towers less than three miles away across an intervening abyss with tortured cliffs and rock slides amply distributed among its western slope.

If climbing Cannon for the day, locate the Kinsman Ridge Trail to the left of the tramway base (N 10.126 min, W 41.226 min). One climbs through forest and leaves the casual tourist behind. The pitch is steep and unrelenting, but the ascent takes slightly over two hours. STAY OFF THE SKI TRAILS. Summertime brush grows poorly near the top, and frequent tramping causes a severe erosion problem. In 1995, the fine for off-season ski trail hiking was $300.

Adherents of the Appalachian Trail may feel that this mountain is not appropriate for their use. The A.T. turns away from Cannon at the Lonesome Lake AMC Hut. But one can hike from the Hut to Cannon and reverse course to finally spend the night at the Liberty Spring Tentsite, a total non-stop hike of six hours. Add another hour if the trek began at Kinsman Pond and ascended Cannon via Lonesome Lake. Should the weather be inclement, avoid all the high peaks and take the direct route from Lonesome Lake to Greenleaf Hut, a hike of less than four hours. To do so, you must give up a small section of the A.T.

Stand on Cannon's summit and note the Franconia Range trailing away to the southeast into the lesser hills of the Pemigewasset Valley. Mounts Osceola and Tecumseh stand tall beyond. Southward sprouts Plymouth Mountain and the southern Kearsarge. Turn the head once more, and the hills grow again as we look back upon Mount Moosilauke, the Kinsmans and the Cannonballs. We recognize Vermont's Killington and Pico Peak sixty-eight miles away just to the right of North Kinsman.

Cannon Mountain belongs to everyone, regardless of whether he or she is a tourist, skier or hiker. No one can forget the towering cliffs seen from the floor of the Notch. The view of the Franconia Range from Cannon's summit is impossible to erase from memory. No one can forget the Old Man.

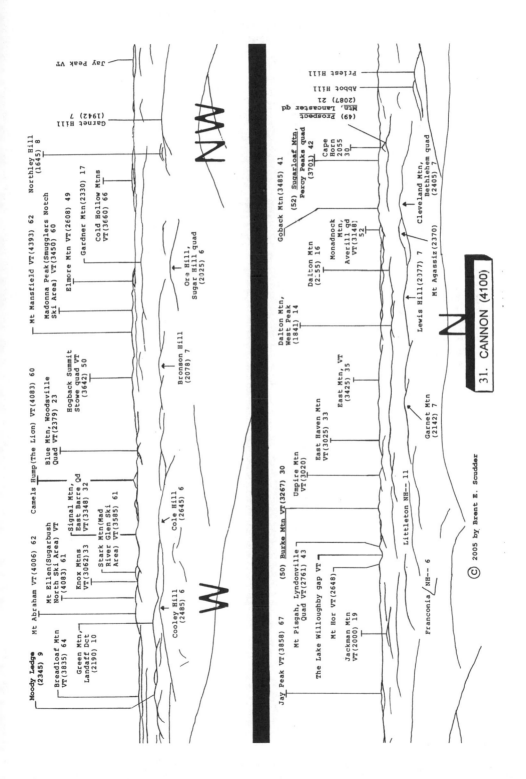

© 2005 by Brent E. Scudder

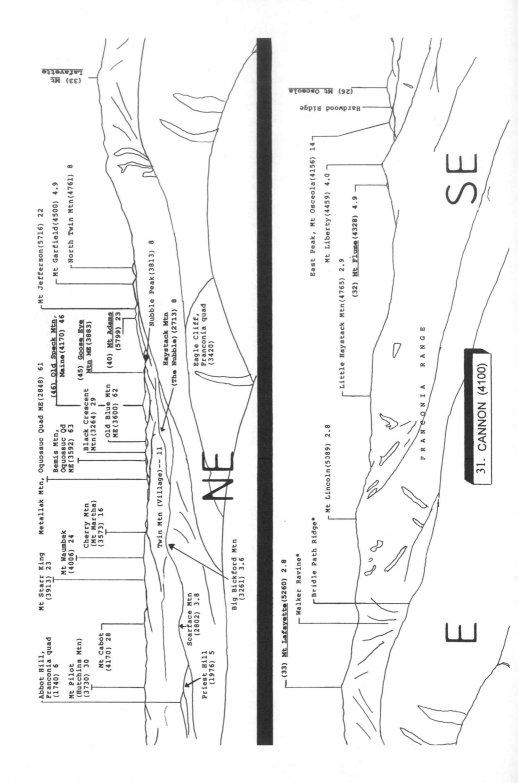

31. CANNON (4100)

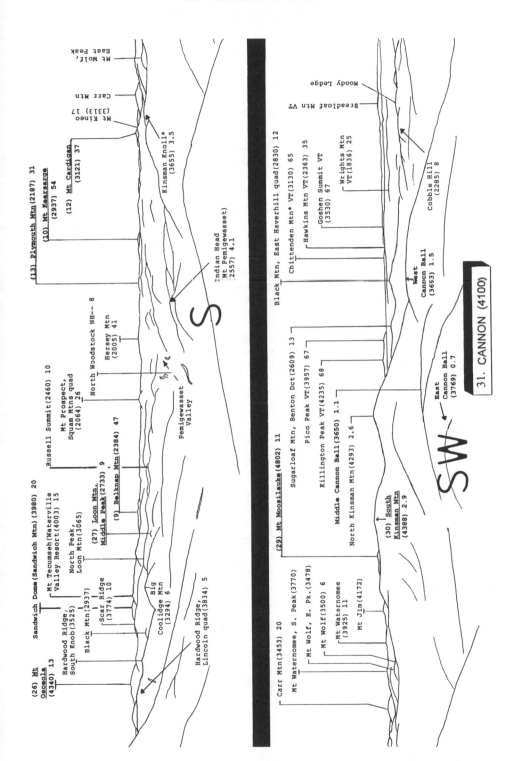

31. CANNON (4100)

S

SW

(32) MOUNT FLUME

N 44° 06.517'
W 71° 37.671'

(Elevation 4328 feet)

Diagrams based on slides taken by
Dan H. Allen

We arrive upon the Franconia Range itself at the southernmost of several peaks that exceed four thousand feet in elevation. The view is awe-inspiring. Arresting the eye is the ridge itself extending northward to the ever-higher mountains of Liberty, Little Haystack, Lincoln and Lafayette. To the right, Garfield stands tall and alone. If we continue to scan to the right, our eyes pass the nearer Owl's Head Mountain and the more distant Galehead, North and South Twin Mountains.

The diagrams of many earlier chapters depict Mounts Flume and Liberty. Their conical shapes make excellent reference landmark mountains. If one drives northbound on I-93, this pair is easy to spot off to the right especially near milepost 93.

To reach two of the routes to the summit, get off of I-93 at Exit 33 and proceed northward on Route 3 until you pass the entrance to the Flume Gorge parking lot. From there drive 0.2 miles to the parking lot of the Whitehouse trailhead (N 06.643 min, W 40.884 min). Walk northward on the trail finally to join the Liberty Spring Trail 0.8 miles later. Climb 0.6 miles on Liberty Spring to where the Flume Slide Trail leads off to the right.

At this point, the hiker must make an important decision. One can take either way. The Flume Slide Trail is shorter. But this more direct ascent climbs an incredibly steep section of slab rocks which are wet most of the time and could lead to a slipping accident. It is safer to continue straight up the Liberty Spring Trail to where it joins the Franconia Ridge Trail. Turn south and follow the latter path over Mount Liberty, down a little ways and up to Flume. The direct more dangerous Flume Slide Route takes just under four hours. Add a half an hour for the safer Liberty route.

Mount Flume is a little out of the way of the Appalachian Trail hiker but not out of reach. The weather forecast should determine the feasibility of going to that summit. If the hiker is proceeding from Lonesome Lake AMC Hut to Greenleaf AMC Hut and wishes to include Mount Flume as part of the itinerary, add two hours and twenty minutes to an already six-hour hike.

Reaching Flume is easier if you spent last night at the Liberty Spring Tentsite. A five-hour walk will allow you to include Mount Flume and be able to reach Greenleaf Hut. If one's next destination is the Garfield Ridge Campsite, then including Mount Flume involves eight hours.

On the summit, look over at nearby Mount Liberty's eastern flank and see a slight projection that does not seem to be part of that peak. You are looking at the tiny tip of Cannon Mountain. To the left appear the Kinsmans and Mount Moosilauke. We can see into Vermont with Jay Peak appearing in the gap to the right of Liberty and Vermont's highest elevation, Mount Mansfield is just to the left at a distance of 66 miles. Camels Hump has been identified beyond and between the Kinsmans but clouds blocked the view when we were there. According to Smith and Dickerman's *The 4000-footers of the White Mountains,* Dix Mountain in New York's Adirondacks may be seen in the same general direction.

To the south we see the familiar Ascutney, Cardigan, Sunapee, Kearsarge – even the Uncanoonucs near Manchester. At our feet lies the ski-trailed Loon Mountain. Looking to the left, mountains such as Tecumseh, Sandwich Dome and Osceola hide the lower elevations beyond.

East of us, Mounts Kancamagus, Hancock, Carrigain and the Bonds punctuate the rough Pemigewasset Wilderness. Bill Merrill Mountain in Maine is visible through Hancock Notch at a distance of 42 miles. Mount Washington stands tall 20 miles away. To the right may be found Mount Hight and Carter Dome directly over the top of Bondcliff.

Much of the Franconia Ridge has endless views in all directions. Traversing it on a clear day from one end to the other is an experience not to be forgotten.

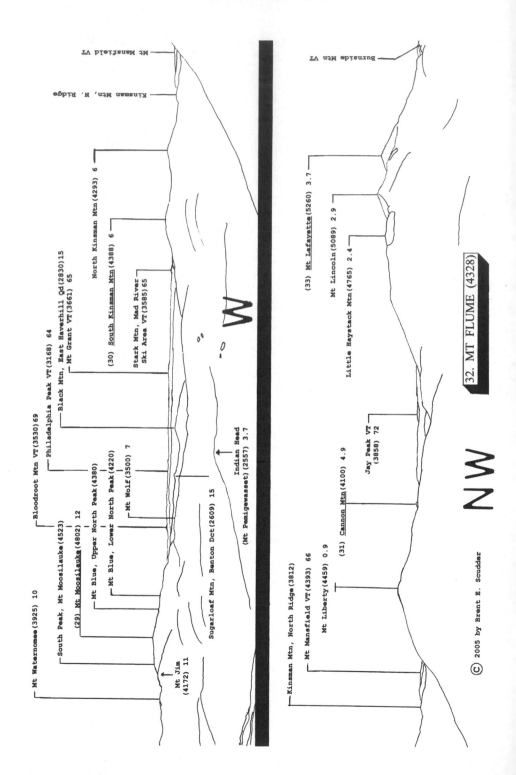

Mt Mansfield VT

Kinsman Mtn, N. Ridge

North Kinsman Mtn (4293) 6

Bloodroot Mtn VT (3530) 69

Philadelphia Peak VT (3168) 64

Black Mtn, East Haverhill Qd (2830) 15

Mt Grant VT (3661) 65

South Kinsman Mtn (4388) 6

Mt Waternomee (3925) 10

South Peak, Mt Moosilauke (4523)

(29) Mt Moosilauke (4802) 12

Mt Blue, Upper North Peak (4380)

Mt Blue, Lower North Peak (4220)

Mt Wolf (3500) 7

(30) South Kinsman Mtn (4388) 6

Stark Mtn, Mad River Ski Area VT (3585) 65

Mt Jim (4172) 11

Sugarloaf Mtn, Benton Dct (2609) 15

Indian Head (Mt Pemigewasset) (2557) 3.7

W

Burnside Mtn VT

(33) Mt Lafayette (5260) 3.7

Mt Lincoln (5089) 2.9

Little Haystack Mtn (4765) 2.4

Kinsman Mtn, North Ridge (3812)

Mt Mansfield VT (4393) 66

Mt Liberty (4459) 0.9

(31) Cannon Mtn (4100) 4.9

Jay Peak VT (3858) 72

NW

32. MT FLUME (4328)

© 2005 by Brent E. Scudder

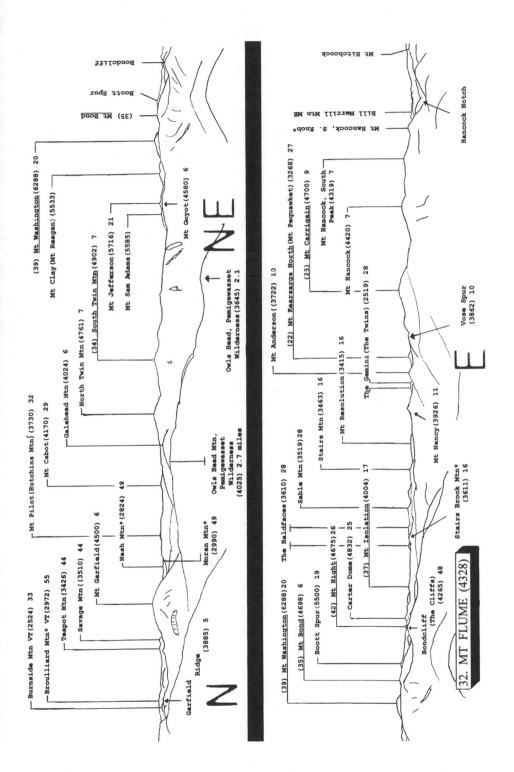

32. MT FLUME (4328)

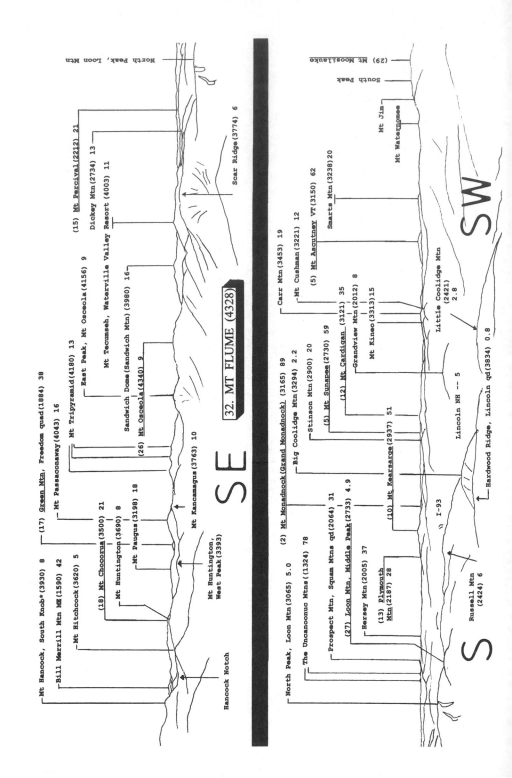

32. MT FLUME (4328)

(33) MOUNT LAFAYETTE

N 44° 09.631'
W 71° 38.662'

(Elevation 5260 feet)

Originally called Great Haystack, the view from this summit takes in vast lands. In 1825, the local citizens commemorated the hero of the Battle of Yorktown. They changed the name of the highest peak in western New Hampshire to honor him, the Marquis de Lafayette.

From the top, look along the Franconia Ridge and note the knife-like ridge extending towards Mounts Lincoln and Liberty. At the horizon 84 miles away stands Joe English Hill. The twin Uncanoonucs are there also, very small and very far. Much closer are the ski trails on Loon Mountain.

To the southwest, Mount Moosilauke stands 13 miles distant. Normally the bulk of this mountain looks large, dominating the imagination. From here its mass is quite apparent. But one looks down on Moosilauke and is not impressed. More startling is the steep cleft of Franconia Notch extending from North Woodstock up past Echo Lake. The hiker is awed to have come up from there without the aid of technical climbing equipment.

If the day is exceptionally clear, glance slightly to Moosilauke's left and discover Vermont's Stratton Mountain 98 miles away. To the right locate Camels Hump on the Green Mountain skyline. Measure six sun diameters farther right and discover New York's Alder Brook Range 120 miles away.

Climbing Lafayette is not nearly as tough as its elevation suggests. One starts 1760 feet above sea level thereby reducing the vertical climb to 3500 feet. Find the trailhead by driving north on the Franconia Parkway 1.7 miles past the turnoff for "The Basin." Look for the Lafayette Place parking lot on the right. Those driving south will find a parking lot of the same name on their side of the road and reach the trailhead by walking eastward through an underpass.

The Old Bridle Path and Falling Waters Trail begin jointly at an information stand located there (N 08.516 min, W 40.848 min). After 0.2 miles the trails divide with the Falling Waters ascending little Haystack and the Old Bridle Path, Mount Lafayette. Along the latter trail may be found the AMC's Greenleaf Hut which, when open, serves as a waypoint for light refreshment. One can reach the top in less than four hours.

Overnight campers may have started the day at the Liberty Spring Tentsite some four miles along the ridge to the south. A two-hour hike brings one to Lafayette. On the other hand, if the A.T. hiker had "overnighted" at the Greenleaf Hut, that person can reach the summit within an hour. Tonight's target will be either the Garfield Ridge Campsite or else the AMC's Galehead Hut. Allow three and a half hours of hiking to the former and five hours to the latter.

Lightning with its tendency to strike the highest object has caused remarkably few fatalities in the White Mountains over the years. At the first sign of thunder, hikers generally move swiftly down the mountain into the relative safety of the forest. But the barren Franconia Ridge line is especially dangerous. Cliffs and slippery pitches fall away on both sides. One has to walk occasionally more than twenty minutes along the ridge *(sometimes even climbing)* in order to find a trail leading downwards. Even then the forest is still many minutes away. In 1982, an Outward Bound party was caught in just this predicament. Lightning struck and killed one member.

If the forecast calls for a chance of scattered thunderstorms stay off the Franconia Ridge. Once thunder is heard, it is too late to reach relative safety.

Today the skies are crystal clear. From the top of Lafayette, we gaze into northeastern Vermont and note Canada visible beyond. Directly through the Lake Willoughby gap rises Quebec's Mont Foster 83 miles away. Farther right, Mont Orford is harder to identify and may require binoculars.

If we look to the north-northeast, we are back in New Hampshire. Glance farther right and we find ourselves already seeing Maine; East Kennebago, Elephant, Old Speck and Goose Eye Mountains being among the principal peaks.

To the east we see that we are certainly part of the White Mountains. Owls Head and the Pemigewasset Wilderness lie right at our feet. Beyond stand the Twins, the Bonds, Mount Carrigain, the Hancocks and the Sandwich Range. To the left is seen Mount Washington.

Truly a day of excellent visibility is the time to select Mount Lafayette. But if one is short on vacation, and the weather is hazy, climb it anyway. It is not the horizon skyline but rather the nearby abyss that inspires awe.

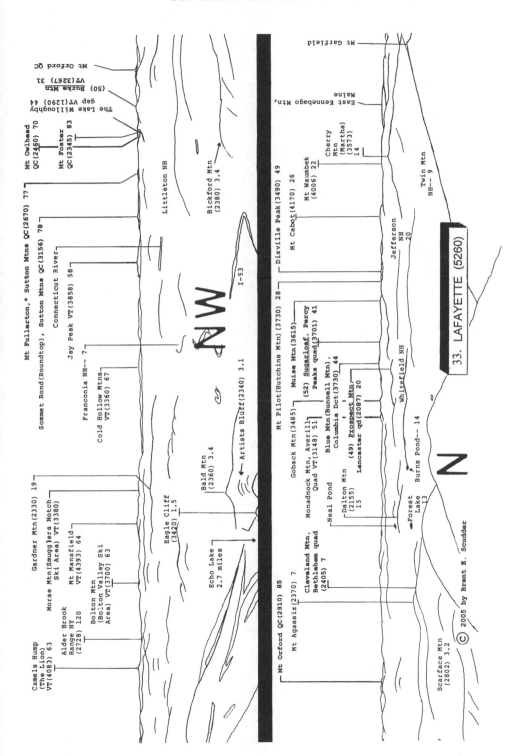

Camels Hump
(The Lion)
VT(4083) 63

Alder Brook
Range NY
(2728) 120

Gardner Mtn(2330) 19

Morse Mtn(Smugglers Notch
Ski Area) VT(3380)

Mt Mansfield
VT(4393) 64

Bolton Mtn
(Bolton Valley Ski
Area) VT(3700) 63

Mt Fullerton,* Sutton Mtns QC(2670) 77

Sommet Rond(Roundtop), Sutton Mtns QC(3156) 78

Connecticut River

Jay Peak VT(3858) 58

Franconia NH-- 7

Cold Hollow Mtns
VT(3360) 67

Mt Orford QC
(2767) 31

Burke Mtn (50)
VT(3267) 31

The Lake Willoughby
gap VT(1290) 44

Mt Owlhead
QC(2460) 70

Mt Foster
QC(2345) 83

Mt Garfield

East Kennebago Mtn,
Maine

Cherry
Mtn
(Martha)
(3573)
14

Twin Mtn
NH-- 9

Littleton NH

Bickford Mtn
(2380) 3.4

Eagle Cliff
(3420) 1.5

Bald Mtn
(2360) 3.4

Artists Bluff(2340) 3.1

Echo Lake
2.7 miles

I-93

NW

Mt Orford QC(2810) 85

Mt Agassiz(2370) 7

Cleveland Mtn,
Bethlehem quad
(2405) 7

Goback Mtn(3485)

Monadnock Mtn, Averill
Quad VT(3148) 51

Neal Pond

Dalton Mtn
(2155)
15

Mt Pilot(Hutchins Mtn) (3730) 28

Muise Mtn(3615)

(52) Sugarloaf, Percy
Peaks quad(3701) 41

Blue Mtn (Bunnell Mtn),
Columbia Dct(3730) 44

(49) Prospect Mtn
Lancaster qd(2087) 20

Dixville Peak(3490) 49

Mt Cabot(4170) 26

Mt Waumbek
(4006) 22

Jefferson
NH
20

Whitefield NH

Forest
Lake
13

Burns Pond-- 14

N

Scarface Mtn
(2802) 3.2

© 2005 by Brent E. Scudder

33. LAFAYETTE (5260)

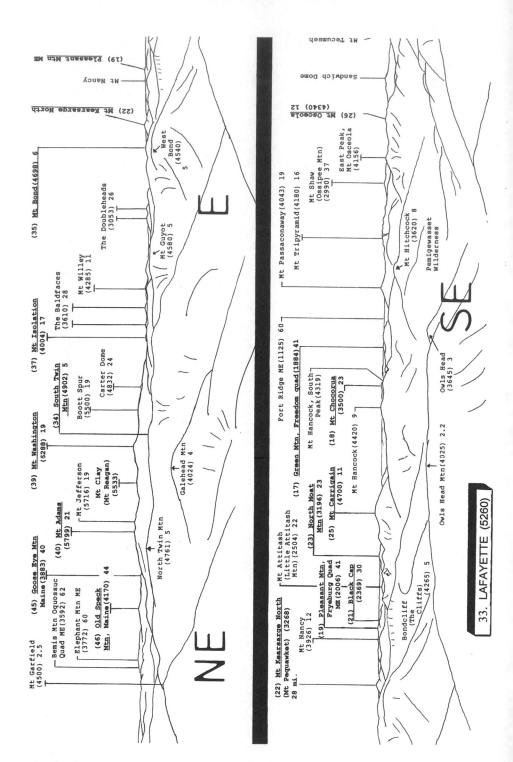

33. LAFAYETTE (5260)

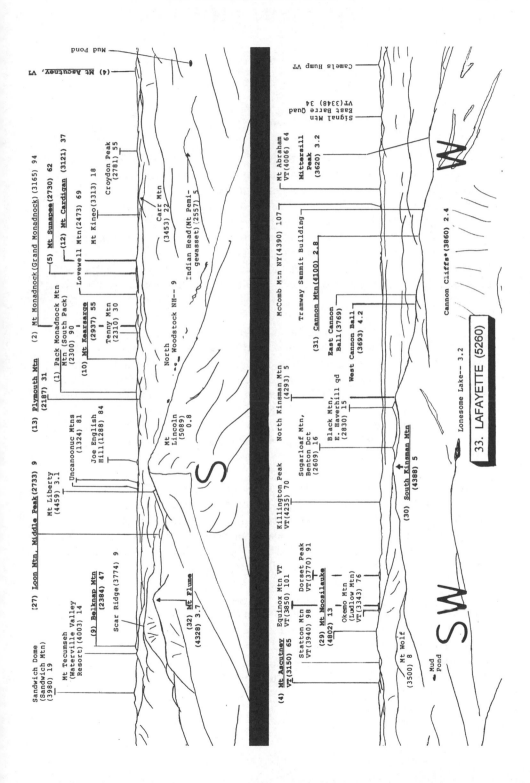

33. LAFAYETTE (5260)

(34) SOUTH TWIN MOUNTAIN

N 44° 11.247'
W 71° 33.262'

(Elevation 4902 feet)

About half way between the notches of Franconia and Crawford stands a very tall mountain with ridges trailing away in several directions. The westward ridge stretches over Mount Garfield and soon meets the northern end of the Franconia Range. A second ridge runs southeastward and arrives at Mount Guyot thereafter branching out with Zealand Ridge on the left and the Bonds on the right. The third ridge reaches north to a companion peak about a mile away and then dips sharply into the Ammonusuc River Valley. Dense forest covers all of the slopes. Trees thin out quickly as one nears the junction of these ridges. One sees a complete panorama from the top of South Twin Mountain.

The Presidential Range looms much larger now. We are five miles closer. As with the previously featured mountain, one easily sees the northern Presidential Peaks standing sharply against the sky. To the right of Mount Washington, one begins to recognize the outlines of those southern Presidentials that are standing below and in front of Boott Spur – Mounts Eisenhower and Pierce. To the right Mounts Jackson and Webster are seen nestled amid the individual summits of the nearer Willey-Rosebrook range. This southern group, while tall in their own right, are insignificant among their neighbors.

Again witness the tortured nature of the White Mountains. To the southwest lies the deep Pemigewasset valley bounded on the west by the great Franconia wall. Northwestward the land is gentler, the higher mountains being more than sixty miles distant. Farther right, the nearer tops begin to shut us in once more. But we see well into northern New Hampshire and nearby Maine with East Kennabago Mountain showing clearly eighty miles away.

The Gale River Trail is the shortest way up. On Route 3, either drive 5.3 miles west from the intersection with 302 in Twin Mountain Village or travel 5.2 miles east from the Franconia Parkway. Turn South opposite Treudeau Road onto Gale River Road (N 14.649 min, W 38.027 min). Following the turn, drive 0.6 miles down the latter road and bear left. After that proceed 0.7 miles and turn right. Park 0.3 miles farther on (N 13.928 min, W 36.611 min).

SOUTH TWIN MOUNTAIN

Once on the trail, a person eventually passes the AMC Galehead Hut and then is confronted with a steep relentless tiring scramble up the final thousand feet. Even so, the route from car to summit takes only four hours.

Those who are bound for Mount Katahdin within a few weeks may have slept at the Garfield Ridge Campsite the previous night. They need three hours of hiking to arrive at South Twin's summit. Others who began the day at the Galehead AMC hut need but an hour. Both groups face that steep final pitch before being rewarded with a marvelous view.

From the top, can the eastbound backpacker see where he might be spending the night? The trail passes over Mount Guyot. With your eyes, follow the crest line to the right of Guyot into the final dip before Mount Bond. Hidden to one side is the Guyot Campsite. You stand about an hour and a half from there.

Anyone intending to reach AMC's Zealand Hut by nightfall will also pass over Mount Guyot. Visually follow the crest line from Guyot's summit but this time to the left along Zealand Ridge until you line up with Mount Field. The Hut is located out of sight in front of Field but behind Zealand Ridge. Although the hike to Zealand Falls is mostly downhill from South Twin Mountain, anticipate four hours before arriving there.

We are not far below Lafayette's altitude, and thus we see several summits in Quebec. Mont Owl Head's apex is discovered on the horizon between Vermont's Burke and Umpire Mountains. Sommet Rond is observed farther left while Mont Orford appears on the right still 85 miles away. The nearest Canadian summit has not been previously pointed out. Look to the right of North Twin and note New Hampshire's Prospect Mountain protruding above its eastern slope. On the right is Quebec's Hereford Mountain only 62 miles away.

The author has seen people reach South Twin's summit on a crystal clear day with its vast view and stay only five minutes. Is that all they wish to see after four hours of climbing?" "Peak bagging" has its rewards of boasting rights. But everyone should remain at awhile and savor a scene that a large majority of the population never witnesses. The peak bagger can still boast.

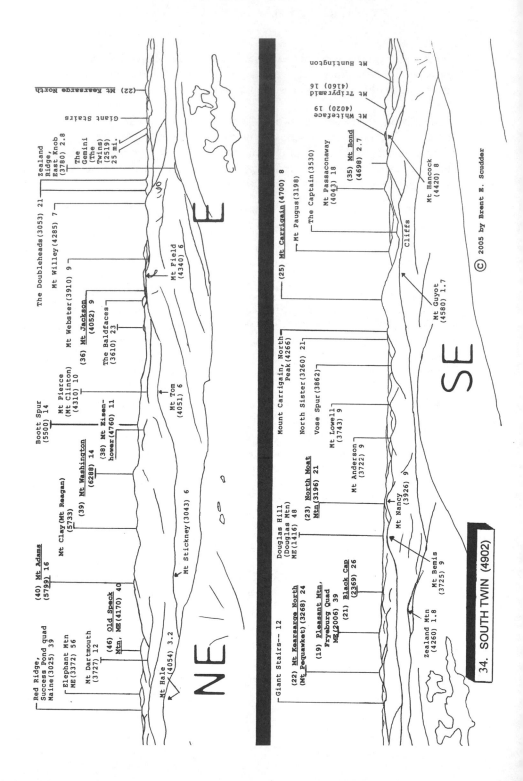

34. SOUTH TWIN (4902)

© 2005 by Brent E. Scudder

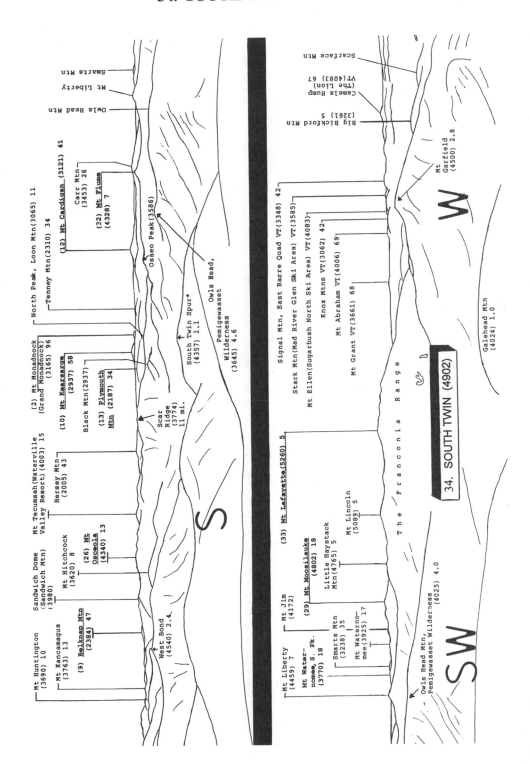

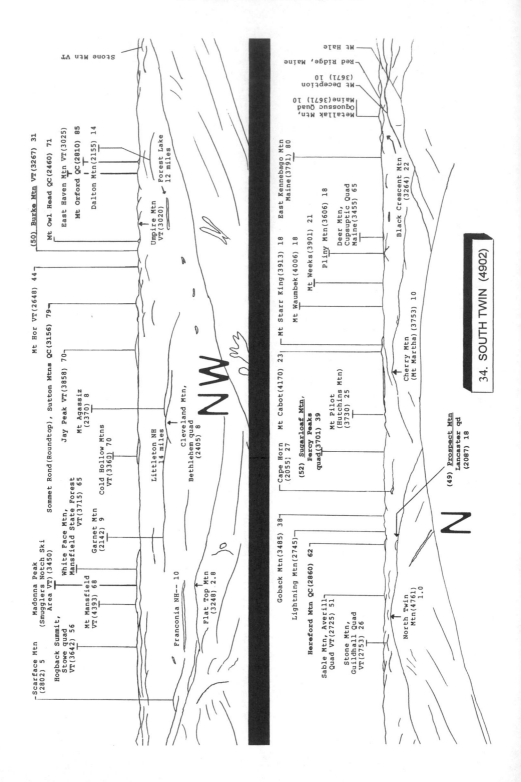

34. SOUTH TWIN (4902)

(35) MOUNT BOND

N 44° 09.173'
W 71° 31.865'

(Elevation 4698 feet)

Antarctica has not just one pole but several. The true South Pole, where all the meridians meet, is known to all. But there is also the South Magnetic Pole, the place away from which compass needles point. Many persons would be surprised to learn that these two places were "poles apart," separated by over 1800 miles. Geographers define a third pole, the point in Antarctica located farthest from the sea. Nor does this hard-to-reach spot lie at the true South Pole but more than 500 miles away in the direction of the Indian Ocean. Few people have stood on the Pole of Inaccessibility.

New Hampshire's 'Pole of Inaccessibility" would be that peak located farthest from the nearest road. A certain mountain located three miles south of Mount Guyot may qualify for this honor. Named for Professor G. P. Bond who mapped the area in 1853, this peak rises along a north south ridge that includes Guyot and, farther on, Bondcliff.

Little of man's works are visible from here. One sees ski trails on Loon and a smudge of black smoke on the left side of Mount Washington not to mention its summit buildings. Other than that, only hill and forest appear along with the tan and gray scars of former rock slides.

Look westward and trace in our mind's eye the course of the Appalachian Trail. The A.T. emerges on the Franconia Ridge just to the right of Mount Liberty. Thereafter it climbs over Little Haystack, Mounts Lincoln and Lafayette. Then it turns eastward as it passes over Mount Garfield and later South Twin. Next this path approaches us obliquely winding over Mount Guyot and then off to the right along Zealand Ridge. It disappears behind Zeacliff to the northeast and then reappears in Zealand Notch as it continues to the right finally touching Ethan Pond. The trail vanishes once again behind the lower end of Mount Willey reappearing later on Mount Jackson and later Mounts Pierce, Eisenhower Monroe, Washington, Clay and Jefferson.

MOUNT BOND

The Appalachian Trail hiker traveling between AMC's Galehead and Zealand Falls Huts does not need Mount Bond for the featured daily panorama. He or she will have already climbed South Twin Mountain. But those who are trudging between the Guyot and Ethan Pond Campsites have no mountain that we cover. A side trip to Bond will only add 45 minutes to a 4 1/2 hour hike. AMC Hut hoppers do not pass as close to Bond. If they wish to climb it, they must add an hour and a half to their existing five-hour journey. These figures do not, of course, allow for the time spent up on Bond enjoying the view.

The day hiker has a grueling trip. In approaching Bond from the north, one first has to climb South Twin and then descend over Guyot and turn for Bond. (See the last chapter for directions in order to locate the trailhead.) Count on hiking 5 1/2 hours to reach the mountain and an hour less to return. This adds up to a hiking day of ten hours. You should plan the climb during June and July when the days are the longest and get an early start. Alternatively, one could hike from the road and spend the night at the Galehead Hut. This cuts the climbing time the next day to a far more manageable seven hours.

From the top of Mount Bond, we see exactly 25 of the other 53 summits featured in this book. The southern Monadnock, Kearsarge and Plymouth mountains almost line up, Monadnock being 94 miles away. Mounts Sunapee and Cardigan rise a bit to the right of this conjunction while Carrigain, Osceola and Belknap appear on the left. The remaining featured summits are scattered randomly around the horizon.

Although we are lower in elevation than South Twin, we still see parts of Quebec. Sommet Rond pokes above the horizon left of South Twin. Hereford Mountain stands left of New Hampshire's Lightning-Goback-Sugarloaf group, while Gosford is seen to the right of Waumbek. If today's visibility reveals the southern Monadnock, we should be able to see all three Canadian tops. They stand nearer.

Besides featuring mountains attainable by summer chair lift, we must also reward those who are willing to lose themselves in the wilderness. The view from Mount Bond may not be better than many, but it is a perspective that few get to see. From the sweeping majesty of the Presidentials to the massive Carrigain and the Franconia Range, the panorama from Mount Bond is unique.

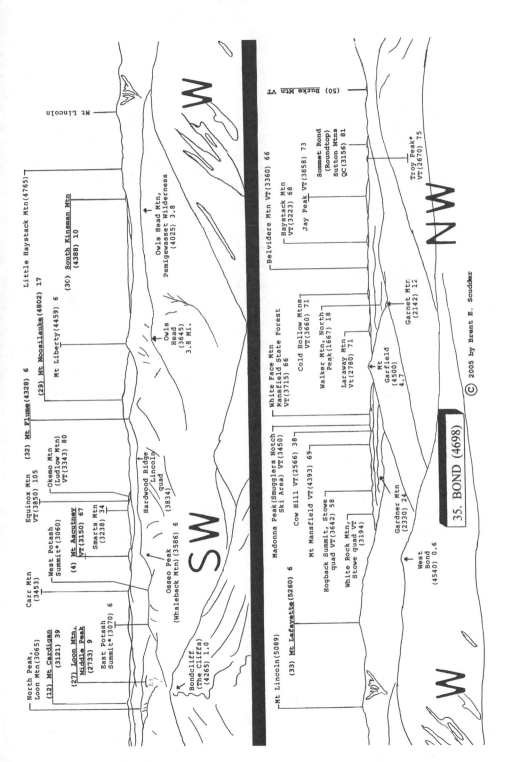

35. BOND (4698)

© 2005 by Brent E. Scudder

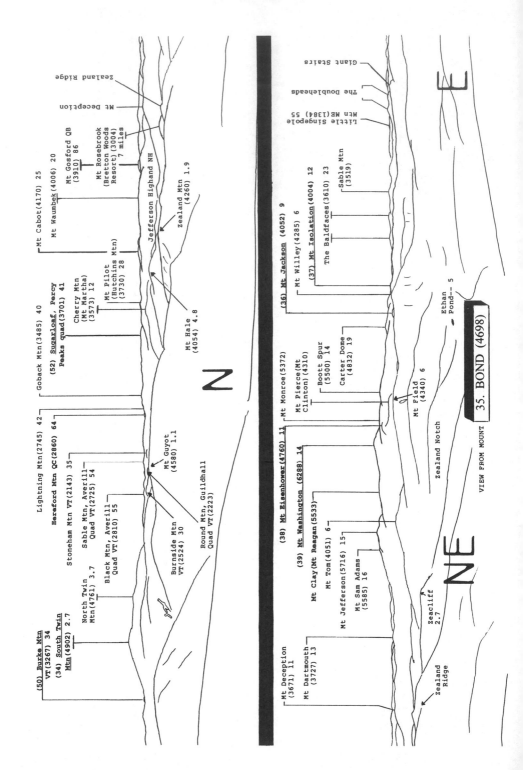

VIEW FROM MOUNT

35. BOND (4698)

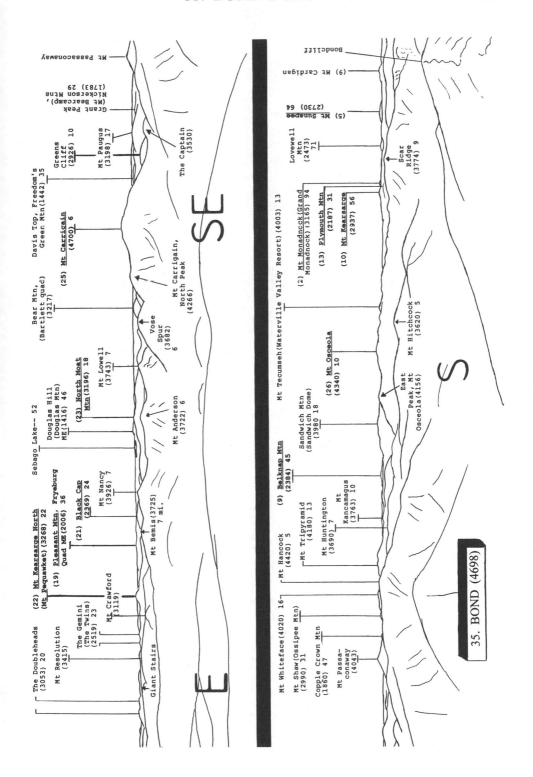

Mt Passaconaway

Grant Peak
(Mt Bearcamp),
Nickerson Mtns
(1783) 29

Greens
Cliff
(2926) 10

Mt Paugus
(3198) 17

Davis Top, Freedom's
Green Mtn(1442) 35

The Captain
(3530)

(25) Mt Carrigain
(4700) 6

Mt Carrigain,
North Peak
(4266)

Bear Mtn,
(Bartlett quad)
(3217)

Vose
Spur
(3682)
6

Mt Lowell
(3743) 7

Mt Anderson
(3722) 6

Douglas Hill
(Douglas Mtn)
ME(1416) 46

Sebago Lake-- 52

(23) North Moat
Mtn (3196) 18

Mt Nancy
(3926) 7

(21) Black Cap
(2369) 24

Mt Bemis(3725)
7 mi.

(19) Pleasant Mtn,
Fryeburg
Quad ME(2006) 36

(22) Mt Kearsarge North
(Mt Pequawket) (3268) 22

Mt Crawford
(3119)

The Gemini
(The Twins)
(2519) 23

Mt Resolution
(3315)

The Doubleheads
(3053) 20

Giant Stairs

SE

E

Bondcliff

Mt Cardigan (9)

Mt Sunapee (5)
(2730) 64

Lovewell
Mtn
(2473)
71

Scar
Ridge
(3774) 9

(2) Mt Monadnock(Grand
Monadnock) (3165) 94

(13) Plymouth Mtn
(2187) 31

(10) Mt Kearsarge
(2937) 56

Mt Tecumseh(Waterville Valley Resort) (4003) 13

Mt Hitchcock
(3620) 5

East
Peak, Mt
Osceola (4156)

(26) Mt Osceola
(4340) 10

Sandwich Mtn
(Sandwich Dome)
(3980) 18

(9) Belknap Mtn
(2384) 45

Mt Tripyramid
(4180) 13

Mt Huntington
(3690) 7

Mt
Kancamagus
(3763) 10

Mt Hancock
(4420) 5

Mt Whiteface(4020) 16

Mt Shaw(Ossipee Mtn)
(2990) 31

Copple Crown Mtn
(1860) 47

Mt Passa-
conaway
(4043)

S

35. BOND (4698)

(36) MOUNT JACKSON

N 44° 12.185'
W 71° 22.518'

(Elevation 4052 feet)

Standing as a tall sentinel along the southern Presidential Range, Mount Jackson commands a sweeping view in all directions. Although mostly tree-covered, its rocky summit cone projects above the forest thereby guaranteeing a complete panorama. The highest point in New England looms nigh for it towers a mere six miles away. We stand on the same range as Mount Washington!

The Presidential Range extends away to the northeast and features such peaks as Mounts Pierce, Eisenhower, Franklin and Monroe. These serve as stepping stones to Mount Washington. A second spur, the rather flat Montalban Range, leads away from Washington to the right. Along it lie Mounts Isolation, Davis, Stairs, Resolution and then, towards the south, Mount Crawford. This ridge blocks all but the higher mountains in the Jackson Village region.

Oakes Gulf is situated where the two ranges join. It is one of Mount Washington's several glacial cirques, the term describing a steep-walled semicircular valley carved out by former glacial action. Nestled up against the shoulder of Mount Pierce we see tonight's possible target, the AMC's Mizpah Spring Hut. The hike from Mount Jackson to Mizpah takes forty-five minutes.

Those persons traveling eastward from Zealand Falls have two routes to Mount Jackson. The first is via the Appalachian Trail. Starting as the Ethan Pond Trail, this path treks southward along a former railroad bed through Zealand Notch. It turns left passing the lovely Thoreau Falls and Ethan Pond. There follows a steep descent into Crawford Notch (N 10.016 min, W 23.161 min) to meet the Webster Cliff Trailhead (N 10.258 min, W 23.234 min). Now one rises quickly up Mount Webster and on to Jackson. The total hiking time from Zealand Falls to Mizpah Spring via Webster Cliff and Mount Jackson is 8 1/2 hours.

The Nauman Tentsite is located right next to Mizpah Hut. Those who started the day at the Ethan Pond Campsite would continue along the route described above and take but seven hours.

The second route from Zealand Falls is more sheltered from the weather. Hike straight eastward along the A-Z trail, which climbs up into the saddle between Mounts Field and Tom. It later joins the Avalon Trail as it drops down into Crawford Notch about three miles north of where the first route emerges (N 13.058 min, W 24.696 min). Locate the Webster-Jackson Trailhead 0.1 miles south of the old Crawford Depot (N 12.902 min, W 24.472 min) and begin the climb once more. Seven hours are required from Zealand Falls to Mizpah.

Should the elements warrant, Mount Jackson may be skipped entirely. Instead of the Webster-Jackson Trail, take the Crawford Path starting at the point where it leaves Route 302 (N 13.207 min, W 24.590 min). Branch right at the Mizpah cutoff and arrive at Mizpah after only six hours of hiking.

An overnight stop to consider is the nearby Appalachian Mountain Club's Highland Center at Crawford Notch. This visitor center complex is open to the public year round featuring not only food and lodging but also an extensive educational program in mountain enjoyment and safety. One will find it on Route 302 at a distance of 20 miles west of North Conway and 8.5 miles east of the intersection with Route 3 in Twin Mountain Village.

Mount Jackson by itself is a rather short hike. One can climb this peak via the Webster-Jackson Trail and return to the car in less than four hours.

Looking southwest from the summit, the companion Mount Webster rises less than a mile away. Beyond stand the previously featured Mounts Carrigain, Osceola and Loon. Westward, the imposingly steep Willey-Rosebrook Range hides most of Mounts Bond, Lafayette and South Twin. We have no blocking ridges to the northwest. We look through Crawford Notch well into Vermont and make out Mount Mansfield and Jay Peak.

Behind us, observe Maine's Pleasant Mountain, Sebago Lake, Ossipee Hill and Mount Agimenticus, the last mentioned being 76 miles away. To the south the view is blocked somewhat by the Sandwich Range. But we are able to recognize the Ossipees and some of the Belknaps. Closer to us, Chocorua's sharp peak is easy to spot. This apex stands as a singular beacon embracing the heavens.

The best features of Mount Jackson are twofold. There is the marvelous prospect of Crawford Notch as well as the close-up view one gets of Mount Washington.

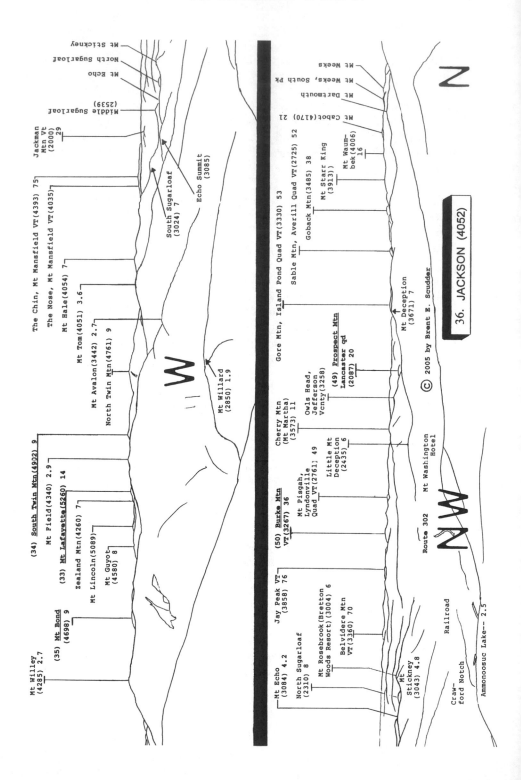

Mt Stickney

North Sugarloaf

Mt Echo

Middle Sugarloaf
(2539)

Jackman
Mtn Vt
(2000)
29

The Chin, Mt Mansfield VT(4393) 75

The Nose, Mt Mansfield VT(4035)

Mt Hale(4054) 7

Mt Tom(4051) 3.6

Mt Avalon(3442) 2.7

North Twin Mtn(4761) 9

South Sugarloaf
(3024) 7

Echo Summit
(3085)

W

Mt Willard
(2850) 1.9

(34) South Twin Mtn(4902) 9

Mt Field(4340) 2.9

(33) Mt Lafayette(5260) 14

Zealand Mtn(4260) 7

Mt Lincoln(5089)

Mt Guyot
(4580) 8

(35) Mt Bond
(4698) 9

Mt Willey
(4285) 2.7

Mt Weeks

Mt Weeks, South Pk

Mt Dartmouth

Mt Cabot(4170) 21

N

Mt Waum-
bek (4006)
16

Mt Star King
(3913)

Goback Mtn(3485) 38

Sable Mtn, Averill Quad VT(2725) 52

Gore Mtn, Island Pond Quad VT(3330) 53

Mt Deception
(3671) 7

36. JACKSON (4052)

© 2005 by Brent E. Scudder

Cherry Mtn
(Mt Martha)
(3573) 11

Owls Head,
Jefferson
Vcnty(3258)

(49) Prospect Mtn
Lancaster qd
(2087) 20

(50) Burke Mtn
VT(3267) 36

Mt Pisgah,
Lyndonville
Quad VT(2761) 49

Little Mt
Deception
(2435) 6

Mt Washington
Hotel

Route 302

NW

Jay Peak VT
(3858) 76

Mt Echo
(3084) 4.2

North Sugarloaf
(2310) 8

Mt Rosebrook(Bretton
Woods Resort)(3004) 6

Belvidere Mtn
VT(3360) 70

Mt
Stickney
(3043) 4.8

Railroad

Craw-
ford Notch

Ammonoosuc Lake-- 2.5

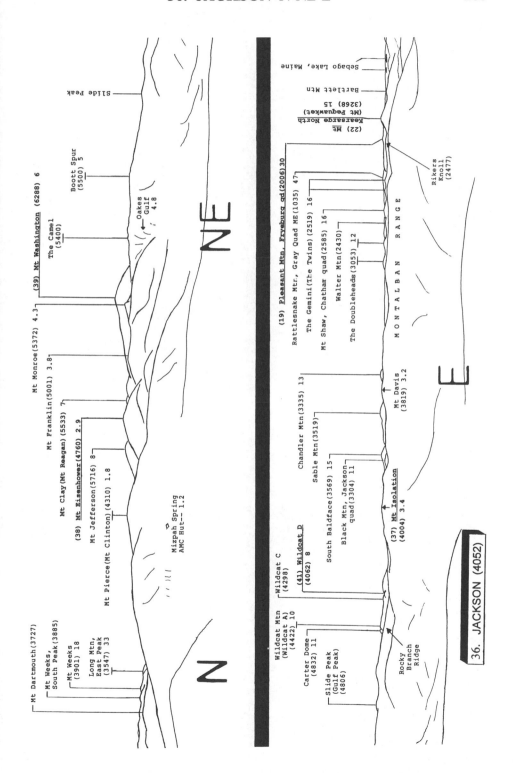

Mt Dartmouth(3727)
Mt Weeks, South Peak(3885)
Mt Weeks (3901) 18
Long Mtn, East Peak (3547) 33
Slide Peak (Gulf Peak) (4806)
Carter Dome (4832) 11
Wildcat Mtn (Wildcat A) (4422) 10
Wildcat C (4298)
(41) Wildcat D (4062) 8
South Baldface (3569) 15
Sable Mtn(3519)
Black Mtn, Jackson quad(3304) 11
Chandler Mtn(3335) 13
(37) Mt Isolation (4004) 3.4
Mt Davis (3819) 3.2
Rocky Branch Ridge

Mt Pierce(Mt Clinton) (4310) 1.8
Mizpah Spring AMC Hut-- 1.2
(38) Mt Eisenhower(4760) 2.9
Mt Jefferson(5716) 8
Mt Clay(Mt Reagan) (5533) 7
Mt Franklin(5001) 3.8
Mt Monroe(5372) 4.3
(39) Mt Washington (6288) 6
The Camel (5400)
Oakes Gulf 4.8
Boott Spur (5500) 5
Slide Peak

N

NE

E

MONTALBAN RANGE

Mt Shaw, Chatham quad(2585) 16
Walter Mtn(2430)
The Doubleheads(3053) 12
The Gemini(The Twins) (2519) 16
Rattlesnake Mtn, Gray Quad ME(1035) 47
(19) Pleasant Mtn, Fryeburg qd(2006)30
(22) Mt Kearsarge North (Mt Pequawket) (3268) 15
Bartlett Mtn
Sebago Lake, Maine
Rikers Knoll (2477)

36. JACKSON (4052)

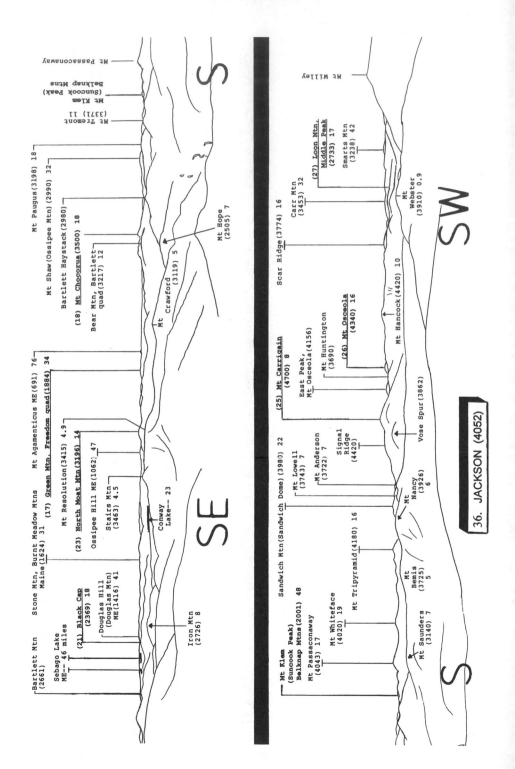

36. JACKSON (4052)

(37) MOUNT ISOLATION

N 44° 12.883'
W 71° 18.556'

(Elevation 4004 feet)

Isolation! The very name evokes images of the farthest peak from civilization, the hardest mountain to reach. As the name implies, there are no roads around its base. In the minds of those seeking to complete their list of New Hampshire's 4000 footers, Isolation seems a major obstacle, an experience best to be looked back upon.

Yet the hill is not the monster that it seems. The miles pass quickly due to a gentle ascent. The Bonds, Pemigewasset's Owl's Head, Mounts Washington and Adams all require more time and effort.

On top the hiker sees that he or she is standing in the middle of three great spurs that converge upon Mount Washington. To the west there runs the left-hand spur, the southern Presidentials which hide most of the terrain beyond. We start with Mount Webster and swing our gaze to the right past Jackson, Pierce, Eisenhower, Franklin and Monroe.

The central spur is the previously mentioned Montalban Range, which starts far to the south out of sight and runs northward towards us along Mounts Resolution, Stairs and Davis. After passing under us, this range merges with Boott Spur and joins the Mount Washington massif less than four miles away. Again we stare into Oakes Gulf which is startlingly steep.

To the east extends the right hand spur, the Rocky Branch Ridge consisting of tops nearly 4000 feet high. Beyond this ridge, Wildcat Mountain and the Carter Range appear close at hand.

While views to the north are hidden by the Presidentials, we see far to the south. To the left stands Maine's Pleasant Mountain as well as the farther off Douglas Mountain. Looking to the right, we come to New Hampshire's Moose Mountains near Wolfeboro, the Sandwich Range, Mount Moosilauke and the Franconias. Even western New Hampshire's Smarts Mountain casts a distant horizon image.

From The AMC Mizpah Spring Hut, the northbound overnight hiker has three route choices. The first is to proceed directly to AMC's Lakes of the

MOUNT ISOLATION

Clouds Hut, a hike of only three hours. It is also a hike over rock and crag exposed to the furious gales that often sweep over the Presidentials.

In stormy weather, stay off the ridge. Using the Dry River Cutoff, descend into the valley below. Assuming that the Dry River is not in flood (despite its name), hike northward along the trail and climb out through Oakes Gulf to find the Lakes not too far over the lip. This trip takes five hours.

Option three includes Mount Isolation. Again drop into the Dry River Valley but turn south a short distance to meet the Isolation Trail. Climb the latter to the ridge until you run into the Davis Path. Turn south again and travel more than a mile to the top of Isolation. In order to reach Lakes of the Clouds from here, go north. After ascending the exposed Boott Spur, swing around to the west to arrive at your destination. Estimate seven hours from hut to hut.

Anyone intending to hike up and back will find that the gentlest route to Isolation is the Rocky Branch Trail leaving from Route 16 (N 12.285 min, W 14.436 min). Drive 5.5 miles north on that highway from the Jackson village cutoff and look to the left for the trail sign. Parking space is ample. The path climbs westward over a saddle in the Rocky Branch Ridge, angles downward into a small valley and turns left. Turn right instead. The Isolation Trail starts here climbing north and then west to join the Davis Path. Turn left for the summit. Allow nine hours for the round trip.

You may ask, "From the Rocky Branch Trail, why can't I just bushwhack straight west across to Davis Path and go north?"

The map certainly invites you to do so. One would save plenty of distance but little time, a half an hour at best. Hiking through trackless forest slows and tires a person far more than he or she may realize. Each step through brush is the equivalent of taking three steps along a path. First you raise the foot higher than normal to step over underbrush. As you place the foot forward, your backpack has caught upon branches. You thrust your body forward to free it, not always with success. We tried this route but elected to return the long way. No, this bushwhack is not recommended.

No casual tourist sees Mount Isolation's unique view. The three ridges converging upon Mount Washington along with the towering Oakes Gulf is a picture reserved only for the dedicated climber.

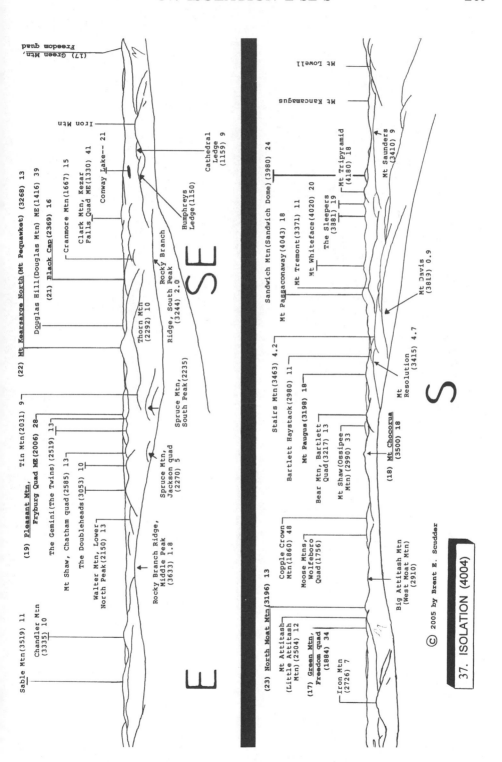

37. ISOLATION (4004)

© 2005 by Brent E. Scudder

E

Sable Mtn(3519) 11
Chandler Mtn (3335) 10

(23) North Moat Mtn(3196) 13

Mt Attitash (Little Attitash Mtn)(2504) 12

(17) Green Mtn, Freedom quad (1884) 34

Iron Mtn (2726) 7

Copple Crown Mtn(1860) 48

Moose Mtns Wolfeboro Quad(1756)

Rocky Branch Ridge, Middle Peak (3633) 1.8

Walter Mtn, Lower North Peak (2150) 13

The Doubleheads(3053) 10

Mt Shaw, Chatham quad(2585) 13

The Gemini(The Twins) (2519) 13

(19) Pleasant Mtn, Fryburg Quad ME(2006) 28

Tin Mtn(2031) 9

Spruce Mtn, Jackson quad (2270) 5

Spruce Mtn, South Peak (2235)

(22) Mt Kearsarge North (Mt Pequawket) (3268) 13

Douglas Hill(Douglas Mtn) ME(1416) 39

(21) Black Cap(2369) 16

Thorn Mtn (2292) 10

Ridge, South Peak (3244) 2.0

Rocky Branch

Cranmore Mtn(1667) 15

Clark Mtn, Kezar Falls Quad ME(1330) 41

Conway Lake— 21

Humphreys Ledge(1150)

Iron Mtn

(17) Green Mtn, Freedom quad

Cathedral Ledge (1159) 9

SE

Sandwich Mtn(Sandwich Dome)(3980) 24

Mt Passaconaway (4043) 18

Mt Tremont(3371) 11

Mt Whiteface(4020) 20

The Sleepers (3381) 19

Mt Tripyramid (4180) 18

Mt Saunders (3410) 9

Mt Kancamagus

Mt Lowell

Stairs Mtn(3463) 4.2

Bartlett Haystack(2980) 11

Mt Parker(3198) 18

Bear Mtn, Bartlett Quad(3217) 13

Mt Shaw(Ossipee Mtn) (2990) 33

(18) Mt Chocorua (3500) 18

Mt Resolution (3415) 4.7

Mt Davis (3819) 0.9

Big Attitash Mtn (West Moat Mtn) (2910)

S

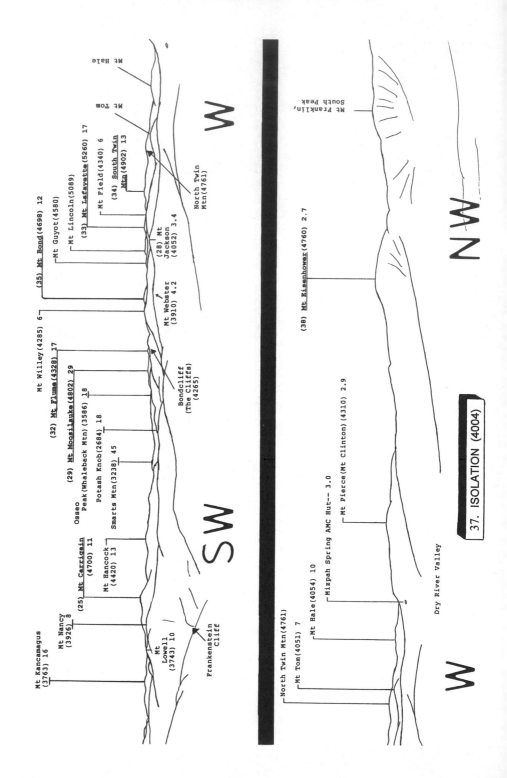

37. ISOLATION (4004)

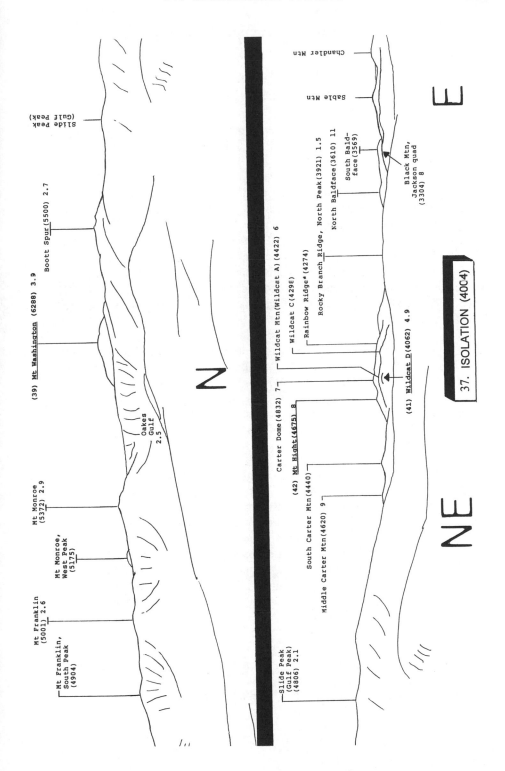

Mt Franklin (5001) 2.6

Mt Franklin, South Peak (4904)

Mt Monroe, West Peak (5175)

Mt Monroe (5372) 2.9

(39) Mt Washington (6288) 3.9

Boott Spur (5500) 2.7

Slide Peak (Gulf Peak)

Oakes Gulf 2.5

N

Slide Peak (Gulf Peak) (4806) 2.1

Middle Carter Mtn (4620) 9

South Carter Mtn (4440)

(42) Mt Hight (4675) 8

Carter Dome (4832) 7

Wildcat Mtn (Wildcat A) (4422) 6

Wildcat C (4298)

Rainbow Ridge* (4274)

Rocky Branch Ridge, North Peak (3921) 1.5

North Baldface (3610) 11

South Baldface (3569)

Black Mtn, Jackson quad (3304) 8

(41) Wildcat D (4062) 4.9

Sable Mtn

Chandler Mtn

NE

E

37. ISOLATION (40C4)

(38) MOUNT EISENHOWER

N 44 deg 14.443'
W 71 deg 21.002'

(Elevation 4760 feet)

Have you ever noticed that several mountains along the Presidential Range have not been named after chief executives? State Geologist Charles Jackson along with Messers. Daniel Webster and Benjamin Franklin were never inaugurated. The Julyan's book, *PLACE NAMES OF THE WHITE MOUNTAINS,* describes the effort which took place early in the Nineteenth Century to have the names of New Hampshire's highest mountains honor our presidents. Mount Washington had been mentioned in map and manuscript since 1792. Why not label adjacent high peaks with the names of subsequent heads of state?

In 1820, seven people guided by local resident Ethan Allen Crawford hiked into these mountains on a Presidential naming expedition. Of the mountains in New Hampshire's highest range, there are nine. But only five presidents had been sworn in. Consequently, a certain rounded peak three miles southwest of Mount Washington escaped a presidential label. Initially known as Dome Mountain (a perfect name), the 1820 expedition changed it to Mount Pleasant.

The effort to name a mountain for Dwight D. Eisenhower first met with a chilly reception. It was not the idea of honoring a famous World War II general and subsequent two-term president that aroused anger. It was the mountain originally selected to bear "Ike's" name – Chocorua. Carrying this project through would have trampled upon the wonderful associations and memories that hundreds of thousands of people have had for this legendary peak. A more agreeable decision was reached. As with Chocorua, Mount Pleasant stood out against the sky in sharp relief, its elevation far higher. Best of all, this summit is part of the Presidential Range. In 1972, Mount Pleasant officially became Mount Eisenhower.

At the top, look to the southwest and note that our 4760-foot elevation transforms the once gigantic Mounts Pierce, Jackson and Webster into mere mounds. Turn around and behold Mounts Jefferson, Clay and Washington still looking down at us. We have much higher to climb.

MOUNT EISENHOWER

No AMC huts are in sight. The place where we may spend the night, Lakes of the Clouds, is hidden by Mount Monroe

Perhaps the shortest way from the road is via the Edmands Path, which approaches the Presidential Range from the west. Drive northbound on Route 302 into Crawford Notch. After passing the AMC Highland Center, take your first right (Signs will point to Crawford Path parking). This is the Clinton Mountain Road (named for De Witt Clinton, an early governor of New York). Go 2.4 miles to reach the Edmands Path trailhead (N 14.925 min, W 23.501 min). The climb should take two hours and forty-five minutes. Clinton Mountain Road is closed during the coldest months. Winter hikers would then have to seek Mount Eisenhower via the Crawford Path (featured two chapters ago).

Again at the summit, one turns his gaze southeastward and easily sees beyond the Montalban Range to discover Kearsarge North sixteen miles away. One also recognizes Maine's Sebago Lake distant to the left. Farther right the land becomes flatter as we look out upon Maine's Atlantic coastal plain peppered by the occasional Clark Mountain, Ossipee Hill and Fort Ridge.

Directly south, the Dry River Valley lies at our feet with Mounts Chocorua, Shaw and Belknap on the horizon. Sandwich Range appears to the right and hides the more distant Monadnock, Kearsarge and Cardigan.

Look west. Because we are higher than Mount Jackson, the Willey-Rosebrook range is less of a shield. Yet such towering masses as Moosilauke, Lincoln and Lafayette remain nearly hidden by the Bonds and the Twins.

To the northwest, gaze upon the golf course near the Mount Washington Hotel, upon Twin Mountain village ten miles away and upon the Vermont skyline. See Camels Hump on the left and Mount Mansfield on the right, the latter requiring careful scrutiny to locate. Also needing a good eye to find is Quebec's Sommet Rond. First look for Cherry Mountain's Owls Head ten miles away. Using the sun as a mental yardstick, go to the horizon past Owls Head and then look one solar diameter to the right. If we can see 84 miles, Sommet Rond appears between Vermont's Mounts Hor and Pisgah.

To the north below us lies Mount Washington's Cog Railway. The dense black smoke of the steam engine is apparent even before one recognizes the train. As tourist upon tourist pours aboard the "pufferbilly," take satisfaction that you are about to climb Mount Washington under your own steam.

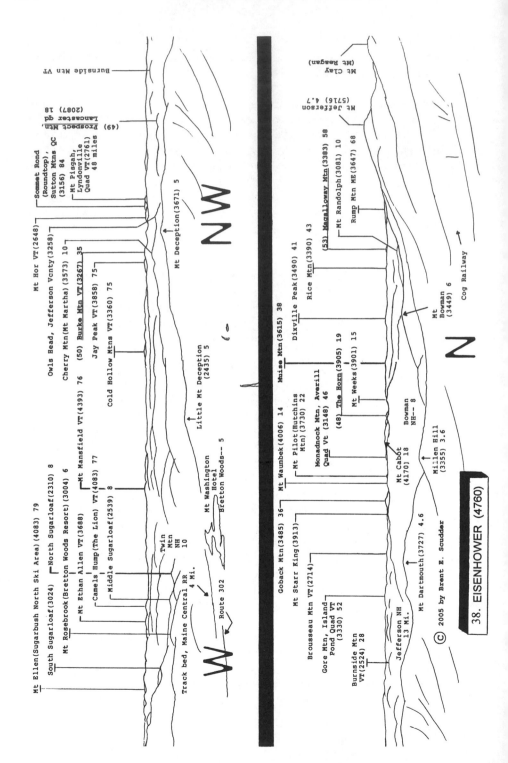

38. EISENHOWER (4760)

© 2005 by Brent E. Scudder

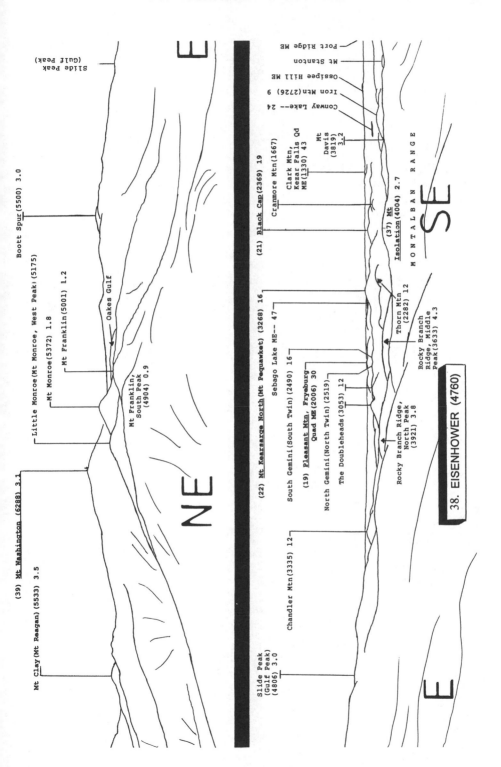

(39) Mt Washington (6288) 3.1

Mt Clay (Mt Reagan) (5533) 3.5

Boott Spur (5500) 3.0

Slide Peak
(Gulf Peak)

Little Monroe (Mt Monroe, West Peak) (5175)

Mt Monroe (5372) 1.8

Mt Franklin (5001) 1.2

Oakes Gulf

Mt Franklin,
South Peak
(4904) 0.9

NE

(22) Mt Kearsarge North (Mt Pequawket) (3268) 16

Sebago Lake ME-- 47

South Gemini (South Twin) (2490) 16

(19) Pleasant Mtn, Fryeburg
Quad ME (2006) 30

North Gemini (North Twin) (2519)

The Doubleheads (3053) 12

Chandler Mtn (3335) 12

Slide Peak
(Gulf Peak)
(4806) 3.0

Rocky Branch Ridge,
North Peak
(3921) 3.8

Rocky Branch
Ridge, Middle
Peak (3633) 4.3

Thorn Mtn
(2282) 12

(21) Black Cap (2369) 19

Cranmore Mtn (1667)

Clark Mtn,
Kezar Falls Qd
ME (1330) 43

Mt
Davis
(3819)
3.2

(37) Mt
Isolation (4004) 2.7

M O N T A L B A N   R A N G E

Port Ridge ME

Mt Stanton

Ossipee Hill ME

Iron Mtn (2726) 9

Conway Lake-- 24

SE

E

38. EISENHOWER (4760)

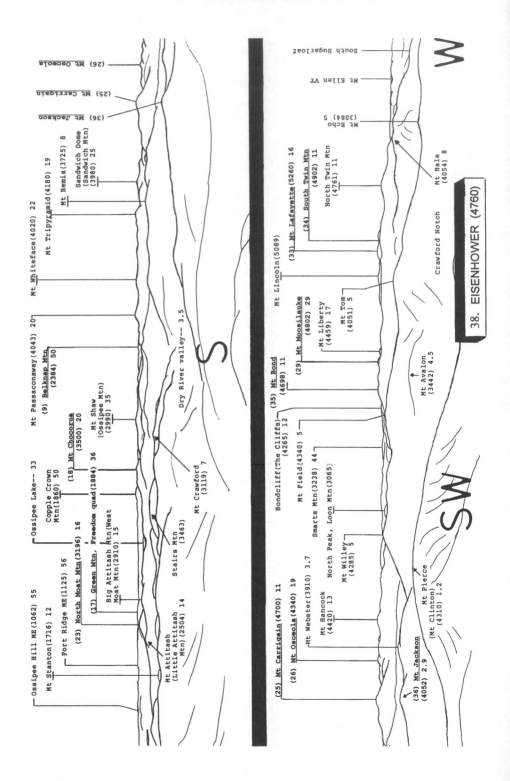

(39) MOUNT WASHINGTON

N 44° 16.224'
W 71° 18.184'

(Elevation 6288 feet)

"STOP!"

"THE AREA AHEAD HAS THE WORST WEATHER IN AMERICA"

"MANY HAVE DIED THERE FROM EXPOSURE,

EVEN IN THE SUMMER"

"TURN BACK IF THE WEATHER IS BAD"

"....White Mountain National Forest"

We encountered this stark warning years ago while climbing in the Presidential Range just prior to breaking out above timberline....and do they mean it! One or two lives are lost annually not to mention several people who suffer injury. Search and rescue activity is well organized and largely handled by volunteer work. But if a hiker requires rescue due to his own blatantly stupid decisions, New Hampshire law requires said person to pay for his own rescue to the tune of several thousand dollars.

Have you ever been outdoors during the summer when the temperature stands at 40 degrees Fahrenheit, and a sixty mile an hour wind blows thick fog into your face? You can barely see a cairn of rocks just fifty feet away. We are describing a wind chill equivalent temperature of 25 degrees, conditions that often occur on Mount Washington during June, July and August.

Have you ever been outdoors during winter, when the temperature stands at minus 20 degrees Fahrenheit, and an 80 mile per hour wind raises powder snow into a whirling white that totally obscures your companion who is standing only ten feet away? The wind chill temperature is now minus 66 degrees – typical Antarctic weather – conditions occurring frequently on Mount Washington during December, January and February.*

---

* See footnote on next page

A hidden danger exists when interpreting the wind chill formula. Wind chill is expressed as an equivalent temperature, but actually measures how quickly heat is removed from a body – a DRY warm body. A person may be damp from perspiration during the exertion of a climb. He may have been thoroughly wetted by a brief but heavy cold shower of rain. Not only does the gale experienced above timberline carry away body heat, it also evaporates the moisture on a person cooling him far more. There may not exist a wind chill factor chart for someone who is soaking wet, but given the worst summertime weather on Mount Washington, the hiker will swear that the actual temperature is far below zero.

"MANY HAVE DIED HERE....EVEN IN SUMMER"

"TURN BACK NOW IF THE WEATHER IS BAD"

Most summer climbs of other New Hampshire Peaks require that a person just take along a sweater. The sheltering woods usually grow to within a few feet of the summit. One only needs to poke his head slightly above tree line in order to have before him an excellent view. But Mount Washington not only rises above timberline; it projects heavenward well into the freely moving upper air stream. Expect the summit to be 22 degrees colder than in Pinkham Notch and 30 degrees colder than in North Conway. Here we assume that no cold front passes during the climb. Plan on the wind, even in summer, to be 35 miles per hour or stronger....usually stronger.

Allow the newcomer to Mount Washington to lack sufficient clothing for comfort. We are not proposing that the initiate place himself in danger. But let his shivering body and chattering teeth tell him that this mountain can kill!

Many casual visitors are so initiated. As sleet pelts the top in late June, I have seen them wearing a sweater or light windbreaker over shorts and polo shirts as they emerge from the Cog Railway train, the Glen House Stage or their own cars. They race into the summit building jumping around and blowing into cupped hands for warmth. The view is clouded with swirling mist causing disbelief among those eyeing the post cards in the gift shop depicting Mount Washington's top as tranquil with open views.

---

* (See the previous page) Since the last edition, meteorologists have felt that the existing wind chill formula was unrealistic in that it gave values that seemed too extreme. The equation has been revised. Using the old formula, the winter example given on page 217 gave you a wind chill value of –88 degrees. But even the milder –66 degrees is much too cold for anything but the best of Polar clothing.

Estimating distance above tree line is deceptive. The rocks flanking this mountain are of no particular size, and so the eye cannot guess the distance to the top. Gaze from Lakes of the Clouds, and the summit seems but twenty minutes away. But examine the scene more closely. Do you see those hikers who are half way to the top? Do you see how tiny they are? I was never able to cover that distance in less than 75 minutes.

During adverse conditions, the decision not to turn back is often influenced by the warm shelter of the summit buildings. These structures are closed during the colder months. Climb only in groups headed by experienced leaders and with proper equipment. Any member not in the best of health and physical shape can jeopardize the lives of the rest of the party.

The Mount Washington weather report may be found on the Internet at <www.mountwashington.org>. The report is also posted at the Cog Railway Base, at Glen House, the Appalachian Mountain Club's Pinkham Notch Visitor's Center on Route 16 and also their Highlands Center at Crawford Notch. The AMC centers mentioned here are open year round. In checking these postings, note whether the forecast calls for worse than the present summit conditions. Even if it does not, people tend to forget that a weather forecast is not a statement etched in stone. It is not a guarantee.

Mount Washington is in cloud during all or part of 315 days a year. While the A.T. hiker may be resigned to passing this great peak during reduced visibility, day hikers hope for better conditions, especially if they have come from a great distance. As mentioned in the Introduction, Appendix A lists six simple weather forecasting rules for predicting days of excellent viewing.

In 1642, Darby Field made Mount Washington's first recorded climb. At that time Algonquins called it Waumbik, meaning "White Rocks," while Abenakis said Kodaak Wadjo, the "Highest Summit." Others labeled it Waumbeket Methna, "Mountain of the Snowy Brow," and some said Agiocook, "Dwelling of the Great Spirit." Crystal Hill, White Hill and Sugarloaf were names given by early Colonial settlers. Mount Washington appeared in manuscript in 1792 and thereby honored the great Revolutionary War general while he was still alive.

Tourism to this peak began when Ethan Allen Crawford along with his father built the first trail to the top in 1819. Trips became frequent by tourists from the hotels that slowly sprouted during the Nineteenth Century. The present Crawford Path follows much of the original course and is considered to be the oldest trail in America that has been under continuous maintenance.

Residents in the year 1861 saw the opening of the Carriage Road (now the Auto Road)) which runs from Pinkham Notch to the top. From the west comes the Cog Railway completed eight years later. These two ways to the summit were the first of their kind in America if not the world.

The first "Summit House" was built in 1852. One could stay overnight and enjoy some of the spectacular effects of aurora, moonlight, sunrises and sunsets over the clouds below. Environmental concerns led to the phasing out of overnight facilities. The present Sherman Adams Building provides food service, a gift shop, telephones, a post office and a museum. The Mount Washington Observatory has operated continuously since 1932. The world's highest wind speed recorded by an on-site instrument occurred here in 1934, namely 231 miles per hour. Such a gale will lift you off the mountain. Higher winds occur in tornadoes of the F5 classification as well as in the stronger F4. But these whirlwinds destroy any instruments set up for direct measurement.

When visiting North Conway, stop by at the Mount Washington Center located across Main Street from the Eastern Slope Inn. It is a combination museum and book shop dealing with all aspects of the mountain. The Mount Washington web site (www.mountwashington.org) lists times when it is open.

The summit view stretches from the Atlantic Ocean to Grand Monadnock, from New York's Mount Marcy to Vermont's Mansfield and from Quebec's Orford to Maine's Bigelow. One looks across more than four degrees of latitude and six degrees of longitude – an area larger than Pennsylvania.

Most spectacular is the view to the north. Watch the Presidential Peaks march away in the forms of Mounts Clay, Jefferson, Adams and Madison. Peer down into the deep abyss between here and Mount Adams – the Great Gulf. On the horizon is Canada. See Hereford Mountain on the left, Megantic in the center and Gosford on the right. Closer to us, the Mahoosuc Mountains start near Mount Madison and draw away towards the northeast exhibiting such names as Hayes, Baldcap, Success, Goose Eye and Old Speck. Mahoosuc means "Land of hungry animals." The Appalachian Trail hiker will soon encounter these.

On the skyline, we see Maine's Kennebagos, Bigelow and Abraham. Maine's highest mountain, the 5267-foot Katahdin has never been visible from here. While the extreme range of 163 miles does not rule out our ever seeing it, the Earth's curvature does. A strategically placed mountain 1640 feet high would hide Katahdin from Washington. Standing in the way is the visible 4049-foot Mount Abraham and the hidden 3520-foot Baker Mountain located east of Moosehead Lake. It would take perfect visibility and too much atmospheric refraction for us to ever be able to spot Katahdin from Mount Washington.

Glen House can be seen below us to the east. Above it rises the Carter-Moriah range. We gaze past these peaks and see that the mountains have grown smaller as the eye approaches the Atlantic. Look for the ocean over the crest of Wildcat D. You must be on Mount Washington before 9 a.m. during July and August in order to catch the sun's glint off the Gulf of Maine. As mentioned earlier, the sun's angle changes rapidly after Labor Day requiring one to reach the top earlier and earlier in order to see the ocean.

We get a second chance to see the Atlantic. At 11:30 a.m. (11 a.m. after October first) the sun lights up the waters of Massachusetts Bay. Look for a bright spot on the horizon well beyond Conway Lake. If it is too late in the day, then there is no way to see it. As earlier stated, during other times of the day, the water as seen through the haze becomes the same color as the land and is therefore hard to spot.

Maine's Pleasant Mountain stands before Sebago Lake on the left and the pointed Kearsarge North on the right. In between, note how the twin peaks of the Gemini are lined up above the Doubleheads. Descend by way of the Lion Head Trail, and the effect becomes more spectacular. At about the 5000-foot level, the more distant Gemini are seen between the Doubleheads. The effect is that of sighting along a rifle barrel.

To the south, Boott Spur divides into the Rocky Branch Ridge and the Montalban Range. To the right, the southern Presidentials begin with the nearby steep-sided Mount Monroe and extends all the way to Mount Webster.

New Hampshire's insignificant Piscataquog Mountain normally blocks the Bay State's Wachusett Mountain. But bring your binoculars and hope for a day not only of super visibility but of sufficient atmospheric refraction. You may see Wachusett.

If we take in the view to the southwest, we behold a tangle of peaks familiar only if we have climbed them. From Chocorua on the left to Lafayette on the right, we count fifteen peaks that we have featured in this book. Beyond them one sees far into southern Vermont as we take note of Okemo Mountain and Killington Peak.

To the west, we can easily see the Bretton Woods ski area on Mount Rosebrook. But the horizon has more interest. We recognize the principal peaks of Vermont's Green Mountains with Camels Hump cutting the most distinctive profile. If visible, New York's Mount Marcy will be found 134 miles away a little to the left of Camels Hump. Mansfield shows forth over the top of nearby Mount Deception, but its flat profile belies its importance as Vermont's highest crest. Gaze northwest to the right of nearby Owls Head and note Quebec's Sutton Mountains 86 miles away. To the left stands Vermont's northernmost ski area, Jay Peak.

The northbound A.T. hiker may have either started his day at the Hermit Lake shelters in Tuckerman Ravine or at AMC's Lakes of the Clouds Hut. It takes 2 1/2 hours to reach the summit from Hermit Lake and about 90 minutes from the Hut. The choices for tonight's destination include one of several shelters or else the AMC Madison Hut. The nearest shelter, The Perch, is located near Edmands Col. One reaches the Col in a little over two hours and the shelter after an additional 30 minutes. Should you choose the loop trails over Mounts Clay and Jefferson, add another forty minutes. Madison Hut can be reached 3 1/2 hours after leaving Mount Washington. The loop trails over Clay, Jefferson and Adams will add another 70 minutes.

Day hikers may choose among several trails. One can climb Washington numerous times and never see the same trail twice. Climb during the summer before branching out into other seasons.

Suppose your party is hiking up a trail with the wind at your back. Eventually you find yourselves well above treeline. A storm descends and the breeze behind you picks up to 50 knots. Soon members of your group are shivering. They may become hypothermic. You do not feel all that warm yourself. No one wishes to retreat towards timberline into the teeth of this numbing storm. It might seem easier to take the possibly fatal choice of climbing with the wind towards the summit buildings. Had you chosen a trail where you were climbing against the wind your obvious choice would have been to let the gale chase you quickly towards the welcoming warmer forest.

Weather worsens very quickly with altitude. How quickly? Late one April I was climbing Passaconaway. The snow depth increased from one inch at the 3000-foot level to hip deep at 4000 feet. I did not have snowshoes. Leaving post holes in the snow is extremely tiring.

Since the most persistent gales blow from the northwest, try your first climb from the southeast. Take Route 16 from North Conway up into Pinkham Notch. Anyone may stop in at AMC's Pinkham Notch Visitor Center and soak up some of the alpine ambiance prior to ascent. The Tuckerman Ravine Trail starts here (N 15.466 min, W 15.191 min). Two hours of climbing through forest brings you into the open onto the floor of the ravine where a massive semicircular wall of rock towers all about. Continue up the ravine, but do not climb on or under the snow arch at the other end, which may persist into July. Its collapse once claimed a victim. Although the summit wind can roar down the ravine floor, most often the gale passes above. The advantage of this trail is that one is usually protected from the full force of the elements until late in the climb. Once exposed at the ravine's rim, the party can retreat quickly back to relative safety. **Forget this route during winter and early spring!** You are climbing an incredibly steep snow slope, which is icy and prone to avalanche. Use the Lion Head Trail instead but climb it with extreme caution!

If you ascend from the west, consider the Ammonusuc Ravine Trail. Here, one has the advantage of being in sheltering forest and scrub up to within several hundred yards of the "Lakes" Hut. If the building is not open, then its leeward side provides a windbreak. However, the upper part of this trail is hazardous during wet or icy conditions.

To reach this trail, drive to the intersection of Route 302 with the road to the Cog Railway. Proceed up the latter road 5.6 miles and find a parking lot on the right (N 16.022 min, W 21.645 min). The trail is steep in sections but with many excellent views. Three hours are required to reach the AMC hut with an additional 90 minutes under normal conditions to reach the top.

Mount Washington is dangerous if not treated with respect. Still, tens of thousands people climb its slopes annually with no more injury than stiff knees or sore feet. The view of countless mountains with an infinite variety of profiles is not to be missed. Rare in the Northeast are the deep ravines and glacial cirques. The view has changed little since the days of Darby Field. Think of the bushwhacking that he had to do!

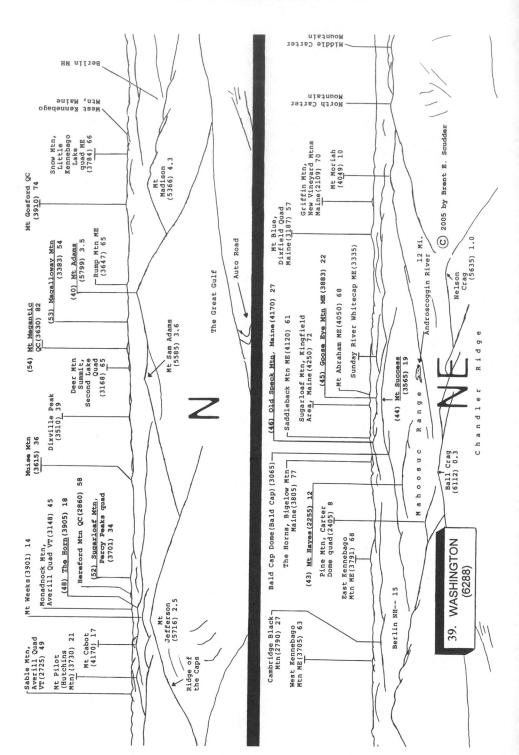

39. WASHINGTON (6288)

© 2005 by Brent E. Scudder

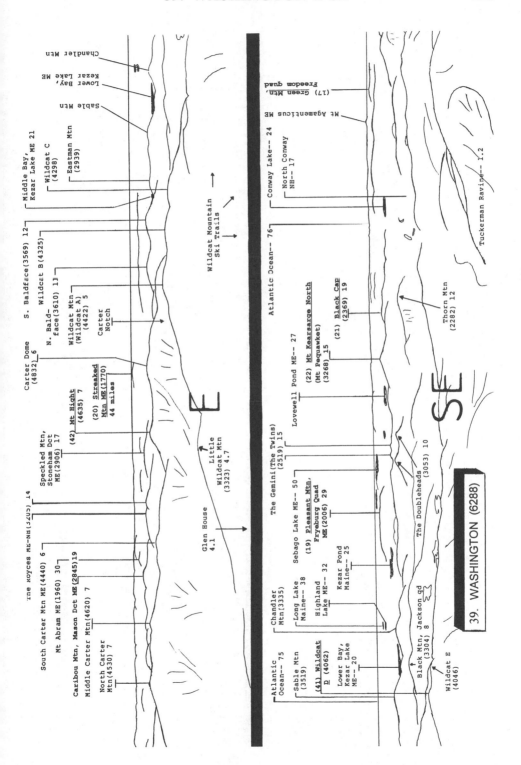

39. WASHINGTON (6288)

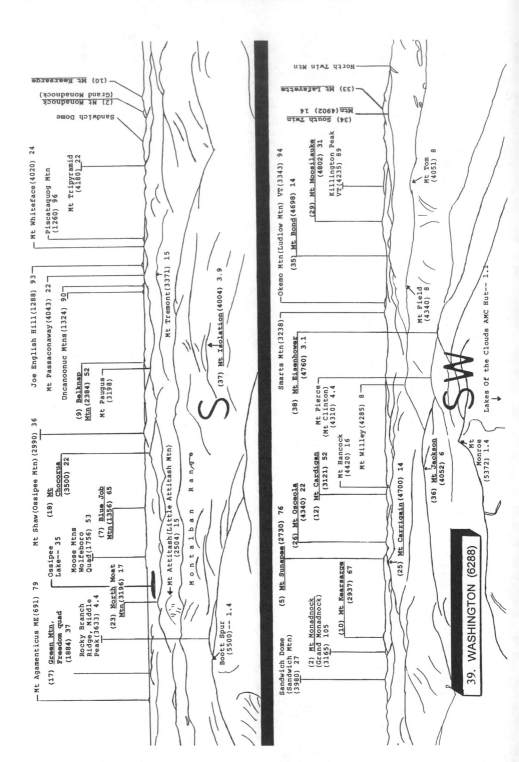

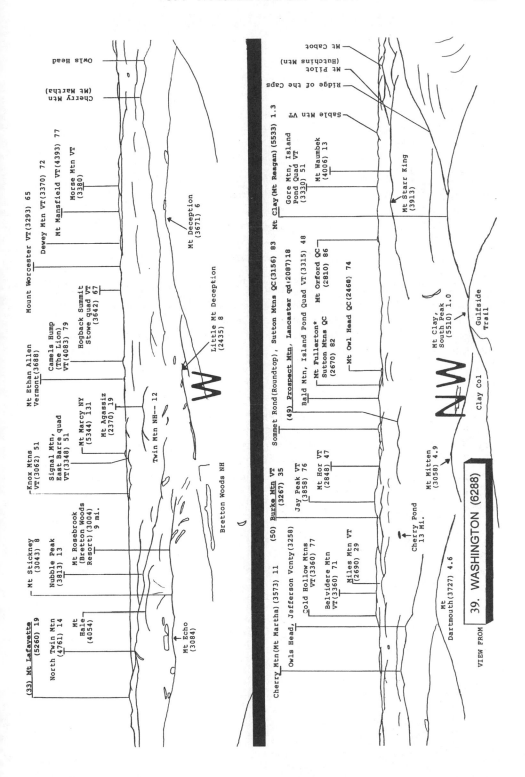

(33) Mt Lafayette
(5260) 19

North Twin Mtn
(4761) 14

Mt Hale
(4054)

Mt Echo
(3084)

Mt Stickney
(3043) 8

Nubble Peak
(3813) 13

Mt Rosebrook
(Bretton Woods
Resort)(3004)
9 mi.

Knox Mtns
VT(3062) 51

Signal Mtn,
East Barre quad
VT(3348) 51

Mt Marcy NY
(5344) 131

Mt Agassiz
(2370) 19

Twin Mtn NH-- 12

Bretton Woods NH

Mt Ethan Allen
Vermont(3688)

Camels Hump
(The Lion)
VT(4083) 79

Hogback Summit
Stowe quad VT
(3642) 67

Little Mt Deception
(2435) 8

W

Mount Worcester VT(3293) 65

Dewey Mtn VT(3370) 72

Mt Mansfield VT(4393) 77

Morse Mtn VT
(3380)

Mt Deception
(3671) 6

Cherry Mtn
(Mt Martha)

Owls Head

VIEW FROM   39. WASHINGTON (6288)

Mt
Dartmouth(3727) 4.6

Cherry Mtn(Mt Martha) (3573) 11   (50) Burke Mtn VT
(3267) 35

Owls Head, Jefferson Vcnty(3258)

Cold Hollow Mtns
VT(3360) 77

Belvidere Mtn
VT(3360) 71

Miles Mtn VT
(2690) 29

Jay Peak VT
(3858) 76

Mt Hor VT
(2848) 47

Cherry Pond
13 Mi.

Mt Mitten
(3058) 4.9

NW

Clay Col

Sommet Rond(Roundtop), Sutton Mtns QC(3156) 83

(49) Prospect Mtn, Lancaster qd(2087)18

Bald Mtn, Island Pond Quad VT(3315) 48

Mt Fullerton*
Sutton Mtns QC
(2670) 82

Mt Orford QC
(2810) 86

Mt Owl Head QC(2460) 74

Mt Clay,
South Peak
(5510) 1.0

Gulfside
Trail

Mt Clay(Mt Reagan) (5533) 1.3

Gore Mtn, Island
Pond Quad VT
(3330) 51

Mt Waumbek
(4006) 13

Mt Starr King
(3913)

Sable Mtn VT
(3380)

Ridge of the Caps

Mt Pilot
(Hutchins Mtn)

Mt Cabot

(40) MOUNT ADAMS

N 44° 19.245'
W 71° 17.531'

(Elevation 5799 feet)

Climbing Mount Adams may be the toughest trail ascent in the northeast. One gains 4500 feet of elevation from the road. Compare that with Mount Washington where, from Pinkham Notch one rises 4250 feet. If you climb Mount Adams, think of it as climbing Mount Washington – only higher.

Mount Adams towers well above timberline and so must be accorded the same respect for wicked weather as with Mount Washington. Winter storms assail the top with great ferocity. During the warm season, the pointed summit cone makes Adams a particularly attractive lightning target. In a similar vein the Atherius Society believes that beings from outer space have charged this peak with spiritual energy. Certain religious cults are positive that malevolent spirits haunt the top. We may have kept these poltergeists at bay because we had checked the weather beforehand as carefully as we would have for Mount Washington.

From the apex, one cannot help but look south along the Presidential Range. One gazes across such deep glacial indentations as Jefferson Ravine and the Great Gulf upward to the rising crests that culminate with Mount Washington. We scan much of the Auto Road serpentinely slithering up upon Chandler Ridge. One can almost see the January gale sweeping huge masses of white powder snow across the Great Gulf and up the steep pitch on the far side dumping foot after foot upon the hapless toll road.

If we scan to the right, the Clay and Jefferson summits approach us. We see beyond them and discover such New Hampshire tops as Kearsarge and Cardigan. Closer in are the White Mountains such as Sandwich Dome, Tecumseh, Osceola, Willey and Bond.

Nearby to the west lies Cherry Mountain with its famous Owls Head on the north end. We must gaze outward eighty miles in order to encounter the magnificent landmark of Vermont's Camels Hump along with the flat-ridged Mount Mansfield.

To the northwest look beyond the nearby towns of Jefferson and Lancaster. Vermont's Burke Mountain and Jay Peak rise up from left to right, respectively. New Hampshire's tall Cabot does not impress us from here. But on Cabot's eastern ridge, the steep cones of The Bulge and The Horn rise precipitously. Closer in lies the Pond of Safety; so named because four supposed deserters from the Revolutionary War had taken refuge there. The group was later exonerated due to extenuating circumstances.

The day hiker has a vast trail choice. The shortest way is from the north. Drive west out of Gorham on Route 2. When you have left Route 16 behind by 5.5 miles, seek a parking lot on the left (N 22.238 min, W 17.351 min). Signs indicate several ways up the mountain. Try the Airline Trail for you gain altitude quickly while you are still fresh.

Those who are headed for Maine along the Appalachian Trail may have awakened this morning at the shelter located near the top of Cascade Ravine called The Perch. They can reach Mount Adams in ninety minutes. Anyone who watched the sunrise at AMC's Lakes of the Clouds Hut needs but five hours to get here plus an extra half hour if Mount Washington was to have been included along the way. Had you started from Madison Hut this morning with tonight's target the AMC's Pinkham Notch Visitor Center on Route 16 (N 15.466 min, W 15.191 min) you encounter no peak with a diagrammed view. However, make a side trip up Mount Adams via the Star Lake Trail and add only an hour and forty minutes to a 4 1/2 hour hike.

At the top of Adams look north. Quebec's Mount Megantic is but a welt on the horizon. Farther right appear Rump Mountain, Aziscohos and the Kennebagos. Umbagog Lake is dimly seen in the middle distance while the towns of Milan, Berlin and Gorham's Upper Village lie before it.

Beyond Mount Madison stand the Mahoosuc Mountains, each of which is hard to distinguish because we look down the length of the range. To the east, the Carter-Moriahs loom forth with the lesser Maine tops beyond. We culminate our scan with Wildcat Mountain, seen farther off than before but with its ski trails plainly visible.

To stand near the north end of the Presidential Range is to look into wild country. We have left familiar lands. We have left the casual tourist behind. (Or have we)?

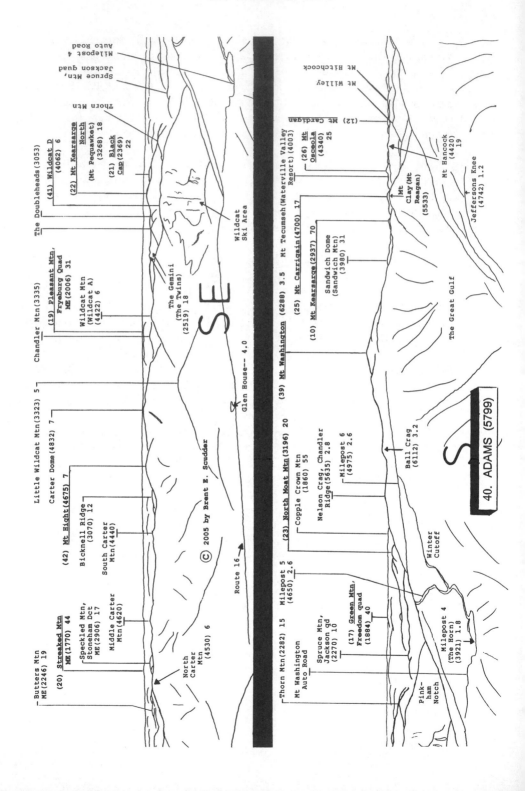

40. ADAMS (5799)

© 2005 by Brent E. Scudder

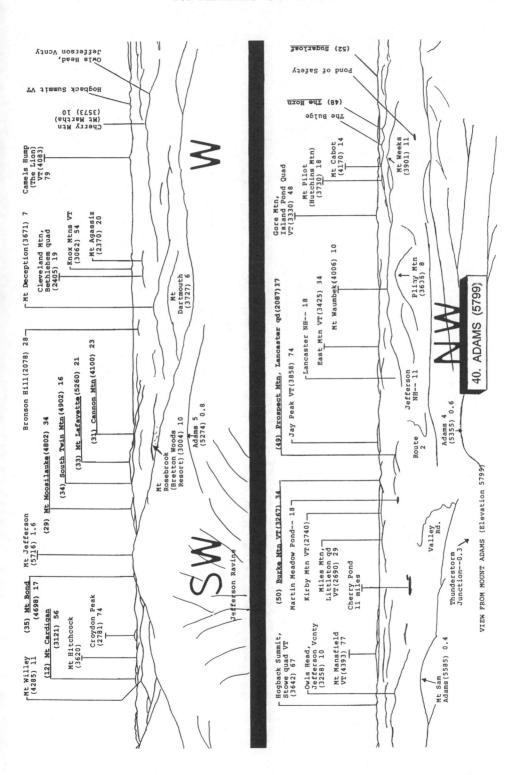

VIEW FROM MOUNT ADAMS (Elevation 5799)

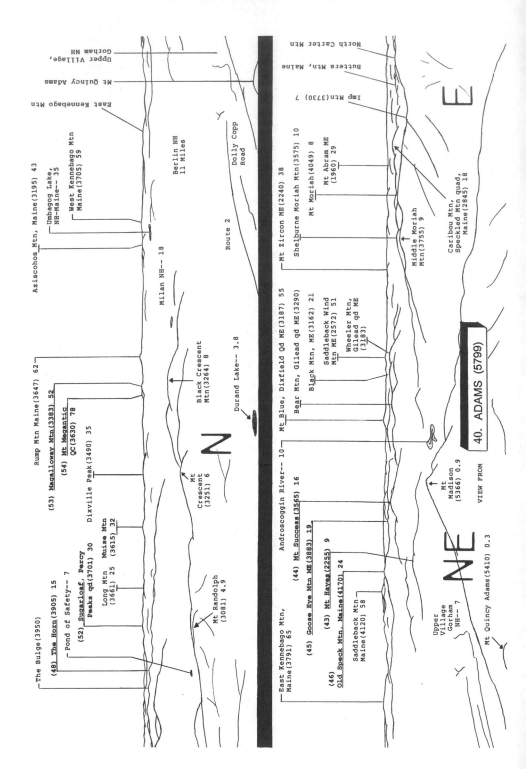

40. ADAMS (5799)

VIEW FROM

The Bulge(3950)

(48) The Horn (3905) 15

Pond of Safety-- 7

(52) Sugarloaf, Percy
Peaks qd(3701) 30

Long Mtn
(3661) 25

Muise Mtn
(3615) 32

Mt Randolph
(3081) 4.9

Rump Mtn Maine(3647) 62

(53) Magalloway Mtn(3383) 52

(54) Mt Megantic
QC(3630) 78

Dixville Peak(3490) 35

Mt
Crescent
(3251) 6

Aziscohos Mtn, Maine(3195) 43

Umbagog Lake,
NH-Maine-- 35

West Kennebago Mtn
Maine(3705) 59

Berlin NH
11 Miles

Milan NH-- 18

Black Crescent
Mtn(3264) 8

Durand Lake-- 3.8

N

East Kennebago Mtn
Maine(3705) 59

Mt Quincy Adams

Upper Village,
Gorham NH

Gorham NH

Route 2

Dolly Copp
Road

East Kennebago Mtn,
Maine(3791) 65

(45) Goose Eye Mtn ME(3883) 19

(44) Mt Success(3565) 16

Androscoggin River-- 10

(43) Mt Hayes(2255) 9

Old Speck Mtn, Maine(4170) 24

(46)

Saddleback Mtn
Maine(4120) 58

Mt Zircon ME(2240) 38

Mt Blue, Dixfield Qd ME(3187) 55

Bear Mtn, Gilead qd ME(3290)

Black Mtn, ME(3162) 21

Saddleback Wind
Mtn ME(2572) 51

Wheeler Mtn,
Gilead qd ME
(3183)

Shelburne Moriah Mtn(3575) 10

Mt Moriah(4049) 8

Mt Abram ME
(1960) 29

Middle Moriah
Mtn(3755) 9

Caribou Mtn,
Speckled Mtn quad,
Maine(2845) 18

North Carter Mtn

Butters Mtn, Maine

Imp Mtn(3730) 7

E

NE

Upper
Village
Gorham
NH-- 7

Mt
Madison
(5366) 0.9

Mt Quincy Adams(5410) 0.3

(41) WILDCAT D

N 44° 14.962'
W 71° 13.411'

(Elevation 4062 feet)

"Why on Earth did you work up a view from a bump along the Wildcat Ridge instead of from the main summit?" the reader asks.

Wildcat D was chosen so that skiers and casual visitors as well as climbers could enjoy the view. The Wildcat Ski Area chair lift arrives nowhere near the main summit but rather at the saddle between two peaks called Wildcat D and Wildcat E. A short hike from the saddle takes the visitor to the top of "D." From here we can see the rest of the mountain. The main summit, also known as Wildcat A, is the apex visible to the northeast just to the left of Carter Dome. "B" and "C" appear to the right respectively. Then comes "D" where we are and behind us, to the southwest, follows Wildcat "E." All these lettered protrusions have been dubbed the Wild Kittens.

We stand at the top of a small observation platform and can hear the clanking of the chair lift invisible beyond the trees below. This lift takes a person from the right side of Pinkham Notch (N 15.852 min, W 14.282 min) and rises up to within a quarter of a mile of where we are standing. It operates not only during the ski season but also during the warmer months. Check www.skiwildcat.com for days and hours of operation.

Tree growth is beginning to obscure some of the view from the platform. But if we combine its views with the views seen from the saddle, we can look in just about all directions.

The Wildcats form part of Pinkham Notch's eastern wall. The Presidential Range hems it in from the west. As a result, we see a magnificent close up of Mount Washington with its attendant gulfs and ravines. Deep indentations are found along the range starting with Gulf of Slides on the left followed by Tuckerman and Huntington Ravines on the right. Farther on we see Madison Gulf. Chandler Ridge hides the Great Gulf. Be it May, June and sometimes July, you will know Tuckerman by the snow patch below the headwall.

Glance northward into the Notch and note the start of the Mount Washington Auto Road before it disappears into the forest. We see it emerge once more near Milepost Four and again a mile later. To the right, Route 16 winds away towards the horizon. Berlin's principal factory spews out a white plume and dims the view beyond. While this smoke may offend the sense of wilderness, the problem had been much worse in years past. If the winds are brisk, the pollution disperses and we can see far into northern New Hampshire and Maine. Such names as Kennebago, Aziscohos and Magalloway inspire the feeling of forest teeming with beaver and bear. Just to the right of Mount Dustan is a small protuberance that straddles the Maine-Quebec border. It has no name but we temporarily designate it as Mount Woburn after a village in the region. The nearby Carter Range interrupts the distant view as it rises to the right and forms the remaining eastern wall of Pinkham Notch.

If you are climbing from the Pinkham Notch Visitor Center, locate the Lost Pond Trail on the other side of the road (N 15.377 min, W 15.133 min). Soon one encounters the Wildcat Ridge Trail. The climber will discover that not only are there Wildcats A through E to reckon with, but also Wildcats F, G, H, I and J not to mention several more. In other words, Wildcat Ridge is serrated, the constant up and down making the trip take far longer than one might suppose. Allow three hours to reach the top of Wildcat D.

The northbound backpacker may have stopped for the night at the Pinkham Notch Visitor Center. The next destination will probably be the AMC's Carter Notch Hut. After Wildcat D, three more hours of hiking are needed to climb over the remaining Wildcats and descend steeply into Carter Notch.

Except for Pleasant Mountain, most of the horizon to the east and south is rather flat. If the time is morning, a silver glare identifies Sebago Lake. Nearby are the Doubleheads, the conical Kearsarge North and the flatter Black Cap. Beyond Thorn Mountain, we look straight down the Saco River Valley. On the horizon stands tiny Mount Agamenticus, its 76-mile distance possibly requiring binoculars.

Boott Spur hides several mountains to the southwest. We cannot see Mounts Eisenhower and Pierce, nor can we make out the Franconia Range. But the others – Bond, Moosilauke, Hancock, Carrigain, Osceola, Tripyramid, Whiteface and Passaconaway are all there.

The massive Presidential Range to the west is what makes the view from Wildcat D so fascinating. If hiking time is lacking, then a brief trip up the chair lift is well worth the small cost.

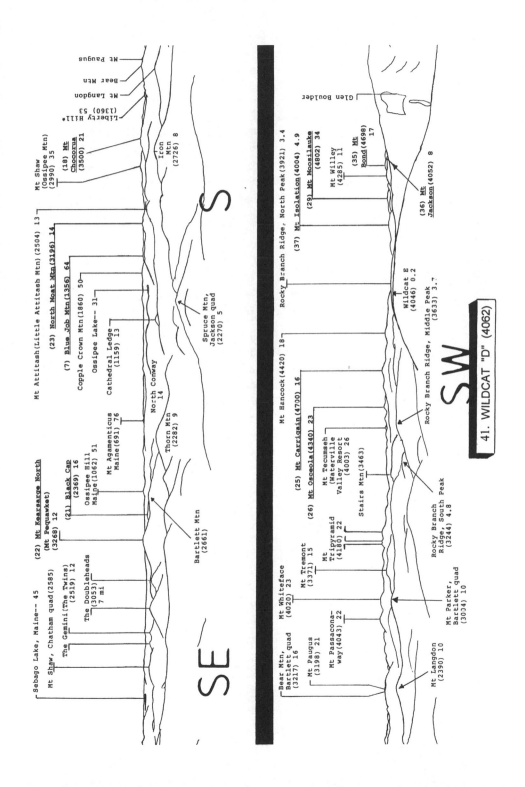

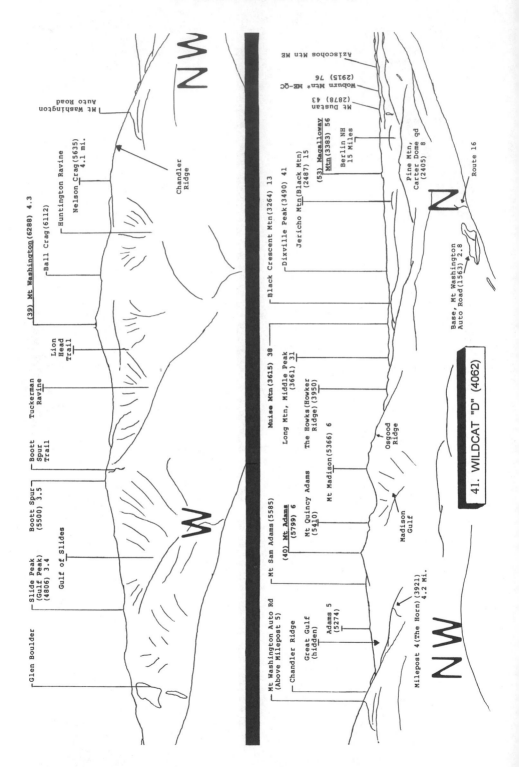

NW

N

Mt Washington Auto Road

Glen Boulder

Slide Peak (Gulf Peak) (4806) 3.4

Boott Spur (5500) 3.5

Gulf of Slides

Boott Spur Trail

Lion Head Trail

(39) Mt Washington (6288) 4.3

Ball Crag (6112)

Huntington Ravine

Nelson Crag (5635) 4.1 mi.

Chandler Ridge

Tuckerman Ravine

W

Mt Sam Adams (5585)

(40) Mt Adams (5799) 6

Mt Quincy Adams (5410)

Mt Madison (5366) 6

Muise Mtn (3615) 38

Long Mtn, Middle Peak (3661) 31

The Howks (Howker Ridge) (3950)

Black Crescent Mtn (3264) 13

Dixville Peak (3490) 41

Jericho Mtn (Black Mtn) (2487) 15

(53) Magalloway Mtn (3383) 56

Berlin NH 15 miles

Aztscohos Mtn ME

Woburn Mtn* ME-QC (2915) 76

Mt Dustan (2878) 43

Pine Mtn, Carter Dome qd (2405) 8

N

Mt Washington Auto Rd (Above Milepost 5)

Chandler Ridge

Great Gulf (hidden)

Adams 5 (5274)

Madison Gulf

Osgood Ridge

Base, Mt Washington Auto Road (1563) 2.8

Route 16

Milepost 4 (The Horn) (3921) 4.2 Mi.

NW

41. WILDCAT "D" (4062)

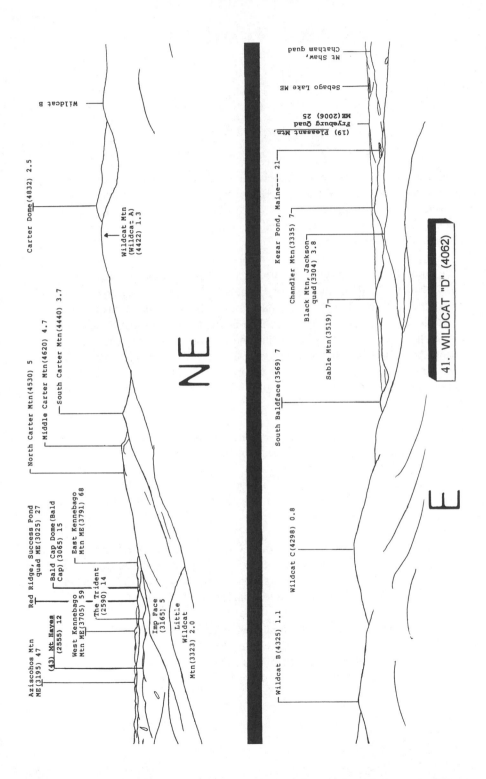

41. WILDCAT "D" (4062)

(42) MOUNT HIGHT

N 44° 16.543'
W 71° 10.229'

(Elevation 4675 feet)

And we had set out to feature Carter Dome! After huffing and puffing our way up a steep trail out of Carter Notch we arrived at a summit that lacked a full circle view. But then another climber suggested that we head over to adjacent Mount Hight, a lower summit perhaps, but one with a view unobstructed by nearby greenery.

We chose the lower peak. To be sure, Carter Dome (N 16.042 min, W 10.744 min) stands in the way of Hight's view to the southwest. But several times before, we solved a similar problem by the graphic method that we call "looking through the mountain." Scenery blocked by Carter was photographed from Carter's summit and then melded into the skyline chart showing the view from Mount Hight. Carter's profile is represented on the same chart, but as a dashed line. It requires much effort to ascend Mount Hight. Once that is achieved, little additional work is needed to climb the Dome.

To the southeast we gaze upon the low hills of coastal Maine. The wide Pleasant Mountain is seen set amid many lakes. As we turn our gaze to the right towards New Hampshire, the Saco River Valley leads away into the distance boxed in by Kearsarge North on the left and the Moat Range on the right. The Sandwich Range begins with the pointed Chocorua, and it disappears behind Carter Dome.

As seen from Carter, the Sandwich Range continues westward with Mounts Passaconaway, Whiteface and Osceola. Nearer to us, the Montalban Range runs north featured by Mounts Davis and Isolation. The southern Presidentials are hidden by nearby Slide Peak and Boott Spur.

To climb Mount Hight, find the Nineteen Mile Brook trailhead located off Route 16 about a mile north of Glen House (N 18.118 min W 13.339 min). One takes this path for about two miles and turns left on the Carter Dome Trail for a direct ascent. Plan on nearly four hours for the climb.

Travelers making the trek from Springer Mountain to Katahdin will have started the day at the AMC's Carter Notch Hut. Two hours is needed to reach Mount Hight. Then it is seven hours over the remaining Carters, Imp Mountain and two Moriahs in order to descend to the Rattle River Shelter for the night. The Imp Campsite is closer, it being about three hours away.

The best part of the view, of course is the Presidential Range. We see directly into the well-known Tuckerman and Huntington Ravines. The Auto Road up Mount Washington is clearly visible with sunlit gleam being reflected from the chrome and glass of moving cars as they find their way past Mileposts Three and Four.

Gaze farther north and see the Presidentials ending with Howker Ridge. Beyond stands the King-Waumbec or Pliny Range with a couple of Vermont tops low on the horizon. Straight away to the north begin the Carter-Moriahs. The westernmost part of the Mahoosuc Range is hidden, but there springs to the right of North Carter Mountain the more distant Trident, Baldcap Dome, Mount Success, Goose Eye and Old Speck. Canada is visible 73 miles away. Towards the Trident, look beyond the next ridge past Aziscohos Mountain. Just to the right and very faint is Quebec's Mont Gosford.

Far into Maine are seen the ski mountains of Saddleback and Sugarloaf. The conical Mount Blue of Dixfield comes next. Farther east the mountains lose altitude and flatten out. Miles of forest spread everywhere. Several bare-topped peaks rise up nearby each with their own eye-catching views. These include Caribou Mountain, Eagle Crag, Bicknell Ridge and the Baldfaces.

We have seen the Presidential Range from a slightly new perspective and have looked northeastward into the wild country. The Mahoosuc Range has become near and takes on a new majesty. It is but a day's hike to the first Mahoosuc Mountain – a day's hike to the "land of hungry animals."

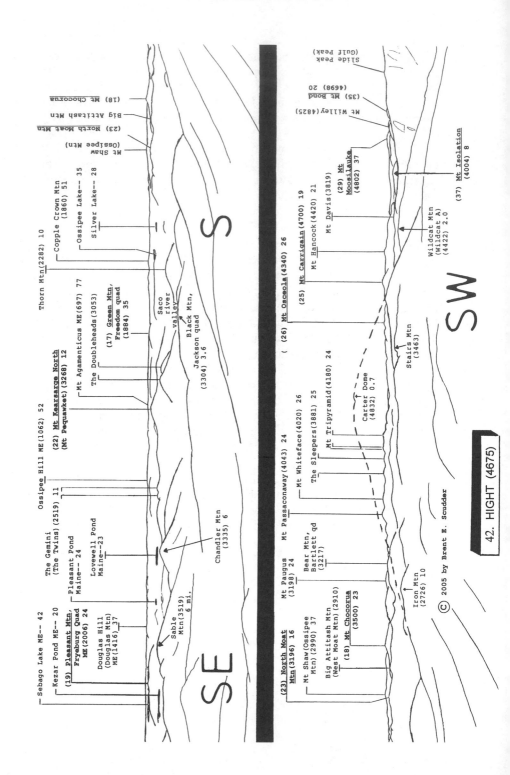

42. HIGHT (4675)

© 2005 by Brent E. Scudder

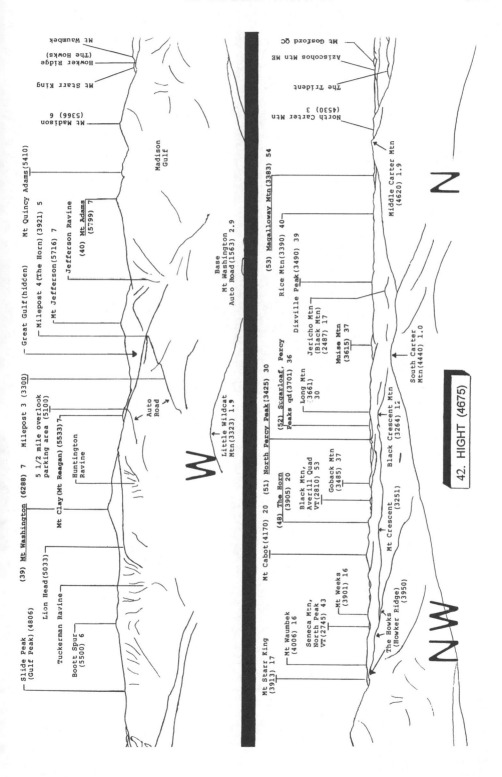

42. HIGHT (4675)

Slide Peak (Gulf Peak) (4806)
Lion Head (5033)
Tuckerman Ravine
Boott Spur (5500) 6
(39) Mt Washington (6288) 7
Mt Clay (Mt Reagan) (5533) 7
5 1/2 mile overlook parking area (5100)
Huntington Ravine
Milepost 3 (3300)
Great Gulf (hidden)
Milepost 4 (The Horn) (3921) 5
Mt Jefferson (5716) 7
Jefferson Ravine
(40) Mt Adams (5799) 7
Mt Quincy Adams (5410)
Mt Madison (5366) 6
Mt Starr King
Howker Ridge (The Howks)
Mt Waumbek
Madison Gulf
Auto Road
Base Mt Washington Auto Road (1563) 2.9
Little Wildcat Mtn (3323) 1.9

W

Mt Starr King (3913) 17
Mt Waumbek (4006) 16
Seneca Mtn, North Peak VT (2745) 43
Mt Weeks (3901) 16
The Howks (Howker Ridge) (3950)
Mt Crescent (3251)
Mt Cabot (4170) 20
(48) The Horn (3905) 20
Black Mtn, Averill Quad VT (2810) 53
Goback Mtn (3485) 37
(51) North Percy Peak (3425) 30
(52) Sugarloaf, Percy Peaks qd (3701) 30
Long Mtn (3661) 30
Jericho Mtn (Black Mtn) (2487) 17
Muise Mtn (3615) 37
Dixville Peak (3490) 39
Rice Mtn (3390) 40
(53) Magalloway Mtn (3383) 54
Black Crescent Mtn (3264) 12
South Carter Mtn (4440) 1.0
Middle Carter Mtn (4620) 1.9
North Carter Mtn (4530) 3
The Trident
Aziscohos Mtn ME
Mt Gosford QC

N

NW

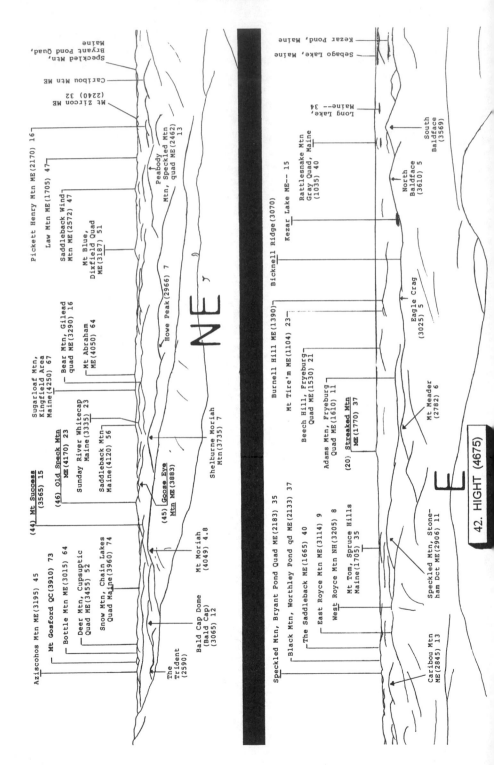

Aziscohos Mtn ME(3195) 45

Mt Gosford QC(3910) 73

Bottle Mtn ME(3015) 64

Deer Mtn, Cupsuptic
Quad ME(3455) 52

Snow Mtn, Chain Lakes
Quad Maine(3960) 74

The
Trident
(2590)

Bald Cap Dome
(Bald Cap)
(3065) 12

Mt Moriah
(4049) 4.8

(44) **Mt Success**
(3565) 15

(46) **Old Speck Mtn**
ME(4170) 23

Sunday River Whitecap
Maine(3335) 23

Saddleback Mtn
Maine(4120) 56

(45) **Goose Eye
Mtn ME**(3883)

Sugarloaf Mtn,
Kingfield Area
Maine(4250) 67

Bear Mtn, Gilead
quad ME(3290) 16

Mt Abraham
ME(4050) 64

Shelburne Moriah
Mtn(3735) 7

Howe Peak(2966) 7

Pickett Henry Mtn ME(2170) 16

Law Mtn ME(1705) 47

Saddleback Wind
Mtn ME(2572) 47

Mt Blue,
Dixfield Quad
ME(3187) 51

Peabody
Mtn, Speckled Mtn
quad ME(2462) 13

Caribou Mtn ME

Mt Zircon ME
(2240) 32

Speckled Mtn,
Bryant Pond Quad,
Maine

NE

Speckled Mtn, Bryant Pond Quad ME(2183) 35

Black Mtn, Worthley Pond qd ME(2133) 37

The Saddleback ME(1665) 40

East Royce Mtn ME(3114) 9

West Royce Mtn NH(3205) 8

Mt Tom, Spruce Hills
Maine(1705) 35

Speckled Mtn, Stone-
ham Dct ME(2906) 11

Caribou Mtn
ME(2845) 13

Burnell Hill ME(1390)

Mt Tire'm ME(1104) 23

Beech Hill, Fryeburg
Quad ME(1530) 21

Adams Mtn, Fryeburg
Quad ME(1610) 11

(20) **Streaked Mtn
ME**(1770) 37

Mt Meader
(2782) 6

Bicknell Ridge(3070)

Kezar Lake ME-- 15

Rattlesnake Mtn
Gray Quad, Maine
(1035) 40

Eagle Crag
(3025) 5

North
Baldface
(3610) 5

South
Baldface
(3569)

Long Lake,
Maine--34

Kezar Pond, Maine

Sebago Lake, Maine

E

42. HIGHT (4675)

(43) MOUNT HAYES

N 44° 24.929'
W 71° 09.583'

(Elevation 2555 feet)

Rutherford B. Hayes was our nation's president from 1877-1881. But according to *Place Names of the White Mountains* by Robert and Mary Julyan, this elevation had honored Margaret Hayes since 1852. She had been the first proprietor of the White Mountains Station House in Gorham. Therefore, Mount Hayes is not another Presidential Peak.

The Presidentials overwhelm the view however. To the southwest, one gazes up at Mounts Madison, Adams and the unlabelled Quincy Adams. On the left stands Mount Washington more distant and therefore appearing less tall. The remaining Presidential Peaks are obscured behind these massive mountains. Farther left, Route 16 can be seen disappearing into Pinkham Notch. Looking south, one sees the crests that the northbound hiker has just traversed. These peaks and the town of Gorham spread out below create a magnificent scene.

The rugged Mahoosuc Range begins with Mount Hayes. Although this initial peak is gentle enough, the Mahoosucs comprise one of the more difficult portions of the Appalachian Trail. There are thirty-one miles of steep climbs and descents over trails that range from rocky to boggy. Springs are few. Mosquitoes and black flies are rife during May, June and July. The back packer may be able to achieve the range in three days, but one should allow for five. Despite these obstacles, a person is rewarded with frequent views from many open ledges.

The best route up Mount Hayes is by way of the Centennial Trail. Drive northbound on Route 16 into Gorham and turn right onto Route 2. Proceed east 3.3 miles and turn left on North Road. Cross the Androscoggin River and take your first left onto a dirt road known as Hogan Road. (Note: What appears to be the first left is not a road at all. Hogan appears just beyond). Drive 0.2 miles to the Centennial trailhead (N 24.249 min, W 07.193 min) which is found on the right. Parking is limited. If necessary park on North Road so that Hogan road is not blocked.

Upon reaching the top you will see no view. However, turn left. Follow the Mahoosuc Trail and hike for ten minutes to a ledge that has the views described above.   Also, from the ledge (approximately N 24.7 min, W 09.9 min), one can scan far down the Androscoggin Valley into Maine and identify such tops as Bear Mountain, Mount Abram, Peabody and Caribou Mountains.   Now look in the opposite direction past the Presidentials.   Note Cherry Mountain and Owls Head near the town of Jefferson.   The Crescent Range dominates the foreground to the west, and farther over, we get a peek at Mount Cabot, the highest New Hampshire mountain north of here.

For the rest of the view, return to the main summit and go beyond the Centennial Trail junction about 0.2 miles (N 25.078 min, W 09.425 min).   One will find the prospect somewhat limited by tree growth.   But look northwest and note a double-humped pair called the Percy Peaks.   North Percy Peak will be featured in a later chapter.   To the right there appear Long and Whitcomb Mountains, respectively.   Our low elevation precludes observing anything in Quebec.   We barely see Magalloway, a mountain forty-five miles due north but located well within New Hampshire.   We will feature Magalloway later on as well.

Hikers who are bound for Maine probably camped out last night at the Rattle River Shelter located just across the Androscoggin River and part way up the opposite mountain.   They descend onto Route 2, locate and cross the nearby North Road Bridge and find the Centennial Trail as described above. The Appalachian Trail hiker will require an hour to reach the Centennial trailhead and two and a half hours to scale Hayes.

Northeastward from the top, the Mahoosuc Trail leads away into the distance over Cascade Mountain and down into Trident Pass.   The overnight backpacker requires two more hours in order to reach the Trident Col Tentsite giving that person a hiking day of five and a half hours (not counting breaks for lunch and viewing).

Have we arrived at "the land of hungry animals?"   We were taking a breather along the Centennial Trail when a rabbit came dashing down the path at full throttle straight towards us.   It managed to see us at the last instant and jumped to the left.   Seconds later, a weasel-like creature appeared in hot pursuit, also nearly crashing into us before jumping aside.   No, the hungry animals may never eat you.   But you could get run over!

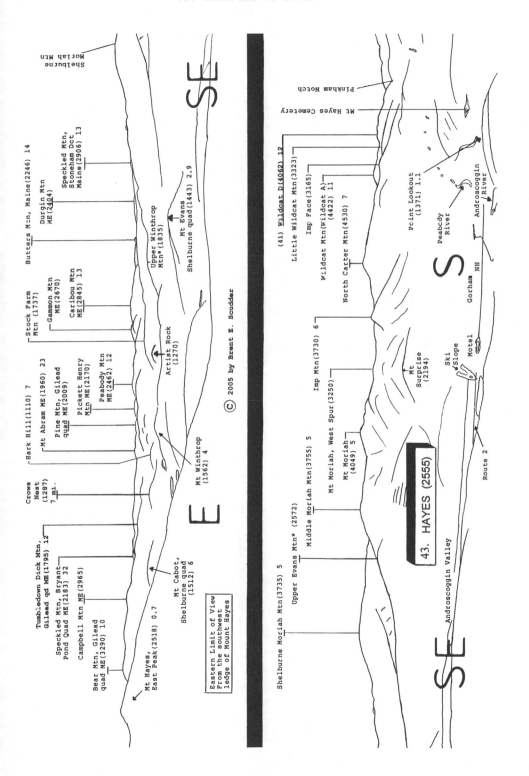

© 2005 by Brent E. Scudder

43. HAYES (2555)

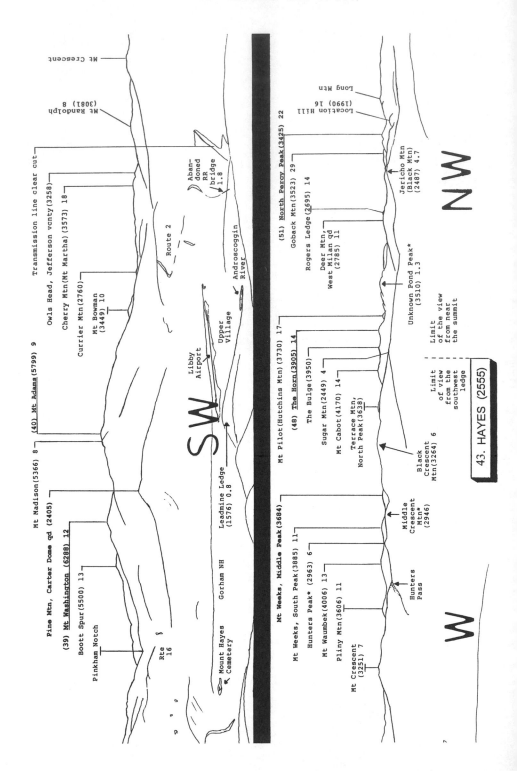

43. HAYES (2555)

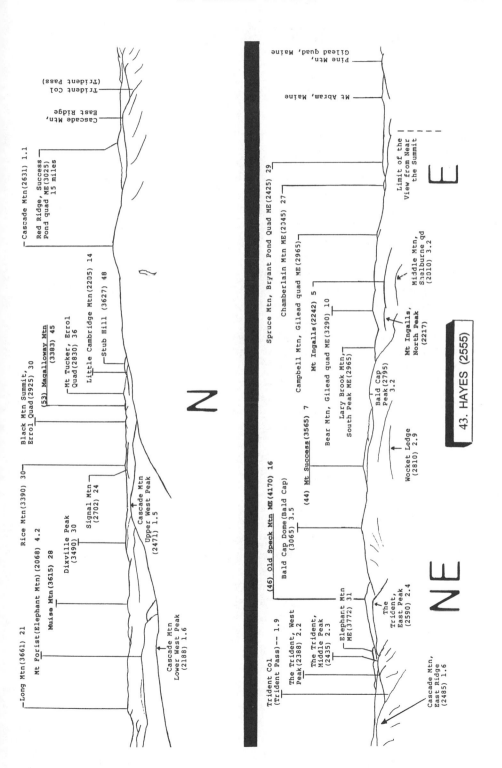

N

Long Mtn(3661) 21
Mt Forist(Elephant Mtn)(2068) 4.2
Muise Mtn(3615) 28
Rice Mtn(3390) 30
Black Mtn Summit, Errol Quad(2925) 30
[53] Magalloway Mtn (3383) 45
Dixville Peak (3490) 30
Signal Mtn (2702) 24
Cascade Mtn Upper West Peak (2471) 1.5
Cascade Mtn Lower West Peak (2188) 1.6
Mt Tucker, Errol Quad(2830) 36
Little Cambridge Mtn(2205) 14
Stub Hill (3627) 48
Cascade Mtn(2631) 1.1
Red Ridge, Success Pond quad ME(3025) 15 miles
Cascade Mtn, East Ridge
Trident Col (Trident Pass)

NE

Cascade Mtn, East Ridge 1.6
Trident Col (Trident Pass)-- 1.9
The Trident, West Peak(2388) 2.2
The Trident, Middle Peak (2435) 2.3
Elephant Mtn ME(3772) 31
The Trident, East Peak (2590) 2.4
(46) Old Speck Mtn ME(4170) 16
Bald Cap Dome(Bald Cap) (3065) 3.5
(44) Mt Success(3565) 7
Bear Mtn, Gilead quad ME(2965)
Bald Cap Peak(2795) 3.2
Wocket Ledge (2810) 2.9
Lary Brook Mtn, South Peak(2965)
Mt Ingalls(2242) 5
Mt Ingalls, North Peak (2217)
Campbell Mtn, Gilead quad ME(2965)
Spruce Mtn, Bryant Pond Quad ME(2425) 29
Chamberlain Mtn ME(2345) 27
Middle Mtn, Shelburne qd (2010) 3.2
Mt Abram, Maine
Pine Mtn, Gilead quad, Maine
Cascade Mtn, East Ridge
Trident Col (Trident Pass)
Limit of the View from Near the Summit

E

43. HAYES (2555)

(44) MOUNT SUCCESS

N 44° 28.282'
W 71° 02.350'

(Elevation 3565 feet)

Success! You have come this far along the Appalachian Trail! Somehow the name of a mountain influences the way you feel about it. Yet this summit is similar to the next mountain over – the one with the mediocre name – just another pile of rocks, dirt and forest. Read John Mudge's book THE WHITE MOUNTAINS, *Names, Places and Legends.* It suggests that the charter for Success Township was granted in 1773 at a time when many colonists viewed with success either the repeal of the Stamp Act or else their refusal to allow tea to be shipped into Boston. The township name was later applied to a hill, a pond, a road and finally the mountain.

The flat summit of Success allows the nearby ridge line to obscure much of the nearer terrain. As a result, we worked up the view in a manner similar to the one created for Mount Moosilauke where we photographed from several locations near the summit. From the top, we hiked 400 yards to the southwest to a place where we developed the view in that direction (N 28.110 min, W 02.480). At this spot, we can see most of the Southern Mahoosucs such as Mount Hayes, Wocket Ledge and the Baldcaps.

On the left the Presidential and Carter-Moriah Ranges still loom tall. Look south and note a small summit so near that it stands beneath our feet. The peak is Mount Ingalls named for an early pioneer family of the area. Of interest to the author, however, is the trail up Ingalls which was named for a distant relative Vida Scudder. She had been a Wellesley College professor around the turn of the Twentieth Century, active in social welfare, a notable author and a summer resident at the Philbrook Farm Inn at nearby Shelburne.

The second location used for diagram development was the main summit itself. Close below to the northwest, Success Pond Road weaves towards us from Berlin. On the horizon, Vermont rises up in the forms of East and Seneca Mountains. To the right come lesser known New Hampshire tops; Long, Castle, Whitcomb, Dixville Peak and Magalloway.

Although more scenery is visible from here, allow us to perform some heavy bushwhacking some 100 yards to the eastern look-off point (N 28.325 min, W 02.316 min). To the north-northeast, Saddle Hill, on the Maine-Quebec border, appears along with Quebec's Gosford Mountain. Farther right, the northern Mahoosucs extend away from us stepping ever higher and higher to culminate at Old Speck in Maine eight miles distant.

Dominating the foreground to the east are several summits of Black and Bear Mountain. Scan to the right. Caribou and Speckled Mountains pass our eyes in quick succession until we arrive at East and West Royce Mountains, a pair split down the middle by the New Hampshire-Maine border.

The Appalachian Trail hiker who awakened this morning at the Trident Col Tent Site will arrive here after five and a half hours of hiking. Another hour and twenty-five minutes is needed to cross into Maine and arrive at the Carlo Col Shelter creating a nearly seven hour hiking day. (Note: Some of the shelters in the Mahoosuc Range are scheduled for demolition and these areas will revert to tent sites.)

The day climber need not hike as long. Drive north on Route 16 out of Gorham. As you approach Berlin, turn right at the first bridge that crosses the Androscoggin River. When you are 0.8 miles from Route 16, the road skirts right and left around the huge smokestacks of the Nexfor-Fraser-Papers Company. You are now on Hutchins Street. Proceed on Hutchins until you have left Route 16 behind by 1.9 miles (N 28.708 min, W 09.835 min). Turn right onto Success Pond Road (no sign), a dirt road often used by logging trucks. On such roads, these trucks have the right-of-way. Drive slowly when approaching blind curves and stay to the right as far as possible. When you are 5.4 miles from Hutchins Street, look right and see a wide path leading away to the right with the west peak of Success appearing beyond. Park here. A small sign announces the Success Trail (N 29.051 min, W 04.595 min). Plan on a two-hour climb.

With each successive mountain featured along the Mahoosuc Range, we watch Mount Washington and the other Presidential Peaks fade into the distance. We see them from a direction witnessed by relatively few hikers. The Mahoosuc elevations may be lower, but the landscape is equally as rugged. Increasingly we come into lake country. Forest is everywhere. Towns are few. The flavor of the early wilderness is still there.

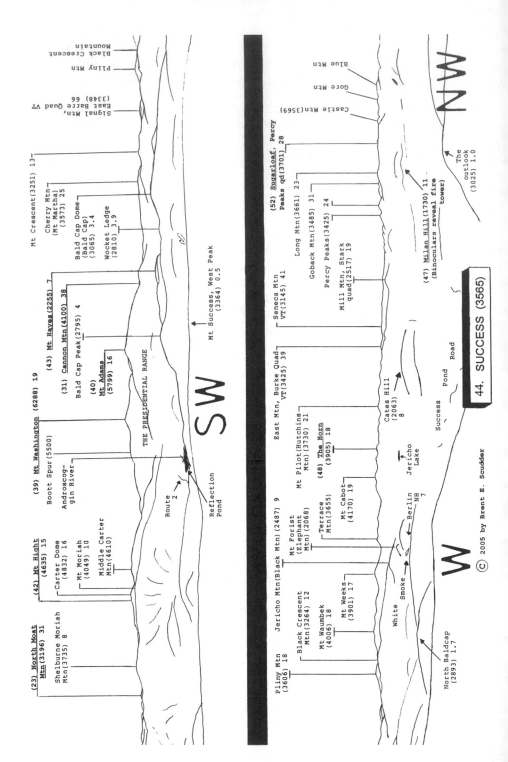

SW

W

NW

(23) **North Moat Mtn**(3196) 31

Shelburne Moriah Mtn(3735) 8

(42) **Mt Hight** (4635) 15

Carter Dome (4832) 16

Mt Moriah (4049) 10

Middle Carter Mtn(4610)

(39) **Mt Washington** (6288) 19

Boott Spur (5500)

Androscog-gin River

Route 2

THE PRESIDENTIAL RANGE

Reflection Pond

Mt Crescent(3251) 13

Cherry Mtn (Mt Martha) (3573) 25

Bald Cap Dome (Bald Cap) (3065) 3.4

Wocket Ledge (2810) 3.9

(31) **Cannon Mtn**(4100) 38

Bald Cap Peak(2795) 4

(40) **Mt Adams** (5799) 16

(43) **Mt Hayes**(2255) 7

Mt Success, West Peak (3364) 0.5

Pliny Mtn

Black Crescent Mountain

Signal Mtn, East Barre Quad VT (3348) 66

Pliny Mtn(3606) 18

Jericho Mtn(Black Mtn) (2487) 9

Black Crescent Mtn(3264) 12

Mt Waumbek (4006) 18

Mt Weeks (3901) 17

Mt Forist (Elephant Mtn)(2068)

Terrace Mtn(3655)

Mt Cabot (4170) 19

(48) **The Horn** (3905) 18

Mt Pilot(Hutchins Mtn)(3730) 21

East Mtn, Burke Quad VT(3425) 39

Seneca Mtn VT(3145) 41

Cates Hill (2063) 8

(52) **Sugarloaf, Percy Peaks qd**(3701) 28

Long Mtn(3661) 23

Goback Mtn(3485) 31

Percy Peaks(3425) 24

Mill Mtn, Stark quad(2517) 19

Castle Mtn(3569)

Gore Mtn

Blue Mtn

(47) **Milan Hill**(1730) 11 (Binoculars reveal fire tower)

White Smoke

Berlin NH 7

Jericho Lake

Success Pond Road

North Baldcap (2893) 1.7

44. SUCCESS (3565)

The outlook (3025) 1.0

© 2005 by Brent E. Scudder

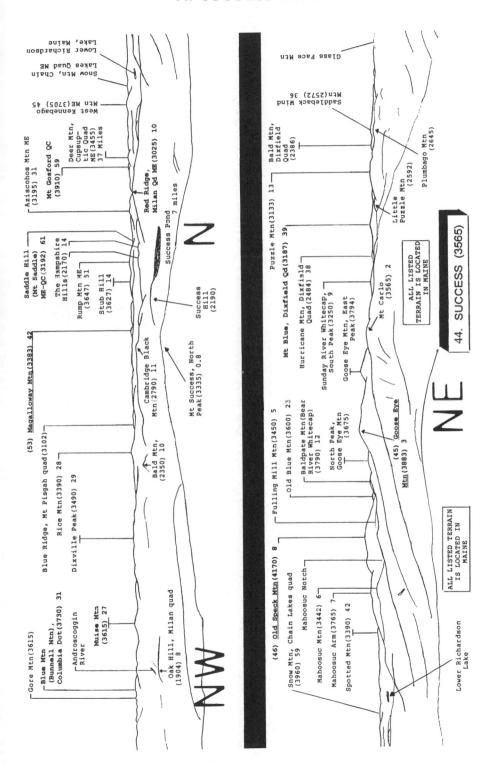

Gore Mtn(3615)

Blue Mtn
(Bunnell Mtn),
Columbia Dot(3730) 31

Blue Ridge, Mt Pisgah quad(3102)

Rice Mtn(3390) 28

(53) Magalloway Mtn(3383) 42

Saddle Hill
(Mt Saddle)
ME-QC(3192) 61

Azischohos Mtn ME
(3195) 31

Mt Gosford QC
(3910) 59

Snow Mtn, Chain
Lakes Quad ME

Lower Richardson
Lake, Maine

West Kennebago
Mtn ME(3705) 45

Deer Mtn,
Cupsup-
tic Quad
ME(3455)
37 Miles

Red Ridge,
Milan Qd ME (3025) 10

The Hampshire
Hills(2170) 14

Rump Mtn ME
(3647) 51

Stub Hill
(3627) 14

Androscoggin
River

Mrise Mtn
(3615) 27

Dixville Peak(3490) 29

Bald Mtn,
(2350) 10

Cambridge Black
Mtn(2790) 11

Success Pond
7 miles

Success
Hill
(2190)

N

Oak Hill, Milan quad
(1904) 8

Mt Success, North
Peak(3335) 0.8

NW

(46) Old Speck Mtn(4170) 8

Fulling Mill Mtn(3450) 5

Old Blue Mtn(3600) 23

Puzzle Mtn(3133) 13

Bald Mtn,
Dixfield
Quad
(2386)

Saddleback Wind
Mtn(2572) 36

Glass Face Mtn

Snow Mtn, Chain Lakes quad
(3960) 59

Mahoosuc Notch

Mahoosuc Mtn(3442) 6

Mahoosuc Arm(3765) 7

Spotted Mtn(3390) 42

Baldpate Mtn(Bear
River Whitecap)
(3790) 12

North Peak,
Goose Eye Mtn
(3675)

Mt Blue, Dixfield Qd(3187) 39

Hurricane Mtn, Dixfield
Quad(2484) 38

Sunday River Whitecap,
South Peak(3250) 9

Goose Eye Mtn, East
Peak(3794)

Mt Carlo
(3565) 2

Little
Puzzle Mtn
(2592)

Plumbago Mtn
(2645)

ALL LISTED
TERRAIN IS LOCATED
IN MAINE

(45) Goose Eye
Mtn(3883) 3

NE

44. SUCCESS (3565)

ALL LISTED TERRAIN
IS LOCATED IN
MAINE

Lower Richardson
Lake

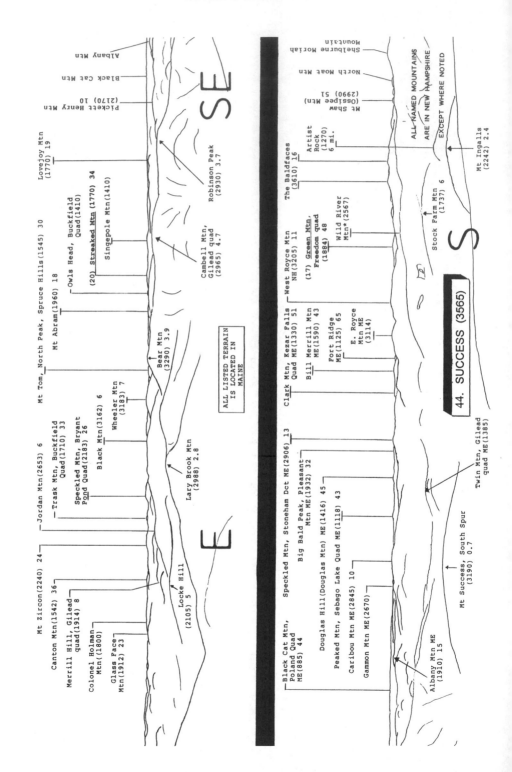

(45) GOOSE EYE MOUNTAIN

Maine

N 44° 30.160'
W 70° 59.967'

(Elevation 3883 feet)

Diagrams based on slides taken by
Dan H. Allen

There is some controversy regarding the height of this mountain. The standard published altitude is 3870 feet, which is up from 3794 feet of an earlier survey. Pick up a copy of the Success Pond 7.5-minute USCG topographical map. Take out a magnifying glass and study the summit of Goose Eye Mountain located near the lower right corner. Inside the 3860 contour line is a tiny circle that may merely mark the summit location. But it could also be the 3880 contour line. We state the elevation as 3883 fully aware that it could be thirteen feet lower.

From the top we see that New Hampshire's Presidential Range is further diminished by distance. More and more of Maine begin to appear to the right of Old Speck Mountain such as Saddleback, Abraham and Sunday River Whitecap. The actual Sunday River Ski Area is located among several tops in the vicinity of Barker Mountain standing a considerable distance to the right. Baldpate and Old Blue Mountains show up in more detail than could be seen from our last featured summit. Far to the southeast, the silver streaks of Sebago and Long Lakes gleam forth reflecting the late morning sun.

If you are traversing the Mahoosuc Range from southwest to northeast, you might have spent the previous night at the Carlo Col Shelter. Eighty-five minutes will bring you to this summit. Count on five more hours to reach the next night's possible stopping point, the Speck Pond Campsite for a total hiking day of 6 1/2 hours. To arrive there, one has to drop precipitously into Mahoosuc Notch and climb steeply out the other side. The Appalachian Trail's most rugged mile is considered to lie along this stretch. If one is tired or behind schedule, a person should stop for the night at the Full Goose Shelter, a ninety-five minute hike from the top of Goose Eye Mountain.

The shortest route for the day climber is by way of Success Pond Road, which runs northeastward from Berlin, New Hampshire. Return to the last chapter for instructions to the Success trailhead. But this time do not go 5.4 miles up Success Pond Road from Hutchins Street. Make it 8.1 miles instead. At this point (N 30.644 min, W 02.600 min), the Carlo Col Trail leads off to the right as a Jeep road. When you have hiked 100 yards up this pathway, the blue-blazed Goose Eye Trail drops down a steep embankment to the left, crosses a brook and turns towards the mountain. Expect to make the summit in two and three-quarter hours.

Due to extensive logging in the area, the Success, Carlo Col and Goose Eye Trails may pass through recently logged sections of forest. If these clear-cut areas consist of several acres, one's navigational skills in hiking may be tested to the utmost. This is because local hiking clubs may not yet have had time to re-blaze or even relocate the trail. It would be wise to add an hour to the estimated hiking time to allow for possible trail searching.

When you emerge from the woods into a large clear-cut area, turn around and look for a suitable landmark that locates the trail for your return trip. If you have a GPS unit, create a waypoint. Now face back across the clearing in your original direction of travel and try to determine where the trail reenters the forest. Use the map to determine if the path might have turned sharply in the middle of the clearing. If you cannot see where the trail re-enters, estimate a spot where you think that it might. Now cross the clearing to a location that is about a hundred yards to one side of your estimate. Walk back along the edge of the logged area toward where you think the trail might continue and, if necessary, walk for another hundred yards. Gaze into the woods and look for a sure sign of the trail, a blaze on a tree for example.

If you have not found the path, turn straight into the woods bushwhacking until the clearing behind you is indicated only by a brightness in the sky beyond the trees. Take a compass bearing on the logged area. Now walk parallel to the edge of the clearing back towards where you think the trail might be. Look both towards and away from the clearing for unmistakable trail signs. If necessary, continue 100 yards past where you think the trail might be. You still have not found the path? You will have to use the same procedure on another section of the clearing. If you still cannot locate the trail and are unwilling to bushwhack to the summit, consider abandoning the hike.

The summit views to the west and north of Goose Eye look well into upper New Hampshire. We seldom hike north of the Presidentials and thus the mountains have unfamiliar names. Later chapters take us there and help us know these peaks in addition to their better-known cousins to the south.

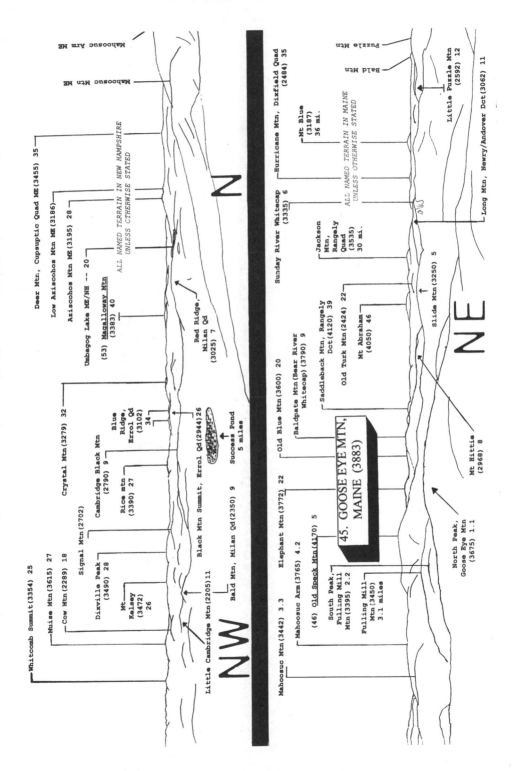

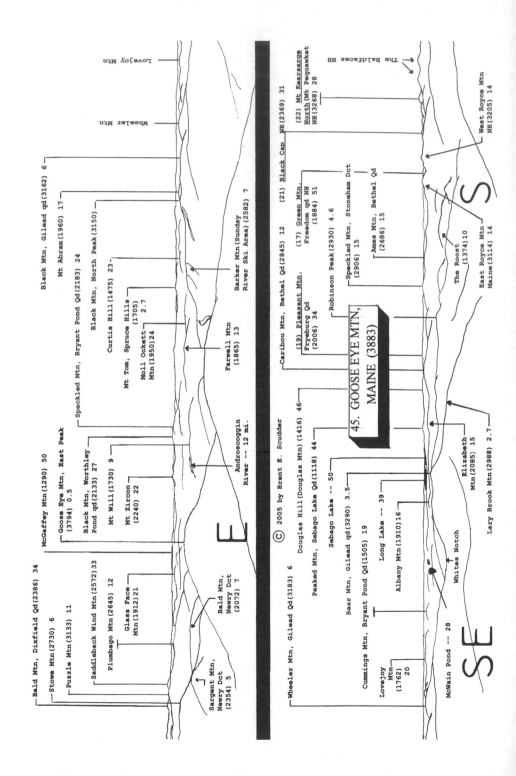

45. GOOSE EYE MTN, MAINE (3883)

© 2005 by Brent E. Scudder

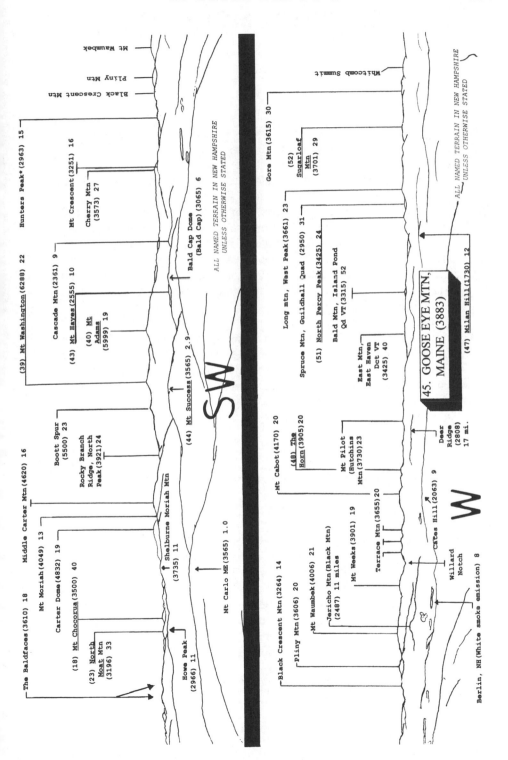

45. GOOSE EYE MTN, MAINE (3883)

(46) OLD SPECK MOUNTAIN

Maine

N 44° 34.233'
W 70° 57.213'

(Elevation 4170 feet)

No backpacking trip along the Mahoosuc Range is complete without climbing Maine's fourth highest peak, Old Speck Mountain.* From its top, the Appalachian Trail hiker can look back upon New Hampshire's ranges and recall the joys and hardships of the numerous mountains that rose more than four thousand feet. He or she gazes far ahead into Maine at what must yet be accomplished. In the mind's eye, one sees the path winding over the Baldpates, Elephant, Saddleback, Sugarloaf and Bigelow Mountain. That person cannot yet see the end of the journey, Mount Katahdin.

Anyone planning to be up and back by evening will find that the easiest trail choice starts from Grafton Notch. Drive up Route 26 some 12 miles or so northwest of Bethel, Maine. At 2.7 miles past Screw Auger Falls, locate a parking lot to the left (N 35.399 min, W 56.828 min). The Old Speck Trail begins here and leads you to a wooded summit in about three hours. An observation tower rises well above the tallest tree. One climbs a steep ladder but is safely caged in by surrounding struts during the ascent.

At the top of the tower, we gaze northwards and see Route 26 disappearing towards Errol, New Hampshire. Lakes appear on both sides. Umbagog on the left lies almost entirely within New Hampshire. To the right appear Lower and Upper Richardson Lakes respectively. And then there is Mooselookmeguntic Lake. Rangely Lake cannot be seen.

We look well into Canada. To the right of Dixville Peak sits Hereford Mountain. Megantic lies low on the horizon between Magalloway and Bosebuck. Gosford is seen to the left of lower Richardson Lake.

To the east, the mountains lose their elevation as we approach the coastal plain. Mount Blue is that "volcano" on the horizon. Below us slope the steep sides of Grafton Notch as Route 26 winds it's way southeast. Nearby, one recognizes Slide Mountain, Puzzle Mountain and Sunday River Whitecap.

---

* Here the word "peak" is defined as an elevation that rises at least 200 feet above any ridge that connects it to a higher mountain.

More water is visible. The nearer Androscoggin River and the more distant Pennesseewasee Lake are seen to the left of Barker Mountain while Sebago Lake appears on the right.

Gaze towards the west and note several New Hampshire summits. From Freedom quadrangle's Green Mountain to Cannon Mountain, we count thirteen peaks featured earlier in this book. We cannot see Mount Hight for it lies up against Carter Dome and is of the same color. But if you catch one of the pair in full sunlight and the other in cloud shadow, both will appear.

Old Speck is noted for its summit wildlife. In *Fifty Hikes in Maine,* author John Gibson mentions having several one-sided conversations with a large friendly rabbit. We did not see the rabbit but two voracious Canada jays tried to steal our lunch. These birds were often fed at lumber camps and have become accustomed to man. But it is disconcerting to hold a sandwich waist high while turning to talk to someone and have the bird go after it. One easily recalls an Alfred Hitchcock movie of more than a generation ago.

Invisible between Goose Eye and Fulling Mill Mountain stands the Full Goose Shelter, where the backpacker may have spent the previous night. It takes 6 1/2 hours to reach Old Speck from Full Goose. On the other hand, it takes only 90 minutes to climb from the Speck Pond Campsite. If the next night's accommodation is to be the Baldpate Lean-to, hike an additional three hours.

A mile away below us to the southwest is seen the gleam of the southern end of Speck Pond, Maine's highest lake. The rest of this body of water lies behind a shoulder of Old Speck. Farther out stands Berlin, New Hampshire, easily recognized by a pillar of white smoke. Look to the right and follow the Pliny-Pilot Ranges topped by Mount Cabot. We can see two states away with Burke Mountain, Vermont, appearing as a tiny horizon swelling beyond Success Pond. Other peaks in Vermont include East Haven, East and the northern Monadnock.

And so we end our progression of nineteen mountains located one day's hike apart on or near the Appalachian Trail. Mount Cube to Old Speck was quite a journey – 140 miles, nearly seven per cent of the entire A. T. Let us leave this famous path and allow the lonely backpacker to continue on his way to Katahdin.

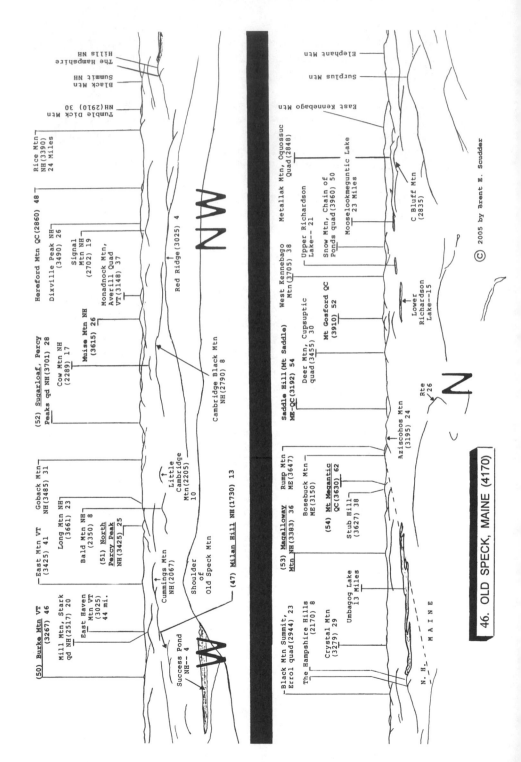

50) Burke Mtn VT (3267) 46

Mill Mtn, Stark qd NH(2517) 20

East Haven Mtn VT (3025) 44 mi.

East Mtn VT (3425) 41

Long Mtn NH (3661) 23

Bald Mtn NH (2350) 8

(51) North Percy Peak NH(3425) 25

Goback Mtn NH(3485) 31

Cummings Mtn NH(2067)

Shoulder of Old Speck Mtn

(47) Milan Hill NH (1730) 13

Success Pond NH-- 4

W

(52) Sugarloaf, Percy Peaks qd NH(3701) 28

Cow Mtn NH (2289) 17

Muise Mtn NH (3615) 26

Little Cambridge Mtn(2205) 10

Cambridge Black Mtn NH(2790) 8

Hereford Mtn QC(2860) 48

Dixville Peak NH (3490) 26

Signal Mtn NH (2702) 19

Monadnock Mtn, Averill Quad VT(3148) 37

Red Ridge(3025) 4

NW

Rice Mtn NH(3390) 24 Miles

Tumble Dick Mtn NH(2910) 30

Black Mtn Summit NH

The Hampshire Hills NH

53) Magalloway Mtn NH(3383) 36

Bosebuck Mtn ME(3150)

(54) Mt Megantic QC(3630) 62

Stub Hill (3627) 38

Rump Mtn ME(3647)

Aziscohos Mtn (3195) 24

Saddle Hill(Mt Saddle) ME-QC(3192) 54

Deer Mtn, Cupsuptic quad(3455) 30

Mt Gosford QC (3910) 52

Rte 26

N

West Kennebago Mtn(3705) 38

Upper Richardson Lake--21

Lower Richardson Lake--15

Metallak Mtn, Oquossuc Quad(2848)

Snow Mtn, Chain of Ponds quad(3960) 50

Mooselookmeguntic Lake 23 Miles

C Bluff Mtn (2835)

East Kennebago Mtn

Surplus Mtn

Elephant Mtn

Black Mtn Summit, Errol quad(2944) 23

The Hampshire Hills (2170) 8

Crystal Mtn (3279) 29

Umbagog Lake 13 Miles

N. H.   M A I N E

© 2005 by Brent E. Scudder

46. OLD SPECK, MAINE (4170)

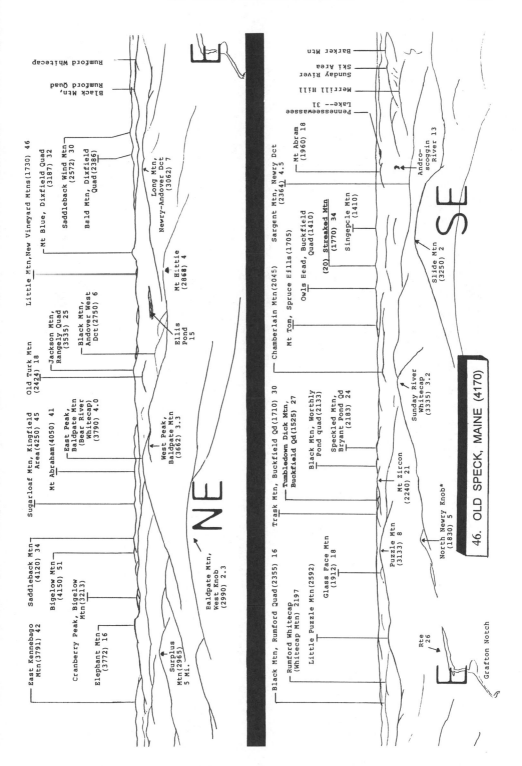

46. OLD SPECK, MAINE (4170)

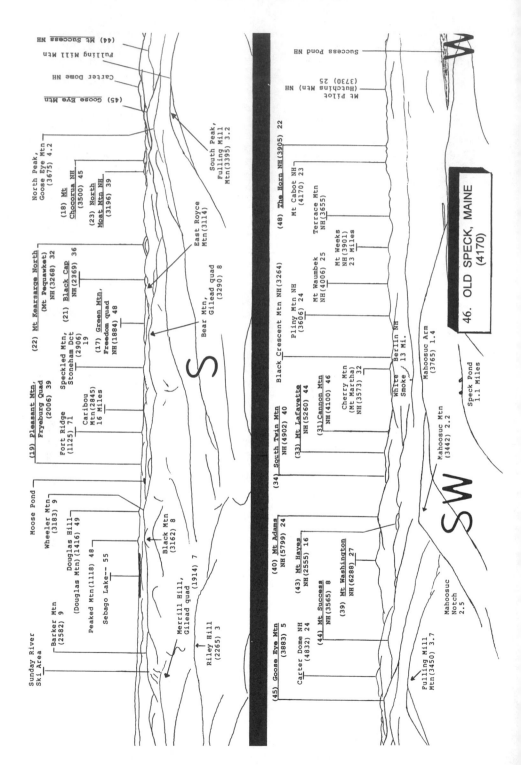

(44) Mt Success NH
Pulling Mill Mtn
Carter Dome NH
(45) Goose Eye Mtn

North Peak,
Goose Eye Mtn
(3675) 4.2

South Peak,
Pulling Mill
Mtn(3395) 3.2

(18) Mt
Chocorua NH
(3500) 45

(24) North
Moat Mtn NH
(3196) 39

East Royce
Mtn(3114)

(22) Mt Kearsarge North
(Mt Pequawket)
NH(3268) 32

Speckled Mtn,   (21) Black Cap
Stoneham Dct   NH(2369) 36
(2906)
19   (17) Green Mtn,
Freedom quad
NH(1884) 48

Bear Mtn,
Gilead quad
(3290) 8

(19) Pleasant Mtn,
Fryeburg Quad
(2006) 39

Fort Ridge
(1125) 71

Caribou
Mtn(2845)
16 Miles

Moose Pond

Wheeler Mtn
(3183) 9

Douglas Hill
(Douglas Mtn)(1416) 49

Peaked Mtn(1118) 48

Sebago Lake-- 55

Black Mtn
(3162) 8

Merrill Hill,
Gilead quad
(1914) 7

Riley Hill
(2265) 3

Sunday River
Ski Area

Barker Mtn
(2582) 9

South Peak

The Horn NH(3905) 22

(48)

Mt Cabot NH
(4170) 23

Terrace Mtn
NH(3655)

Mt Weeks
NH(3901)
23 Miles

Mt Waumbek
NH(4006) 25

Pliny Mtn NH
(3606) 24

Black Crescent Mtn NH(3264)

Cherry Mtn
(Mt Martha)
NH(3573) 32

(31)Cannon Mtn
NH(4100) 46

(33) Mt Lafayette
NH(5260) 44

(34) South Twin Mtn
NH(4902) 40

White   Berlin NH
Smoke 13 Mi.

Mahoosuc Arm
(3765) 1.4

Mahoosuc Mtn
(3442) 2.2

Speck Pond
1.1 Miles

(40) Mt Adams
NH(5799) 24

(43) Mt Hayes
NH(2555) 16

(39) Mt Washington
NH(6288) 27

(45) Goose Eye Mtn
(3883) 5

Carter Dome NH
(4832) 24

(44) Mt Success
NH(3565) 8

Mahoosuc
Notch
2.5

Pulling Mill
Mtn(3450) 3.7

Success Pond NH

Mt Pilot
(Hutchins Mtn) NH
(3730) 25

46. OLD SPECK, MAINE
(4170)

S

SW

W

(47) MILAN HILL

N 44° 34.331'
W 71° 13.391'

(Elevation 1730 feet)

Welcome to the North Country! The land is wild and tourists are few. One can hike an entire day without seeing anyone. But we start this section with a rather tame rise of terrain – in fact, one can travel by automobile to the summit. In later chapters, we provide more challenge.

Drive north on Route 16 through Gorham and Berlin. The next town is Milan. Turn left on Route 110B (Milan Hill Road). Two miles later, one arrives at the entrance to Milan Hill State Park appearing on the left (N 34.652 min, W 13.532 min). During the off-season, the entrance gate may be closed and this would mean a 15-minute hike. If you drive up, expect to pay a small parking fee. One can check on the status of the park by calling (603) 482-3373.

The park has a campground, so you may expect restroom facilities. A fire tower stands at the top. If the cab is not open, one can climb to the floor below and still catch marvelous views.

Those attuned to the mountains farther south may find the panorama unfamiliar. But quickly the climber recognizes the Presidential Range. With a bit of intuition, he or she can sort out the Mahoosuc Range. Mount Hayes stands low well to the left of towering Mount Adams and is backed up against the more distant Mount Moriah. The Mahoosucs extend farther left over Cascade Mountain and then take over the horizon as we look eastward over The Trident, the Bald Caps, Mount Success, Goose Eye and, of course, Old Speck.

In order to learn the panoramas of the North Country, perhaps it is best to do what was done in the early chapters – memorize a few landmark mountains, and then look for these again on subsequent tops that we climb.

Southwestward arises a tall rounded peak called Mount Weeks. To the west-southwest is the highest New Hampshire Mountain north of the Presidentials – Mount Cabot. Bring the eye farther right until you see a pair of pyramids located almost northwest. These are the Percy Peaks. To the north-northwest arises Muise Mountain.   These landmarks will be seen repeatedly later on.

Because of our low elevation, we are unable to see many mountains that are the subject of earlier chapters. We cannot distinguish the top of Mount Washington – only Ball Crag which is located close to the summit. South Twin Mountain is visible. Other than these, no mountain appears that is featured before Chapter Forty.

High terrain to the north prevents observing anything in Quebec. But a number of peaks in Maine are visible. Scan from north to south starting with the more distant West Kennebago Mountain. We turn our head to the right and come to the nearer Aziscohos Mountain, the Baldpates and the eastern portion of the Mahoosuc Range. These all appear prominently.

Closer in are smaller hills in New Hampshire located to the east of the Androscoggin River. These range from Veezey Hill to the north extending southeastward to Errol Hill, Doubletop, Little Roundtop, Little Cambridge and Cambridge Black Mountains.   Then comes Bald and Chickwolnepy. Roundtop stands in front of Little Roundtop but is not featured in the diagram. Little Roundtop is 25 feet taller!

Milan Hill has a low elevation but a sweeping view. If the remaining vacation time is short and Mother Nature provides you with one of those sparkling days of limitless visibility, then consider this trip to the North Country. From the heart of the White Mountains, one can drive to Milan Hill in a surprisingly short time.

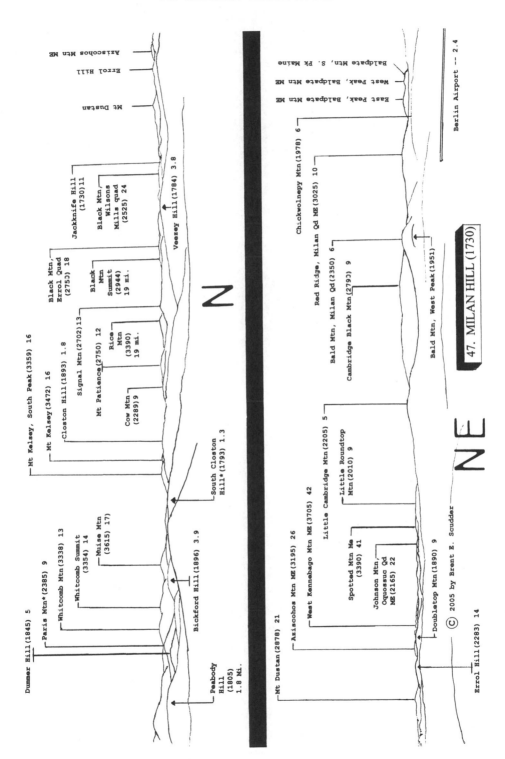

47. MILAN HILL (1730)

© 2005 by Brent E. Scudder

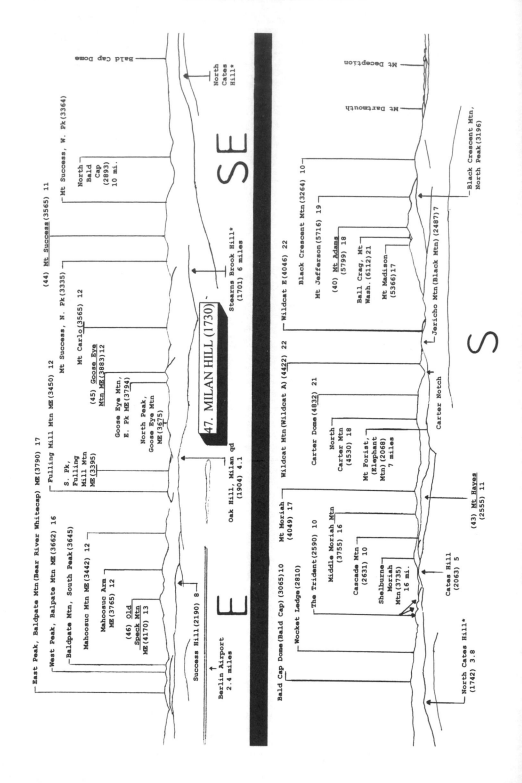

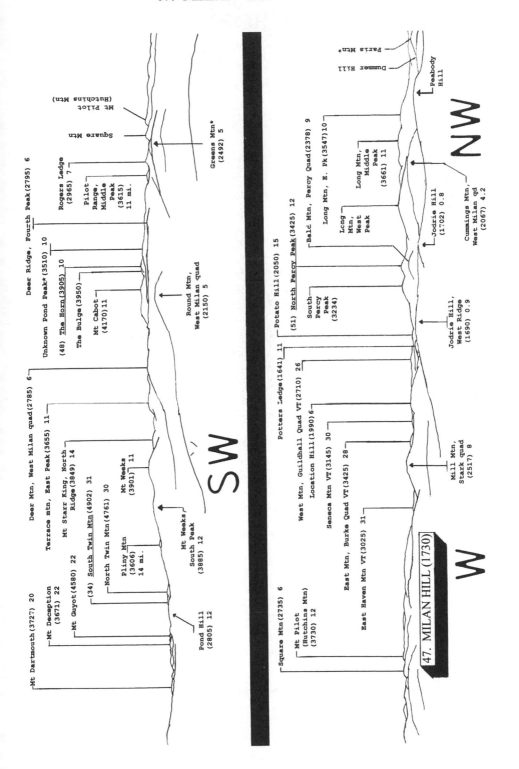

Mt Dartmouth (3727) 20

Deer Mtn, West Milan quad (2785) 6

Mt Deception (3671) 22

Terrace mtn, East Peak (3655) 11

Mt Gayot (4580) 22

Mt Starr King, North Ridge (3849) 14

South Twin Mtn (4902) 31

(34) North Twin Mtn (4761) 30

Pliny Mtn (3606) 14 mi.

Mt Weeks (3901) 11

Mt Weeks South Peak (3885) 12

Pond Hill (2805) 12

Deer Ridge, Fourth Peak (2795) 6

Unknown Pond Peak* (3510) 10

(48) The Horn (3905) 10

The Bulge (3950)

Mt Cabot (4170) 11

Rogers Ledge (2965) 7

Pilot Range, Middle Peak (3615) 11 mi.

Mt Pilot (Hutchins Mtn)

Square Mtn

Greens Mtn* (2492) 5

Round Mtn, West Milan quad (2150) 5

SW

Square Mtn (2735) 6

Mt Pilot (Hutchins Mtn) (3730) 12

East Mtn, Burke Quad VT (3025) 31

East Haven Mtn VT (3025) 31

Seneca Mtn VT (3145) 30

West Mtn, Guildhall Quad VT (2710) 26

Location Hill (1990) 6

Potters Ledge (1641) 11

Potato Hill (2050) 15

(51) North Percy Peak (3425) 12

South Percy Peak (3234)

Bald Mtn, Percy Quad (2378) 9

Long Mtn, West Peak

Long Mtn, E. Pk (3547) 10

Long Mtn, Middle Peak (3661) 11

Jodrie Hill, West Ridge (1690) 0.9

Mill Mtn, Stark quad (2517) 8

Jodrie Hill (1702) 0.8

Cummings Mtn, West Milan qd (2067) 4.2

Peabody Hill

Dummer Hill

Paris Mtn*

NW

W

47. MILAN HILL (1730)

(48) THE HORN

N 44° 31.070'
W 71° 24.004'

(Elevation 3905 feet)

Projecting as the horn of a rhinoceros on the end of a ridge, this peak is well named. Steep pitches drop away on three sides and the summit is tiny. The vista stretches away in all directions and tree growth will never take over within our lifetimes.

If you are unfamiliar with the North Country mountains, orient yourself the same way as was done on Milan Hill. Start with the Presidential Range to the south. To the right of Mount Washington is the unlabelled Mount Monroe and farther over the dome-shaped Mount Eisenhower. To the left, there follows Adams, the Carter-Moriahs and the Mahoosucs.

Now seek the four "landmark" mountains identified in the last chapter. Mount Weeks stands four miles away in front of Mount Washington. Cabot is that big thing blocking the view to the southwest. Look slightly left of north and behold the twin conical Percy Peaks that stand nearly in line. Muise Mountain is almost due north but only cuts a tiny profile on the horizon beyond the nearer Mill and Bald Mountains.

Let us add two additional landmarks to the list. Extending away to the northwest is the Pilot Range with multiple unnamed summits. Mount Pilot (Hutchins Mountain) is the highest, the word "pilot" suggesting that early trappers sighted that peak as a means for navigation through the trackless wilderness. For our second landmark, note Vermont's Burke Mountain to the west. This prominent rise is visible from many peaks in the region.

On the northern skyline, we see scattered parts of Quebec. Just to the right of Mount Pilot appears the easternmost peak of the Sutton Range, Mont Fullerton*. Then follows the well-known Mont Owl Head. To the northeast rises Gosford, a broad summit sixty miles away. Between Owl Head and Gosford lie the mountains of northern New Hampshire, little known because of the more impressive heights behind us. From left to right, we have the Stratford Mountain group, Long Mountain's several summits, Dixville Peak, Magalloway Mountain and Stub Hill.

---

* Temporary designation

Look eastward into Maine and discover East Kennebago and Bigelow Mountains along with Maine's version of The Horn, which is a part of Saddleback Mountain -- Saddlehorn perhaps? At our feet lies unceasing tree cover. But nearby Rogers Ledge and Square Mountain have excellent views.

As of this writing a person can no longer legally approach The Horn from the west over Cabot as suggested in the First Edition. The first mile of the Mount Cabot Trail has been closed by the landowner. Although it may have been shut down for entirely other reasons, this closing illustrates the need for the hiker to exercise due respect for any property where the owner has been more than generous to allow a trail through his lands.

To climb the Horn from the east, Take Route 110 northwestward from Route 16 in Berlin a distance of 7.4 miles and turn left on the York Pond Road following signs to the Berlin Fish Hatchery. Proceed 4.9 miles to its gate (N 30.129 min, W 19.893 min). If you cannot return by the 4 p.m. closing time, park here and hike in. Otherwise drive 2.2 miles to the Unknown Pond trailhead (N 29.917 min, W 21.510 min) which is found on the right. Hike this trail to and past Unknown Pond. There you will encounter the intersection with the Kilkenny Ridge Trail (N 31.722 min, W 23.540 min) which leaves to the left up the mountain. After an additional mile, a short side trail to the left takes you up The Horn. Expect the climb to take four hours.

At the top of The Horn we once again resort to the graphic technique of "looking through the mountain." The intervening Mount Cabot and The Bulge interrupt the view to the southwest. On the skyline diagram, we represent these peaks as dashed lines and fill in the hidden scenery with the view from Cabot's south peak. Unfortunately, the climber must hike an additional hour to reach Cabot's summit (N 30.356 min, W 24.861 min) and proceed a short distance to the site of a former fire tower (N 30.203 min, W 24.605 min).

But look at the view! Look southwest from Cabot, and see the craggy Lafayette and the rounded Moosilauke. To the right stands the Vermont horizon from Killington Peak northward past Camels Hump. At times, we can identify Dorset Peak 115 miles away. The hiker can make a round trip of it by continuing over Cabot down the Kilkenny Ridge Trail and turning left on the Bunnell Notch Trail to return to York Pond Road 100 feet from where he or she started. However, at press time, this latter path was not well marked and rather challenging.

This is the wild country, the North Country. Certainly some civilization is visible, but forest and mountain extend in all directions.

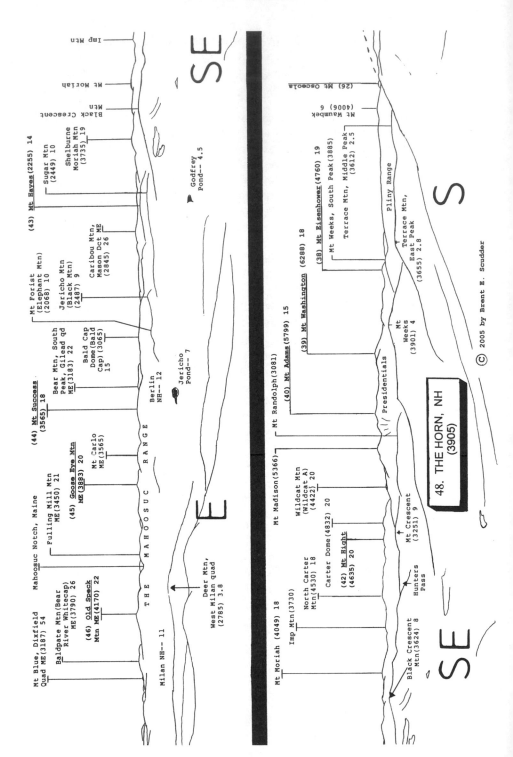

48. THE HORN, NH (3905)

© 2005 by Brent E. Scudder

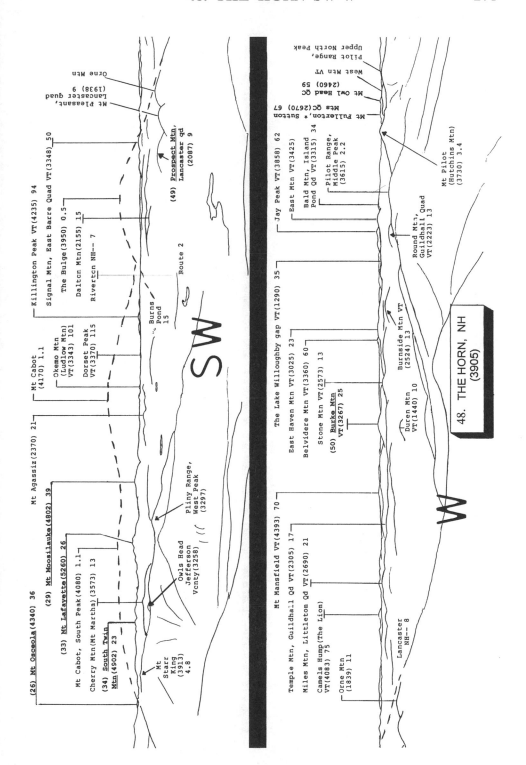

(26) Mt Osceola(4340) 36   Mt Agassiz(2370) 21

(29) Mt Moosilauke(4802) 39

(33) Mt Lafayette(5260) 26

Mt Cabot, South Peak (4080) 1.1

Cherry Mtn(Mt Martha) (3573) 13

(34) South Twin
Mtn (4902) 23

Mt
Starr
King
(3913)
4.8

Owls Head
Jefferson
Vcnty(3258)

Pliny Range,
West Peak
(3297)

Mt Cabot
(4170) 1.1

Okemo Mtn
(Ludlow Mtn)
VT(3343) 101

Dorset Peak
VT(3370) 115

Killington Peak VT(4235) 94

Signal Mtn, East Barre Quad VT(3348) 50

The Bulge (3950) 0.5

Dalton Mtn(2155) 15

Riverton NH-- 7

Burns
Pond
15

Route 2

Mt Pleasant,
Lancaster quad
(1938) 9

Orne Mtn

(49) Prospect Mtn,
Lancaster qd
(2087) 9

SW

Mt Mansfield VT(4393) 70

Temple Mtn, Guildhall Qd VT(2305) 17

Miles Mtn, Littleton Qd VT(2690) 21

Camels Hump(The Lion)
VT(4083) 75

Orne Mtn
(1839) 11

Lancaster
NH-- 8

The Lake Willoughby gap VT(1290) 35

East Haven Mtn VT(3025) 23

Belvidere Mtn VT(3360) 60

Stone Mtn VT(2573) 13

(50) Burke Mtn
VT(3267) 25

Duren Mtn
VT(1440) 10

Burnside Mtn VT

Jay Peak VT(3858) 62

East Mtn VT(3425)

Bald Mtn, Island
Pond Qd VT(3315) 34

Pilot Range,
Middle Peak
(3615) 2.2

Round Mtn,
Guildhall Quad
VT(2223) 13

Mt Fullerton,* Sutton
Mts QC(2670) 67

Mt Owl Head QC
(2460) 59

West Mtn VT

Pilot Range,
Upper North Peak

Mt Pilot
(Hutchins Mtn)
(3730) 3.4

48. THE HORN, NH
(3905)

W

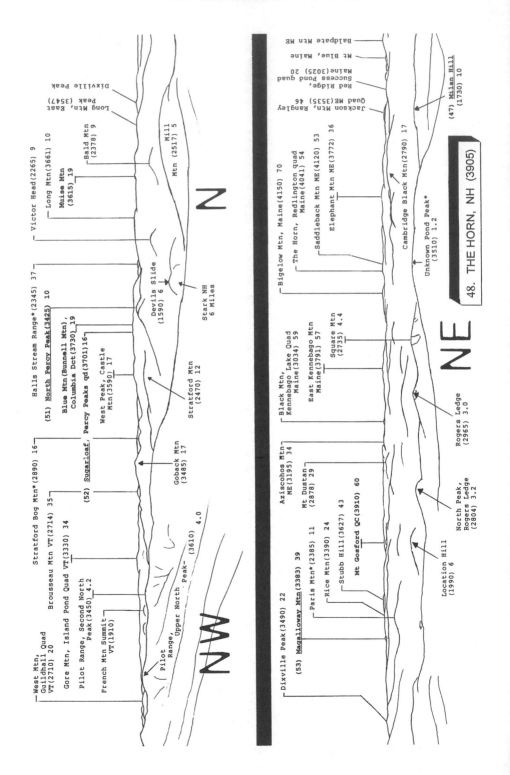

NW

N

NE

48. THE HORN, NH (3905)

West Mtn,
Guildhall Quad
VT(2710) 20

Gore Mtn, Island Pond Quad VT(3330) 34

Pilot Range, Second North
Peak(3450) 4.2

French Mtn Summit
VT(1910)

Pilot
Range,
Upper North
Peak-
(3610)   4.0

Brousseau Mtn VT(2714) 35

Stratford Bog Mtn*(2890) 16

Halls Stream Range*(2345) 37

(51) North Percy Peak(3425) 10

Blue Mtn(Bunnell Mtn),
Columbia Dct(3730) 19

(52) Sugarloaf, Percy Peaks qd(3701)16

West Peak, Castle
Mtn(3590) 17

Goback Mtn
(3485) 17

Stratford Mtn
(2470) 12

Devils Slide
(1590) 6

Stark NH
6 Miles

Victor Head(2265) 9

Long Mtn(3661) 10

Muise Mtn
(3615) 19

Bald Mtn
(2378) 9

Long Mtn, East
Peak (3547)

Dixville Peak

Mill
Mtn (2517) 5

Dixville Peak(3490) 22

(53) Magalloway Mtn(3383) 39

Paris Mtn*(2385) 11

Rice Mtn(3390) 24

Stubb Hill(3627) 43

Mt Gosford QC(39l0) 60

Aziscohos Mtn
ME(3195) 34

Mt Dustan
(2878) 29

Black Mtn,
Kennebago Lake Quad
Maine(3034) 59

East Kennebago Mtn
Maine(3791) 57

Square Mtn
(2735) 4.4

Bigelow Mtn, Maine(4150) 70

The Horn, Redlington quad
Maine(4041) 54

Saddleback Mtn ME(4120) 53

Elephant Mtn ME(3772) 36

Rogers Ledge
(2965) 3.0

North Peak,
Rogers Ledge
(2804) 3.2

Location Hill
(1990) 6

Cambridge Black Mtn(2790) 17

Unknown Pond Peak*
(3510) 1.2

48. THE HORN, NH (3905)

Jackson Mtn, Rangley
Quad ME(3535) 46

Red Ridge
Success Pond quad
Maine(3025) 20

Mt Blue, Maine

Baldpate Mtn ME

(47) Milan Hill
(1730) 10

(49) PROSPECT MOUNTAIN

Lancaster Quadrangle

N 44° 27.046'
W 71° 34.269'

(Elevation 2087 feet)

We descend from the lofty heights of Mount Cabot and The Horn to try a summit that is barely two thousand feet high. From its top, the distant peaks seem more massive. Prospect was selected because of its strategic location. We stand just south of Lancaster, New Hampshire and can review many of the peaks that are on or near the Appalachian Trail.

Glance to the south-southwest and locate Mount Moosilauke standing somewhat low on the horizon 32 miles away. Turn the head to the left slowly past South Kinsman, Cannon, Lafayette, South Twin, Jackson, Eisenhower, Washington and Adams. We have climbed all of them as well as several between. Their majesty is enhanced by the lack of intervening hills as we take in this magnificent profile across the valley of the Johns and Ammonusuc Rivers.

We arrive here by taking Route 3 six miles north out of Whitefield. This road climbs steeply into the saddle between Pleasant and Prospect Mountains. On the left there is ample parking (N 27.185 min, W 34.727 min). To the east, a gated entrance disappears into the forest with signs for Weeks State Park. The road leads to the summit, a place adorned with picnic tables, a fire tower and the Weeks Memorial Mansion.

John W. Weeks once owned this mansion. He had been the Congressman who sired the Weeks Act of 1911. This act resulted in the development of the White Mountain National Forest. He was also the father of Sinclair Weeks, the Secretary of Commerce under President Eisenhower. John W. had as a progenitor another John W. who had been a member of the Presidential Range naming expedition of 1820 led by Ethan Allen Crawford. The home is now a museum containing historic photographs, mounted bird specimens and an exhibition of text and art featuring the Weeks Act. The museum is open most days from late June through Labor Day. One may visit the website www.nhstateparks.org and click on "John Wingate Weeks Historical Site" for information.

Off-season, the Park's entrance gate is closed, and this requires a climb on foot.   The road wraps its way around Prospect during its 1.2-mile ascent giving one an open view of the large ponds to the south and the Pliny-Pilot range to the east.   At the top is seen a huge sweep of New Hampshire's highest peaks.

The fire tower is not the usual cab perched astride a structure of girders and open steps intimidating those who fear heights.   Instead, it resembles a lighthouse in that it is enclosed all the way up but having many openings for viewing.   With the common fire tower, the warden need not be there for a person to be able to reach the landing below the cab where one generally has a clear view.   The enclosed tower on Prospect Mountain can be locked at the base and may require the warden's presence for it to be open. Its times of being open are more related to the fire season rather than the mansion's hours.

If the tower is closed, then the only view is to the south, but a view well worth the hike.   Today, the tower is open and we have climbed its hundred or so steps.   Immediately we become aware that Prospect Mountain is the easternmost of three abrupt hills starting with Orne Mountain two miles away along with the nearer Mount Pleasant.   Off to the left we see Martin Meadow Pond and the smaller Blood Pond.   (Before we speculate upon how many ax murders it took to christen the latter, please note that the Coos County telephone directory lists five families named Blood.)

Because we are lower in elevation, we fail to see the more distant ranges. Vermont's Mount Mansfield shows up over the top of Orne Mountain but only in part.   We cannot see the Lake Willoughby gap, the Lowell Mountains nor the Jays.   There is just one Quebec summit – Hereford Mountain seen 44 miles away past Bear Mountain.   Nearby New Hampshire tops loom large eclipsing what lies beyond.   Starting with Lightning Mountain on the left and ending with Long on the right, a veil of peaks shuts off seeing the northern Monadnock, Magalloway and Stub Hill.   The Pliny-Pilot range hides all of Maine.

But a disadvantage is often a reverse advantage.   When looking down at lesser summits from greater heights, we often fail to see their individuality. From 2087 feet, such "molehills" stand high.   We not only see their skyline profiles, but also the indentations formed by ravines, diagonal ridge lines and open ledges.   The numerous details, seen from lesser tops, create a marvelous view of their own.

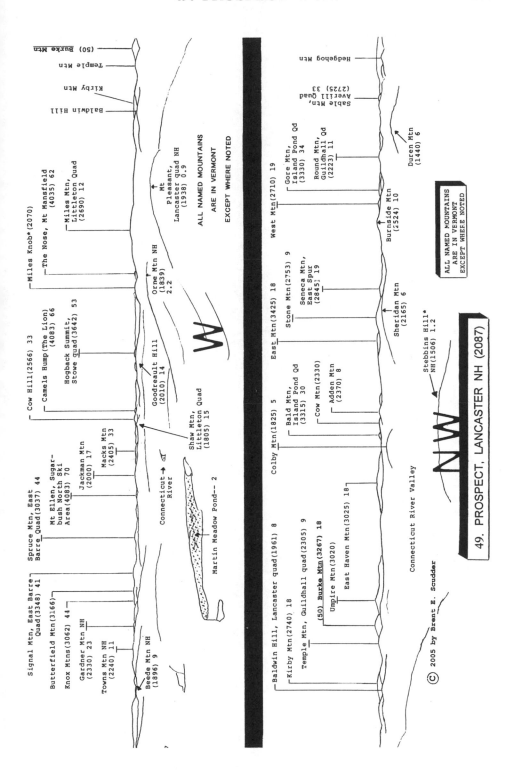

Signal Mtn, East Barre Quad(3348) 41

Butterfield Mtn(3166)

Knox Mtns(3062) 44

Gardner Mtn NH (2330) 23

Towns Mtn NH (2240) 11

Beede Mtn NH (1896) 9

Spruce Mtn, East Barre Quad(3037) 44

Mt Ellen, Sugar-bush North Ski Area(4083) 70

Jackman Mtn (2000) 17

Macks Mtn (2405) 33

Cow Hill(2566) 33

Camels Hump(The Lion) (4083) 66

Hogback Summit, Stowe quad(3642) 53

Goodreault Hill (2010) 14

Shaw Mtn, Littleton Quad (1805) 15

Connecticut → River

Martin Meadow Pond-- 2

Miles Knob* (2070)

The Nose, Mt Mansfield (4035) 62

Miles Mtn, Littleton Quad (2690) 12

Orne Mtn NH (1839) 2.2

Mt Pleasant, Lancaster quad NH (1938) 0.9

Baldwin Hill

Kirby Mtn

Temple Mtn

(50) Burke Mtn

W

ALL NAMED MOUNTAINS

ARE IN VERMONT

EXCEPT WHERE NOTED

Baldwin Hill, Lancaster quad(1961) 8

Kirby Mtn(2740) 18

Temple Mtn, Guildhall quad(2305) 9

(50) Burke Mtn(3267) 18

Umpire Mtn(3020)

East Haven Mtn(3025) 18

Colby Mtn(1825) 5

Bald Mtn, Island Pond Qd (3315) 30

Cow Mtn(2330)

Adden Mtn (2370) 8

East Mtn(3425) 18

Stone Mtn(2753) 9

Seneca Mtn, East Spur (2845) 19

Sheridan Mtn (2165) 6

West Mtn(2710) 19

Gore Mtn, Island Pond Qd (3330) 34

Round Mtn, Guildhall Qd (2223) 11

Burnside Mtn (2524) 10

Hedgehog Mtn

Sable Mtn, Averill Quad (2725) 33

Duren Mtn (1440) 6

Stebbins Hill* NH(1506) 1.2

Connecticut River Valley

NW

ALL NAMED MOUNTAINS
ARE IN VERMONT
EXCEPT WHERE NOTED

49. PROSPECT, LANCASTER NH (2087)

© 2005 by Brent E. Scudder

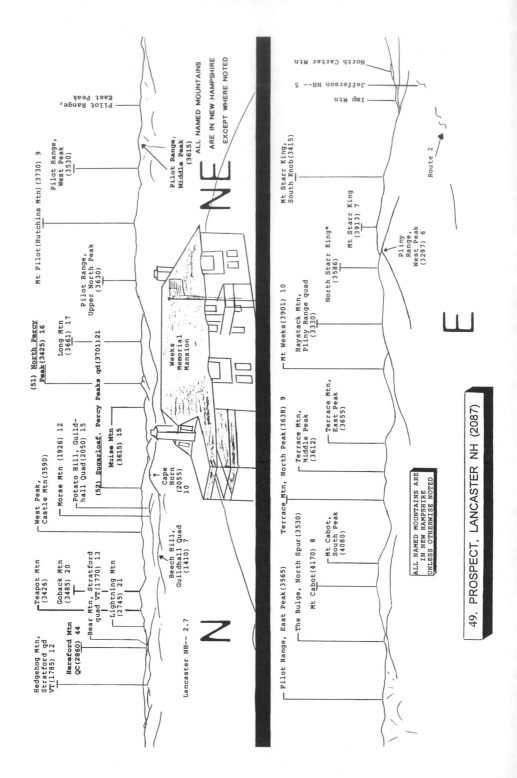

49. PROSPECT, LANCASTER NH (2087)

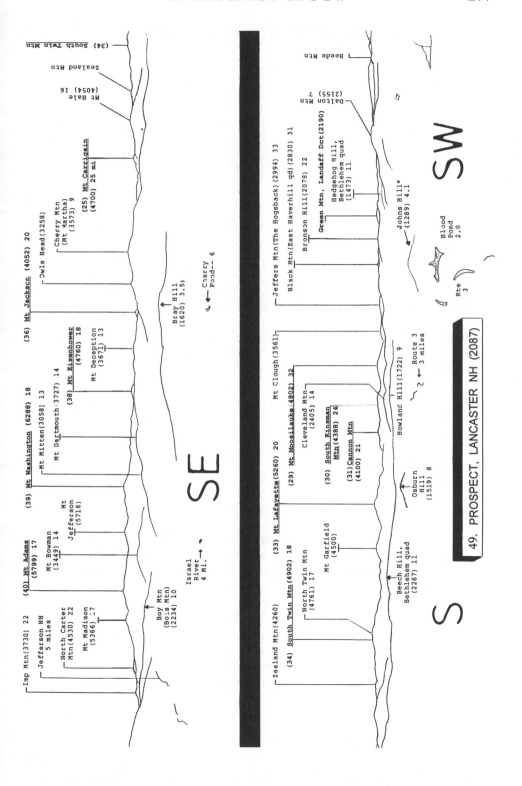

49. PROSPECT, LANCASTER NH (2087)

(50) BURKE MOUNTAIN

Vermont

N 44° 34.198'
W 71° 53.532'

(Elevation 3267 feet)

Again we cross a political boundary in order to reach another of the northern peaks. Just what are these demarcations called state lines but artificial barriers of the mind created by only one of Earth's thousands of species. Gaze at a map of the Granite State and note that it becomes progressively narrower in the upper part. Seeing the White Mountains from all directions requires viewpoints from outside New Hampshire.

Welcome to Vermont's Northeast Kingdom. Here stands a broken ridge of heights running from south to north that gradually bends towards the right. This range forms a wall of high terrain that forced road builders to go around. Starting with the multi-summited Kirby Mountain to the south, the range extends northward past Burke, Umpire, East Haven, East and Seneca Mountains, respectively. Driving to Burke Mountain from New Hampshire means passing south of this range on I-93, and then up I-91 past St. Johnsbury to exit 23. Travel north on Route 5 a distance of 2.4 miles and fork right onto 114. An additional 4.8 miles brings you to the turnoff on the right that leads to the Burke Mountain ski area. Continue straight, passing the Burke Mountain Academy, until you reach the toll road. You have driven around the mountain range in order to ascend from the opposite side.

Burke's charm is several-fold. From the top, not only do you see a view of the White Mountains unfamiliar to many, but also the Lake Willoughby gap only thirteen miles almost in the reverse direction. There we note the steep slopes formed on either side of the gap by Mounts Hor and Pisgah. We also recognize Quebec's Sutton Mountains beyond. Vermont's Green Mountains start with Killington Peak visible to the southwest. They extend all the way past Camels Hump, Mount Mansfield and Jay Peak. Between Mansfield and Butternut, a slight protrusion on the horizon reveals Johnson Mountain, New York, a mere 94 miles away. In the reverse direction arises Maine's Saddleback Mountain. We scan four states and two countries – quite a feat for a mere three-thousand footer.

Burke Mountain's ski area is of some size yet little known. Stowe, Jay Peak, Cannon, Loon and Waterville Valley with their large "verticals," multiple lifts and apres-ski activities combine to lure away the thousands and thousands of suburban skiers. Yet this area has all these features not to mention overnight lodging and a condominium community.

If planning to drive up this forested peak, check beforehand as to whether the toll road is open to vehicles (www.skiburke.com). If hiking, one can climb either via the toll road or by means of the ski trails during other than the winter season. The ski trails, themselves, are not suggested hiking after May due to excessive weed growth. Yet, during the ascent, one gets ever expanding views towards the Lake Willoughby gap. Hiking the mountain by either route takes an hour and a half.

One may also hike up the old CCC road, an unblazed trail that leaves the toll road to the right (N 35.091 min, W 53.697 min) about 0.4 miles above the tollhouse. This path works across the ski trails and winds around to the west side of the mountain. The West Peak Trail then leaves to the left passing over West peak, then dropping and rising to finally reach the summit.

At the top there stand two spires, one a fire tower and the other the television antenna for WVTB Channel 20, a PBS station. The latter blocks some of the view from the tower. Yet what is missing from the panorama can be seen from various outlooks near the summit parking lot.

The scene from Burke differs markedly from those of recent chapters. Among northern New Hampshire summits, forest extends in all directions. But from here we make out extensive open fields to the west and north. The soil of northern Vermont is either more fertile or else it has been easier to till over the centuries. Away from Vermont we see the usual forest.

New Hampshire's White Mountains continue to impress us as always. In April, Cannon's snow-covered ski trails show clearly. Beyond looms the gleaming white Presidential Range. Closer to us stand Mounts Lafayette and Moosilauke. To the left follow the horizon past Old Speck and The Horn.

No longer do the tall mountains of northern New Hampshire block the view towards Quebec. From Sommet Rond to Hereford's north peak, we see many Canadian tops. In the opposite direction arises Mount Ascutney, 83 miles away. From Burke Mountain – four states and two countries – truly a great view.

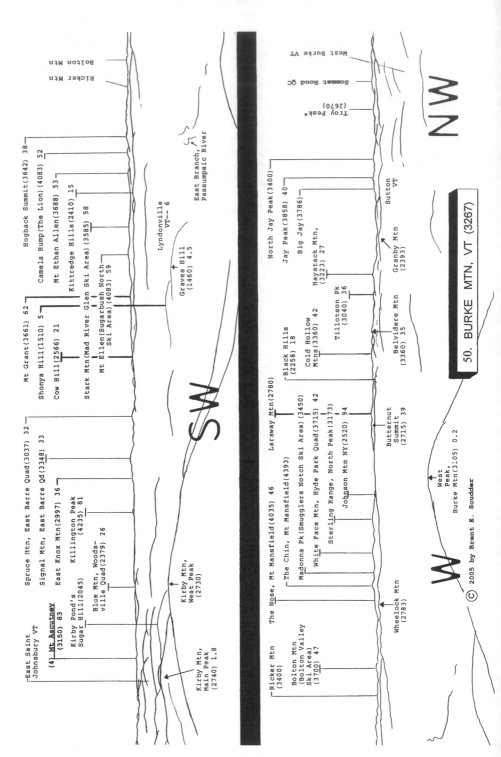

50. BURKE MTN, VT (3267)

SW panorama labels:

East Saint Johnsbury VT
(4) **Mt Ascutney** (3150) 83
Kirby Pond's Sugar Hill (2045)
Blue Mtn, Woodsville Quad (2379) 26
Kirby Mtn, Main Peak (2740) 1.8
Kirby Mtn, West Peak (2730)
Spruce Mtn, East Barre Quad (3037) 32
Signal Mtn, East Barre Qd (3348) 33
East Knox Mtn (2997) 36
Killington Peak (4235) 81
Mt Grant (3661) 62
Shonya Hill (1510) 5
Cow Hill (2566) 21
Stark Mtn (Mad River Glen Ski Area) (3585) 58
Mt Ellen (Sugarbush North Ski Area) (4083) 59
Hogback Summit (3642) 38
Camels Hump (The Lion) (4083) 52
Mt Ethan Allen (3688) 53
Kittredge Hills (2410) 15
Lyndonville VT--6
Graves Hill (1460) 4.5
East Branch, Passumpsic River
Bolton Mtn
Ricker Mtn

W panorama labels:

Ricker Mtn (3400)
Bolton Mtn (Bolton Valley Ski Area) (3700) 47
The Nose, Mt Mansfield (4035) 46
The Chin, Mt Mansfield (4393)
Madonna Pk (Smugglers Notch Ski Area) (3450)
White Face Mtn, Hyde Park Quad (3715) 42
Sterling Range, North Peak (3173)
Johnson Mtn NY (2520) 94
Laraway Mtn (2780)
Black Hills Mtns (3360) 42
Cold Hollow Mtns (3360) 42
Black Hills (2258) 18
Tillotson Pk (3040) 36
Butternut Summit (2715) 39
Belvidere Mtn (3360) 35
Haystack Mtn, (3223) 27
North Jay Peak (3400)
Jay Peak (3858) 40
Big Jay (3786)
Granby Mtn (2393)
Sutton VT
Wheelock Mtn (2783)
West Peak, Burke Mtn (3105) 0.2

NW panorama labels:

Troy Peak* (2670)
Sommet Rond QC
Ricker Mtn
Bolton Mtn
West Burke VT

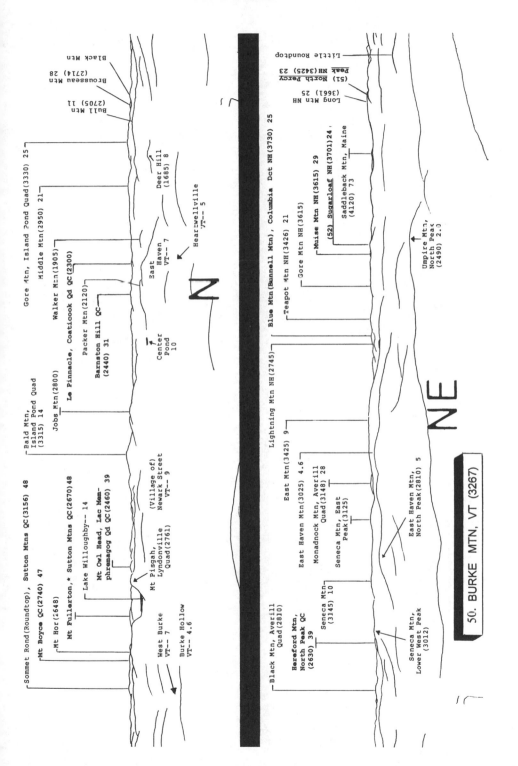

50. BURKE MTN, VT (3267)

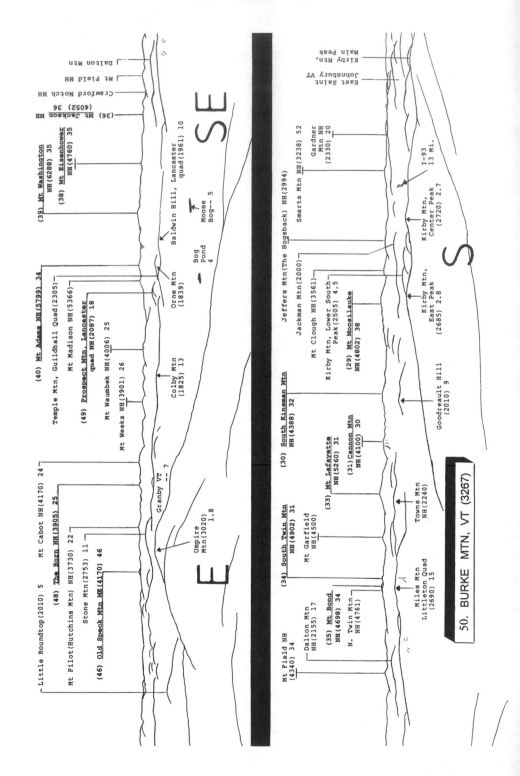

SE

E

S

Little Roundtop(2010) 5   Mt Cabot NH(4170) 24

(48) **The Horn** NH(3905) 25

Mt Pilot(Hutchins Mtn) NH(3730) 22

Stone Mtn(2753) 11

(46) **Old Speck Mtn** ME(4170) 46

Dalton Mtn

Mt Field NH

Crawford Notch NH

(36) **Mt Jackson NH**
(4052) 36

(39) **Mt Washington**
NH(6288) 35

(38) **Mt Eisenhower**
NH(4760) 35

(40) **Mt Adams** NH(5799) 34

Temple Mtn, Guildhall Quad(2305)

Mt Madison NH(5366)

(49) **Prospect Mtn, Lancaster**
quad NH(2087) 18

Mt Waumbek NH(4006) 25

Mt Weeks NH(3901) 26

Baldwin Hill, Lancaster,
quad(1961) 10

Moose
Bog-- 5

Bog
Pond
4

Orne Mtn
(1839)

Colby Mtn
(1825) 13

Granby VT -- 7

Umpire
Mtn(3020)
1.8

Mt Field NH
(4340) 34

Dalton Mtn
NH(2155) 17

(35) **Mt Bond**
NH(4698) 34

N. Twin Mtn
NH(4761)

(34) **South Twin Mtn**
NH(4902) 31

Mt Garfield
NH(4500)

(33) **Mt Lafayette**
NH(5260) 31

(31)**Cannon Mtn**
NH(4100) 30

(30) **South Kinsman Mtn**
NH(4388) 32

Jeffers Mtn(The Hogsback) NH(2994)

Jackman Mtn(2000)

Mt Clough NH(3561)

Kirby Mtn, Lower South
Peak(2505) 4.5

(29) **Mt Moosilauke**
NH(4802) 38

Towns Mtn
NH(2240)

Miles Mtn
Littleton Quad
(2690) 15

Goodreault Hill
(2010) 9

Smarts Mtn NH(3238) 52

Gardner
Mtn NH
(2330) 20

I-93
13 Mi.

Kirby Mtn,
Center Peak
(2720) 2.7

Kirby Mtn,
East Peak
(2685) 2.8

East Saint
Johnsbury VT

Kirby Mtn,
Main Peak

50. BURKE MTN, VT (3267)

(51) NORTH PERCY PEAK

New Hampshire

N 44° 39.781'
W 71° 26.102'

(Elevation 3425 feet)

The Percy Peaks form two cones that rise abruptly to the east of the Nash Stream Wilderness. Their odd presence immediately arouses one's curiosity and also a desire to climb at least one of them. The view from the top of the north peak is certainly worth the arduous ascent.

When measuring across a map, the direct distance from road to summit is barely more than a mile. The trail meanders thereby increasing the hike to 2.2 miles. A steep pitch is assured by the 2200-foot elevation gain. The first half of the trail has a shallow grade of ten per cent leaving a sharp twenty-eight percent pitch for the last half. This incline is comparable to the stiff climb from Greeley Ponds up to the summit of East Osceola or to the relentless rise from the AMC Galehead Hut up to the top of South Twin Mountain.

At the top, look to the southeast and see lovely Christine Lake at our feet. Christine forms the headwaters of the Upper Ammonoosuc River. Well beyond is Berlin with the Mahoosucs to the left and the Presidentials on the right. Nearer and to the right of Mount Washington stands The Horn. Between the two, not only in angle but also in distance, rises Mount Weeks.

Turn our gaze to the right of The Horn over to Mount Cabot. The highest elevation farther over is Mount Pilot, and then the ridge descends to allow us to see several earlier featured peaks from Lafayette to Moosilauke. To the southwest lies the town of Groveton at a distance of six miles. Look left and take note of Cape Horn, a pointed peak that is not too impressive from here but one which towers majestically when seen from the road.

We see much of Vermont as we scan all the way from Signal Mountain near East Barre all the way to Jay Peak. Vermont's highest elevation, Mount Mansfield, barely appears over the northern ridge of East Haven Mountain.

In order to find the trailhead, approach the village of Groveton, New Hampshire from the south on Route 3. Turn right on Route 110 and let the odometer reel off 2.7 miles. Go left on Emerson Road and continue until you are 2.1 miles from Route 110. Turn left again onto Nash Stream Road, a dirt road which the Diamond International Paper company once owned and maintained. At that time, the road was not cleared of snow in winter and closed between the Spring snow melt and late May. Once you are on Nash Steam Road drive 2.7 miles and look for the Percy Peak Trail sign on the right (N 39.937 min, W 27.457 min).

Follow the path that is charted on the Percy Peaks USCG topographical map (7.5 minute series) to the junction of the trail that circles the north peak. Hike counter-clockwise around the circle to and slightly beyond the saddle between the Percys. A steep trail that is not on the map leads left uphill over rocky ledges to finally reach the summit. Extreme care must be taken on these rocky out-croppings if they are wet with dew, misty rain or fog. Ice and snow are even more dangerous.

We do not see much of Quebec. The Savage Mountain group blocks us to the northwest along with the Blue Mountain Range to the north. But we can identify Sommet Rond, Mont Megantic and several lesser peaks that we have not labeled. In Maine we see two Snow Mountains standing to the left of nearby Long Mountain. To the right of Long, there appear a number of peaks ranging from Saddleback Wind Mountain to Mount Carlo.

On the morning we selected to climb North Percy, the air was crystal clear. We had been on the trail only a half an hour when we met a couple who were moving rapidly down the mountain.

"You must have started up at the crack of dawn, I said.

The man replied, "I thought I heard a bear growl. We're leaving!"

Read Kilham and Gray's delightful book *Among the Bears* (listed in Appendix H), and you will feel far less nervous about ursine encounters than this couple. We found no trace of the furry creature.

The magnificence of North Percy Peak is known by relatively few hikers. Too many of them ignore the North Country with its miles of forest, lake and mountain. Some of us would prefer that this state of affairs remain that way. But if we spread out the use of the woods over a greater area, then the more popular sections become more of a wilderness experience.

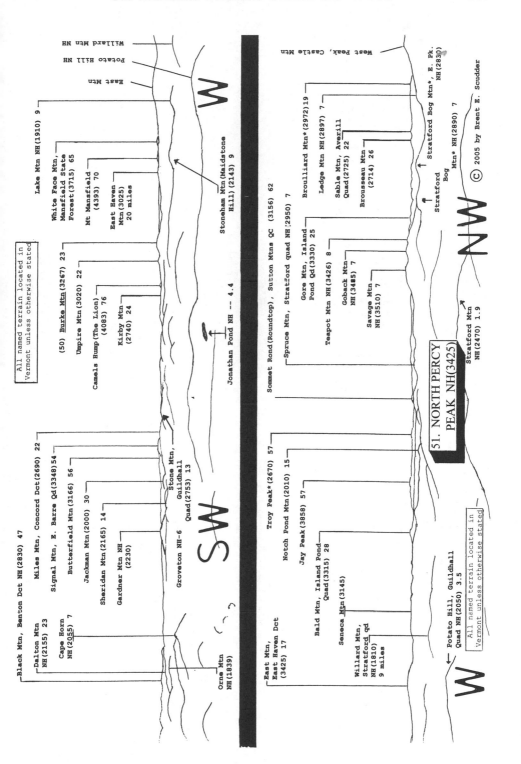

All named terrain located in Vermont unless otherwise stated

Black Mtn, Benton NH (2830) 47
Dalton Mtn NH (2155) 23
Cape Horn NH (2055) 7
Miles Mtn, Concord Dct (2690) 22
Signal Mtn, E. Barre Qd (3348) 54
Butterfield Mtn (3166) 56
Jackman Mtn (2000) 30
Sheridan Mtn (2165) 14
Gardner Mtn NH (2230)
Stone Mtn, Guildhall Quad (2753) 13
Groveton NH-6
Orne Mtn NH (1839)

Lake Mtn NH (1910) 9
White Face Mtn, Mansfield State Forest (3715) 65
(50) Burke Mtn (3267) 23
Umpire Mtn (3020) 22
Mt Mansfield (4393) 70
Camels Hump (The Lion) (4083) 76
East Haven Mtn (3025) 20 miles
Kirby Mtn (2740) 24
Stoneham Mtn (Maidstone Hill) (2143) 9

East Mtn NH
Potato Hill NH
Willard Mtn NH

W

Jonathan Pond NH -- 4.4

SW

East Mtn, East Haven Dct (3425) 17
Notch Pond Mtn (2010) 15
Jay Peak (3858) 57
Bald Mtn, Island Pond Quad (3315) 28
Seneca Mtn (3145)
Willard Mtn, Stratford qd NH (1810) 9 miles

Troy Peak* (2670) 57

Sommet Rond (Roundtop), Sutton Mtns QC (3156) 62
Spruce Mtn, Stratford quad NH (2950) 7
Gore Mtn, Island Pond Qd (3330) 25
Teapot Mtn NH (3426) 8
Goback Mtn NH (3485) 7
Savage Mtn NH (3510) 7
Broulliard Mtn* (2972) 19
Ledge Mtn NH (2897) 7
Sable Mtn, Averill Quad (2725) 22
Brousseau Mtn (2714) 26
Stratford Bog Mtn*, E. Pk. NH (2830)
Stratford Bog Mtn* NH (2890) 7

West Peak, Castle Mtn

NW

© 2005 by Brent E. Scudder

Potato Hill, Guildhall Quad NH (2050) 3.5

All named terrain located in Vermont unless otherwise stated

Stratford Mtn NH (2470) 1.9

51. NORTH PERCY PEAK NH (3425)

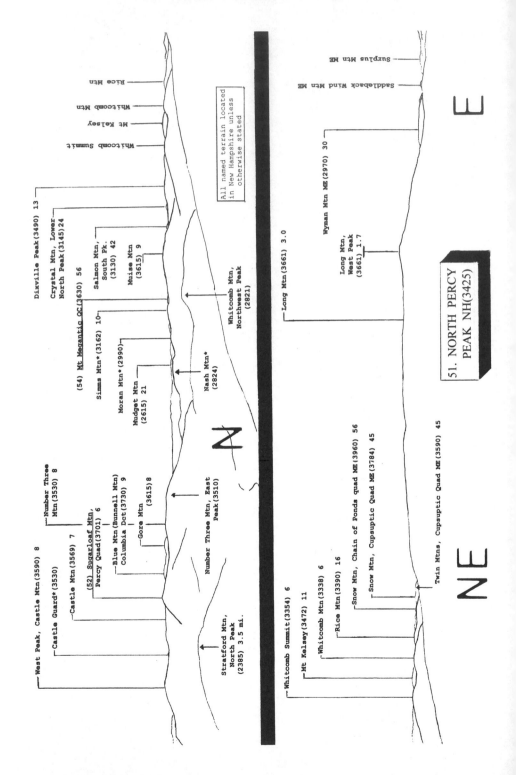

All named terrain located
in New Hampshire unless
otherwise stated

West Peak, Castle Mtn (3590) 8
Castle Guard* (3530)
Castle Mtn (3569) 7
(52) Sugarloaf Mtn,
Percy Quad (3701) 6
Blue Mtn (Bunnell Mtn)
Columbia Dot (3730) 9
Gore Mtn
(3615) 8
Number Three Mtn, East
Peak (3510)
Stratford Mtn,
North Peak
(2385) 3.5 mi.

Number Three
Mtn (3530) 8

Dixville Peak (3490) 13
Crystal Mtn, Lower
North Peak (3145) 24
(54) Mt Megantic QC (3630) 56
Salmon Mtn,
South Pk.
(3130) 42
Muise Mtn
(3615) 9
Simms Mtn* (3162) 10
Moran Mtn* (2990)
Mudget Mtn
(2615) 21
Nash Mtn*
(2824)
Whitcomb Mtn,
Northwest Peak
(2821)

Whitcomb Summit
Mt Kelsey
Whitcomb Mtn
Rice Mtn

Rice Mtn

N

Whitcomb Summit (3354) 6
Mt Kelsey (3472) 11
Whitcomb Mtn (3338) 6
Rice Mtn (3390) 16
Snow Mtn, Chain of Ponds quad ME (3960) 56
Snow Mtn, Cupsuptic Quad ME (3784) 45
Twin Mtns, Cupsuptic Quad ME (3590) 45

Long Mtn (3661) 3.0
Wyman Mtn ME (2970) 30
Long Mtn,
West Peak
(3661) 1.7

Saddleback Wind Mtn ME
Surplus Mtn ME

E

NE

51. NORTH PERCY
PEAK NH (3425)

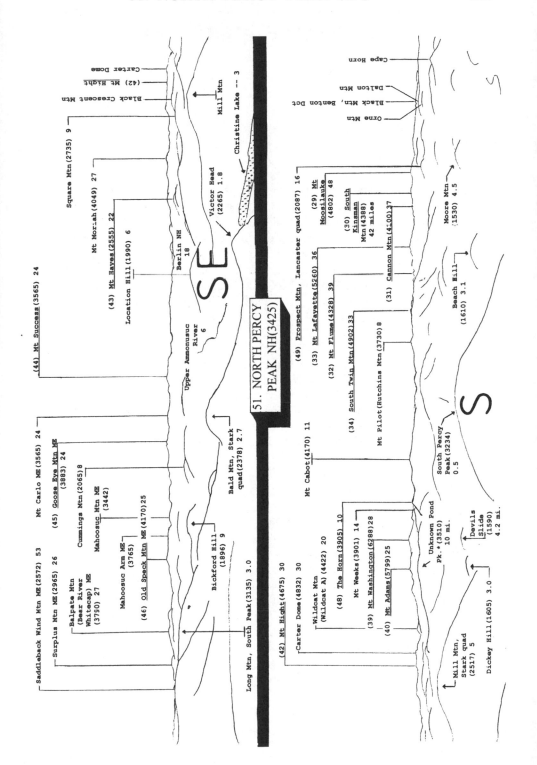

51. NORTH PERCY PEAK NH(3425)

(52) SUGARLOAF MOUNTAIN

N 44° 44.649'
W 71° 28.070'

(Elevation 3701 feet)

Selecting the mountains to be featured in this book was often difficult. Among a wealth of summits with all-encompassing views, we had to choose upon the basis of popularity versus challenge. Among a dearth of such tops, we were narrowed to deciding among a group of wooded peaks, the views from which require either the presence of a temporal fire tower, or the existence of sufficient partial outlooks near the summit. Among the Blue Mountains extending from Stratford to Columbia, all tops seem wooded, and they are, except for one. The summit of Sugarloaf is barely an outcrop of rock above the trees. Yet it would take decades of growth for the forest to take over the view, if ever.

Southward from Sugarloaf, we see the major tops of the White Mountains about forty miles away. Mount Washington stands nearly in line with the Percy Peaks. If we turn the head towards the right, our eyes sweep past Mounts Carrigain, Bond, South Twin, Lafayette, Cannon, Kinsman and Moosilauke. Closer in lies The Horn and we see its relationship with Lancaster's Prospect Mountain seen to the right of and closer than Lafayette. Look to the southwest across the Connecticut River Valley and discover Vermont's Killington Peak over 100 miles away. Our gaze glides northward past Burke, Mansfield and Jay Peak.

To find the beginning of the Sugarloaf Trail, use the instructions in the last chapter to locate the Percy Peaks trailhead. But this time, after turning north from Emerson Road onto Nash Stream Road, drive 8.3 miles. The stream of that name will always be on your left until you are practically at your destination. Then you will cross it and find a driveway on your left. A sign says "Finally Inn." Across the road facing back is a sign which says "Sugarloaf Jct" (N 44.229 min, W 26.349 min). Park so as not to block the driveway. The Sugarloaf Trail starts up this driveway past a shingled cabin and across an open field into the woods. After walking about five hundred feet, the trail forks with the Cohos Trail going left and the Sugarloaf Trail continuing straight. Anytime that the path forks, choose the steeper alternative.

Allow two hours for the climb up a well-marked trail. Once you have reached the ridge, turn left or towards the south. The summit should reveal itself within 200 yards.

We stand on the southeast corner of the Blue Mountains, a collection of tops of approximately the same altitude. One sees the nearby tops of Savage, Goback, and Lightning Mountains to the west with Castle, Blue (Bunnell), Gore and Fitch Mountains to the northwest and north. All are without published trails their summits allowing no views.

Beyond stands Vermont's Monadnock almost identical in size to its southern cousin. Quebec's Sutton Range graces the horizon nearly sixty miles away. The Canadian Orford, Hereford and Megantic peaks follow on the right. Farther over, the United States border splits Salmon Mountain, Saddle Hill and Gosford's east peak.

The wilder mountains of Maine lie farther east. There is Bigelow, Bemis, Elephant and Old Speck. Half of the Mahoosuc Range is visible, the other half being hidden behind Long Mountain.

Where is Nash Bog Pond? We could not see it. A later look at the photographs we took revealed no pond but a bog. Once a person knows what to look for, the shoreline of this green carpet stands out in sharp relief.

Climbing Sugarloaf puts you well into the North Country enabling you to have seen the White Mountains from all sides. Most hiking guides either skip this mountain or give it few pages with the result that there are few hikers. The country is indeed wilder. The forest is thicker and more remote. But why stop here? Let us move even farther north.

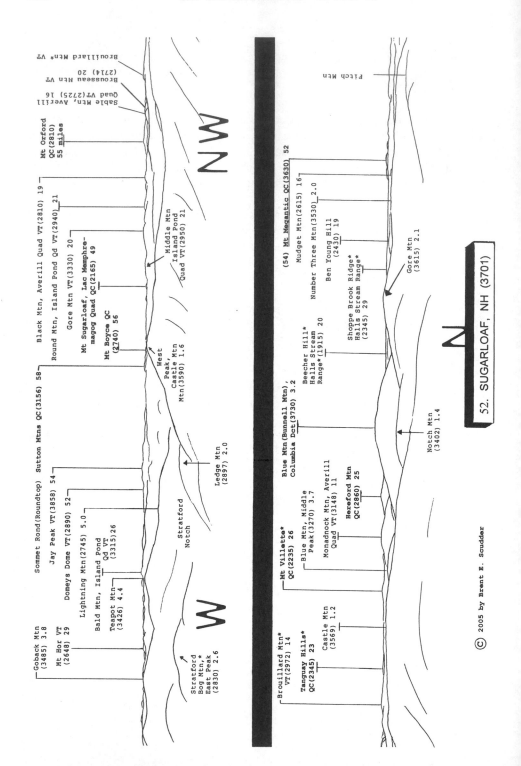

© 2005 by Brent E. Scudder

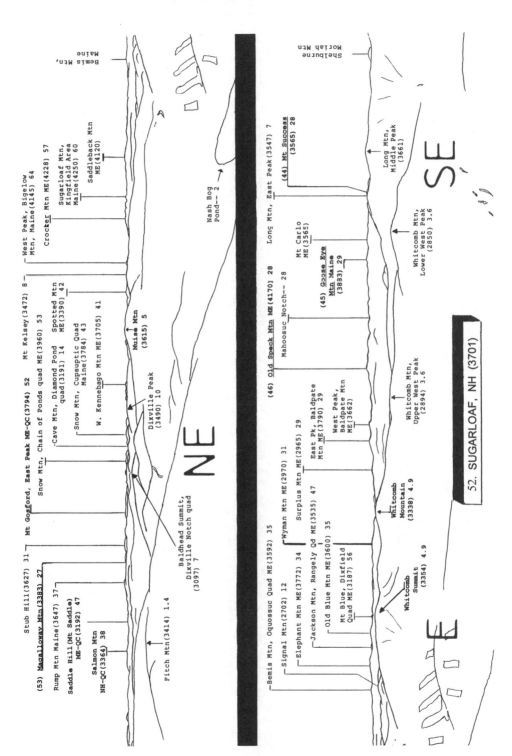

NE

Stub Hill(3627) 31 — Mt Gosford, East Peak ME-QC(3794) 52 — Mt Kelsey(3472) 8 —

(53) Magalloway Mtn(3383) 27

Snow Mtn, Chain of Ponds quad ME(3960) 53

Rump Mtn Maine(3647) 37

Saddle Hill (Mt Saddle) ME-QC(3192) 47

Cave Mtn, Diamond Pond quad(3191) 14

Spotted Mtn ME(3390) 42

Snow Mtn, Cupsuptic Quad Maine(3784) 43

Salmon Mtn NH-QC(3364) 38

W. Kennebago Mtn ME(3705) 41

Muise Mtn (3615) 5

Dixville Peak (3490) 10

Baldhead Summit, Dixville Notch quad (3097) 7

Fitch Mtn(3414) 1.4

West Peak, Bigelow Mtn, Maine(4145) 64 —

Crocker Mtn ME(4228) 57

Sugarloaf Mtn, Kingfield Area Maine(4250) 60

Saddleback Mtn ME(4120)

Nash Bog Pond-- 2

Bemis Mtn, Maine

E

Bemis Mtn, Oquossoc Quad ME(3592) 35

Signal Mtn(2702) 12

Wyman Mtn ME(2970) 31

Surplus Mtn ME(2965) 29

Elephant Mtn ME(3772) 34

Jackson Mtn, Rangely Qd ME(3535) 47

Old Blue Mtn ME(3600) 35

Mt Blue, Dixfield Quad ME(3187) 56

Whitcomb Summit (3354) 4.9

Whitcomb Mountain (3338) 4.9

West Peak, Baldpate Mtn ME(3662)

East Pk, Baldpate Mtn ME(3790) 29

Whitcomb Mtn, Upper West Peak (2894) 3.6

SE

(46) Old Speck Mtn ME(4170) 28

Long Mtn, East Peak(3547) 7

Mahoosuc Notch-- 28

Mt Carlo ME(3565)

(45) Goose Eye Mtn Maine(3833) 29

(3565) 28

(44) Mt Success 28

Whitcomb Mtn, Lower West Peak (2850) 3.6

Long Mtn, Middle Peak (3611)

Shelburne Moriah Mtn

52. SUGARLOAF, NH (3701)

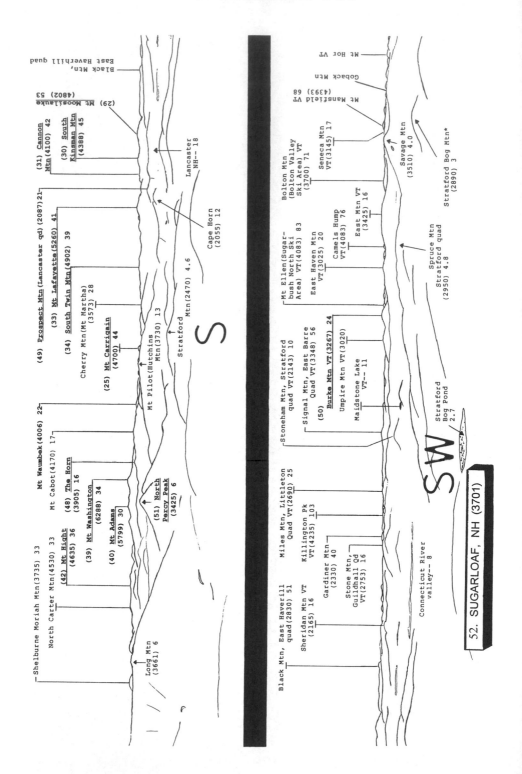

52. SUGARLOAF, NH (3701)

(53) MAGALLOWAY MOUNTAIN

N 45° 03.790'
W 71° 09.806'

(Elevation 3383 feet)

We arrive at the headwaters of the Connecticut River. From Magalloway's summit, nothing is seen but lakes and forest. One sees no city or town – only the habitat of the beaver, deer, fox, bear and moose. The bear tends to avoid man, but the moose stands invisible in the leafy shadows watching these irrational human creatures hike past, understanding them not in the least.

Magalloway lies only thirteen miles from Quebec. Indeed, the mountain is situated so far north that from its top, one not only sees parts of Vermont beyond intervening Canadian territory but also parts of Maine. To the west, Barnston Hill, Quebec, is seen to the left of Vermont's more distant rise, temporarily named Lucas Ridge. In the opposite direction, Quebec's Gosford appears to the right of Maine's farther off Merrill Mountain.

At the summit look south and see a relatively hazy Presidential Range. We are farther north of Mount Washington (54 miles) than Belknap Mountain is to the south. We can turn our head to the right looking past Mounts Jefferson, Eisenhower and Field, but the remaining White Mountains pass behind such tops as Waumbec, Cabot and Dixville Peak. Sugarloaf is seen on the horizon farther right complete with its characteristic steep eastern slope.

Our first stretch of water is the lovely Lake Francis situated almost due west of us followed by First Connecticut Lake to the northwest and Second Connecticut Lake to the north. Farther away, Canada appears and the place names become decidedly French. To be sure, Quebec offers us such English names as Barnston Hill, Hereford Mountain and Mount Foster. But gaze upon Mont Chagnon, Colline Chabot, Mont des Trois Lacs, Bon Durban and others.

Reaching Magalloway Mountain requires a compass, a road map and a topographic chart. The recently published Magalloway "topo" shows many of the logging roads in the area. However, one can also navigate with either of the two earlier charts – the American produced "Second Lake," or the Canadian-published "Malvina."

North of Pittsburg, New Hampshire, take Route 3 until you are 4.8 miles past the dam on First Connecticut Lake. Turn right on Magalloway Road (N 07.764 min, W 13.403 min) and arrive 1.2 miles later at a bridge over the Connecticut River. The width of this famous waterway may surprise you. Continue straight. Once beyond the river, various lumber roads lead off to the left and right. Stay on the best-traveled road.

Having left Route 3 behind by three miles, the road forks left and begins to climb. It passes over a height of land (an elevation marked 2407 on all three charts). Shortly thereafter (5.3 miles from Route 3), turn sharply right onto a side road that leads downhill (N 05.490 min, W 09.780 min). Eventually you will see another road leading downhill to the left. Ignore it and continue straight. Drive to the end which is 8.4 miles from Route 3 (N 04.163 min, W 10.314 min). Park here. A badly eroded jeep roads leads off to the right. This is the path to the top. Whenever the trail forks, take the steeper choice. Allow fifty minutes from car to summit.

The top is forested, but excellent views are seen from the fire tower as well as from the top of the cliff that faces east. Gaze northeast and gather in our best view of Maine's Rump Mountain. Rump's distinctive profile makes it easy to recognize from here as well as from mountains farther south. Look past the 3607-foot Stub Hill and past Maine's Kennebago Divide. Bigelow Mountain stands to the right of East Kennebago. Closer in lies Aziscohos Lake and nearer still the valley of the Dead Diamond River.

With central New Hampshire's excellent trail system, we tend to forget the compass. Quite often I have discovered that I never removed it from my pack. Take frequent compass readings here! Paths are few and often obscure. GPS units can fail. Cell phone coverage in the mountains is sporadic at best. A hike in the wrong direction will result in miles and miles of walking in order to reach the nearest paved road. The added precaution of frequently ascertaining your bearings preserves the aura of exhilaration that is the essence of mountain hiking in this vast northern forest.

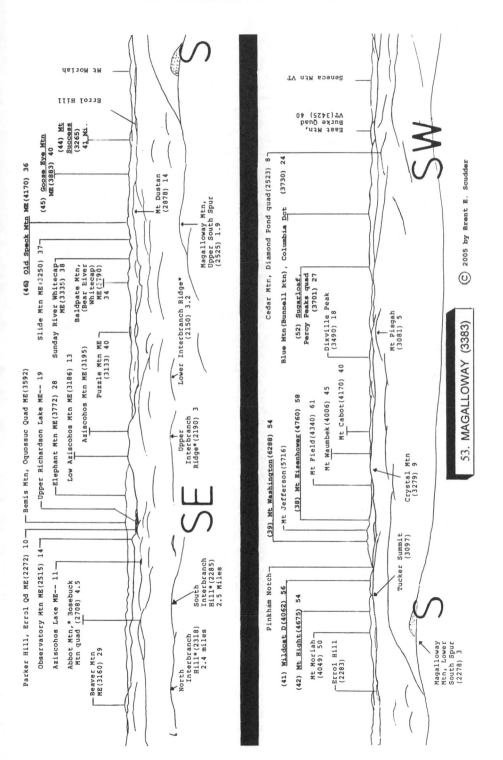

Parker Hill, Errol Qd ME(2272) 10 ─┐

Observatory Mtn ME(2515) 14 ─┐

Aziscohos Lake ME── 11 ─┐

Abbot Mtn,* Bosebuck
Mtn quad (2708) 4.5

Beaver Mtn
ME(3160) 29

Bemis Mtn, Oquossuc Quad ME(3592) ─┐

Upper Richardson Lake ME── 19 ─┐

Elephant Mtn ME(3772) 28 ─┐

Low Aziscohos Mtn ME(3186) 13 ─┐

Aziscohos Mtn ME(3195) ─┐

Puzzle Mtn ME
(3113) 40

Slide Mtn ME(3250) 37 ─┐

Sunday River Whitecap
ME(3335) 38

Baldpate Mtn,
(Bear River
Whitecap)
ME(3790)
34

(46) Old Speck Mtn ME(4170) 36

(45) Goose Eye Mtn
ME(3883) 40

(44) Mt
Success
(3265)
41 Mi.

Errol Hill

Mt Moriah

Mt Dustan
(2878) 14

Magalloway Mtn,
Upper South Spur
(2525) 1.9

Lower Interbranch Ridge*
(2150) 3.2

Upper
Interbranch
Ridge*(2190) 3

North
Interbranch
Hill*(2318)
2.4 miles

South
Interbranch
Hill*(2285)
2.5 Miles

SE

S

Pinkham Notch ─┐

(41) Wildcat D(4062) 56 ─┐

(42) Mt Hight(4675) 54 ─┐

Mt Moriah
(4049) 50

Errol Hill
(2283)

Magalloway
Mtn, Lower
South Spur
(2278) 3

S

Tucker Summit
(3097)

(39) Mt Washington(6288) 54

Mt Jefferson(5716) ─┐

(38) Mt Eisenhower(4760) 58 ─┐

Mt Field(4340) 61 ─┐

Mt Waumbek(4006) 45 ─┐

Mt Cabot(4170) 40

Crystal Mtn
(3279) 9

Blue Mtn(Bunnell Mtn), Columbia Dot ─┐

Cedar Mtn, Diamond Pond quad(2523) 8

(52) Sugarloaf,
Percy Peaks quad
(3701) 27

Dixville Peak
(3490) 18

Mt Pisgah
(3081) 5

East Mtn,
Burke Quad
VT(3425) 40

Seneca Mtn VT

(3730) 24

SW

© 2005 by Brent E. Scudder

53. MAGALLOWAY (3383)

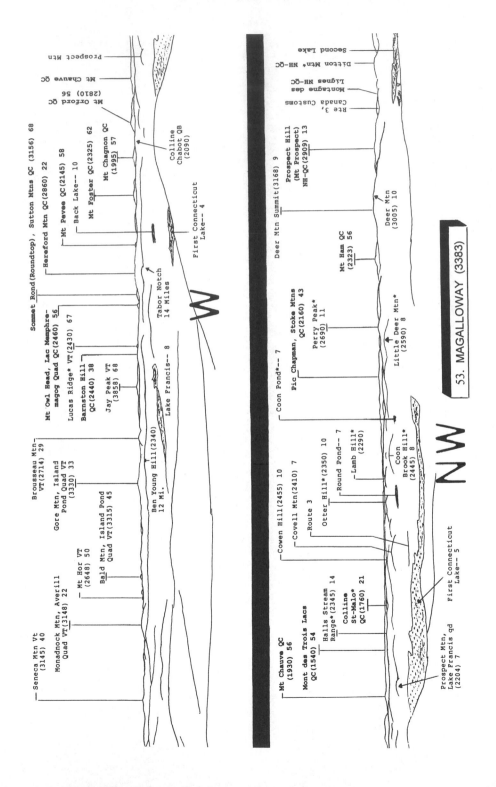

53. MAGALLOWAY (3383)

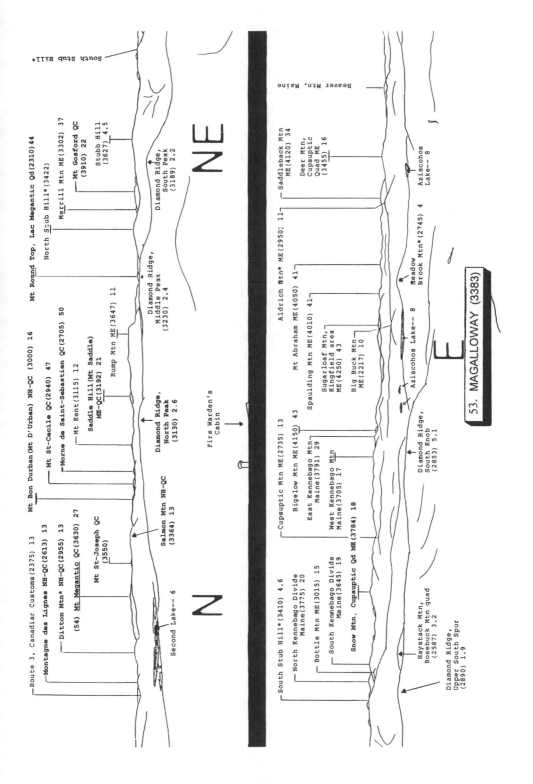

53. MAGALLOWAY (3383)

(54) MONT MEGANTIC

Quebec, Canada

N 45° 27.343'
W 71° 09.176'

(Elevation 3630 feet)

Along Route 3 north of Pittsburg, New Hampshire, one drives mile after mile through thick forest. Rich blue lakes appear, but soon they become invisible due to intervening trees. A four-room cabin sweeps past along the road followed by a hunting camp. A sign says "Firewood." Another advertises canoes. One fails to realize how much the forest shuts him in. The sky is there but only as a narrow blue ribbon of brightness overhead. To the left and right is a verdant green that is deep, dark and almost foreboding.

The road climbs. In the rear view mirror, one sees mountains stretching across. To the left appears a placid lake. The forest has thinned out somewhat. After several minutes, we perceive ourselves to be approaching a mountain pass. At the crest there appears a small building on the left with a large American flag fluttering freely on a pole out front. Farther on, but to the right, we see another building also displaying a banner on a similar pole. The banner's colors are red and white emblazoned with a maple leaf. We have arrived in Canada!

After clearing customs, a fantastic view opens before us. We are seven hundred feet above a vast open countryside that stretches forty miles into the distance. Tiny towns, each dominated by a church spire, are set about eight miles apart. One could swear to have stepped back a century into rural France. To be sure, modern automobiles are the principal mode of transport. TV antennas and satellite dishes adorn many homes. Other than these, the valley reflects a gentler, quieter time.

The centerpiece of this lovely view is a large, lumpy, dark green cake – a mountain over four miles wide. Maps reveal it to be circular in shape, Quebec's version of a geological ring dike complex. The ring structure is not complete and erosion through an opening has taken out some of the interior. But what remains suggests a castle wall. What we see before us is our final elevation – Mont Megantic.

The old New Hampshire Route 3 has now become Quebec Route 257. Drive down off the pass into Chartierville and continue north to La Patrie. Speed limit signs are in kilometers per hour. Multipy by 6/10 to get miles per hour. At La Patrie, turn right onto Route 212 and then left again nine miles later at Notre-Dame-des-Bois. Go two more miles and turn left. The entrance to Parc National du Mont Megantic is reached 2.5 miles later (N 25.490 min, W 09.780 min). Stop at the Information Center to obtain a code number that lifts the automatic gate. Fees as of this writing are $3.00 per person in US currency. A paved road takes you 3.3 miles to the top. Hiking trails abound but hikers are also charged. The road is not open during winter, but snow shoeing and cross-country skiing are allowed. During busy times of the summer, the gate may be closed to the passenger car. At that time, a shuttle bus will take you up to the summit.

Mont Megantic is crowned with an astronomical observatory managed jointly by Laval University and the University of Montreal. From this lofty height, one can see in all directions, but be prepared to move about. At the very top, one can look eastward back down the road. One can also gaze to the southwest and up to 90 degrees of the horizon to either side. In order to look in other directions, walk a tenth of a mile down the road below the parking lot and spot a steep paved road climbing to the right. The house that you see immediately above you is the Pavilion de la Voie-Lactee containing soda machines and rest rooms. There is also a balcony from which you can look to the northeast and 90 degrees to the left and right..

Climb farther up the side road to another observatory, the so-called "Observatoire Populaire du Mont Megantic." Beyond is a viewing area that looks to the southeast and up to 90 degrees along the horizon on both sides.

Do not skip nearby Mont Saint-Joseph. The chart on page 305 is the view to the east and southeast of that very peak (N 26.840 min, W 07.216 min). Mont Saint-Joseph can be reached by turning right on a gravel road found 1.6 miles up from the gate (turning left if you are descending). A mile brings you to a Catholic sanctuary on the top. Although the public is welcome to visit, please respect the fact that it is a religious retreat.

Mont Megantic was selected because the view not only reveals what lies beyond the Canadian Border, but also looks back on the White Mountains from a direction seen by few Americans. Atop Mount Washington, we saw such northern peaks as Snow, Gosford and the Kennebagos as mere pinpricks on the horizon. Now we are near enough to see their individual profiles. We note that both Snow Mountains have rounded tops, that Gosford is one tall apex with several smaller bumps trailing away to the south and that the Kennebago Divide consists of at least three peaks.

The subtitle of this book refers to fifty-four northern New England Mountains. While number fifty-four is actually in Quebec, more than half of the horizon seen from its summit rests in the United States. In this sense we think of Megantic as being a northern New England mountain.

The view to the north is fairly empty of high terrain. There is just an occasional hill or mountain. We see meadows upon meadows sprinkled with trees, lakes and villages. The St. Lawrence River approaches no nearer than seventy miles and, thus, cannot be seen. To the left of nearby Mont Sainte-Cecile, the Notre-Dame Mountains stretch from seventy to ninety miles away to the northeast. The Notre Dames are also visible from the city of Quebec.

Behold! The highest points in Vermont, New Hampshire and Maine can be seen simultaneously! Mount Mansfield is found 103 miles away on the horizon past La Patrie just to the right of Barnston Hill. Mount Washington is closer – 82 miles – visible to the south a little to the right of Magalloway. Katahdin is harder to spot. Gaze eastward down the road from Megantic's summit and note the hump on the outer castle wall that is called Mont Victoria. Just to the right, Maine's Big and Little Spencer Mountains appear prominently as one summit. From this direction the Spencers are often mistaken for Mount Katahdin. The air must be sufficiently clear so that Big and Little Spencer Mountains appear in sharp contrast with the horizon. Then you will see Maine's tallest on the left 113 miles away. Sometimes Katahdin is so faint that although you do not see it, you sense that something is there. When this happens, binoculars reveal its presence.

Katahdin is also visible from Mont Saint-Joseph. But the Spencers no longer serve as a guide. Both are hidden behind the temporarily-designated Keenes Mountain. Locate Katahdin between Keenes and Mont Cliché.

As we head back to New Hampshire, we see a sign reading "Frontiere (E.U.) 18." The E.U. means Etats-Unis or United States but what about the word "Frontiere?" While Quebec natives use the word simply to mean "border," it is a frontier in the English sense. The known ends and the unknown begins. A child growing up in La Patrie must view the world in just this way. Nearby are the familiar fields, farms and villages. At the USA frontier, the forested mountains begin, full of mystery, dark spirits and hungry animals.

And so, we conclude this comprehensive coverage of the White Mountains. We could have chosen other peaks from which to develop panorama diagrams; but these, I trust, cover a broad spectrum from the easily attainable Pitcher and Blue Job Mountains to the more strenuous Bond, Adams, Isolation and The Horn. The fit and trim hiker will belittle the easier ascents now. But as the climber advances in years, he or she will appreciate that skyline diagrams exist for those mountains still physically attainable.

We began this book with Pack Monadnock Mountain located not far from the Massachusetts border. From chapter to chapter, we worked our way northward weaving left and right to assure a continuum that allowed each subsequent panorama to overlap the previous one.

From Pack Monadnock to Blue Job Mountain, we featured the southern New Hampshire area. Here the land was flat but with isolated mountains that were easy to recognize. Far to the north stood the White Mountains visible only on a day of remarkable clarity, their dark, serrated outline arousing a sense of awe and mystery.

From Mount Major to Maine's streaked Mountain, we covered the Lakes Region. Large island-studded bodies of water stood before us while the White Mountains, much nearer now, towered beyond.

The southern White Mountain area followed. This was the Black Cap to Loon Mountain region. Here we skirted the "Sandwich Front," a range of mountains that separated the lowlands to the south from the high peaks to the north.

Central to the book was the Appalachian Trail. Starting with Mount Cube near the Connecticut River to Maine's Old Speck, we described nineteen mountains located a day's hike apart on or near this famous path.

Finally we came to the North Country featuring such peaks as The Horn, Sugarloaf and Magalloway. Towns were few. Forest was everywhere.

We finished in Quebec where the land was rather flat but with isolated mountains that were easy to recognize. Far to the south stood the White Mountains visible only on a day of remarkable clarity, their dark serrated outline arousing a sense of awe and mystery.

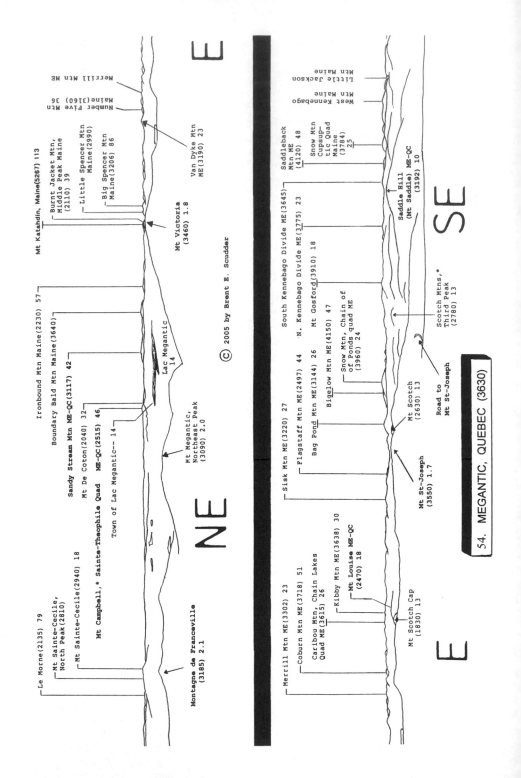

54. MEGANTIC, QUEBEC (3630)

© 2005 by Brent E. Scudder

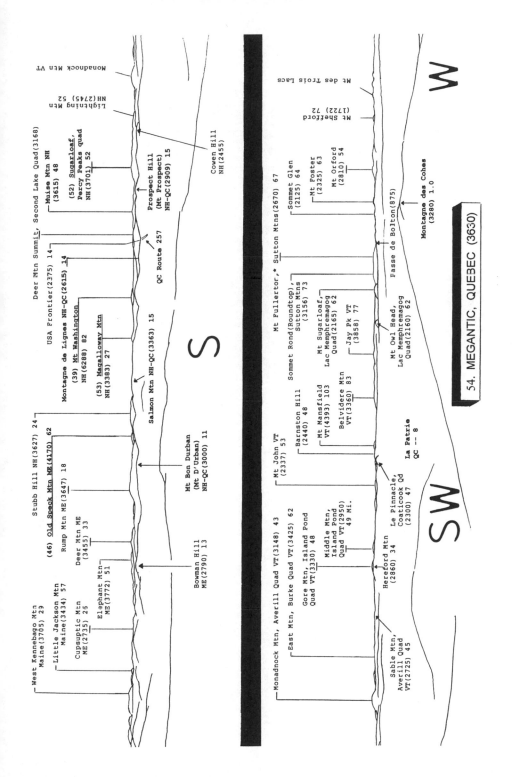

54. MEGANTIC, QUEBEC (3630)

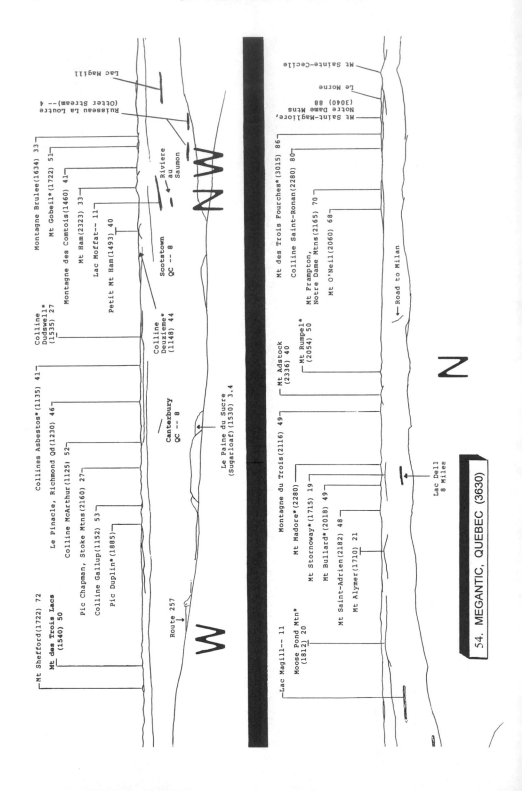

54. MEGANTIC, QUEBEC (3630)

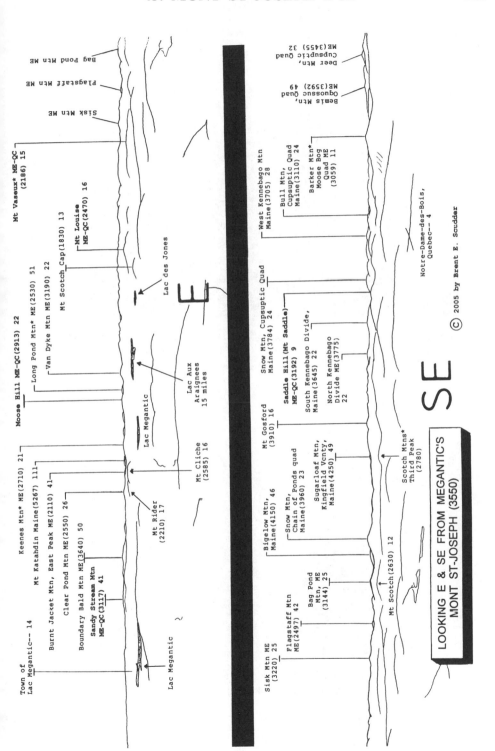

LOOKING E & SE FROM MEGANTIC'S
MONT ST-JOSEPH (3550)

SE

© 2005 by Brent E. Scudder

Town of
Lac Megantic-- 14

Mt Katahdin Maine(5267) 111

Keenes Mtn* ME(2710) 21

Burnt Jacket Mtn, East Peak ME(2110) 41

Clear Pond Mtn ME(2550) 26

Boundary Bald Mtn ME(3640) 50

Sandy Stream Mtn
ME-QC(3117) 41

Lac Megantic

Mt Rider
(2210) 17

Mt Cliche
(2585) 16

Lac Megantic

Lac Aux
Araignees
15 miles

Sisk Mtn ME
(3220) 25

Flagstaff Mtn
ME(2497) 42

Bag Pond
Mtn, ME
(3144) 25

Bigelow Mtn,
Maine(4150) 46

Snow Mtn,
Chain of Ponds quad
Maine(3960) 23

Sugarloaf Mtn,
Kingfield Vcnty,
Maine(4250) 49

Mt Gosford
(3910) 16

Snow Mtn, Cupsuptic Quad
Maine(3784) 24

Saddle Hill (Mt Saddle)
ME-QC(3192) 9

South Kennebago Divide,
Maine(3645) 22

North Kennebago
Divide ME(3775)
22

Mt Scotch (2630) 12

Scotch Mtns*
Third Peak
(2780)

West Kennebago Mtn
Maine(3705) 28

Bull Mtn,
Cupsuptic Quad
Maine(3110) 24

Barker Mtn*
Moose Bog
Quad ME
(3059) 11

Notre-Dame-des-Bois,
Quebec-- 4

Moose Hill ME-QC(2913) 22

Long Pond Mtn* ME(2530) 51

Van Dyke Mtn ME(3190) 22

Mt Scotch Cap(1830) 13

Mt Louise
ME-QC(2470) 16

Lac des Jones

Sisk Mtn ME

Flagstaff Mtn ME

Bag Pond Mtn ME

Mt Vaseux* ME-QC
(2186) 15

Bemis Mtn,
Oquossuc Quad
ME(3592) 49

Deer Mtn,
Cupsuptic Quad
ME(3455) 32

Clouds at sunrise cover Mount Washington as seen from Lakes of the Clouds Hut. These clouds poured over the ridge from the east, descended a short distance and then got caught an updraft to return back eastward over the summit.

Looking down Tuckerman Ravine from the top of the headwall. Wildcat Mountain ski trails beyond

APPENDIX A

FORECASTING EXCELLENT VISIBILITY

In researching this book, crystal clear weather of long duration was required. As with all peaks, Mount Washington had to be cloud-free so that it could be photographed from any other summit. The National Weather Service did not make this type of forecast. But we needed the information.

A forecasting study was needed. We sent away for appropriate weather records and then discovered patterns that were consistent with subsequent events of high visibility. This method is known as analog forecasting. When used properly, the result is deadly accurate.

We wished to be able to predict periods lasting twelve hours or longer that Mount Washington observers would be able to report a visibility of 80 miles or higher. Armed with this forecast, we would have time to get to any mountain in the area, climb to the top and be able to see "forever."

Soon we discovered six forecasting rules that the layman could use to make this prediction. The required weather knowledge may be found in a middle school Earth science course. One can also become "weather-wise" by watching television weather shows on a daily basis and making an effort to correlate what the forecaster is saying with what is actually happening outside.

In addition, the layman needs to have a geographical understanding of national weather maps that are presented on TV. States are not identified. You must know the name of the state from its profile, and you must what other states share its borders. Florida, California and Texas are easily identifiable on such a map, but can you pick out Indiana or Wyoming?

Since Edition One was published, the sources of weather information available to the public have changed radically. In 1995, you did not need the Internet. Between television and recorded telephone messages one could obtain enough information to satisfy the six rules needed to forecast excellent visibility. Today a person needs the Information Superhighway. What is desired is for one to look at a series of two or more weather maps spread out over several hours so that one can track the paths of fronts as well as high and low pressure areas. You can see the maps on television. But you need some information regarding pressure values. The Internet readily supplies the latter.

FORECASTING A HIGH VISIBILITY EVENT IN THE WHITE MOUNTAINS

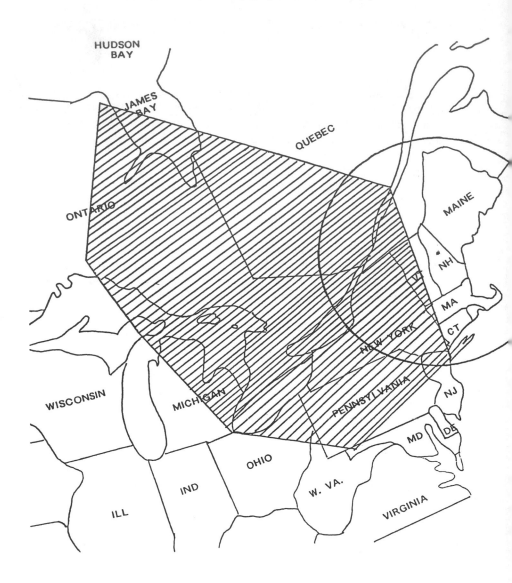

A high pressure center must be in the hatched zone
and approaching the circular area

In order to forecast a day where the visibility on top of Mount Washington is to be eighty miles or greater the following six rules apply:

1. There must not be any areas of low pressure centered over Maine, New Brunswick, Nova Scotia nor over the waters between.

Suppose that on the night before the proposed hike, the weather map shows a low over Nova Scotia. Is the rule violated? Not necessarily. If the low is moving steadily out to sea it should be well offshore by morning.

2. There must be no weather fronts over New England.

3. A high-pressure center **must be approaching** a circle of 300 miles radius that is centered on Mount Washington. The high **need not** be inside this magic circle.

4. This same high must be on a path causing the center to pass into the United States to the east of central North Dakota. This high is not required to be in the United States on the day of the hike. It can remain in Canada.

5. As this high approaches the magic circle, it must be centered within the hatched area found on the map on the facing page. This area is described by connecting a line from New York City to Cumberland, Maryland; Toledo, Ohio; Escanaba, Michigan; Port Arthur, Ontario; the northwestern corner of James Bay; the city of Quebec and back to New York.

Rule five seems nebulous. Mount Washington may clear off when the high is still over Michigan. Yet the event may not occur until the high is crossing the Hudson River. It can take an entire day for the high to drift from Michigan to upstate New York. I need to know with far more precision when Mount Washington is to become free of cloud.

6. On the day of the hike, the barometer must read or exceed 30.20 inches of mercury in **at least one** of the following locations: Sherbrooke, Quebec; Burlington, Vermont; Albany or Buffalo, New York. If other pressure units are used, the equivalent figure is 1023 millibars or 102.3 kilopascals.

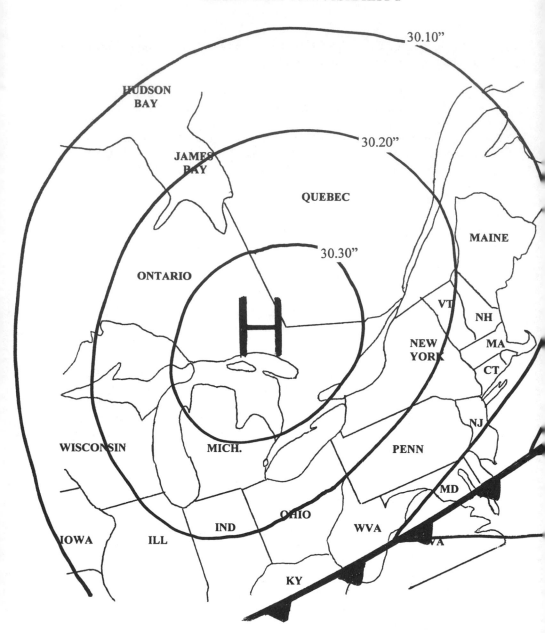

TYPICAL WEATHER MAP DURING AN EVENT OF HIGH VISIBILITY

IN THE WHITE MOUNTAINS

Why should Rule Six work? A strong high over Michigan with a central pressure of 30.70 will probably cause the clouds to lift off of Mount Washington. A weak high of 30.25 inches centered over the upper Hudson Valley is likely to cause the same event. In both cases, the pressure in at least one of the above-mentioned four cities will be at or exceed 30.20 inches. These rules work with an accuracy of 95 per cent.

On the morning of the hike, be not alarmed if you wake up to pea soup fog or else discover Mount Washington to be capped by cloud. The six forecasting rules predict a situation where drier air is constantly moving in. Add to that the natural drying effects caused by the advancing heat of the day, and you will discover all summits in the clear by the time you reach your destination.

The six rules forecast not only excellent visibility but also below normal temperatures often accompanied by a strong wind. The result is a more severe wind chill temperature. Keep this in mind as you dress for the climb.

The best hiking months are September and October followed by May and June. During July and August, Canadian highs are weaker and seldom achieve the prerequisite 30.20 inches of mercury. Highs are much stronger in the winter and there are frequent periods of excellent visibility. But refrain from most climbing activity during the colder months until you have been on winter hikes with experienced all-season climbers. Special dress and equipment are needed for the hip-deep snows of the forest and the windswept icy crust above tree line.

High visibility events often occur when the six rules are not satisfied. But these seldom last twelve hours.

Exceptional visibility seems to occur up to a week after the passage of a fast-moving tropical storm or hurricane. Typically, a hurricane approaches the Bahamas from the western Atlantic. When it nears Florida, the gale curves around the north and then northeast as it passes harmlessly out to sea. The aftermath of such storms have little effect upon the clarity of the air.

But during their turns to the north, some hurricanes are literally "kicked in the tail" by the jet stream and hurled straight into the Canadian Maritime Provinces or the northeastern United States. Forward speeds exceed 40 miles per hour as they pass the latitude of New York City. It does not seem to matter whether the storm center passes as far west as Ohio or as far east as

Nova Scotia. But one does not wish for New Hampshire to suffer a direct hit as it did in 1938. The problem was not the visibility but rather that extensive flooding and tree damage along the trail made the normal bushwhack seem a picnic by comparison. After the storm, you will still need to satisfy the six forecasting rules. But the reward can be a visibility exceeding 150 miles.

Such fantastic visibility occurred when I climbed Mount Chocorua shortly after Hurricane Hugo had ravaged South Carolina and zipped northward through Ohio in a greatly weakened state. From Chocorua's summit, I was startled by the clarity with which the 49-mile distant southern Kearsarge revealed itself. But then I turned to the right and recognized the real Kearsarge. I had been staring at Monadnock! The latter lies 86 miles away.

While the best source of weather information is the Internet, there are some drawbacks. The author can recommend several web sites and advise you where to click the mouse once you have signed on. But web sites come and go with maddening regularity. Even the more stable sites make frequent and radical changes in their format several times a year. Therefore some of following information may be invalid even before this book is published!

The Weather Channel sponsors a magnificent web site: www.weather.com. Go to "Maproom." Under "Map type" select "Weather Details." Move the mouse over to "Select a weather details map collection." Click on "Short term forecast." Now look below the displayed map for another selection box. There you click on "US Morning forecast," "US Midday Forecast" and "US Evening Forecast." These are surface weather maps forecasting the positions of highs, lows, fronts, unlabeled isobars and areas of precipitation and fog.

There is a possibility that a map has yet to be updated. If it is morning, we hope that the "US Morning Forecast" is a weather map valid for 24 hours from now. But you could be looking at a "nowcast" for today. How can you tell? Weather systems generally move from west to east. If these systems have appeared to move west, you are likely to be looking at a forecast map that has not been updated. Remember to satisfy Rule 6 by entering the name of the city in the appropriate space and asking for current conditions.

Also visit www. theweathernetwork.com. This is the web site of Canada's weather channel. Click on 'Weather maps" and then click on "system." Here you can examine the high when it is in the vicinity of James Bay. It also may be used to receive Sherbrooke's weather. But you had better get used to temperatures in Celsius, rainfall in millimeters, pressure in kilopascals and wind speeds in kilometers per hour.

On a web site of weather information, it is sometimes difficult to find the forecast maps of surface weather conditions because the selection lists often have obscure names. Look for terms like "surface map," "forecast map," "surface analysis," "surface prog," "fronts," "Pressure systems," "today's forecast," "tomorrow's forecast," "synoptic chart," "synoptic forecast," "synoptic prog," "synopsis" and possibly a few others.

As for other sources of information, pull up www.nws.noaa.gov for an extensive web site run by the National Weather Service.

A great web site is www.mountwashington.org for Mount Washington's weather. Included are current web cam shots of the mountain from the town of Jackson along with shots taken on the mountain. These video cams are not too useful for the hiker who is starting out for the day because the weather is often different by the time Mount Washington or nearby peaks are climbed. But you can use these images to test how well the six forecasting rules work without ever having to leave the comfort of your computer room.

Do not overlook visiting the following:

http://iwin.nws.noaa.gov/iwin/nh/zone.html for NH zone forecasts or
http://iwin.nws.noaa.gov/iwin/nh/public.html for predictions covering the higher mountains of New Hampshire.

CNN and other news organizations have extensive weather information at their web sites. Also play with the following addresses:

http://www.intellicast.com
http://www.accuweather.com
http://www.wunderground.com
http://vortex.plymouth.edu
http://apollo.lsc.vsc.edu

Forecast surface weather maps show where the predicted positions of highs, lows and fronts will be at a particular time in the future. This time is known as the valid time or "VT" of the forecast often given as a six digit number with a slash after the first two digits followed by the letter Z. An example would be "VT 14/1800Z." The 14 is the day of the month and 1800 refers to 18 hours after midnight of a 24 hour clock (in other words 6 p.m.) The Z refers to the world standard time zone called Z or Zulu Time (same as GMT or UTC for our purposes). Subtract four hours (0400 hours) to get

Eastern Daylight Time and 5 hours for Eastern Standard. So a weather map valid at 1200Z Wednesday is also valid at 0800 hours (8 a.m.) Eastern Daylight time. But the 0000Z Thursday map is in effect at 8 p.m. Wednesday. Confusing? Think of the time 0000Z Thursday as being 2400Z Wednesday. Subtract 0400 hours and you get 2000 hours, which converts to 8 p.m.

Those who have no access to the Internet can watch the Weather Channel via cable or satellite television. A thorough geographical knowledge is necessary because the required weather maps are often aired very briefly. As of this writing, the most useful maps are seldom displayed. Sometimes a local TV news program gives you better results. However, it is extremely difficult for the public to obtain the proper pressure information needed for rule six without going on line.

There are alternatives to Rule Six. If you live in Massachusetts, Vermont, New Hampshire, western Maine or even slightly over the border in Quebec, certain local weather measurements will tell you that Rule Six is probably in effect. First correct your barometer to the approximate sea level reading by matching it to the reading given in the latest weather report from the nearest radio or TV station. NOAA Weather Radio is also useful for this purpose. To adjust the pressure reading, turn the little screw or dial on the back of the instrument a tiny amount. Now, if your barometer reads 30.10 inches or higher, and the wind is blowing from the northwest or north at twelve miles per hour or greater (preferably greater), then Rule Six is probably in effect.

If the TV weather broadcast has a stream of arrows passing over New England showing the wind flow at the ground, you may be able to use this as a Rule Six substitute. Pretend you are riding on a "canoe" down the wind stream. If the current bends to the right, then Rule Six is probably in effect. Downstream flow to the right is called anticyclonic curvature. Such flow inhibits cloud-causing vertical air motion. Rule Six was actually set up to ensure that the wind flow was anticyclonic.

Newspaper forecasts are based on weather information that is up to 12 hours old. As a result, their forecast accuracy is lower.

Periods of high visibility come at random. Often it means last-minute cancellation of social plans or perhaps arranging a day off from work or school. Too many obligations will prevent you from climbing with any frequency on days of excellent visibility. From time to time, you may have to cast off the human race in order to be out on a crystal clear day. Good hiking!

APPENDIX B

HIKING SAFETY

This chapter in its brevity cannot pretend to cover every base on hiking safety. It is to voice the concerns of a person, the author, who has enjoyed nearly a lifetime of safe hiking (some of it through dumb luck!).

Unique among survival books is Dan H. Allen's 1998 edition of *Don't Die on the Mountain,* published by Diapensia Press of New London, New Hampshire. Mr. Allen backs up his safety advice with a lifelong experience of hiking and camping. The book stands out from others because it covers the dynamics of group interaction and is a must for anyone contemplating leading a hike. Many mountain climbing accidents stem from inadequate leadership. A good leader can never eliminate the possibility of an accident. But he or she can greatly reduce the risk.

Accidents requiring rescue stem from losing one's way, heat prostration, heart attacks, slips causing concussions, sprains and broken bones; not necessarily in that order. In winter and above tree line during other seasons, hypothermia and frostbite are added major hazards requiring rescue. There is also the danger of avalanche. Many accidents result from poor judgment due to inexperience. This is why we encourage you to sample the mountains in order from south to north as the book does. When you have completed the first seventeen summits in no particular order, you will have navigated over a number of trail conditions, experienced several kinds of weather and have some ideas of your capabilities before getting into the remote high country.

Inadequate planning leads to many of these accidents. Getting a late start and rushing to complete the hike before dark leads to hasty decisions (navigation problems included) not to mention trying to move faster over the trail than safety or body will allow.

The day hiker can easily avoid being caught out in the woods at night. Before setting out, determine the time of sunset in a local New Hampshire newspaper or alternatively do a search on the Internet for "time of sunset." On the web site you select, choose a location in New Hampshire and check whether the times are listed in Eastern Standard or Eastern Daylight. As the hike begins, note the present time. Calculate the minutes remaining until sunset. Divide that time in half. Add the result to the time you began your hike. When those minutes have elapsed, reverse course even if you are short of your goal. Admittedly, this is a very hard thing to do (especially for climbers of Mount Everest who died for failing to do just that). The reverse course tends to be downhill which means faster walking. You may acquire a time reserve of as much as an hour. This strategy prevents the twisted ankle or minor navigation error from causing darkness to overtake you in the forest.

Many hikers plan one-way trips with a car parked at each end of the trail. Timing is trickier but generally these people have had more hiking experience.

Is being caught in the woods at night really an emergency? If there has been no accident and if hypothermia or frostbite is not a problem, the answer is an emphatic NO! Scary, perhaps. Inconvenient, certainly. But getting benighted under these circumstances does not require rescue. Keep the food at a distance and bears will take no interest.. The remaining fauna is benign. If you are equipped with a powerful flashlight and are on a well-marked trail, you can still move albeit very slowly. Once you lose the path, looking for it may make the situation worse. SIT DOWN AND WAIT FOR DAYLIGHT. You will only be a few feet on either side of the trail.

Before setting in a small group or alone, you should always tell someone of your hiking plans so that they can "call out the dogs" if you are overdue. While getting benighted is not necessarily an emergency, the person you informed may still request rescue. Such operations are expensive. If there is no emergency, volunteer rescuers will feel that their time has been wasted. Not only that, but as we mentioned earlier, if you made hiking decisions based on poor judgment, you may be fined thousands of dollars to pay for the rescue of your precious hide. This is where the cell phone can be advantageous. You can update your informant of your change of hiking plans so that he or she does not act too hastily. However there are many dead spots in the mountains where cell phones do not work. Either that or you forgot to recharge the batteries. Perhaps you were bushwhacking, and a branch flipped the phone off of your belt without you noticing. (That happened to me). Plan your hike as though you had not brought a cell phone.

This brings us to the wilderness experience versus technology. A major reason for hiking in the forest is to return to a time when mankind was more dependent on his own resources. This is part of the great adventure. Placing electronic gadgets in one's backpack greatly offends the purist. The author believes in having these instruments, but only as a backup. Nothing angers the nature lover more than standing on the summit of Mount Chocorua next to a man who is on his cell phone consulting his stockbroker.

There has been much editorial debate over the use of cell phones and GPS equipment in the forest. People have suggested that these gadgets would increase the amount of solo hiking not to mention the participation of the inexperienced in situations beyond their capability, because they could always call for rescue. Whether this is true is immaterial. There are incompetent fools in all activities of risk. If these gizmos can save lives, then it is folly to leave them home. But if your attention is focused more on numerical readouts rather than the rustling breeze in the trees, the hammering of the woodpecker, the blue of the sky above the green canopy, the princess pine on the ground or the flowers in a clearing, then you are not on a hike. You are still at home pushing buttons.

Before the days of cell phones, I carried (and still carry) a small A.M. transistor radio. I never used it for music. In fact, the radio never came out of the pack unless the sky suggested that there might be thunderstorms about. Then I would turn it on and tune between stations in order to detect the characteristic static created by thunderstorms that are within fifty miles. One stroke of lightning creates a sharp burst of static lasting about a half a second. The radio often gave me up to two hours prior warning of thunderstorms and prevented my being on rocky summits or outcroppings with lightning darting about. Beware! While most thunderstorms form somewhere else and give audible warning before passing overhead, there is the rare occasion that the storm actually does form overhead. Then there is no warning

Generally New Hampshire ticks are not a major problem. But with the recent spread of Lyme disease through the deer tick, one must be extra careful. Areas near the seashore seem to have more of them. In any case grassy areas should be avoided. If that is not possible, then the body should be inspected after the hike. The deer tick is tiny, not much bigger than a pinhead.

Stinging insects are not a common problem. But if you are allergic, be sure that you have the antidote with you. Some wasps build ground nests that are right on the trail. Beware of bees near any large cairn, even at high altitude.

During May, June and July, one should never be in the White Mountains without insect repellent. Black flies, mosquitoes and no-see-ums do not attack you singly or in pairs. They come as squadrons, they come in hoards. Once I had to abandon a hike due to my lack of bringing protection. The result was an ignominious one-mile dash to reach shelter.

It is always tempting to fill canteens from a cold running brook. But as the White Mountains continue to increase in popularity, so does the risk of drinking contaminated water. One is not necessarily safe even if he or she has determined that there is no permanent human activity upstream. Not all moose and bear have read the camping manual emphasizing that latrines be no closer to a stream than one hundred paces. Not all humans have read this book either. Carry in all your drinking water. Otherwise, use disinfectant tablets or boil what you have scooped out of a stream.

One of the charms of New Hampshire hiking is the lack of poisonous snakes. During fifty years of hiking in the White Mountains, I have seen but two snakes on the trail...both harmless. A number of moose have crossed my path. I have seen several bears and none took an interest in me. Do follow basic bear precautions. Do not feed them or keep food near you overnight while camping. This includes the chocolate bar in your pocket. Do not sleep in any clothing in which you prepared or ate food. Do not get between a mother and her cub. To get a feel for the nature of New Hampshire black bears, we have already mentioned Kilham and Gray's book *Among the Bears* which is listed in the bibliography in Appendix H.

On a lighter note, I was once a counselor at Androscoggin Jr., a boarding camp for youngsters in Wayne, Maine. We took the campers on an overnight hike. After dark, a precocious eight-year old declared that he wished to camp alone. We bowed to his wish knowing that he would not last long in those dark woods. We counselors helped him set up a tent and built him a campfire away from the other campers. Later on, as his fire was dying, another counselor and I sneaked up on him deliberately cracking sticks as we went.

A frightened voice cried out into the blackness "You don't scare me! Bears are two-thirds vegetarian!"

Quipped the other counselor, "Yes, we are eating two thirds of the tent and one third of you!"

The boy quickly rejoined the others.

APPENDIX C

THE HIKING ALTIMETER

It has only been a few years that an accurate wrist altimeter has been available at stores that sell outdoor equipment. Not only does the altimeter give you your present elevation but it also can be a navigation aid.

As an example, we were hiking from the east to Mount Isolation via the Rocky Branch Trail. This path leaves Route 16 near Jackson, New Hampshire. After 3.7 miles, the Isolation Trail leaves to the right and passes northward below the summit to a point a mile past it before it turns west to meet the Davis Path. A person then backtracks south another mile along the latter route in order to reach the summit of Isolation. We thought we might save distance by leaving the Rocky Branch Trail at the 3.7-mile mark and bushwhack westward until we intersected the Davis Path. From there we would approach our goal from the south thus saving two miles.

We brought along no GPS but we did have an altimeter. The Davis Path was less frequently traveled at the spot where we had planned to join it. How well worn would the trail be? There was a possibility of the footway being so obscured that we might miss it completely. The map showed that the Davis Path had been laid out almost level at between 3600 and 3700 feet of elevation. Once we had passed the ridge line of the Montalban Range, a 3700-foot altitude reading would alert us to look carefully for the trail. We had no trouble finding it.

The wrist altimeter has other uses. I wear it on long automobile trips in order to get a better feel for the nature of the terrain across a state. In addition, when driving in rain with temperatures are close to freezing, an elevation change of a couple of hundred feet alerts me of a possible change to hazardous road conditions.

I take the unit skiing. Besides its entertainment value as a toy in determining one's vertical velocity down the slopes, I can tell how close I am to the bottom of the mountain without being able to see where the trail ends. Sometimes a cloud hugs the top and the ski lift raises me up into it. Visibility becomes practically zero. With the altimeter I have an accurate reading on how soon I need to disembark.

Such altimeters read to the nearest ten feet. In a sense they are too accurate. One may spend a couple of hundred dollars in order to buy such a gadget and within a day or two decide that the readings are way off. That is because the user does not understand how an altimeter functions.

Wrist altimeters do not measure elevation. They measure atmospheric pressure. Inside the unit is a scale that assigns an elevation for each pressure that it measures. The altitude is then displayed digitally. Even if the altimeter is left in one place over a period of time, its readings will constantly change due to pressure changes. So what changes pressure? Four things:

1. Passing weather systems cause pressure (thus "altitude") to fluctuate. If a low-pressure area approaches, the altimeter will begin reading values that are too elevated. An approaching high will result in values that are too low. Vigorous approaching weather systems can create a 200-foot error after just two hours of hiking. Such an extreme is infrequent. If you are spending the night outdoors, be sure to read the altitude the moment you reach your campsite. When you leave in the morning, reset the altimeter to that same height. It may surprise you to learn the extent to which the campsite "rose" or "fell" overnight.

2. Thermal waves cause the pressure to fluctuate. Often referred to as "atmospheric tides" these waves travel about four hours behind the sun as the Earth rotates. An additional wave is induced on the opposite side of the planet away from the sun. This effect will cause your altimeter to fluctuate sinusoidally, averaging about ten feet per hour to reach low values around 10 a.m. and 10 p.m. with highs at 4 p.m. and 4 a.m. This effect is greatest at the Equator and absent at the Poles.

3. The Venturi effect causes pressure changes. Strong winds over a ridge can "raise" the elevation. You get the same effect in a moving car. Open the window and you will create an altitude jump of about 30 to 40 feet.

4. A change in atmospheric density will cause the pressure to fluctuate.

In order to understand this effect, one must realize what causes pressure. Above every horizontal square inch of the Earth's surface exists a set number of gas molecules that constitute air (give or take a few). This volume of air stacks up several hundred miles to the limits of Outer Space. Each molecule has weight and presses down upon the molecules below to give you pressure.

If the air is cold, the same molecules are packed more closely together (more dense). This means that on a frigid day, if I increase my elevation to

APPENDIX C....THE ALTIMETER

a certain level, I will leave more molecules below me than I would have done on a warm day. It also means that at that new elevation, I have fewer molecules pressing down from above. Freely translated, the air pressure will be lower at that new elevation on a cold day than it would have been on a warm day. The altimeter reads higher when the air is cold.

There is no altimeter error due to air density if the air temperature is 59 degrees Fahrenheit at sea level and decreases by 3.6 degrees for every thousand feet one climbs. But if temperatures at sea level are around 20, the altimeter will read, on the average, 43 feet too high for every thousand-foot gain in elevation. Similarly, if the temperature is 90, the altimeter is likely to read about 35 feet too low for every thousand feet that is gained.

Once we were skiing on Ragged Mountain when a strong cold front moved in. Air pressure falls in advance of a cold front and then rises after frontal passage. When the cold air hit, the pressure began rising at the base of the mountain while continuing to fall at the top. In other words, the altitude reading at the base of the mountain began to drop while the altitude reading at the top continued to rise. This strange phenomenon was merely the result of the increasing air density of the colder air.

Student and licensed pilots should beware. This discussion of air density is not the same concept at density altitude.*

To minimize these errors in altitude, use your "topo" map to set your altimeter to the correct reading before you start the climb. Using the same map, find places along the trail such as sharp bends that you will recognize upon arrival so that you can reset the altimeter. Correcting the instrument every two hours rarely gives you errors in excess of 30 feet most of the time.

---

*Putting it simplistically, density altitude is the elevation that the aircraft "feels" when taking off or landing. For example, the runways at Salt Lake City, Utah, are at an elevation near 4000 feet. Even on a hot day, the air pressure will be close to that normally found at 4000 feet. But the air density will be so low that the plane will "feel" as though it is taking off from a runway that is, say, 7000 feet above sea level. You must load the airplane and calculate takeoff distance and climb angle as though you were actually at 7000 feet. If this means leaving behind some payload (passengers and/or cargo) – even if this means leaving behind half of your fuel supply, that is aerodynamics for you. It beats crashing.

I have personally experienced a high equivalent altitude due to low air density. We took off from Salt Lake City in an old Cessna 140. The temperature was 107 degrees. Normally such a plane uses 1000 to 2000 feet of runway to lift off. We needed the entire 6000 feet of pavement and barely cleared the fence at the far end.

APPENDIX D

HIKING WITH A HEART MONITOR

If the hiker does not feel too encumbered after equipping himself with a compass, watch, cell phone, wrist altimeter, GPS, thermometer, turn and bank indicator, tachometer, artificial horizon, on board radar, ILS equipment, landing lights, fuel gauge, oil pressure indicator and stall warning horn, then he or she might consider wearing a heart monitor.

Seriously, sports people in many activities wear heart monitors once in a while in order to judge their level of fitness. These are sold at some outdoor stores for about $100. One wears a flexible band around the chest. The band picks up one's heart beat and broadcasts it to a wrist watch that reads out in beats per minute. A person measuring more than 42 inches around the rib cage may find the chest band too small. But with a little Velcro™ and ingenuity, the larger person may be able to come up with a solution. The watch can be set to give an alarm when the heartbeat exceeds or falls below a certain value. Charts come with the monitor telling what these limits should be for healthy people at various ages.

An older climber might be concerned that his heart rate is getting too high for his level of fitness and could use the monitor to adjust his pace accordingly. There can be a problem for that climber because of the social pressure involved with keeping up with a group. Although most hikers do not mind being in the back of a group, the older person might have to choose between a safe heart rate and keeping up.

The monitor is very useful in setting a proper climbing pace. As a teenager, I would race up the mountain for fifteen minutes and then have to take a ten to fifteen minute rest. I learned that if I became the tortoise and not the hare by slowing my pace to the point where I needed a five-minute rest once an hour, I reached the summit a lot more quickly. (The older person might have to rest more often no matter how slow his pace).

Of course when you climb, the heart is beating at an elevated level. When you take a break, the rate comes down to the resting level in a set amount of time. As your heart tires, it beats less efficiently and takes longer for the rate to come down. Not only that but it takes less effort to push the heart rate higher. **If you have a heart condition, you should never consider using the monitor as a safe method of mountain climbing without consulting your doctor.**

APPENDIX E

LIST OF PEAKS

GIVEN TEMPORARY DESIGNATION

As mentioned in the preliminary chapter labeled "Using the Diagrams," found on page 17, we found it necessary to give various unlisted peaks temporary names. This was a convenient device that saved a lot of long-winded description. Some readers may wish to locate these summits, not just on a panorama diagram but also on a topographic map. Other reasons exist to list them. First, some of these mountains will be named in the future. If each terrain feature has already been assigned a temporary tag, then the reader will be able to update his panorama charts by using maps, a ruler and protractor. Second, some of these elevations already have local names that have yet to appear on updated maps. Readers are asked to supply these names for future editions of this book.

In the following table, the temporary mountain name is listed first. Peaks located beyond New Hampshire are listed with their two-letter state codes. In the second column, there is listed the name of the topographical map where the mountain is located. Chart names with asterisks refer to the older Geological Survey maps known as the 15-by 15-minute series. All Canadian maps will be similarly designated, because their map scale is close to the older United States series. Chart names lacking the asterisk will be from either the newer 7.5-by 7.5-minute series or the newest 7.5 by-15-minute series. This distinction eliminates a potential problem when identical names occur in more than one map set.

In the third column one finds the geographical entity from which we derived the temporary mountain name. The fourth column lists a reference mountain found on the same topographical map. The compass bearing (relative to True North) and the distance from the reference mountain to the temporarily named peak are found in the last column.

For example: At the top of the list, the peak which we are calling Abbot Mountain, New Hampshire is located on one of the newer maps entitled Bosebuck Mountain. It was named after nearby Abbott Brook. One can locate Abbott Mountain by taking a ruler and protractor and extending a line from Haystack Mountain in the direction of 166 degrees (relative to True North) and then measuring a length of 4.2 miles. The list follows:

TEMPORARY NAMES	TOPO-GRAPHIC MAP	NAME SOURCE	REFERENCE PLACE	Azi-muth & Range
Abbott Mtn	Bosebuck Mtn	Brook	Haystack Mtn	166/4.2
Acteon Peak	Waterville Valley	Ridge	Sachem Peak	267/0.8
Aldrich Mtn ME	Lincoln Pond	Brook	Deer Mtn	322/1.5
Atwell Summit	Cardigan	Brook	Mt Cardigan	004/3.1
Avenchur Hill	Alton	Camp	Prospect Mtn	330/5.4
Barker Mtn	Moose Bog	Pond	Bowman Hill	064/1.7
Beaver Hill	Marlborough	Pond	Skatutakee Mtn	165/1.8
Beecher Hill	Pittsburg	Falls	Ben Young Hill	285/3.6
Bidle Path Ridge	Franconia	Trail	Greenleaf Hut	SSW
Broulliard Mtn VT	Averill Lake	Stream	Sable Mtn	114/2.6
Mt Bullard QC	Thetford Mines*	Stream	Mt Saint-Adrien	048/2.5
Mt Campbell ME/QC	St-Theophile*	Pond	Sandy Stream Mtn	012/5.3
Campton Hill	Squam Mtns	Township	Mt Weetamoo	286/2.2
Cannon Cliffs	Franconia	Mountain	Cannon Mtn	082/0.4
Castle Guard	Blue Mtn	Mountain	Gore Mtn	228/1.4
Cemetery Hill	Holderness	Note (1)	Dolloff Hill	109/4.3
Chapin Hill	Ascutney	Pond	Ironwood Hill	108/4.0
Chateauguay Mtn VT	Delectable Mtn	River	Mt Hunger	172/4.3
Chittenden Mtn VT	Mt Carmel	Town	Mt Carmel	134/2.2
Cold Rain Hill ME	North Sebago	Pond	Peaked Mtn	036/1.0
Colline Deuzieme QC	Warwick*	Stream	Petit Mt Ham	292/5.7
Colline Dudswell QC	Dudswell*	Town	Pic Chapman	022/7.2
Colline St-Malo	Coaticook*	Town	Colline Theroux	125/2.3
Collines Asbestos QC	Dudswell*	Town	Wottenville QC	268/3.1
Mt Constance	East Haverhill	Lake	Jeffers Mtn	240/4.1
Coon Brook Hill	Cowen Hill	Brook	Cowen Hill	093/2.6
Coon Pond	Cowen Hill	Brook	Cowen Hill	091/3.5

TEMPORARY NAMES	TOPO-GRAPHIC MAP	NAME SOURCE	REFERENCE PLACE	Azi-muth & range
Crosby Hill MA	Winchendon	Road	Thrasher Hill	187/2.8
Crown Point	Baxter Lake	School	Blue Job Mtn	147/3.5
Curtiss Hill	Milford	Note (2)	Dram Cup Hill	351/1.9
Dexter Hill	Alton	Hamlet	Prospect Mtn	152/1.6
Ditton Mtn NH/QC	2nd Conn. Lake	River	Deer Mtn	044/3.2
Dry Hill	Baxter Lake	Road	Blue Job Mtn	129/5.2
Dunbarton Hill	Goffstown	Town	Dunbarton NH	019/0.6
Durrell Mtn	Belmont	Road	Whiteface Mtn	181/0.9
East Ball Hill VT	Chester	Hill	Old Shincracker	285/2.5
East Gilford Hill	West Alton	Town	Belknap Mtn	031/2.4
East Jackson Hill	Lovewell Mtn	Hill	Jackson Hill	090/0.4
East Mink Hill	Warner	Hills	Stewarts Peak	040/1.0
East Mudgetts Mtn	Wentworth	Pond	Streeter Mtn	350/1.7
East Pocket Mtn	Ossipee	Mountain	Pocket Mtn	117/2.2
East Potash Summit	Mt Osceola	Knob	Potash Knob	027/0.5
Edminister Hill	Ascutney	Cemetery	Ironwood Hill	069/1.4
Forest Hill	Holderness	Pond	Dolloff Hill	350/0.6
Mt Fullerton QC	Note (3)	Lake	Mt Sugarloaf	280/6.6
Mt Gobeil QC	Arthabaska*	Stream	Mt Christo	105/7.1
Greens Mtn	West Milan	Ledge	Square Mtn	088/0.7
Halls Stream Range	Indian Stream*	Stream	Halls Stream	To SE
Mt Hancock, S. Knob	Mt Carrigain	Mountain	Mt Hancock	161/1.3
Heartwell Mtn VT	Readsboro	Town	Castle Hill	255/4.2
Hebron Hill	Ashland	Town	Plymouth Mtn	253/1.0

TEMPORARY NAMES	TOPO- GRAPHIC MAP	NAME SOURCE	REFERENCE PLACE	Azi- muth & range
Hobbs Knob	Silver Lake	Brook	White Ledge	298/1.4
Horseshoe Hill	Andover	Pond	Beech Hill	048/1.3
Hunters Peak	Pliny Range	Pass	Mt Crescent	010/1.5
Jacquith Hill	Marlborough	Brook	Skatutakee Mtn	153/1.2
Jenness Mtn	Pittsfield	Pond	Catamount Mtn	134/2.2
Jenny Coolidge Mtn	(in VT) Weston	Brook	Holt Mtn	339/2.7
Johns Hill	Lancaster	River	Prospect Mtn	213/4.1
Keenes Mtn ME	Boundary Pond	Station	Clear Pond Mtn	255/4.6
Kelley Hill	Pittsfield	Brook	Nudds Hill	001/7.4
Kinsman Knoll	Lincoln	Mountain	Mt Liberty	263/4.0
Lamb Hill	Cowen Hill	Brook	Cowen Hill	022/1.4
Liberty Hill	Laconia	Road	Gunstock Mtn	238/3.4
Little Deer Mtn	2nd Conn. Lake	Mountain	Black Cat Spur	236/3.0
Lockes Hill	Alton	Hamlet	Prospect Mtn	178/2.2
Long Pond Mtn ME	Long Pond	Pond	Parlin Mtn	317/4.2
Lower Berrys Pond	Baxter Lake	River	Blue Job Mtn	116/2.0
Lower Hedgehog Hill	Stoddard	Hill	Pitcher Mtn	082/0.9
Lwr Interbranch Ridge	Magalloway Mtn	Note (4)	Magalloway Mtn	148/3.2
Lucas Ridge VT	Jay Peak	Brook	Jay Peak	008/4.9
Madison Boulder Hill	Silver Lake	Boulder	Oak Hill	242/4.1
Mt Madore QC	Thetford Mines*	Stream	Mt Saint-Adrien	064/3.8
McCutcheon Hill	Wentworth	Pond	Black Hill	175/2.7
Meadow Brook Mtn	Bosebuck Mtn	Brook	Haystack Mtn	150/2.3
Middle Crescent Mtn	Pliny Range	Range	Mt Crescent	023/1.8
Middle Ossipee Mtn	Tamworth	Mtns	Black Snout	125/9.9

TEMPORARY NAMES	TOPO-GRAPHIC MAP	NAME SOURCE	REFERENCE PLACE	Azi-muth & range
Miles Knob VT	Miles Pond	Mountain	Miles Mtn	176/1.2
Mirror Lake Hill	Woodstock	Lake	Barron Mtn	223/2.4
Moose Pond Mtn QC	Scotstown*	Pond	Mt Alymer	226/3.7
Moran Mtn	Blue Mtn	Notch	Fitch Mtn	050/3.7
Muise Mtn	Blue Mtn	Note (5)	Fitch Mtn	068/4.2
Nash Mtn	Blue Mtn	Pond	Fitch Mtn	045/3.2
North Abbott Hill	Milford	Hill	Dram Cup Hill	233/0.8
North Cates Hill	Milan	Hill	Oak Hill	222/2.6
North Fitch Hill ME	North Sebago	Hill	Fitch Hill	039/0.9
North Interbranch Hill	Bosebuck Mtn	Note (4)	Haystack Mtn	192/2.7
N. Newry Knob ME	Puzzle Mtn	Town	Puzzle Mtn	289/3.8
North Pembroke Hill	Suncook	Hill	Garvin Hill	217/2.2
N. Pete Parent Pk. VT	Danby	Peak	Peru Peak	038/3.4
North Starr King	Pliny Range	Mountain	Mt Starr King	316/0.8
North Stub Hill	Bosebuck Mtn	Hill	Stub Hill	346/0.8
North Tuttle Hill	Stoddard	Hill	Holmes Hill	149/2.7
Otter Hill	Cowen Hill	Brook	Cowen Hill	036/0.8
Paris Mtn	Dummer Ponds	Hamlet	Dummer Hill	332/3.5
Passumpsic Hill VT	Concord	River	Jackman Mtn	261/4.4
Perry Peak	Cowen Hill	Stream	Cowen Hill	031/4.4
Pic Duplin QC	Dudswell*	Village	Pic Chapman	225/3.3
Proctor Ski Hill	Andover	Academy	Mt Kearsarge	026/3.4
Prospect Hill ME	Milton	Cemetery	Miller Corner ME	185/4.6
Prospect Hill NH	Concord	Local	Jerry Hill	106/1.4
Province Hill	Gilmanton I.W.	Road	Pine Mtn	216/8.1

TEMPORARY NAMES	TOPO-GRAPHIC MAP	NAME SOURCE	REFERENCE PLACE	Azi-muth & Range
Rainbow Ridge	Carter Dome	Trail	Carter Dome	157/0.8
Readsboro Mtn VT	Readsboro	Town	Castle Hill	233/4.0
Reservoir Hill	Dover East	Reservoir	Great Hill	309/5.3
Ridgepole Mtn	Squam Mtns	Trail	Mt Percival	065/2.2
Robbins Hill MA	Winchendon	Pond	Thatcher Hill	207/3.1
Mt Rumpel QC	Thetford Mines*	Town	Cap a Thom	102/4.6
Scotch Mtns, 3rd Pk.	(in QC) Woburn*	Mountain	Mt Scotch	206/2.5
Searsburg Mtn VT	Readsboro	Town	Castle Hill	274/4.9
Shoal Pond Mtn	Crawford Notch	Pond	Whitewall Mtn	191.2.3
Shoppe Brook Ridge	Malvina*	Brook	Cowen Hill	282/4.1
Simms Mtn	Blue Mtn	Stream	Fitch Mtn	058/4.1
South Closten Hill	Milan	Hill	Closten Hill	178/0.5
South Hookset Hill	Manchester North	Town	Campbell Hill	161/1.9
S.Interbranch Hill	Bosebuck Mtn	Note (4)	Haystack Mtn	190/3.1
South Stub Hill	Bosebuck Mtn	Hill	Stub Hill	119/0.6
South Tuttle Hill	Stoddard	Hill	Holmes Hill	161/2.8
South Twin Spur	South Twin Mtn	Mountain	Mt Guyot	281/1.4
Stairs Brook Mtn	Stairs Mtn	Brook	Mt Isolation	200/2.1
Stearns Brook Hill	Success Pond	Brook	Chickwolnepy Mtn	187/4.4
Stebbins Hill	Lancaster	School	Prospect Mtn	310/1.2
Mt Stornoway QC	Scotstown*	Town	Mt Alymer	111/4.0
Stratford Bog Mtn	Stratford	Pond	Goback Mtn	097/0.8
Strat. Bog Mtn E. Pk,	Stratford	Pond	Goback Mtn	073/1.2
Tanguay Hills QC	Coaticook*	Hamlet	Hereford Mtn	240/7.2
Mt des 3 Fourches QC	St-Magliore*	Forks	Le Bonnet QC	302/8.3
Thornton Hill	Woodstock	Town	Blake Mtn	027/2.9
Troy Peak VT	North Troy	Town	Gilpin Mtn	003/6.0

TEMPORARY NAMES	TOPO-GRAPHIC MAP	NAME SOURCE	REFERENCE PLACE	Azimuth & Range
Unknown Pond Peak	Stark	Pond	The Horn	053/1.2
Upper Evans Mtn	Wild River	Mt Evans	Howe Peak	291/2.8
U. Interbranch Ridge	Magalloway Mtn	Note (4)	Magalloway Mtn	142/3.0
Upper Winthrop Mtn	Shelburne	Mountain	Mt Winthrop	187/1.3
Mt Vaseaux ME-QC	Woburn*	Stream	Louise Mtn	217/3.4
Mt Villette QC	Coaticook	Town	Hereford Mtn	268/4.3
Walden Peak	Mt Chocorua*	Trail	Mt Paugus	262/2.2
Walker Ravine	Franconia	Brook	Mt Lincoln	270/0.8
Walnut Hill ME	Mousam Lake	Road	Abbott Mtn	166/6.1
West Potash Summit	Mt Osceola	Knob	Potash Knob	358/0.7
Woburn Mtn ME/QC	Arnold Pond	QC town	Twin Peaks	066/2.4
Wonalancet Ridge	Mt Chocorua	Mountain	Carrigain Outlook	270/1.0
Woodstock Spur	Mt Moosilauke	Town	Mt Wolf	182/2.2

NOTES

1. This hill is flanked by three cemeteries.

2. Named for the New Hampshire State Reservation inside of which it lies.

3. The Canadian topographical map called Lac Memphremagog.

4. Located between the middle branch and the east brach of the Dead Diamond River.

5. Muise Mountain is an official name. But it has yet to appear on most maps.

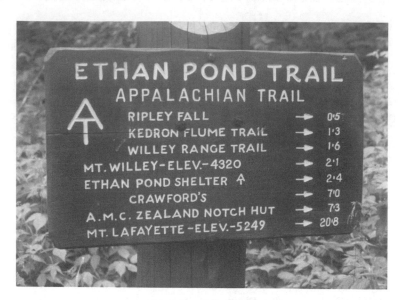

Ethan Pond Trail sign

Zealand Notch
Mount Carrigain on the right

APPENDIX F

A FURTHER WORD ON MOUNTAIN NAMES

Appendix E lists 141 nameless summits on the diagrams to which we assigned temporary labels. We can spot such mountains on the charts because each will have an asterisk. Yet the skyline charts contain more than 300 blank peaks to which we gave names but omitted the asterisk. For example:

Mt Franklin, South Peak(4904) 9

No map carries this name. But it is a component peak of Mount Franklin which is listed on every chart. Any designation such as North Peak, Middle Peak, South Spur, East Knob and Lower West Peak along with others is listed without an asterisk as long as it is the lesser peak of a principal mountain. Think of it as a "generic" name.

What about generic names that are officially recognized and therefore appear on the maps? For example:

South Peak, Mount Moosilauke(4523) 11

If the name of a component peak is official, it is listed ahead of the principal mountain. If the name is an unofficial generic label, it follows.

Such usage would require us to label the more southerly of the Kinsman pair "South Peak, Kinsman Mountain." More often we hear "South Kinsman" and label it as such.

There are some mountains the names of which appear on no nationally published topographical map but the names of which are recognized by a considerable number of people. These peaks are not given asterisks either. An example is The Captain, observable from Potash and South Twin Mountains as well as from Mount Bond. Other examples are Mount Hibbard, visible from Chocorua and Mont St-Joseph which is part of the view from Magalloway and Megantic.

One remaining type of unnamed mountain to which a temporary label was assigned is asterisk-free. Quite often the lower peak of a larger mountain is awarded the name for the entire mass. This is because the early settler from his valley location could only see the lower peak which he named. That very summit blocked from view the higher crest behind it. From the opposite

APPENDIX F....MORE ON NAMES

direction, one sees the nameless top but not the lesser peak. For example, in northern Vermont, Hogback Mountain stands forth with an elevation of 3240 feet. From New Hampshire we never see it. Hogback is blocked by the main elevation that we call

Hogback Summit, Stowe quad VT(3642) 49

"Summit" tells us that it is the highest point of what should have been named Hogback Mountain even though the maps keep it nameless. An exception is Clark Summit near Hillsborough, New Hampshire, which is an official name.

Highlands Mountain (Bean Hill)(1506) 25

We stated earlier that if a second mountain name was shown in parentheses, it was an alternate label and probably less preferred. In this case, Bean Hill is the name that appears on topographic charts. Yet thousands of skiers remember it as Highlands Mountain. Even though the ski area of this name went out of business a while back, Highlands is going to remain the name of choice for many years to come.

Mt Clay (Mt Reagan)(5533) 1.3

In 2003, the New Hampshire Legislature decided that a mountain should honor Ronald Reagan and chose to rename Mount Clay in honor of the former President. The U.S. Board of Geographic Names has certain rules to which it adheres, one being that the honoree has been deceased at least five years before recognizing the name change.* Because of the publication date of this book, we have decided to continue using Mount Clay as the principal name.

Mt Prospect, Squam Mtns quad(2064) 16

Previously we explained that two mountains of the same name are distinguished by our including the title of the topographical map quadrangle where each peak is located. You will note on the panorama charts that the word "quad" is sometimes capitalized and at other times in the lower case. The reason is that there is more than one set topographical charts.   Two

---

- The United States Board of Geographic names does not always adhere to this policy of waiting five years after the death of an honoree to award him a place on a map. I happen to know personally that the second Scudder Peak in Antarctica was named after someone who is very much alive as of this writing.

charts, one in each set, may carry the same map title. But their scales differ with the older chart series covering more area.

If "Quad" has an initial capital letter, it refers to the older chart set covering 15 minutes of latitude and 15 minutes of longitude. Canadian charts have a scale similar to the older U.S. map set and are also listed with the upper case "Quad,". The newer American maps covering 7.5 minutes of both latitude and longitude along with those covering 7.5 by 15 are given the lower case "quad." The convention used here is that a map name labeled "Quad" covers more area than its lower case cousin.

Sugarloaf Mountain, Benton Dct(2609) 11

Occasionally one does not see the word "Quad" but rather "Dct" or district – usually a township. This may occur when two mountains of the same name are found on the same map thereby requiring a unique distinction. At times the use of "Dct" avoids redundancy. As an example, the nearest Sugarloaf Mountain seen from Mount Moosilauke happens to lie within the Moosilauke quadrangle. To eliminate this redundancy, we show it as lying within New Hampshire's Benton Township.

Sometimes the quad designation is omitted entirely. It contributes to chart clutter and often is not needed. As a case in point, there are fourteen Black Mountains in our area of study. One is actually part of Mount Kearsarge and can be mistaken for no other. The "quad" is left out.

"Quad" is rarely listed when referring to major peaks. Most hikers are not familiar with the 1512-foot Mount Cabot located near Shelburne, New Hampshire. But many are well aware of the 4170-foot Mount Cabot standing northeast of Lancaster. In this case, we list the name of the quadrangle after the lesser-known Cabot but not after the more famous one.

In and about Mount Washington, we deferred to the elevations determined on the Bradford Washburn map. Elsewhere in the White Mountains we used those elevations listed on the new 7.5-minute and 7.5 by 15-minute series. Peripheral areas were sprinkled with elevations found on the older 15-minute series. South Kinsman and Goose Eye Mountains were given higher elevations for reasons explained in those chapters.

The reader should now have a thorough understanding of how to interpret the mountain listings.

Looking
north along
Cathedral
Ledge.
Carter Notch
on horizon
left of center.

Famous Presidential Range sign

APPENDIX G

GPS CONVERSIONS & WAYPOINT CALCULATIONS

In this book, we express GPS co-ordinates of latitude and longitude in degrees, minutes and decimal parts of a minute (DD° MM.mmm'). Most GPS units allow you to express latitude and longitude in any system you want. But for those units that lack this feature, the following applies:

A. To convert **from DD° MM' SS" to DD° MM.mmm'** -- (To convert from degrees, minutes and seconds to degrees, minutes and decimal parts of a minute, the following applies): Change the seconds (SS) to decimal parts of a minute (mmm) by multiplying SS by 1/60. Thus a latitude of 42 degrees 12 minutes and 30 seconds becomes 42 degrees 12 minutes and 0.5 minutes or 42 degrees 12.500 minutes.

B. To convert **from DD° MM.mmm' back to DD° MM' SS",** just take mmm and multiply by 60 to get SS. Thus with 42 degrees 12.500 minutes, multiply the .500 minutes by 60 to get 30 seconds and the result is 42 degrees, 12 minutes and 30 seconds.

C. To convert **from DD.dddddd°** (degrees and decimal parts of a degree) **to DD° MM.mmm',** merely multiply dddddd by 60 to get MM.mmm. Thus with a latitude of 42.125000°, multiply the .125000 by 60 and get 07.500. The result is a latitude of 42 degrees 07.500 minutes.

D. To convert **from DD° MM.mmm back to DD.dddddd°,** multiply MM.mmm by 1/60 to get dddddd. Thus with 42 degrees 07.500 minutes, multiply the 07.500 times 1/60 to equal 0.125000 and you get 42.125000 degrees.

Calculating a waypoint: Waypoints can be calculated on any map that has marks of latitude and longitude along its edges. We use the Geological Survey (USGS) topographical charts because their scale assures tremendous accuracy. Obtain an appopriate map. Buy a two foot plastic straight edge for drawing lines. These are available in fabric stores. Next you need a ruler that measures in centimeters and tenths thereof. Such a ruler may be found in an office supply store, an art supply store, a drafting supply company, college bookstore or anywhere school supplies are sold.

Refer to the diagram the next page.

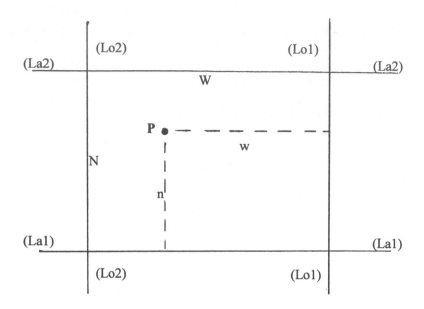

P is the point on the map where the GPS co-ordinates will be calculated.

Units of latitude and longitude are in degrees and decimal parts of a degree out to six places.

(La1) is the latitude of the first latitude line below **P**. It may or may not be the lower edge of the map.

(La2) is the latitude of the first latitude line above **P**. It may or may not be the top of the map.

(Lo1) is the longitude of the first longitude line to the right of **P**. It may or may not be the right hand edge of the map.

(Lo2) is the longitude of the first longitude line of the left of **P**. It may or may not be the left hand edge of the map.

n = the distance that you measured with the ruler from (La1) to **P**.

N = the distance that you measured with the ruler from (La1) to (La2)

w = the distance that you measured with the ruler from (Lo1) to **P**.

W = the distance that you measured with the ruler from (Lo1) to (Lo2).

1. Mark on the map the point **P** for which you wish to calculate a GPS reading.

2. Now look at each corner of the USGS topographical map. A latitude and longitude is given in degrees, minutes and seconds. Use steps A and D on page 335 to convert these numbers to degrees and decimal parts of a degree out to six places.

3. Next look along the vertical edges of the chart exactly one third and two thirds of the distance up to find intermediate tic marks of latitude. These will be labeled in brevity such as 25' or 27' 30". Thus, if a lower corner reading was 42° 22' 30'' (42 degrees, 22 minutes and 30 seconds), the first mark up (25') would mean 42° 25' 00". The second mark up (27' 30") would mean a latitude of 42° 27' 30".

4. Along the top and bottom edges of the chart, repeat step three to locate the intermedate tics of longitude. (The newer 7 1/2 by 15 minute charts will have five intermediate longitude tics instead of two.)

5. With the two-foot straight edge, draw in the intermediate latitude and longitude lines determined by the intermediate tics described in the previous two paragraphs. You will end up with a grid of squares. It will not be necessary to create the entire grid. (Note: The two foot straight edge is not long enough for the width of a 7.5-by-15-minute map. You will have to use the centimeter ruler in combination with it.)

6. Designate the two latitudes and two longitudes that you are going to use for (La1), (La2), (Lo1) and (Lo2). Use steps A and D on page 335 to convert these to degrees and the decimal parts of degrees out to six places.

7. Determine all the quantities used in the diagram on the page opposite and solve the equations below for the latitude and longitude of **P**. Round off the values as little as possible during the calculations.

(**P**lat) = (La1) + n [(La2) - (La1)]/N   where (**P**lat) is the latitude of **P**.

(**P**long) = (Lo1) + w[(Lo2)-(Lo1)]/W where (**P**long) is the longitude of **P**.

8. Using page 335, convert these values to whatever is in your GPS unit. Round off your answer to the whatever precision is used in your device.

9. You may need to make a datum correction. Check the fine print at the bottom of the map you are using. Typically it will read as follows: "Horizontal datum...North American Datum of 1927 (NAD27).   North American Datum of 1983 (NAD83) is shown by dashed corner ticks."

At the corners of such a chart, there are dashed cross hairs located slightly away from each corner. What the fine print means is that the actual map corners are in the NAD27 datum mode. But if the map had been drawn with the actual corners at the dashed cross hairs, then it would be in the NAD83 datum mode. If you had made all of your measurements based on the actual map edges, the coordinates of your waypoint would be in the NAD27 mode.

To convert your reading froom NAD 27 to the WGS84 mode used in this book, merely subtract 0.002 minutes of latitude and 0.032 minutes of longitude. Newer topographical maps use NAD83. WGS84 is so similar to NAD83 in this part of the world that both may be considered identical.

When measuring n, N, w and W; estimate the reading to the nearest tenth of a millimeter. This means that you take two adjacent millimeter marks on the ruler and estimate where the line falls between. You may be off by two or three tenths of a millimeter.. But the reading will be more accurate than if you merely read it to the nearest millimeter. When we deal with the 7.5 minute series charts, being off by of one tenth of a millimeter will give you a map error of eight feet. So a 0.3 millimeter error is nothing over which to loose sleep.

As an example, consider Mount Cardigan. The 1998 provisional edition of the 7.5 minute map called Mount Cardigan was drawn up using the older NAD27 datum. We obtained the following:

$(La1)$ = 43 deg 37 min 30 sec = 43.625000 degrees
$(La2)$ = 43 deg 40 min 00 sec = 43.666667 degrees
$(Lo1)$ = 71 deg 52 min 30 sec = 71.875000 degrees
$(Lo2)$ = 71 deg 55 min 00 sec = 71.916667 degrees
       n = 11.28 centimeters
       N = 19.23 centimeters
       w = 13.36 centimeters
       W= 14.02 centimeters

Plug in the formulas and the Latitude of **P** equals 43.649441 degrees. Use step C on page 335 to convert this number to 43 degrees 38.966 minutes.

The longitude of **P** equals 71.914705 degrees which by using the same step C converts to 71 degrees 54.882 minutes.

Make the datum correction of **P** to WGS84 by subtracting 0.002 minutes of latitude and 0.032 minutes of longitude. The waypoint reading for the summit of Mt Cardigan becomes N 43° 38.964', W 71° 54.850'.

Remember that you can also set a waypoint by taking the GPS unit to the exact site and pressing a couple of buttons on the unit.

When using the ruler to measure on a map, you want the best accuracy possible. To avoid parallax error, make sure you move your head so that your eye is directly above each point where you are taking a reading.

Map edges are thinner than the best pencil line. It increases your accuracy if you can utilize map edges whenever possible. For example, determine the values of N and W by measuring between tics along the edge of the map rather than between drawn pencil lines. One might feel that an error occurs if you fail to measure W at **P**'s exact latitude. This concern is due to the decreasing distance of a longitude degree as one progresses northward. The error is less than that created by the width of a pencil line.

Now suppose that (La2) is represented by the top edge of the map. Instead of measuring n, measure the remainder of the distance from **P** to (La2). This quantity happens to be N - n. Subtract that from N. You are left with n. But instead of having measured from a pencil line to **P**, you have measured from a map edge to **P**.

These calulations may seem tedious. But we are only dealing with ratio and proportion, a concept that the high school mathematics student can easily grasp. As one begins to understand the reasoning behind these formulae, shortcuts may be discovered that reduce the length of each computation to less than a minute. To try and describe these shortcuts would require several more pages and may confuse the reader more than it would help. Developing a spreadsheet would cut down considerably on calculation time.

Finding a location on a map from given waypoints: At times, the GPS user may wish to take information gathered on his unit to pinpoint a location on his map, perhaps the site of his summer cabin. The only thing that is different in this problem is that the latitude and longitude are known while the quantities n and w and are not.

Take your readings of latitude and longitude and convert them to the datum used on the map (if necessary). To go from WGS84 to NAD83, no correction is necessary. To go from WGS84 to NAD27, add 0.002 minutes of latitude and 0.032 minutes of longitude.

Prepare the map as you did before. This means that you will take every latitude and longitude you need and convert them to degrees and decimals out to six places. Measure N and W. Solve the equations on 337 for n and w.

n = N[(**P**lat) - (La1)]/[(La2) - (La1)]

w = W[(**P**long) - (Lo1)]/[(Lo2) - (Lo1)]

Take the map and determine from the GPS reading, in which grid square point **P** will be located. (Refer to the chart on page 336 for clarification.) Go to the lower right hand corner of that grid square and measure off n vertically upward and w horizontally to the left. Mark the end of each distance as *n'* and *w'* respectively. Using a protractor, right angle straight edge or compass, construct perpendiculars to the longitude line at *n'* and the latitude line at *w'*. Where these two new lines cross is your point **P**.

The reader with a GPS unit would probably be more interested in the earlier problem of calculating waypoint co-ordinates to enter into his unit. Such solutions are very useful in planning a future hike. **But always take a map and compass along on any hike and remember how to use them**.

APPENDIX H

REFERENCES

Allen, Dan H., DON'T DIE ON THE MOUNTAIN, Diapensia Press, New London NH, 1998

Appalachian Mountain Club, AMC MAINE MOUNTAIN GUIDE, (3rd - 8th editions), AMC Books, Boston 1971-1999

Appalachian Mountain Club, AMC WHITE MOUNTAIN GUIDE, (17th - 27th editions), AMC Books, Boston 1963-2003

Appalachian Mountain Club, *APPALACHIA* (Semi-Annual Journal), (Vol 34 - 55 No 2.), AMC Books, Boston 1962-2005

Appalachian Mountain Club, SOUTHERN NEW HAMPSHIRE TRAIL GUIDE (1st edition), AMC Books, Boston 1999

Appalachian Trail Conference, APPALACHIAN TRAIL GUIDE TO NEW HAMPSHIRE-VERMONT, (10th Edition) Harpers Ferry WV, 2001

Bent, Arthur B. (Editor), WINTER ON MOUNT WASHINGTON, The Mount Washington Observatory, Gorham NH 1956

Cannon, Le Grand, Jr., LOOK TO THE MOUNTAIN, Holt Rinehart & Winston, Inc., New York 1942 (Golden Apple Edition, New York) 1983

Chocorua Mountain Club, CHOCORUA MOUNTAIN CLUB MAP OF THE CHOCORUA REGION, NH, 1966 (Includes panorama)

Churchill, Winston S., A HISTORY OF THE ENGLISH SPEAKING PEOPLES, Vol 2., Dodd Mead & Co., New York, 1956

Dartmouth Outing Club, D. O. C. TRAIL MAP, Hanover NH, 1990

Dickerman, Mike, ed. THE WHITE MOUNTAIN READER, Bondcliff Books, Littleton NH, 2000

Doan, Daniel, FIFTY HIKES, New Hampshire Publishing Company, Somersworth NH 1973 (Retitled FIFTY HIKES IN NEW HAMPSHIRE)

Doan, Daniel, FIFTY MORE HIKES IN NEW HAMPSHIRE, New Hampshire Publishing Company, Somersworth NH, 1978

Ford, Daniel, "A New Lease on Cranmore," *SKIING*, Nov. 1987

Gibson, John, FIFTY HIKES IN MAINE, New Hampshire Publishing Company, Somersworth NH 1976

Green Mountain Club, DAY HIKERS GUIDE TO VERMONT, (2nd edition) George Little Press, Inc, Burlington VT 1983

Julyan, Robert and Mary, PLACE NAMES OF THE WHITE MOUNTAINS, University Press of New England, Hanover NH 1993

Kilham, Benjamin and Gray, Ed; AMONG THE BEARS, *Raising Orphan Cubs in the Wild*, Henry Holt and Company, First Owl Books Edition, New York 2003

Letham, Lawrence, GPS MADE EASY (4th Edition) The Mountaineers, Seattle, 2003

Maine Appalachian Trail Club in cooperation with the Appalachian Trail Conference, APPALACHIAN TRAIL GUIDE TO MAINE, (13th edition) Augusta ME, 1996

Monadnock-Sunapee-Greenway Trail Club,   MONADNOCK-SUNAPEE GREENWAY TRAIL GUIDE (6th edition), Marlow NH, 2001

Monkman, Jerry and Marcy, DISCOVER SOUTHERN NEW HAMPSHIRE, AMC Books, Boston 2002

Mount Washington Observatory, MOUNT WASHINGTON (Includes Panorama), Gorham NH, 1962

Mount Washington Obsevatory, *WINDSWEPT* (Quarterly Journal) , North Conway NH 1995 - 2005

Mudge, John T.B., THE WHITE MOUNTAINS, *Names Places and Legends,* The Durand Press, Etna NH, 1992

National Weather Records Center: Daily weather maps, surface weather observations from Buffalo and Syracuse NY, Burlington VT, Whitefield, Laconia, Manchester and Mount Washington NH; National Ocean and Atmospheric Administration (NOAA), Ashville NC, 1971.

Parc National du Mount-Megantic, EN COULISSES, Reseau Sepaq, Canada 2004

Pletcher, Larry, HIKING NEW HAMPSHIRE, Falcon Publishing Inc., Helena, Montana, 1995

Randall, Peter, MOUNT WASHINGTON, *A short Guide and History,* (includes panorama), University Press of New England, Hanover NH, 1974

Reifsnyder, William E., HIGH HUTS OF THE WHITE MOUNTAINS, AMC Books, Boston, 1979

Sadler, Ruth and Paul, FIFTY HIKES IN VERMONT, New Hampshire Publishing Comapny, Sommersworth NH 1974

Scudder, Brent E., SCUDDER'S WHITE MOUNTAIN VIEWING GUIDE, (First edition) High Top Press, Belmore NY 1995 (Reprinted by Bondcliff Books, Littleton NH, 2000)

Scudder, Brent E., Slide Collection, Panorama sweeps from 54 summits, 47 in New Hampshire and seven beyond its borders, 1970-2003.

Skalka, Jennifer, *THE CONCORD MONITOR,* Concord, NH, May 4, 2003

Smith, Steven D. and Dickerman, Mike, THE 4000-FOOTERS OF THE WHITE MOUNTAINS, *A guide and History*, Bondcliff Books, Littleton NH 2001

Stier, Maggie and McAdow, Ron; INTO THE MOUNTAINS, Stories of New England's most celebrated peaks, Appalachian Mountain Club Books, Boston 1994

The Sunapee-Ragged-Kearsarge Greenway Coalition and the Country Press, SRKG TRAIL GUIDE, New London NH 2003

Surveys and Mapping Branch, Department of Energy, Mines and Resources: Topographic Maps, Canada Map Office, Ottawa

Sweetser, Moses Foster, THE WHITE MOUNTAINS, *a handbook for travellers*, James R. Osgood & Co, Boston, 1876 (and later editions).

Trails Committee of the Berkshire Chapter, Appalachian Mountain Club, METACOMET-MONADNOCK TRAIL GUIDE (9th edition), Paper House Inc. Amherst MA, 1999

United States Geological Survey: Topographic Maps covering all of New Hampshire, most of Maine and Vermont and a considerable portion of Massachusetts; Reston VA.

Van Diver, Bradford B., A ROADSIDE GEOLOGY OF VERMONT AND NEW HAMPSHIRE, Mountain Press Publishing Co., Missoula MT, 1987

Vermont Agency of Natural Resources, Department of Forests, Parks and Recreation; A RECREATIONAL GUIDE TO ASCUTNEY STATE PARK, 2002

Washburn, Bradford, MOUNT WASHINGTON AND THE HEART OF THE PRESIDENTIAL RANGE (Map), Appalachian Mountain Club, Boston 1988.

Waterman, Laura and Guy, FOREST AND CRAG, *A History of Hiking, Trail Blazing, and Adventure in the Northeast Mountains,* AMC Books, Boston, 1987 and reprinted in 2003.

APPENDIX I...INDEX

This index is divided into the following sub-indices: I-

SUB-INDEX....I-A

MOUNTAINS, HILLS AND VALLEYS

If a name listed below lacks a terrain qualifier such as "Mountain" or "Hill," then the word "Mount" is assumed to precede it. Names in italics have no preceding qualifiers. (Quebec mountains lacking a terrain qualifier will be assumed to be preceded by the word "Mont.") Terrain features with no State abbreviation are located in New Hampshire. Mountains with temporary names will be given the customary asterisk.

A

B

SUB-INDEX I-A....MOUNTAINS, HILLS AND VALLEYS

C

SUB-INDEX I-A....MOUNTAINS, HILLS AND VALLEYS

G

H

SUB-INDEX I-A....MOUNTAINS, HILLS AND VALLEYS

L

M

SUB-INDEX I-A....MOUNTAINS, VALLEYS AND HILLS

O

P

Q - R

S

T

SUB-INDEX I-A....MOUNTAINS, HILLS AND VALLEYS

SUB-INDEX I-A....MOUNTAINS, HILLS AND VALLEYS

X - Y - Z

SUB-INDEX I-B...LAKES, PONDS AND RIVERS

If a name listed below lacks a terrain qualifier such as "Lake" or "Pond," then the word "Lake" is assumed to precede it. Names in italics have no preceding qualifiers. (Bodies of water in Quebec lacking a qualifier will be assumed to be preceded by the word "Lac.") All names lacking a State abbreviation are bodies of water located in New Hampshire.

SUB-INDEX I-B....LAKES, PONDS AND RIVERS

SUB-INDEX I-B....LAKES, PONDS AND RIVERS

SUB-INDEX I-C....TRAILS AND SHELTERS

If a name appears without the the word "Way", "Path", 'Shelter" or similar designation, the word "Trail" is assumed to follow it. Exceptions are listed in italics. Italics are sometimes used for clarity. Trails associated with particular mountains are followed by the name of their respective mountains in parentheses. Trails ascending mountains of the same name are not included.

SUB-INDEX I-D....TOWNS, DISTRICTS AND SITES

SUB-APPENDIX I-E....PEOPLE

SUB-INDEX I-E....PEOPLE

SUB-INDEX I-F....MISCELLANEOUS

Brent Scudder has lived in New Hampshire for twelve years. He graduated from Saint Paul's School in 1956 and Kenyon College in 1960. He holds a masters degree in meteorology from New York University. Brent spent a year at Byrd Station, Antarctica, and three months at the South Pole. Scudder Peak near latitude 75 degrees south and longitude 115 degrees west bears his name. Brent taught physics at Hopkins School in New Haven and later became an adjunct professor at Dowling College on Long Island where he taught aviation weather. He has served both as a weather forecaster and an airline dispatcher. Presently Brent is retired and lives with his wife Regina in New London, New Hampshire. He has climbed New Hampshire's "highest forty-eight" mountains and has belonged to the Appalachian Mountain Club since 1971.

NOTES

ORDER FORM

Please send _____ copy(ies) of *SCUDDER'S WHITE MOUNTAIN VIEWING GUIDE.* A check or money order is enclosed.

The book sells for $18.95 per copy. Shipping and handling charges are $2 per copy. Priority mail is $4 for the first copy and $2 per book for each additional copy. Fedex is $12 for the first copy and $4 per book thereafter. Bookstores and distributors visit HighTopPress.com for terms. All checks must be drawn in United States funds.

Price of book(s) @ $18.95 each _____

Shipping and handling _____

Total enclosed _____

Name_____

Suite or Apartment no._____

Street or P.O. Box no._____

_____

City_____ State or Province_____

Zip or Postal Code_____ Country_____

High Top Press
P.O. Box 299
North Sutton
New Hampshire
03260

This form may be photocopied.